DOGFIGHT

DOGFIGHT

True Stories of Dramatic Air Actions

ALFRED PRICE

Front cover: Cody Images/USAF/Edwin H Ryan

Text of this book was previously published as two separate titles:
Sky Battles and Sky Warriors.

Sky Battles previously published by Arms and Armour Press, 1993
and by Cassell Military Classics, 1998, 2000

Sky Warriors previously published by Arms and Armour Press, 1994
and by Cassell Military Classics, 1998, 1999, 2000

This edition first published in 2009

The History Press
The Mill, Brimscombe Port
Stroud, Gloucestershire, GL5 2QG
www.thehistorypress.co.uk

British Library Cataloguing in Publication Data.
A catalogue record for this book is available from the British Library.

ISBN 978 0 7524 5470 2

Typesetting and origination by The History Press Ltd.
Printed in Great Britain

Contents

PART I
Sky Battles

Introduction

M y aim in writing this work has been to illustrate the actuality of aerial warfare during the past eight decades, by bringing together a series of detailed accounts of air actions spread throughout the period. To portray the multi-faceted nature of the air weapon, the narratives that follow include descriptions of each of the main roles in which aircraft are employed in time of war.

Chapter 1, 'Above the Fields of France', provides a rare insight into fighter operations over the Western Front during the final year of the First World War. Major William Sholto Douglas commanded No 84 Squadron equipped with S.E.5A fighters, and the account is based on a tactical paper that he wrote and also on the unit's records. Following painful lessons learned when the Squadron entered combat, its commander worked out his tactical doctrine almost from first principles. Douglas himself was not a high scorer in combat, but thanks to his tactical leadership his squadron became one of the most effective air fighting units of its time. The techniques he formulated enabled others, notably Captain Andrew Beauchamp Proctor VC, to amass large victory scores while avoiding the risks that eventually claimed the lives of so many successful pilots. No 84 Squadron was continually in action throughout the final twelve months of the conflict, fighting over one of the most active parts of the battle front. Yet, after the first three weeks, the unit suffered relatively few losses.

The Second World War, which began in September 1939, was the first major conflict in which the possession of air superiority allowed one side to impose major constraints on operations by the opposing land and sea forces. Chapter 2, 'The Rise and Demise of the Stuka', describes a type of operation that was relatively easy for the side that possessed air superiority and hazardous if that quality had been lost. During the early *Blitzkrieg* campaigns in Poland, Norway, Belgium, Holland and France, the Junkers Ju 87 'Stuka' dive-bombers attacked targets with pin-point accuracy to support the German armoured thrusts. The Stukas tried to continue their run of successes during the Battle of Britain in the summer of 1940, and although they inflicted severe damage on their targets they suffered heavy losses in the process. Against warships manoeuvring in open water the dive-bombers remained a potent threat, until the vessels were provided with sufficiently strong air cover to make such attacks unproductive.

From time to time an air attack goes terribly wrong, and as a result the raiding force pays a terrible price. Chapter 3, 'Only One Came Back', and Chapter 4, 'Low Altitude Attack', provide examples of a couple of small-scale actions in which the raiders were all but wiped out.

By the autumn of 1940 the *Luftwaffe* had come to the realization that the only way it could mount a sustained air attack on strategic targets in Great Britain was to send its bombers under cover of darkness. Chapter 5, 'Countering the Night Bomber', describes the first large-scale night bombing campaign in history. Initially the raiders suffered minimal losses, but gradually the night defences improved and by the end of the period they had started to take an increasingly heavy toll.

At sea, one notable development during the Second World War was that the aircraft carrier ousted the battleship as the primary instrument of surface naval power. When opposing carrier forces went into action against their own kind the result was a complex interplay between air and naval forces, and the first such encounter, in May 1942, is described in Chapter 6, 'Battle of the Coral Sea'.

Another air campaign that had features quite unlike any other is described in Chapter 7, 'Battle of the Bay'. 'The Bay' was the Bay of Biscay, and the actions were between submarine-hunting aircraft of Royal Air Force Coastal Command on the one side and German U-boats on the other. During this campaign air crews logged vast numbers of flying hours but only rarely did they see anything of their enemy. In parallel with the air-sea battle there ran an equally important struggle between the opposing sides' technicians, with each trying to outwit the other. During the summer of 1943 the strategic bombardment of targets in Germany by US heavy bombers entered its critical phase, with the action described in Chapter 8, 'The Regensburg Strike'. Then it became clear that the defensive firepower from formations of heavily armed Flying Fortresses was insufficient to deter attacks from a determined and well-equipped enemy fighter force. The answer was to push ahead with the development of the long-range escort fighter, with results that will be observed in later chapters.

Reconnaissance is a vitally important aspect of air power. Yet, because it involves single aircraft which seek to avoid combat, there is usually little action and the subject receives less attention than it deserves. Without effective pre-attack reconnaissance, an air commander will lack the information he needs to use his force to greatest effect. And unless he has prompt post-attack reconnaissance, he cannot determine whether or not an attack has been successful. Chapter 9, 'Reconnaissance to Berlin', illustrates the skills and the special kind of bravery needed to fly, alone, deep into enemy territory in an unarmed aircraft.

As has been said, the German 'Blitz' on Britain in 1940 and 1941 was the first-ever large-scale night bombing campaign. Yet this campaign was soon being dwarfed by that mounted by RAF night bombers against targets in Germany. Usually the cloak of darkness shielded the bombers from the ferocity of the German night fighter and gun defences, but on 30/31 March 1944 events conspired to strip away that safeguard. The resultant action is described in Chapter 10, 'The Nuremberg Disaster'.

By the spring of 1944 the US heavy bombers had protection from strong forces of escorting fighters all the way to and from their targets. The cumulative effect of these attacks was the devastation of major parts of the German war economy and in particular the synthetic oil industry. *Reich* Air Defence fighter units found themselves locked into a losing battle of attrition against the American fighters, in which they suffered heavy losses in aircraft and pilots. The history of warfare provides many examples of actions where a few courageous men overcame a numerically superior foe. The *Luftwaffe* sought such an outcome when it introduced the novel attack methods described in Chapter 11, 'Day of the Sturmgruppe'.

The appearance of the Messerschmitt Me 262 jet fighter in action in the autumn of 1944 brought a huge advance in combat performance and firepower compared with anything that had gone before. These are important attributes for a fighter aircraft, but they are not, by themselves, sufficient to bring about the defeat of a well-resourced and well-trained foe. Chapter 12, 'The Jets get their Chance', reviews the problems of bringing the revolutionary Messerschmitt 262 fighter into action in sufficient numbers.

During the late 1930s the accepted wisdom of the time was that manoeuvring combat between fighters was a thing of the past. The RAF *Manual of Air Tactics*, 1938 Edition, solemnly stated that 'Manoeuvre at high speeds in air fighting is not now practicable, because the effect of gravity on the human body causes a temporary loss of consciousness, deflecting shooting becomes difficult and accuracy is hard to obtain.' Apart from the first of those statements, the others were (and, indeed still are) true. The effect of gravity on the human body during high-speed manoeuvres *does* cause temporary loss of consciousness, deflection shooting *does* become difficult and as a result accuracy is hard to obtain. When the matter was subjected to the acid test of combat in the Second World War, however, it soon became clear that although deflection shooting was 'difficult' and accuracy was 'hard to obtain', these were not insurmountable obstacles. Although manoeuvring combat was difficult and tiring, with determination it was certainly possible.

Following the introduction of swept-wing jet fighters able to exceed the speed of sound in a dive, in the late 1940s, it was again fashionable to sound the death-knell of fighter-versus-fighter combat – until the Korean War taught people otherwise. The notion was resurrected a decade later with the emergence of Mach 2 fighters armed with air-to-air missiles – until the air war over North Vietnam laid that particular ghost to rest for all time. The largest dogfight of that period is described in Chapter 13, 'Furball over Hai Duong'.

The action over Hai Duong demonstrated that fighter pilots are sometimes forced to fight on terms quite different from those for which they had trained in peacetime. Another example of this occurred during the Falklands Conflict in 1982, when Sea Harrier pilots defended the amphibious landing operation at San Carlos against attacks by the far larger Argentine Air Force and Navy. Chapter 14 'Low Level Drama in front of San Carlos', describes the heaviest day of air fighting during that conflict.

Air transport is yet another aspect of air warfare that is possible only if one's opponent does not possess air superiority over the operating area. In Chapter 15, 'The Epic of "Bravo November"', the Falklands War provides an example of how a single large helicopter, handled with skill and resolution, had a considerable effect on a land campaign.

The Vietnam War spawned two families of air-to-ground weapons that have brought unprecedented accuracy to attacks on land targets: the laser-guided bomb and the electro-optically guided bomb. During the final years of 'The Cold War', the US 48th

Tactical Fighter Wing equipped with F-111Fs perfected the techniques for delivering these weapons. Chapter 16, 'Precision Attack – By Night', describes the unit's operations during the Persian Gulf conflict in the 1990's.

At any time the act of being shot down is a traumatic experience, as an aircraft suddenly becomes incapable of sustained flight. Chapter 17, 'St Valentine's Day Shoot-Down', describes an example that occurred during the attacks on Iraq.

This series of accounts is intended to provide the reader with a wide-ranging overview of the business of aerial warfare. Some of the impressions gained may not fit easily into the reader's pre-conceived framework of ideas on this complex subject. It is not my intention to be deliberately controversial, but neither have I repeated some of the comforting and comfortable assertions of 'established wisdom' that I consider to be invalid. By setting out the facts in this way, I trust that readers will be able to take a more critical line with the material that appears before them in future.

Author's Note

Unless stated otherwise, in this account all miles are statute miles and all speeds are given in statute miles per hour. Gallons and tons are given in Imperial measurements. Times are given in local time for the area where the incident described took place. Weapon calibres are given in the units normal for the weapon being described, e.g. Oerlikon 20mm cannon or Browning .5in machine gun. Where an aircraft's offensive armament load is stated, this is the normal load carried by that type of aircraft during operations and not the larger maximum figure stated in makers' brochures and reproduced in most aircraft data books.

Acknowledgment

I thank my friend Martin Middlebrook for kind permission to use first-person quotations from his books *The Schweinfurt-Regensburg Mission* and *The Nuremberg Raid*, in Chapters 8 and 10 respectively.

Alfred Price
Uppingham, Rutland
January 1993

Chapter 1

Above the Fields of France

The story of No 84 Squadron Royal Flying Corps, which was sent into action over France in the autumn of 1917, and of its commander Major W. Sholto Douglas, who became one of the leading air combat tacticians of his time.

Air-to-air combat had its origins over the Western Front during the First World War, after reconnaissance planes started to carry machine guns so that they could engage their enemy counterparts if they chanced to meet them. Then in the summer of 1915 the German Air Service introduced the Fokker monoplane, the first aircraft to be an effective destroyer of its own kind. A single-seater, the Fokker had a performance that no two-seater of the time could match. More importantly, its machine gun fired forwards through the propeller disc and had an interrupter system to prevent rounds striking the propeller blades. The deployment of the Fokker monoplane in small numbers enabled German pilots to seize air superiority, but the effect proved transitory as its features were soon copied by the enemy.

From then on each side strove to wrest air superiority from its opponent, or hold on to it. This led to the accelerated development of all aspects of aviation and in particular that of the fighter aircraft. The warring sides fielded a succession of new types that with ever more powerful engines, could fly faster and higher and climb faster. Structures became heavier and a lot stronger and aeroplanes' armaments became more lethal.

As the fighter aircraft became more effective, talented individuals began to amass sizeable victory scores and establish their names as exponents of the new form of warfare: Germans like Max Immelmann, Oswald Boelke and Manfred von Richthofen, Frenchmen like Georges Guynemer, Charles Nungesser and Rene Fonck and from Britain men like 'Mick' Mannock, Albert Ball and James McCudden. Every country needs to have heroes in time of war, and almost overnight the ace pilots became national celebrities.

Yet although these men were prepared to fight each other to the death and on rare occasions did so, they had much in common. Invariably they were gifted with excellent eyesight, which allowed them to see their enemy at great distances and usually before they themselves were seen. They had learned to use the sun or cloud cover to approach an enemy unseen, and they could size up the tactical situation at a glance and assess the quickest way to reach a firing position on their foe. Some of them were exceptionally fine shots, while others compensated for a lack of this ability by closing to short range to deliver their lethal burst. Most of their victims were taken by surprise and never saw their assailant before their aircraft was hit. Contrary to popular belief, the high-scoring aces scored relatively few victories in one-versus-one turning combats, or during the swirling dogfights. Those who survived long enough to reach that status knew that the risks incurred in this type of fighting were too great and the chances of success too small. By the end of 1917 the day of the lone aerial hunter – the man who went out alone to stalk enemy planes – was nearing its end. Few could operate effectively in this way, and the pilots of average ability achieved much more if they flew as part of a well-led unit than if they were left to their own devices. Air fighting had become a team affair and, as in a football match, the well-led team would usually defeat the bunch of talented but undisciplined individualists.

Born in 1893, William Sholto Douglas joined the Royal Flying Corps in 1914. Early the following year he flew his first operational flights with No 2 Squadron. In April 1916 he commanded No 43 Squadron equipped with Sopwith 1½ Strutters and led the unit in action. In August 1917 Douglas took command of No 84 Squadron, then in the process of forming at Lilibourne near Rugby with eighteen S.E.5A fighters. Of the 24 pilots assigned to the unit, only Douglas and his three flight commanders had previous air fighting experience.

In September No 84 Squadron moved to Liettres in northern France, ten miles behind the front line, and underwent a short period of preparation for combat. Its first mission over enemy territory took place on 15 October, when it escorted six de Havilland 4 bombers attacking an ammunition dump. During a tussle with enemy fighters

Lieutenant Edmund Krohn claimed the destruction of an Albatros fighter, the unit's first victory. But any elation that might have been felt was tempered by the loss of Lieutenant Lord, who was shot down and taken prisoner.

Although the S.E.5A had the edge in performance over the Albatros D V, the main German type it met in action, the Squadron suffered painful losses during its initiation into combat. At the time the Battle of Passchendaele was in full swing, and the unit was in action on almost every day and suffered severe losses. During a particularly hard-fought action on 31 October, for example, Captain Leask lead a six-aircraft flight down to attack four hostile aircraft seen below them. Then a dozen Albatros fighters pounced from above and the would-be hunters became the prey. Two S.E.5As were shot down and their pilots killed, while the Squadron claimed the destruction of two enemy aircraft.

During its first sixteen days in action, No 84 Squadron lost nine pilots killed or taken prisoner, more than one-third of its complement. Its total claim over the period amounted to five enemy aircraft. On this inauspicious start Douglas later reflected:

> It was a hard school for a new and untried Squadron and at first, owing to the inexperience of the pilots, we suffered casualties. But bitter experience is a quick teacher ...

In November the Battle of Passchendaele petered out and the ground fighting slackened. This, coupled with a general deterioration in the weather, led to a marked reduction in air activity. Replacements arrived to fill the gaps in the ranks, and those pilots that had survived the harsh initial baptism of fire emerged with a better grasp of the realities of air combat. Now the unit was allowed a breathing space to consider past mistakes and build on its hard-won fighting experience. After a couple of moves it ended the year based at Flez near St Quentin.

Douglas soon revealed himself as a shrewd tactician and a perceptive commander. Although his own victory score would never be impressive, he produced a workable set of tactics and ensured that his pilots complied with them. The lessons of the bloody initiation into combat were well learned and No 84 Squadron evolved into an effective force, confident in its abilities and with a high ratio of victories to losses.

After the war Douglas wrote a long report on his experiences as a fighter commander, in which he set down the techniques that led to success in air combat and those that did not. He quickly grasped the fundamental lesson that has been part of the combat philosophy of every successful fighter pilot, before or since:

> A lesson that we soon learnt was that there are occasions when it is wrong to accept battle, that one must always strive to take the enemy at a disadvantage. Equally, one must not be taken at a disadvantage oneself and this often entails a deliberate refusal of battle and a retirement so that the enemy's advantage may be nullified. If for instance that advantage is height, then one should retreat, climb hard, and go back and seek out the enemy at his own height or higher. Of course there are occasions when battle has to be accepted at a disadvantage – if, for instance, one sees another British squadron being overwhelmed by superior numbers, then obviously whatever the odds one must accept battle. But normally one should force the battle upon the enemy, not have the battle forced on oneself.

Douglas appreciated the strengths and weaknesses of the S.E.5A, compared with the enemy types that his unit met in action. As well as its excellent speed, climbing and diving performance compared its opponents, the S.E.5A had other useful attributes. It was a rugged aircraft that would accept a lot of mishandling, and the commander felt that that was particularly important:

> The S.E. was strong in design and construction, and it did not break up in the air when roughly handled as certain other types were apt to do. *Nothing undermines a pilot's confidence in his machine so much as doubts as to its strength* [author's emphasis].

The pilot's view from the S.E.5A was better than from most other contemporary biplane fighter types – an important characteristic in an air action where the side that was the first to detect its opponent possessed the initiative in any combat that followed. The aircraft was also a stable firing platform, particularly in the dive, and this was another factor that Douglas considered useful:

> It was very steady when diving fast; the pilot could therefore take very careful aim when diving to attack (and nine times out of ten he attacks by diving). This is an advantage pertaining to all stable machines – the faster one dives, the steadier becomes one's gun platform. An unstable machine like a Camel or a Sopwith Dolphin is apt to 'hunt' when diving at high speeds, i.e. to vary its angle of dive from time to time in spite of the

pilot's best endeavours to prevent it . . . Good shooting under these circumstances is rendered very difficult.

If an S.E.5A pilot were forced on to the defensive in combat, a steep dive would enable him to pick up speed quickly and draw away from his opponent, even one that was faster in straight and level flight. It was a useful method of breaking out of an action if a pilot was hard-pressed, if his guns had jammed or if he had run out of ammunition.

The S.E.5A was less manoeuvrable than many contemporary fighter types, though Douglas played down the importance of this attribute in combat:

The S.E. has often been criticised as being heavy on the controls for a single-seater, and so insufficiently manoeuvrable. In the days when aerial fighting was a series of combats between individuals, it is true that the manoeuvrability of the individual machine was all-important. In 1918, however, it was no longer the individual pilot but the flight flying in close formation that was the fighting unit; and the distinction will, I think, become more and more pronounced in future wars. In the present development of aerial fighting it is *the flight that fights as one unit* [author's emphasis]. Therefore it is the manoeuvrability of the flight that counts, not the manoeuvrability of the individual machine. If then a machine is sufficiently handy (as was the S.E.) to keep its place in the formation in any flight manoeuvre, it is of minor importance whether that machine is individually of a high degree of manoeuvrability or not.

It was found that supremely quick manoeuvring was nearly always a defensive measure; when attacked the pilot escaped the immediate consequences by swift manoeuvre. The attack on the other hand was usually delivered by a flight formation diving at high speed, so that in attack it was the manoeuvrability of the flight that counted. Now if you have a machine superior in performance to the enemy (as was the S.E. till the autumn of 1918), and your patrols are well led, you should very rarely be attacked or thrown on the defensive. Instead, you should be able so to manoeuvre your formation that, by virtue of your superior speed and climb, you yourself are always the attacker; which leads us to the conclusion that if your machines are superior in performance to those of the enemy, manoeuvrability is a very secondary consideration.

By trial and error Douglas arrived at what he considered to be the optimum fighting unit: a five-aircraft formation flying in 'V', stepped up from front to rear. Lacking radio, the aircraft flew close to the leader to observe his hand signals. The leader could also communicate by manoeuvres, though there was only a small range of easily understood messages that could be passed in this way. For example, banking gently to one side then to the other meant 'Close up'; flying an undulating path meant 'Open out'; to signal his intention to turn, the leader banked twice in the required direction, then began turning; and 'Enemy in sight' was indicated by banking the aircraft steeply from side to side several times.

Douglas ordered that flight leaders make all of the tactical decisions, and the other pilots in the flight had to concentrate on maintaining position in formation and following instructions. The technique of co-ordinated search, in which every pilot in the formation scans an area of sky keeping watch for the enemy, was unknown. Given the poor training and experience level of the average squadron pilot at the time, it would probably have been unworkable.

By this stage of the war the German fighter units usually flew in formations of a dozen or more. They rarely ventured over the land battle, preferring to engage the enemy over their own territory. Lieutenant-Colonel, the commander of the 22nd Wing of which No 84 Squadron was part, sent multi-squadron formations over hostile territory in an attempt to force the German fighting patrols into action. Typically, such a formation comprised a squadron of Sopwith Camels at 15,000ft, one of S.E.5As 16,000ft and one of Bristol fighters at 18,000ft. The tactic was a complete failure. The force could be seen from several miles, and any German fighting patrol in its path quickly drew away to the east. When the formation turned for home, having punched at an empty sky, the enemy fighters harried it from the sides and flanks and attempted to pick off stragglers.

Douglas took part in a few of these fighter sweeps and was scathing in his criticism of them. In his view the squadron-size offensive patrol was much more successful as a means of engaging the enemy. That, he felt, was the largest force that could be led effectively into action by one man. He developed a technique of using three flights flying some distance apart but in concert, each with a set role. In a typical patrol of this type, 'A' Flight flew in the lead at 15,000ft and its commander was in charge of the entire formation. 'B' Flight, in support, maintained position about half a mile behind 'A' Flight and flew in echelon some 500ft above it. 'C' Flight, also in support, flew farther behind 'A', echeloned on the opposite side to 'B' Flight and at 18,000ft. Describing the tactical employment of this force, Douglas commented:

S.E.5A

Role: Single-seat fighter.

Power: One Wolseley Viper 8-cylinder, liquid-cooled engine developing 200hp at take-off (other types of engine were also fitted, but the Viper was standard on No 84 Squadron's aircraft from March 1918 to the end of the war).

Armament: One Vickers .303in machine gun synchronized to fire through the propeller disc; one Lewis .303in machine gun mounted on top of the upper wing, firing above the propeller disc. There was provision for carrying four 25lb bombs on racks under the fuselage.

Performance: Maximum speed 128mph at 6,500ft; climb to 10,000ft, 10min 50sec; climb to 15,000ft, 20min 50sec.

Normal operational take-off weight: 1,988lb (no bombs carried).

Dimensions: Span 26ft 7hin; length 20ft 11in; wing area (both wings) 245.8 sq ft.

Date of first production S.E.5A: May 1917.

The duty of 'B' Flight is to follow closely and conform to the movements of 'A' Flight. It does not attack on its own initiative – the initiative lies absolutely in the hands of the squadron patrol leader, i.e. the leader of 'A' Flight. This somewhat rigid formalism was found to be necessary owing to the tendency of the following flights to be drawn away into subsidiary combats, leaving the squadron leader unsupported. If the latter attacks, 'B' Flight does one of two things: it either reinforces 'A' Flight, if the enemy is sufficiently numerous to make this worthwhile; or it flies directly over the top of 'A' Flight and affords protection to 'A' Flight against enemy machines attacking from above. The third flight ('C' Flight) is the covering force: it flies as high as possible, and some two or three miles behind and to the flank of 'A' Flight. The leader follows 'A' Flight at a distance, and has orders never to come down to assist 'A' and 'B' Flights except in great emergency. The mere fact that 'C' Flight is circling high up over the combat is usually sufficient to prevent any but a very strong enemy formation from attacking the two lower flights.

Douglas took the view that the well-led and disciplined flight formation was the most effective means of destroying enemy aircraft for minimum losses, and in action he set great store on maintaining flight cohesion:

It was soon discovered that, as soon as the flight lost formation and was split up, casualties occurred. Also, that it was not when attacked that the flight was so liable to break up, as when [it was] attacking. When attacked, pilots naturally hung together for mutual protection; but when an attack was begun, pilots were apt to break off in pursuit of the particular German machine that they had marked down as their prey, and were then set upon while so isolated, and overwhelmed by superior numbers.

After much debate and in spite of opposition from the individualists in the squadron, we finally made a strict order that *no pilot was on any account to leave the formation* [author's emphasis], even to take an apparently easy opportunity of shooting down an enemy machine. The initiative in any attack lay wholly with the flight leader: if he dived to the attack, the whole flight dived with him; when he zoomed away after the attack, even if he had failed to shoot down the enemy attacked, all pilots zoomed away with him still keeping formation. This was found to be the only way of keeping the formation together during a combat; otherwise the flight was split up at the first onset, each pilot breaking off in pursuit of a different enemy machine, and then being defeated in detail.

The natural consequence of this order was that it was usually the flight commander who actually shot down the enemy machine. But, being the most experienced pilot, he was the most capable of doing this quickly and effectively. In addition, with his flight behind him to act as a buffer against any attack from behind, he could afford to concentrate all his powers on the destruction of the enemy machine. There was no need for him to be peering over his shoulder all the time, anxious lest he himself be attacked. His aiming and shooting were therefore the more careful and deliberate.

Unless it were unavoidable, No 84 Squadron refused to engage in dogfights with enemy fighters. The First World War dogfight has been likened to 'a bar room brawl with guns'. Once the opposing forces were committed, their commanders had no control over the action, and that was reason enough for Douglas to order his pilots keep out of them. These disciplined fighting tactics proved highly effective; particularly on 3 April 1918 when the unit engaged a large force of enemy Pfalz and Albatros fighters over Pozières and claimed the destruction of six enemy aircraft without loss to itself. A few weeks later, on the 25th, No 84 Squadron had another successful action when it claimed the destruction of nine Pfalz and Albatros fighters for the loss of one S.E.5A.

From time to time the Squadron was ordered to provide close escort for bomber formations attacking targets in hostile territory. Douglas hated this type of operation, and likened a fighting squadron tied to a bomber formation to a boxer trying to fight with one hand tied behind his back. He continued:

> . . . a fighting squadron on escort duty cannot attack the enemy formations that it encounters because if it did so, the bombers, proceeding on their course, would soon be out of sight and would thus be left unprotected. All that the fighting squadron can do is to wait until the enemy attacks and then to parry the blow. Moreover a bombing formation, if composed of machines with a good performance, of pilots who can fly in close formation and of observers who can shoot straight, can fight a very successful defensive action against even superior numbers.

In the decades to follow, fighter unit leaders of almost every nation would reiterate Douglas's sentiments.

The effectiveness of No 84 Squadron's tactics was quickly reflected in its ratio of victory claims to losses. During the four months from the beginning of December 1917 the unit claimed 68 enemy aircraft destroyed or sent out of control. Like most victory totals amassed during the conflict, it was almost certainly an overclaim, but, whatever the true figure, it was achieved for a loss of only two pilots killed in action, two taken prisoner and one wounded.

On 1 April 1918 the Royal Flying Corps was incorporated into the new Royal Air Force. At the time No 84 Squadron was too busily engaged in the fighting to notice anything different. It would take several months for the changes to filter through the command system, and business continued exactly as before.

As has been said, Douglas himself did not achieve an impressive victory score. But several of his pilots did, notably Lieutenant Andrew Beauchamp Proctor. A diminutive South African only 5ft 1in tall, 'Procky' was so small that his aircraft was fitted with blocks on the rudder pedals so that he could reach them. His contemporaries described him as being extremely aggressive in the air, he had exceptionally keen vision and he was an excellent shot. Although a novice pilot when the unit first went into action, by the end of March 1918 he was a flight leader. By the following month, when he was promoted to Captain, his victory score stood at 5½ enemy aircraft.

ALBATROS D V

(The German fighter type most frequently encountered by No 84 Squadron, up to the spring of 1918)

Role: Single-seat fighter.
Power: One Mercedes D III 6-cylinder, liquid-cooled engine developing 160hp at take-off.
Armament: Two Spandau 7.9mm machine guns synchronized to fire through the propeller disc.
Performance: Maximum speed 102mph at 9,840ft; climb to 9,840ft, 17min 9sec. Normal operational take-off weight: 2,018lb.
Dimensions: Span 29ft 8½in; length 24ft; wing area (both wings) 220.1 sq ft.
Date of first production Albatros D V: May 1917.

During the final three months of the war No 84 Squadron became adept in the specialized technique of destroying enemy observation balloons. By this stage of the war the numerous Allied patrols over the battle front made life extremely hazardous for German planes on gunfire spotting missions. As a result, the German artillerymen came to rely on balloon-borne observers to direct fire against ground targets beyond the front line. If these balloons could be destroyed or kept on the ground, the effectiveness of the German artillery was much reduced and the life of the long-suffering British infantrymen was made much easier – hence the importance given to attacking these sausage-shaped targets.

Since they were filled with potentially explosive hydrogen gas and carried no defensive weapons, it might seem that the balloons were easy prey. As many a fighter pilot discovered to his cost, however, this was not the case. Hydrogen in an enclosed container – such as a balloon envelope – is not inflammable: like petrol, it becomes explosive only when it is mixed with oxygen in the correct ratio. To set the balloon on fire it was first necessary to puncture the envelope to allow the gas to escape and mix with the surrounding air, then ignite the mixture with tracer rounds. That meant that the rounds had to be concentrated on a particular part of the balloon, and attacks had to be pressed to within 50yds to achieve success. If there were rain, or if the air were moist, it was almost impossible to ignite a balloon.

Normally the German observation balloons flew at altitudes of between 1,500 and 4,500ft and had machine guns positioned around them to deter fighter attacks. If he saw enemy fighters approaching, the observer jumped from his basket by parachute and the balloon was winched down as rapidly as possible. Because the balloons flew at a relatively low altitude, anyone attacking one was himself liable to be attacked from above by enemy fighters. Douglas therefore devised a set-piece method of attacking the balloons, a variation of the tactics which had proved successful during the Squadron's offensive patrols. The Squadron crossed the front line in formation at altitudes around 10,000ft, as if flying an ordinary patrol. When the force reached a point above the balloons, the flight designated to attack them dived away. The pilots fanned out and each singled out a balloon to engage. One covering flight descended to 5,000ft to protect the attackers from enemy fighters, while the other flight stayed at 10,000ft to deter enemy planes going down to engage those below. During an attack on balloons, speed and surprise were essential.

Douglas noted:

It was . . . found to be best to dive steeply to a point about half a mile from the balloon and on a level with it; then to flatten out and go straight at the balloon with all the added velocity gained in the dive. At 200 yards' range one took a sighting shot with the Vickers and at fifty yards opened fire with the Lewis gun. One carried straight on to within about twenty yards of the balloon, firing all the time, hopped over it and zoomed away.

These attacks were invariably brisk affairs, with no more than ten minutes from the time the formation first crossed the front line until the last aircraft was back over friendly territory. The tactics were used successfully on several occasions and at the end of the war the Squadron's score stood at 50 balloons destroyed. On its best day for balloon attacks, 24 September 1918, the unit was in action twice. In the morning Beauchamp Proctor led an attack on a line of balloons: he shot down one and his colleagues shot down two more. That afternoon Captain Carl Falkenburg led a similar attack on a line of six balloons which resulted in the destruction of four. On both occasions the covering flights prevented enemy fighter patrols from interfering with the operations. In his report, Falkenburg noted that the attack

. . . took the enemy by surprise and we had four balloons in flames before he began to retaliate from the ground. By the time the Ack Ack and machine gun fire got really intense we were back in the clouds and succeeded in getting home almost unscathed. The top flight, led by Lt Nel, kept a good watch and kept just over us while we were attacking the balloons. They then escorted us home.

In the afternoon of 8 October Beauchamp Proctor engaged a Rumpler reconnaissance aircraft near Maretz and followed it down to low altitude to finish it off. His S.E.5A came under fire from the ground and he was hit in the arm. Nevertheless, he continued with the mission and made an unsuccessful attack on a balloon before returning to base. The wound proved more serious than initially thought, however, and he spent most of the next five months in hospital. By then his victory score stood at 54 enemy aircraft, including 16 observation balloons. Following a strong recommendation from Douglas, supported by corroborating statements by four other pilots, Beauchamp Proctor was awarded the Victoria Cross in recognition of his bravery and determination in combat.

Following their bloody initiation into combat, during which nine pilots were lost in less than three weeks, Douglas and the other survivors learned their craft quickly. During the twelve-month period from the early part of November 1917 until the Armistice exactly a year later, No 84 Squadron was continually in action and it took part in some of the heaviest fighting. The unit was credited with the destruction of 306 enemy aircraft, including 50 balloons. In the absence of effective verification procedures, it would be surprising if these claims were accurate; but, even if only half were true, the unit's score was still remarkable.

Many units achieved high victory scores by employing high-risk tactics and incurring heavy losses in the process. That was not Douglas's way. No 84 Squadron operated as a disciplined unit employing comparatively low-risk tactics, and that was reflected in the relatively low losses suffered in action – 25 pilots killed, two taken prisoner and eighteen wounded. Few units engaged in prolonged heavy fighting over the Western Front got off so lightly.

After the war Douglas gained rapid promotion in the RAF and at the beginning of the Second World War he was Assistant Chief of Air Staff with the rank of Air Vice-Marshal. In the autumn of 1940 he was appointed to lead Fighter Command in succession to Sir Hugh Dowding. Later he became Commander-in-Chief RAF Middle East, and at the end of the war he was Commander-in-Chief Coastal Command. In 1948 he retired as Marshal of the Royal Air Force and soon afterwards, as Lord Douglas of Kirtleside, joined the board of the British Overseas Airways Corporation and played an important part in the development of that airline. He died in 1969.

Chapter 2

The Rise and Demise
of the Stuka

*With its angular outline and screaming siren, the steep-diving
Junkers Ju 87 'Stuka' has come to epitomize the fast-moving,
hard-hitting Blitzkrieg tactics employed with such success by
German armed forces during the early part of the Second World
War. In this chapter we examine the ingredients of the aircraft's
success, and the countermeasures that brought about its defeat.*

Until the advent of guided weapons, the steep dive-attack was
the most accurate method to deliver bombs on a defended
target. Against small targets, bombing accuracy is a matter of para-
mount importance. A 1,000lb bomb missing the hard target by a
few tens of yards will cause it no serious damage. It can be shown
mathematically (though the author will resist the temptation) that
if a bomb's miss distance is halved, its destructive effect is four
times as great. If the miss distance is reduced by three-quarters, the
destructive effect is increased *sixteen-fold*. Or, to put it another way,
the same destructive effect can be achieved using *one-sixteenth* the
weight of bombs. Those figures explain the rationale for the Stuka
and its concept of operation: that a small weight of high explosive
positioned accurately will be much more effective than a considerably greater amount of explosive positioned less accurately. (Today,
this argument justifies the greater cost and complication, but the far
greater accuracy, of the 'smart' weapons.)

The word 'Stuka' is a contraction of the German word
Sturzkampfflugzeug meaning 'dive-bomber'. Strictly speaking, the
term refers to all aircraft capable of performing that role and not

merely to a particular type. Yet by common usage over many years, 'Junkers 87' and 'Stuka' have come to be synonymous, and they will be treated as such in this account.

The Junkers Ju 87 was designed without compromise as a steep-diving bomber, and everything else was subordinated to that requirement. The 'Berta', the main production version until early in 1941 and the one that established the type's reputation, carried a 1,100lb bomb load. The fixed, spatted undercarriage gave the aircraft a decidedly dated look, and in horizontal flight its maximum speed was only 238mph. Yet during a diving attack the drag from the fixed undercarriage was a positive asset, when combined with that from the dive brakes extended under the wings: slowed by these protuberances, the Ju 87 was inherently stable in its near-vertical attack dive. With the engine throttled back, the machine reached a terminal velocity of only about 350mph (a cleaner aircraft would have attained a greater terminal velocity in the dive; that meant that the pilot had to dive less steeply or release the bombs and begin the pull-out at a higher altitude, and either factor would have reduced bombing accuracy).

Once the bombs had been released, a specially designed mechanism initiated a firm but smooth 6g pull-out from the dive. The Ju 87's rugged structure was designed to withstand this manoeuvre with a safety margin in case – as sometimes happened – the bombs failed to leave the aircraft. It was an important consideration: during a 6g pull-out, 1,100 pounds of bombs still in place added more than 3 tons to the load the aircraft's structure had to support.

Just as the requirements of the steep-diving attack dominated the design of the Ju 87, so they dictated the tactics of using the aircraft in action. The description that follows covers a typical 'set piece' dive-bombing attack by these aircraft.

On their way to the target the Ju 87s usually flew at about 11,000ft, the highest altitude at which crews could go safely without resorting to oxygen. The aircraft flew in three-plane 'vics' and, depending on the size and importance of the target, a *Staffel* (up to nine aircraft) or *Gruppe* (up to 30 aircraft) formation flew with the vics in line astern with an interval of 300yds between each.

For an accurate attack, it was important that the aircraft were heading directly into the wind when they commenced their dives. As he neared the target, the formation leader kept an eye open for smoke rising from the ground, to determine the wind direction, and aligned the attack run accordingly. Immediately before he commenced his dive, each Ju 87 pilot re-trimmed the aircraft for the dive and set the briefed bomb-release altitude (above sea level) on the contacting altimeter.

Inset into the floor of the cockpit in front of the pilot's seat was a window, through which he could see the target as it slid into position beneath the aircraft. A few seconds before commencing the dive, he throttled back the engine to idling and operated a lever to rotate the dive brakes to the maximum-drag position. The dive brakes produced a severe nose-up trim change to the aircraft, and to compensate for it a trim tab fitted to the elevators was lowered automatically.

When the formation leader commenced his dive, the rest of the aircraft in the formation followed in turn. For attacks on targets of small horizontal extent, for example bridges or small buildings, the Ju 87s usually approached in echelon formation, peeled into the dive and attacked in line astern. Against larger or better-defended targets, for example harbours or marshalling yards, the dive-bombers would usually bunt into their dives in three-aircraft vics and attack together to split the defensive fire.

Once established in its 80-degree dive, the Ju 87 was a stable platform and it was easy for the pilot to position the target under his reflector sight and hold it there. Speed built up relatively slowly, and it took a dive through 8,000ft for the aircraft to reach its terminal velocity of 350mph. The dive lasted about 20 seconds, allowing plenty of time to line up on the target. The accuracy of the attack depended upon maintaining a constant dive angle, and to assist in this a protractor was etched into the perspex on each side of the cockpit canopy so that the pilot could read off his angle during the dive.

When the aircraft reached a point 2,000ft above the bomb-release altitude previously set on the contacting altimeter, a warning horn sounded in the cockpit. When the aircraft reached the previously set bomb-release altitude, typically 2,300ft above the ground, the warning horn ceased. That was the signal to release the bombs. It will be remembered that before commencing the dive, a trim tab fitted to the elevators was lowered automatically to compensate for the nose-up pitching moment caused when the dive brakes were placed in the high-drag position. Now, the operation of releasing the bombs also activated a powerful spring, which returned the elevator trim tab sharply to the neutral position. The nose of the aircraft pitched up sharply, pulling the aircraft firmly but smoothly out of the dive. In this pre-set manoeuvre, the lowest point reached was about 1,000ft above the target – enough to give a margin of safety from exploding bombs and enemy small-arms fire. As the nose of the aircraft rose above the horizon, the pilot returned the dive brakes in the low-drag position, opened the throttle, re-trimmed the aircraft and turned on to the pre-briefed escape heading.

On completion of their training, German dive-bomber pilots were expected to put half of their bombs within a circle 25m (27yds) in radius centred on the target. (For comparison, the aiming error from a horizontal bomber releasing its bombs from high altitude was about three times as great.) In combat the bombing was invariably less accurate, because of the lack of familiarity with the target and the distractions caused by the enemy defences. As a result, the average bombing errors in combat were two or three times those achieved on the training ranges. Nevertheless, against (say) a circular target with a radius of 80yds, with moderately heavy anti-aircraft gun defences, a nine-aircraft *Staffel* of Ju 87s stood a good chance of scoring direct hits with half the bombs. Against very small, hard targets such as tanks of the period (typical dimensions about 7yds long and 3yds wide), which could survive anything except a direct hit or a very near miss, the Stukas were relatively ineffective.

To sum up, by a combination of its near-vertical dive, relatively low diving speed and low bomb-release altitude, the Ju 87 was able to deliver (unguided) bombs with an accuracy not previously achieved in action and rarely attained since. During the Second World War other types of aircraft also carried out steep-diving attacks, but these released their bombs from altitudes somewhat higher than those of the Ju 87 and their accuracy was correspondingly reduced.

During the invasion of Poland, in September 1939, the Ju 87 established a formidable reputation in combat. These aircraft were used to deliver pin-point attacks on bridges, rail targets and troop concentrations well behind from the front line – what are now termed 'battlefield air interdiction' missions.

Attacks on airfields met with less success. During the period of tension preceding the invasion, the Polish Air Force re-deployed most of its combat flying units to well-camouflaged field landing grounds. As a result, few military planes were lost during the attacks on the larger airfields and most of them were not combat types. Yet, although the Polish Air Force survived much of the initial onslaught, it was too small and its equipment was too outdated to pose a serious threat to German air operations. The Polish forces were poorly equipped with anti-aircraft guns for the protection of targets and, operating with little hindrance, the Ju 87 units struck hard and with great accuracy.

Despite numerous accounts that have suggested otherwise, over Poland the Ju 87 units were rarely used for close air support operations, that is to say against targets within a few hundred yards of friendly ground forces. The Ju 87 could deliver an accurate steep-diving attack only against a target that was clearly visible from

10,000ft (or nearly two miles). Camouflaged troop positions in the battle area were difficult to see from such an altitude, and even more difficult to attack. Moreover, as the wars in the Persian Gulf have shown, positive identification of troops in the battle area is a demanding business, and there is an ever-present risk that bombs might fall on the very troops they are supposed to assist.

The dive-bomber was a new and effective weapon and, above all, it was predominantly a *German* weapon. In those circumstances the German propaganda machine can hardly be blamed for playing the aircraft for all it was worth. Among friends and foes alike, the legend of the invincibility of the Stukas was established. Significantly, the number of Ju 87s in service at any time was never large. Over Poland, for example, the *Luftwaffe* committed every operational Ju 87 unit, but there were only about 370 aircraft.

On 10 May 1940 German forces launched their all-out *Blitzkrieg* campaign in the west, and from the first the Stukas were heavily committed. In one of many attacks flown by the dive-bombers that day, *Major* Walter Hagen led the 30 aircraft of *Trägergruppe 186* into the air from Hannweiler near Bad Kreuznach. (*Träger* = aircraft carrier; the unit was earmarked to operate from the aircraft carrier *Graf Zeppelin* when it was completed, but in the meantime it flew as a normal combat unit.)

The dive-bombers' objective was the major French Air Force base at Frescaty near Metz, some 70 miles away, and the attack was planned to take place at dawn. The aircraft took off and assembled into formation in the dark, each with a 550lb bomb under the fuselage and four 110-pounders on the underwing racks. The dive-bombers had no close escort, but a *Gruppe* of Messerschmitts was sweeping the route ahead of it to drive away any enemy planes that might be airborne. *Hauptmann* Helmut Mahlke described the action, from the time the Stukas arrived in the target area:

In the turn we went into line astern, thirty Ju 87s following each other into the attack. As we lined up for our dives the flak opened up at us, but their shooting was slow and it did not bother us much. The target assigned to my *Kette* [vic] was the airship hangar, I could see it clearly. When it was my turn to attack, I banked my aircraft then pushed into an 80-degree dive. At 700m I released my bombs in a salvo, then began my pull-out. As I did so I looked at the hangar and at first it seemed that nothing had happened. Then the building expanded, rather like a toy balloon when somebody blows into it. Suddenly, the structure collapsed in a cloud of smoke and debris.

After delivering their attacks the Ju 87s reassembled into formation and headed for home, having suffered no losses.

During the next six weeks, Mahlke's unit was in operation on almost every day that the weather allowed, with crews flying as many as four missions a day. By the final week in May, Allied forces in northern France were being pushed relentlessly towards the coast, and Operation 'Dynamo' began to evacuate troops from Dunkirk and the beaches to the east. On 1 June Mahlke took part in an attack on the port and had his first encounter with an RAF fighter:

> It tried to shoot me down but almost certainly it ran out of ammunition before it could do so. The pilot curved around, moved into formation alongside me, saluted and pulled away for home. It was an act of chivalry that could never have happened in Russia . . .

After the Dunkirk evacuation ended, the German ground forces regrouped and moved against the French forces trying to re-establish a defensive line across northern France. The Stukas resumed operations in support of advancing German units, and during this phase there occurred an incident which impressed on Mahlke the risks of attacking targets in the vicinity of friendly forces. On 17 June he was ordered to lead his *Staffel* against a French troop position at Chatillon-sur-Seine near Dijon, in an area some distance ahead of German forces which threatened to hold up the advance. The approach flight was uneventful and Mahlke began his attack-dive, but then he noticed Very lights rising from the ground and men hastily laying out recognition panels. The area was in German hands! Mahlke pulled out of the dive and ordered his crews to abandon the attack. It was a close call: his unit had come close to bombing friendly troops in error. Later it transpired that French resistance in the area had collapsed and that the German advance had been much faster than expected.

During the campaign in the West, *Trägergruppe 186* flew about 1,500 sorties, in the course of which it lost fifteen crews out of its establishment of 40. The overall loss rate was about 1 per cent, not a high figure, but the cumulative loss during the six weeks of hard fighting amounted to 40 per cent of the air crew. At that stage of the war the war losses in crews and aircraft were made good almost immediately from the replacement units, but it was an uncomfortable pointer to the problems that would arise during a lengthy campaign.

The Battle of Britain opened in July 1940, and the large-scale bombardment of targets on the British mainland began on 12 August. That day there were attacks by Stukas on the radar stations at Pevensey, Rye, Dover, Dunkirk (in Kent) and Ventnor. The radars proved difficult targets, however. They were small objectives and their vital parts were protected by blast walls. Although the open-work metal towers supporting the radar aerials might appear fragile, they presented only a small area to blast pressure or bomb splinters and it required almost a direct hit to knock one down. Although most of the radar stations suffered damage, following hasty repairs all except one was back in operation on the following day.

The largest co-ordinated attack ever mounted by Stukas took place on 18 August 1940, 'The Hardest Day'. One hundred and nine Ju 87s drawn from *Sturzkampfgeschwader 3* and *77*, escorted by more than 150 Messerschmitt Bf 109 fighters, set out to attack the airfields at Gosport, Ford and Thorney Island and the radar station at Poling. British radars observed the approaching attack force in good time, and the fighter controllers scrambled 68 Spitfires and Hurricanes to meet it. The defenders were still climbing into position to intercept when the Stuka formations crossed the coast and prepared to begin their attack-dives. The escorting Messerschmitts with each dive-bomber *Gruppe* now split into two parts, one remaining with the dive-bombers at high altitude while the other descended to 3,000ft ready to protect the Ju 87s when they pulled out of the dives and were at their most vulnerable.

At that moment, when the high-level escort was at its weakest, eighteen Hurricanes of Nos 43 and 601 Squadrons bounded into the Ju 87s of *I Gruppe* of *Sturzkampfgeschwader 77* as they were about to commence their attack on the airfield at Thorney Island. *Oberleutnant* Johannes Wilhelm, piloting one of the Stukas, heard the radio warning of the approaching fighters as he prepared to begin his dive. Behind him, *Unteroffizier* Anton Woerner, his rear gunner, squinted into the bright sun, looking for the enemy. Then, appearing as if from nowhere and with guns belching fire, the Hurricanes charged into the German formation. Wilhelm glimpsed three or four British fighters roar past him in rapid succession. To one side of him a Stuka burst into flames and slid out of the formation. Then Wilhelm felt his aircraft shudder and engine oil streamed back over his cabin. Then the cockpit began to fill with smoke: the aircraft was on fire! Wilhelm rolled the dive-bomber on to its back and shouted '*Raus!*' ('Get out!'). Both men slid back their canopies, released their straps and tumbled clear of the stricken dive-bomber.

As the Stukas commenced their attack-dives, individual Hurricanes followed them down, loosing off bursts whenever they could bring their sights to bear. Contrary to what some accounts have suggested, however, a Ju 87 in the dive was *almost invulnerable* to fighter attack.

Flight Lieutenant Frank Carey of No 43 Squadron, who led the Hurricane attack that day, commented:

> In the dive they were very difficult to hit, because in a fighter one's speed built up so rapidly that one went screaming past him. But he couldn't dive forever . . .

Oberleutnant Otto Schmidt released his bombs on Thorney Island and the Stuka was pulling itself out of the dive when something behind him caught his eye – an enemy fighter, looming large. His rear gunner was not firing back, and suddenly he realized why not – the unfortunate man was collapsed lifeless in his seat. In concentrating on making an accurate attack, Schmidt had failed to notice that his own aircraft had been hit. He pushed the Stuka into a sideslip to reduce speed and the British fighter shot past.

As the dive-bombers pulled away from their targets at low altitude, the leading Ju 87s flew at low speed to allow those behind to catch up easily. The aircraft flew in a loose gaggle, and if one came under attack from an enemy fighter it accelerated and flew past one or more of the others. If the fighter attempted to follow, it had to expose itself to fire from other Ju 87s in the gaggle. In the past the tactic had sometimes been effective in forcing fighters to break off the chase, but now several British squadrons were piling into the fight. The 25-mile strip of coastline between Bognor and Gosport became a turmoil of over 300 aircraft twisting and turning to bring guns to bear, or to avoid guns being brought to bear.

Running over the Isle of Wight from the west, Flight Lieutenant Derek Boitel-Gill, at the head of eleven Spitfires of No 152 Squadron, caught sight of the mêlée below. He ordered the unit into line astern and dived into the thick of the fighting. He closed on one of the dive-bombers, fired a four-second burst and saw the enemy go straight into the sea. Pilot Officer Eric Marrs followed his leader and later wrote:

> We dived after them and they went down to 100 feet above the water. Then followed a running chase out to sea. The evasive action they took was to throttle back and do steep turns to right and left, so that we would not be able to follow them and would overshoot. There were, however, so many of them that if one was shaken off the tail of one there was always another to sit on.

Marrs fired at several of the dive-bombers and saw one of them strike the sea, streaming burning petrol from its port wing. He continued his attacks until he ran out of ammunition.

JUNKERS JU 87B-1

Role: Two-seat dive-bomber.

Power: One Junkers Jumo 211 Da 12-cylinder, liquid-cooled engine developing 1,200hp at take-off.

Armament: Normal bomb load one 550lb bomb under the fuselage and four 110lb bombs under the wings; two Rheinmetall Borsig MG 17 7.9mm machine guns in the wings; one Rheinmetall Borsig MG 15 7.9mm machine gun in a flexible mounting firing rearwards.

Performance: (Without bomb load) Maximum speed 238mph at 13,130ft; maximum cruising speed 209mph at 12,145ft; maximum range 490 miles; service ceiling 26,240ft.

Normal operational take-off weight: 9,560lb.

Dimensions: Span 45ft 3¼ in; length 36ft 1 in; wing area 343 sq ft.

Date type entered production: May 1938

The Stukas hit their targets with great precision, scarcely a single bomb falling outside the immediate area surrounding each target. Ford airfield was put out of action for several weeks, while those at Thorney Island and Gosport continued in use though at reduced efficiency. Twenty-one aircraft were wrecked on the ground. The radar station at Poling suffered severe damage, though following repairs it was back in use after a few days.

Of the Stuka *Gruppen* involved, one, *I* of *Sturzkampfgeschwader 77*, was hit particularly hard: of the 28 Stukas taking part in the attack, ten were shot down, one was damaged beyond repair and four returned with serious damage. More than half the unit's aircraft had been destroyed or damaged. The unit's commander, *Hauptmann* Herbert Meisel, was among those killed. The other three *Gruppen* lost only six aircraft shot down and two damaged. Considering the force as a whole, 21 per cent of aircraft had been destroyed or damaged – too great a loss to be accepted as a matter of course.

The action on 18 August 1940 was the first real setback suffered by the Stukas, and it served to highlight a weakness that would be demonstrated again and again as the war progressed: the aircraft was a fine offensive weapon, but only if it could operate without hindrance from enemy fighters. If air superiority had not been secured, the dive-bomber units could expect heavy losses.

The Stukas next went into action over the Mediterranean after 150 of these aircraft were deployed to Sicily to support the Italian bombardment of Malta and the convoys taking supplies to the belea-guered island. On 10 January 1941 the Ju 87 revealed its devastating effectiveness against capital ships of the Royal Navy. In attacks on ships manoeuvring in open water, dive-bombing was far more effective than horizontal bombing. A dive-bomber pilot could follow the ship during its evasive turn, re-aligning his sight to aim at a point in the sea immediately in front of the vessel. The time of flight of the bombs after release, about five seconds, was too short for any subsequent change of helm to take effect.

That day the target was a battle group comprising the aircraft carrier *Illustrious*, two battleships and eight destroyers escorting a convoy of supply ships bound for Malta and Greece. The striking force comprised 43 Ju 87s, drawn from *I Gruppe* of *Sturzkampfgeschwader I* and *II Gruppe* of *StG 2*. At the time the German aircraft were first detected on radar approaching the force, the four Fulmar fighters airborne were at low altitude and nearly out of ammunition, having driven off an attack by Italian torpedo bombers. The carrier turned into wind and launched four more fighters, but it was too late for them to climb to meet the raiders before the attack began. The Ju 87s began their dives without interference from enemy fighters, concentrating on *Illustrious* as their main target. Admiral Cunningham, the Royal Navy force commander, later wrote of their attack:

> There was no doubt we were watching complete experts. We could not but admire the skill and precision of it all. The attacks were pressed home to point blank range, and as they pulled out of their dives, some of them were seen to fly along the flight deck of *Illustrious* below the level of her funnel.

From start to finish the action took only seven minutes, by the end of which the carrier had suffered seven direct hits and one near-miss:

Bomb No 1 hit and destroyed the starboard S.2 pom-pom (anti-aircraft gun) and killed most of the crew.

Bomb No 2 perforated the forward end of the flight deck and passed overboard, exploding 10ft above the waterline. This caused extensive splinter damage to compartments near the waterline and started a fire in one of them.

Bomb No 3 exploded in the after lift well about 10–20ft below the flight deck, causing severe damage to the lift structure and electrical equipment and wrecking a Fulmar fighter on the lift.

Bomb No 4 perforated the armoured flight deck and exploded just above the hangar deck. This caused serious damage to the forward lift and the surrounding hangar deck structure. The blast blew away the fire curtains, causing numerous casualties, and started a serious fire in the hangar. Several aircraft in the hangar were destroyed.

Bomb No 5 hit the after end of the after lift, adding to the damage caused by bomb No 3.

Bomb No 6 perforated a pom-pom gun platform, passed through the ship and went overboard without detonating. A fire was started in two mess decks.

Bomb No 7 hit the after lift well and this completed the destruction of the lift structure.

Bomb No 8 was a near-miss off the starboard side which caused minor damage to the structure and slight flooding.

To add to the damage, a shot-down Ju 87 crashed into the carrier's flight deck near the after lift well, starting a further fire in that much-battered area.

The onslaught left the Royal Navy's newest aircraft carrier in dire distress, with fires blazing out of control below her decks and tongues of flame shooting from the after lift well. The rudders were out of action and she headed for Malta, steered by using differential revolutions on the main engines. The ship could no longer operate her aircraft, and those that were airborne were ordered to fly to Malta.

A follow-up attack during the late afternoon by fifteen Ju 87s caused a further direct hit near the after lift, adding to the damage to that area, and two near-misses close to the stern. That evening, with the fires inside the hull still burning out of control, the pummelled carrier reached Malta and tied up in Valetta harbour. During the attacks 83 of her crew had been killed and 100 wounded.

While *Illustrious* was undergoing repairs in Valetta, she was subjected to further attacks. Yet another direct hit near the after lift caused further damage to that part of the ship. Near-misses caused damage to machinery in the boiler room. Despite these intrusions, essential repairs were completed in a remarkably short time. After dark on 23 January, unnoticed by the enemy, the carrier limped out from Malta and headed for Alexandria. More than a year would elapse before she was again ready for operations. The action established that the waters within range of the Stuka bases in Sicily were now virtually off-limits to Royal Navy capital ships.

The Ju 87s would achieve further destruction against the Royal Navy during the invasion of Crete in May 1941 and the subsequent evacuation of Allied forces. And they would demonstrate their effectiveness yet again when German forces invaded the Soviet Union in the following month. Yet the heyday of the Stuka was fast drawing to a close. From the beginning of 1942 each of Germany's enemies appreciated the potent threat posed by the Ju 87s when they could operate without restriction, and the vital need to contain that threat. The best answer, of course, was to have enough fighters to make attacks by the dive-bombers too expensive to contemplate. That requirement had been easy to assert but difficult to fulfil, but now, as the *Luftwaffe* became over-committed on each battle front in turn, the enemy fighter defences became much more difficult for the Stukas to penetrate.

The other means of countering the dive-bomber, which was now available in large and increasing quantities, was the fast-firing, medium-calibre anti-aircraft gun. Typical of the weapons in this class were the 40mm Bofors used by British forces and the 37mm M 1939 used by the Soviets. The weapons fired at a rate of about 120 rounds a minute, and a Ju 87 would be lucky to survive one hit from their explosive shells. Viewed from the target, a Stuka making a steep-diving attack appeared to hang almost stationary in space. It thus presented a zero-deflection shot, and if the gunners knew their business their fire was lethal.

By mid-1942 most high-value targets had effective gun defences, and the Stukas had to abandon their accurate steep-diving attacks. Increasingly they were used in shallow-dive or low-altitude attacks, which were less risky but also far less effective. Losses in experienced crews mounted rapidly, further reducing the effectiveness of those *Gruppen* equipped with the type. In the autumn of 1943 the *Sturzkampfgeschwader* (dive-bomber *Geschwader*) were renamed *Schlachtgeschwader* (ground attack *Geschwader*) and soon afterwards the majority of units re-equipped with FW 190 fighter-bombers. The day of the Stuka had passed.

Chapter 3

Only One Came Back

*When the Bristol Blenheim entered service with the Royal
Air Force in 1937, the twin-engine bomber was one of the
fastest combat aircraft in the world. Produced in large numbers,
it formed a cornerstone of the Royal Air Force's rearmament
programme. This was a time of rapid advances in aviation,
however, and the Messerschmitt Bf 109E which entered service
early in 1939 had a speed advantage of 70mph over the
Blenheim. In the spring of 1940 the Blenheim squadrons were
the mainstay of the RAF tactical bomber force, and they bore
the brunt of the fighting when the Germans launched their
offensive in the west. All of the units committed suffered heavy
losses, none more so than No 82 Squadron when it attempted
an attack on German troops advancing through Belgium on the
morning of 17 May.*

On 10 May 1940, when the German offensive in the west
opened, No 82 Squadron was based at Watton in Norfolk and
had a strength of 22 Blenheim IV bombers. The unit spent the next
two days on standby, awaiting the order to go into action. In the
afternoon of 12 May it sent nine aircraft to bomb roads in Belgium,
to crater them and render them impassable to enemy traffic. After
another day of inactivity, in the morning of the 14th the Squadron
sent six aircraft to attack rail and road targets in Holland. During
these operations No 82 encountered no determined fighter opposition and all its aircraft returned safely.

Other units flying attack missions had suffered heavily, however,
giving a grim foretaste of what lay in store if the slow bombers were
intercepted by enemy fighters. In the afternoon of the 14th, the RAF

tactical bomber squadrons launched an all-out attack on bridges over the Meuse River near Sedan, across which German troops and supplies were streaming to support the thrust into France. The area was patrolled by large numbers of Messerschmitts and the bombers suffered appalling losses: of the 71 aircraft taking part in the attacks, 40 were shot down. After the war the official historian would record that 'No higher rate of loss in an operation of comparable size has ever been experienced by the RAF'. Meanwhile No 82 Squadron's charmed existence continued. On the 15th it sent twelve aircraft to attack enemy troops concentrating near Montherme and again all of the Blenheims returned safely. The unit's run of luck was about to end, however, and do so in most brutal fashion.

At 2 a.m. in the morning of the 17 May, the crews were roused early and made their way to the briefing room. The unit had orders to bomb an enemy troop column reported to be moving between Namur and Gembloux in Belgium, the attack to be delivered at first light. It was still dark at 4.50 a.m. when Squadron Leader Miles Delap, the unit commander, led the first element of three bombers into the air off the grass runway at Watton. At measured intervals, the other three elements followed. Once airborne, Delap circled the airfield, lights on, while other elements formed up behind him. The formation comprised two flights each of six bombers with two elements flying in tight 'vic' formation one behind the other and stepped down. Each aircraft carried four 250lb bombs. The Blenheims were to rendezvous en route with a squadron of Hurricanes that was to escort them to the target, but because of an administrative hitch the latter failed to show up. The Blenheims were to continue with their attack alone.

Cruising at 9,000ft on the clear spring morning, the raiders were nearing their target when suddenly they were buffeted by anti-aircraft shells bursting all around them. The formation opened out and the aircraft flew a weaving path to present a more difficult target for predicted fire. For one of the Blenheims the evasive action began too late, however, and the unfortunate machine fell out of the formation in a steep descent, trailing flames.

As suddenly as the cannonade began it ended, but this was the lull before the tempest. Before the bombers had time to regain their previous close formation, they came under attack from about fifteen Messerschmitt Bf 109s of *Jagdgeschwader 3* which dived from out of the sun and opened fire with cannon and machine guns. The Blenheims' gunners loosed off long bursts to try to beat off the fighters, but the bombers' light defensive armament was quite insufficient for the task. Delap later recalled:

Some of the bombers dived away, others went off weaving through the sky as they took evasive action. My own aircraft was holed along both the port and starboard wings and the port engine caught fire. Only the armour plating behind my seat saved me. Then a shell exploded in the cockpit and started a fire which produced so much smoke that I could no longer see the instrument panel. That was the last-straw and I gave the order to bail out. With all that smoke I had no hope of reaching the floor escape hatch, so I released the hatch above my head and climbed up on my seat, facing aft, and prepared to jump clear. The next thing I knew, I was out in the cool air. After the heat and smoke in the cockpit that was quite a relief. Fortunately I was well covered and only my eyelashes had got burnt. When I was well clear of the aircraft I thought the time had come to pull the ripcord. I felt for it, but couldn't find it. I looked down for it, but it wasn't there. There was no panic, but I remember thinking 'That's odd!' Then I looked up and saw that parachute was already open. I hadn't lost consciousness and I knew I hadn't pulled the ripcord – it was indeed very odd.

The Messerschmitts had a field day, picking off the Blenheims one after another. That piloted by Sergeant 'Jock' Morrison was hit several times, one engine was knocked out and the aircraft went into a spin. Probably the German fighter pilot thought it was going the same way as the others, and broke off the attack. Morrison regained control of the battered aircraft, however, levelled out close to the ground and set course for Watton flying on his remaining engine. It was the only bomber to survive the engagement.

After several minutes spent dangling from his parachute, Miles Delap was deposited gently in a forest:

BRISTOL BLENHEIM Mk IV

Role: Three-seat light bomber and reconnaissance aircraft.
Power: Two Bristol Mercury 9-cylinder, air-cooled, radial engines each developing 920hp at take-off.
Armament: Normal bomb load 1,000lb. (Defensive) one fixed Browning .303in machine gun firing forwards; two Browning .303in machine guns in the dorsal turret.
Performance: Maximum speed 266mph at 11,800ft; maximum cruising speed 225mph at 15,000ft.
Normal operational take-off weight: 14,500lb.
Dimensions: Span 56ft 4in; length 42ft 9in; wing area 469 sq ft.
Date of first production Blenheim IV: Spring 1939.

MESSERSCHMITT BF 109E-3

Role: Single-seat fighter.
Power: One Daimler Benz DB 601Aa 12-cylinder, liquid-cooled engine developing 1,175hp at take-off.
Armament: Two MF/FFF 20mm cannon mounted in the wings; two MG 17 7.9mm machine guns mounted on top of the engine and synchronized to fire through the airscrew.
Performance: Maximum speed 348mph at 14,560ft; climb to 19,685ft, 6min 12sec.
Normal operational take-off weight: 5,875lb.
Dimensions: Span 32ft 4½in; length 28ft 4¼in; wing area 176.5 sq ft.
Date of first production E sub-type: February 1939.

My parachute caught in a tree so I undid my harness and slid down the trunk. There was a battle going on nearby; I could not see anything but there was an exchange of small-arms fire not very far away. What was incongruous was that the birds were making nearly as much noise as the guns: it was about 6 o'clock in the morning and this was the dawn chorus. I had come down near Villiers, which seemed appropriate as it happens to be my middle name.

Soon after he had landed, the pilot was picked up by French soldiers, and eventually he returned to England via Cherbourg.

Delap knew that his force had suffered heavy losses, but not until he reached Watton a couple of weeks after the incident did he learn that only one Blenheim – Morrison's – had returned from the operation. And it had been damaged beyond repair. At Watton Delap was reunited with his navigator, Sergeant Frank Wyness, who had also returned from France. The latter was able to settle the mystery of Delap's missing ripcord. While the pilot had been standing on his seat, gathering his wits before jumping from the burning aircraft, Wyness thought he had lost consciousness. So he took hold of Delap's ripcord with one hand, and gave the pilot a hefty shove with the other. Then Wyness followed him out of the opening.

Morrison and his crew, Delap, Wyness and the few others who made it back to Watton after parachuting into France had been the lucky ones. Of the 36 air crewmen who had set out on the attack, almost all had been killed or taken prisoner. None of their bombs had reached the intended target. It was a terrible example of the fate likely to befall those who fly obsolete aircraft against an enemy who possesses air superiority.

Chapter 4

Low Altitude Attack

*Sunday 18 August 1940 saw some of the fiercest fighting of the
Battle of Britain. On that day the Luftwaffe planned heavy
attacks on four important fighter airfields near London. The
first of these, Kenley, was hit early that afternoon in an action
involving almost the whole of* Kampfgeschwader 76.

During the campaigns in Poland and France, *Kampfgeschwader 76*
had demonstrated its capabilities as a hard-hitting bomber unit.
By the beginning of the Battle of Britain the *Geschwader* was established at three airfields situated near to each other to the north of
Paris: *I* and *III Gruppen,* based at Beavais and Cormeilles-en-Vexin
respectively, were equipped with Dornier Do 17s, and *II Gruppe*, based
at Creil, had recently re-equipped with Junkers Ju 88s. Most crews in
the *Geschwader* had previous combat experience, and morale was high.

The 9th *Staffel* of the *Geschwader*, part of *III Gruppe*, specialized in
low-altitude attacks on pin-point targets. For the low-altitude attack
role, the Do 17 was considered the best of the German twin-engine
bomber types available. It was the only one powered by air-cooled
radial engines, which were far less vulnerable to battle damage than
their liquid-cooled equivalents. The aircraft of the 9th *Staffel* were
fitted with additional armour to protect the crew and, to provide
extra firepower for engaging ground targets, each carried a 20mm
Oerlikon cannon on a flexible mounting in the nose.

The attack on Kenley was planned to take place in three phases.
First, a dozen Junkers Ju 88s of *II Gruppe* were to carry out a precision dive-bombing attack on the hangars and airfield installations.
Five minutes later, 27 Dornier Do 17s of *I* and *III Gruppen* were
to deliver a horizontal bombing attack from 12,000ft to crater the

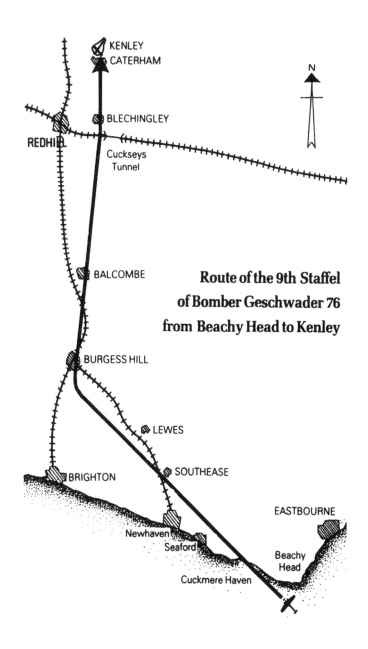

KENLEY
CATERHAM

BLECHINGLEY

REDHILL

Cuckseys
Tunnel

**Route of the 9th Staffel
of Bomber Geschwader 76
from Beachy Head to Kenley**

BALCOMBE

BURGESS HILL

LEWES

SOUTHEASE

BRIGHTON

EASTBOURNE

Newhaven
Seaford

Beachy
Head

Cuckmere Haven

airfield and knock out the ground defences. The high-flying Ju 88s and Dorniers were to attack from the south-east and they would have full fighter escort. Finally, five minutes after the horizontal-bombing attack, nine Do 17s of the 9th *Staffel* were to run in at low altitude from the south to finish off any important buildings that were still standing. It was a bold and an imaginative plan but, like so many of its kind in the history of air warfare, it would be only partially successful. Only the low-altitude attack would cause serious damage, and in the process the 9th *Staffel* itself would suffer heavy losses. The account that follows will centre on the action fought by that unit.

Shortly before noon, the Dorniers and Ju 88s of the high-altitude raiding forces began taking off. The bombers assembled into formation and began their long, slow climb to attack altitude, heading for the Pas de Calais where they were to rendezvous with their escorting fighters. On the way the bombers ran into a layer of cloud that was much thicker than expected, with the result that several aircraft were forced out of formation. Above cloud the leaders had to orbit for several minutes to allow their formations to reassemble. At the time nobody realized it, but the delay was to have terrible consequences for the *9th Staffel* attacking at low altitude.

Since it was to fly a more direct route to the target and remain at low altitude throughout the mission, the 9th *Staffel* left Cormeilles-en-Vexin several minutes after the other bombers. As usual during hazardous attacks, the unit's popular commander, *Hauptmann* Joachim Roth, flew as navigator in the leading Dornier. The nine-aircraft formation flew across northern France and the English Channel at a comfortable 500ft, letting down to 60ft to remain below the *British* radar cover as it approached the coast of Sussex.

Near the coast the bombers passed a couple of Royal Navy patrol boats, which opened an ineffective fire with machine guns. None of the Dorniers was hit and the boats were soon left behind. Soon after 1 p.m. the raiding force crossed the coast just west of Beachy Head.

In the light of what happened later, many Germans thought it was the chance meeting with the patrol boats that robbed the raiders of the advantage of surprise. The air defences of Great Britain rested on surer foundations than that, however. As the bombers neared the coast the Observer Corps post on top of Beachy Head reported their approach to the Observer Group Headquarters at Horsham: nine Dorniers at zero altitude, heading north-west. The report was relayed to Fighter Command's raid reporting net, and passed to each of the Group and Sector operations rooms.

Once past the coast, Roth continued on his north-westerly heading, making for Burgess Hill. He had chosen the small market

---

DORNIER Do 17Z

Role: Four-seat bomber (with folding seat to enable one further person to be carried, if required).

Power: Two Bramo 323 Fafnir 9-cylinder, air-cooled, radial engines each developing 1,000hp at take-off.

Armament: Normal operational bomb load 2,200lb. (Defensive) six Rheinmetall Borsig MG 15 7.9mm machine guns in flexible mountings, two firing forwards, two firing rearwards and one firing from each side of the cabin. The aircraft operated by 9./ KG 76 carried an Oerlikon 20mm cannon in place of one of the forward-firing machine guns.

Performance: Maximum speed 255mph at 13,120ft; normal formation cruising speed at 16,000ft,180mph; normal formation cruising speed at low altitude (9./KG 76), 175mph; radius of action with normal bomb load, 205 miles.

Normal operational take-off weight: 18,930lb.

Dimensions: Span 59ft 0¼in; length 51 ft 9½in; wing area 592 sq ft.

Date of first production Do 17Z: Early 1939.

---

town as his turning point because it lay on the junction of the rail lines from Lewes and Brighton, and from there he could follow the line to London; furthermore, the seven tall chimneys of the town's brickworks would serve as an unmistakable landmark for the low-flying aircraft. The bombers found Burgess Hill without difficulty and turned on to their northerly heading. As they roared low over the town, many of its citizens stood in the open, gazing up at the unaccustomed sight. *Unteroffizier* Günther Unger, piloting one of the Dorniers, recalled:

At first they did not take us for the enemy, not expecting German aircraft to be flying so low. Then the large crosses on our wings taught them otherwise and in the next instant they were scurrying for cover.

Once past the town, the bombers raced northwards over the undulating countryside. War correspondent and photographer Rolf von Pebal, flying as a passenger in one of the Dorniers, later wrote:

We zoomed over the English countryside, a few metres high. Every fold in the ground served as cover for us, each wood was exploited as a hiding place. We bounded over trees, undulating the whole time. A train rushed by underneath us. A couple of cyclists dashed for cover in the ditch by the side of the road.

PARACHUTE-AND-CABLE SYSTEM

Launched vertically into the path of low-flying aircraft, this unconventional weapon was fired in nine-round salvos from a row of launchers on the ground. The weapon comprised a 480ft length of steel cable suspended from a parachute, which opened automatically when the rocket reached the top of its climb at about 600ft. When an aircraft struck the cable and started to carry it forwards, the shock of the impact caused the opening of a second drag parachute attached to the bottom end of the cable. If the contraption snagged on the wing or any other part of the aircraft, the combined drag from the two parachutes imposed a violent deceleration that was usually sufficient to cause the machine to stall and fall out of the sky in an uncontrollable dive.

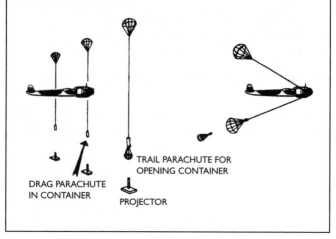

DRAG PARACHUTE
IN CONTAINER

PROJECTOR

TRAIL PARACHUTE FOR
OPENING CONTAINER

The Observer Corps posts along the route continued to issue regular reports on the progress of the low-flying Dorniers. In the Sector operations room at Kenley, the station commander, Wing Commander Thomas Prickman, had watched as his two fighter squadrons were vectored to intercept the high-altitude raiding forces coming in from the south-east. When the 9th *Staffel* turned north over Burgess Hill, it was clear that his airfield or that at Croydon was under threat. Accordingly Prickman ordered all airworthy planes on the ground at Kenley to take off on a 'survival scramble' and head north-west, until the threat had passed. He also ordered No III Squadron, at readiness at Croydon with twelve Hurricanes, to scramble and patrol over Kenley at 3,000ft.

At 1.19 p.m. the Dorniers passed over the Reigate-Tonbridge railway line, one of the navigation features pointed out to crews at the briefing. Joachim Roth had achieved a clever piece of low-altitude navigation. After a 60-mile sea crossing and a flight of 40 minutes over unfamiliar enemy territory, he had brought his force to within three minutes of the target, on time and exactly on the planned route. But where were the pillars of smoke rising from the target, to indicate that the dive-bombing and horizontal attacks had subdued the airfield's defences? Obviously something had gone wrong, but Roth had every reason to believe that his unit still retained the advantage of surprise, and there was no thought of turning back.

At Kenley the anti-aircraft gun and rocket defences were stood-to and ready for action. The airfield's defence against low-flying aircraft comprised four 40mm Bofors guns, two obsolete 3in anti-aircraft guns and about twenty Lewis .303in machine guns. Also, along the northern edge of the airfield was a line of parachute-and-cable launchers, an unconventional 'secret weapon' that had not previously been used in action. Now, as the bombers closed in, the weapons were manned and loaded and the gun barrels were pointed expectantly to the south.

In the operations room at Kenley, Prickman watched the markers representing the enemy raiding forces march relentlessly across the map table towards his station. Now he ordered one of his officers to broadcast a final warning on the public address system: 'Air attack imminent: all personnel not on defence duties to the shelters.'

At 1.21 p.m., a couple of miles south of target, the Dorniers of the 9th *Staffel* leapt the final hundred feet to clear the North Downs and the formation widened out as the crews picked out their assigned targets. Moments later the Hurricane pilots of No 111 Squadron sighted the bombers and began curving into attack positions, while the German rear gunners let fly at them.

As this was happening, the Kenley ground defences opened fire with everything they had. There was the distinctive booming of the rapid-firing Bofors guns, as they loosed off bursts of six or eight rounds at a time. There was the louder, more measured bark of the 3in guns. Then came the stutter of one, then two, then several Lewis guns. In the Dorniers the gunners replied in kind, firing back with their cannon and machine guns.

The first aircraft to go down was a Hurricane, that flown by Flight Lieutenant Stanley Connors leading No 111 Squadron. Whether his fighter was hit by a bomber's return fire or by the Kenley defences, or by both, will never be known with certainty. The Hurricane swerved to one side and dived into the ground with the pilot still in the cockpit. The remaining Hurricanes pulled away violently to escape from the fiery inferno and headed round to the far side of the airfield to catch the bombers as they emerged from the target.

Günther Unger saw a hail of light flak and machine-gun fire shower past his cockpit. He pushed the aircraft yet lower and went for his target, the left-hand hangars. Moments later, Lewis-gun rounds thudded into his right engine and brought it to a smoking stop. The pilot feathered the propeller and struggled to hold the Dornier straight, as his navigator released the bombs in one long stick.

Unteroffizier Schumacher, piloting another of the Dorniers, watched the bombs from the leading aircraft ram into the hangars:

> Other bombs were bouncing down the runway like rubber balls. Hell was let loose. Then the bombs began their work of destruction. Three hangars collapsed like matchwood. Explosion followed explosion, flames leapt into the sky. It seemed as if my aircraft was grabbed by some giant.

Enemy rounds thudded into the bomber, leaving a smell of phosphorous and smouldering cables. Several of the plane's instruments were smashed, and the left engine was hit, belched smoke and started to lose power. As the Dornier leading the right-hand section was closing on its target, a Lewis-gun round hit the pilot squarely in the chest and he slumped forwards. The navigator, *Oberfeldwebel* Wilhelm Illg, leaned over the unconscious man and grabbed the control column to prevent the aircraft smashing into the ground.

After releasing their bombs on buildings on the south side of the airfield, the bombers skimmed low over the landing ground to make good their escape. Beside the line of parachute-and-cable launchers, the operator, saw three enemy bombers coming straight for him and when he judged them to be within range he pushed his firing button. With a *whoosh*, a salvo of nine rockets soared into the sky, each leaving a trail of smoke. *Feldwebel* Wilhelm Raab was at the controls of one of the Dorniers heading towards the trails:

> Suddenly red-glowing balls rose up from the ground in front of me. Each one trailed a line of smoke about 1 metre thick behind it, with intervals of 10 to 15 metres between each. I had experienced machine-gun and flak fire often enough, but this was something entirely new.

Raab had no idea what was in front of him, but obviously the spectacle had not been laid on for his health. He eased the aircraft

HAWKER HURRICANE Mk I

Role: Single-seat fighter.
Power: One Rolls-Royce Merlin III 12-cylinder, liquid-cooled
engine developing 1,030hp at 16,250ft.
Armament: Eight Browning .303in machine guns mounted in the
wings.
Performance: Maximum speed 328mph at 20,000ft; climb to
20,000ft, 3min 30sec.
Normal operational take-off weight: 6,447lb.
Dimensions: Span 40ft; length 31ft 4in; wing area 258 sq ft.
Date of first production Hurricane I: October 1937.

up from the ground, then swung the control wheel to the right to
drop the right wing, to pass between two of the smoke trails:

> Everything seemed to be going well – then I felt a hefty tug
> on my machine. Now they've got us, I thought, we're going to
> smash into the ground.

But Raab's quick thinking had saved the Dornier from disaster. The
aircraft was in a bank when it struck the cable, and the latter slid
along the wing and fell clear before the lower parachute had time
to open and take effect. Once through the line of smoke trails, Raab
levelled out and waggled the controls; to his immense relief, the
aircraft responded normally.

Another Dornier was less fortunate. It had been hit earlier and was
on fire, and it ran straight into one of the hanging cables. The trap
functioned as its designers intended and the combined drag of the
two parachutes caused the bomber to stall and fall out of control. It
smashed into the ground just beyond the airfield boundary and all
five men on board were killed.

Joachim Roth in the leading Dornier was another of those
threatened by the cables. He had released his bombs when the
rockets rose into the sky in front of him. The pilot, *Oberleutnant*
Rudolf Lamberty, eased the aircraft up a little to give more room to
manoeuvre and turned to avoid the threat. In that he was successful,
and the bomber cleared the obstacle easily. But immediately afterwards a Bofors shell struck the left wing beside the engine and
blew a gaping hole in the structure. Petrol gushed from the shattered fuel tank and burst into flames, as Lamberty feathered the
propeller of the dying engine and struggled to hold the Dornier
in the air.

Lamberty passed over the airfield boundary, and immediately afterwards a pair of Hurricanes charged after him from above. The German pilot saw dust spurts rise from the ground in front of him, kicked up by bullets that had missed his aircraft. Those that hit the Dornier made a hollow sound 'like a handful of dried peas thrown against a window pane'. The first fighter overshot, then the other ran in to attack and scored further hits.

The Dornier was now a flying time-bomb: it was only a matter of time before the petrol fire burned through the main spar and the entire structure of the wing collapsed. The three crewmen in the rear cabin baled out, and two of them suffered broken limbs when they struck the ground with partially open parachutes. Lamberty crash-landed in a cornfield and he and Roth suffered burns during their escape from the plane.

With the formation broken up and most of the Dorniers under fighter attack, each bomber crew had to look to its own salvation. That said, however, the action that followed was not one-sided. The RAF pilots had no previous experience of engaging bombers manoeuvring close to the ground, while their opponents were at home in that environment. As a result, the Dornier crews were able to give as good as they got.

Sergeant Harry Newton swung his Hurricane into a firing position behind one of the bombers and saw tracer rounds coming towards him from his intended victim. The German pilot, Günther Unger, edged his Dornier lower to avoid the attack, but, flying on one engine, he had few options. Newton opened fire and saw his tracers go over the bomber's starboard wing:

> I thought, just a slight correction and I've got him! But just at that moment he got me, because my cockpit seemed to burst into flames . . . But I was so annoyed at the thought of that Dornier getting away that I put my hand back into the flames, groped for the stick, made my correction and then loosed off a long burst in the direction of where I thought the Dornier was.

Newton then pulled into an almost vertical climb to gain altitude before baling out, keeping his eyes tightly closed to protect them from the flames licking around him. The fighter's speed fell away rapidly, then the engine coughed to a halt. Newton slammed the stick forwards, kicked himself out of the cockpit and pulled his ripcord. As he did so he opened his eyes, in time to see the tail of his Hurricane flash past about a foot away from his right ear. The next thing he knew was that the parachute had opened and the ground was coming up to meet him.

The frenzied low-level chases over the Sussex countryside continued. In addition to the Hurricane shot down at the beginning of the action and that flown by Harry Newton, two other Hurricanes were hit and damaged by the bombers' return fire.

In an air action, events follow each other with great rapidity. Everything described in this narrative, from the time the 9th *Staffel* commenced its attack on Kenley until the last Hurricane broke off the chase, occurred in a space of just five minutes – from 1.22 to 1.27 p.m. on that fateful Sunday afternoon.

Seven of the nine Dorniers that had attacked Kenley re-crossed the south coast of England on their way home, but most were in a pitiful condition. Two of the bombers were each flying on a single damaged engine, and they ditched in the English Channel. Two more Dorniers with serious damage made it back to France but crash-landed near the coast; one was found to have no fewer than *two hundred hits* from .303in rounds, a testimony to the ruggedness of its structure. A further two Dorniers made wheels-down landings at airfields near the coast, one to allow a wounded crewman to receive medical attention, the other flown by its navigator after the pilot had been mortally wounded. Only one of the Dorniers returned without major damage or a seriously wounded crewman. Of the forty men on board the Dorniers, nine were killed, three were wounded and five were taken prisoner. All five officers taking part in the attack were killed, seriously wounded or captured. Never again would the *Luftwaffe* attempt a low-altitude, deep-penetration attack on a target in England with a formation of twin-engine bombers.

The low-altitude attack destroyed three out of the four hangars at Kenley, and several other buildings. The attack by horizontal bombers a few minutes later inflicted relatively little damage, except for some cratering of the landing ground. The two attacks destroyed four Hurricanes and a Blenheim fighter on the landing ground, and caused damage to two Hurricanes and a Spitfire. The planned attack on Kenley by Ju 88 dive-bombers failed to materialize. These aircraft arrived at the target late, to find the airfield shrouded in smoke from fires caused by the earlier attacks. They bombed their secondary target at West Mailing airfield.

Although they inflicted severe damage, the attacks did not put Kenley airfield out of action for long. It was a relatively simple matter to select the least-cratered area of grass 500yds long and 50yds wide, render safe the unexploded bombs, fill in the craters and then flatten with a steam roller. Within a couple of hours, the airfield had a usable runway and limited fighter operations resumed; and within 24 hours of the attack, Kenley and her resident fighter squadrons were fully operational again.

There are three important operational lessons to be drawn from the attack on Kenley on 18 August 1940. The first is that low-flying aircraft are vulnerable to ground defences, if the former lose the element of surprise on their way to the target. That lesson is as true today as it was in 1940.

The second lesson is that resolute and well-equipped repair teams can restore an airfield to operations remarkably soon after an attack. Equipment that is destroyed or damaged can usually be replaced. Engineering work on aircraft can be carried out in the open, especially during the summer months.

The third lesson is that if there were a well-organized raid reporting system, it was extremely difficult to destroy fighters on the ground in any numbers by bombing their airfields. If there were sufficient warning – and during the Battle of Britain there usually was – fighters at a high state of readiness were airborne and clear of their base before an attack could develop. Aircraft dispersed on the ground or sitting in revetments were difficult to hit. The four RAF fighters destroyed on the ground during the attacks on Kenley represented a rare success for the German bomber force: during three and a half weeks of concentrated attacks on Fighter Command airfields in the Battle of Britain, *fewer than twenty* Spitfires and Hurricanes were destroyed on the ground at those airfields.

Chapter 5

Countering the Night Bomber

*During August 1940 the Luftwaffe began night attacks on cities
in Great Britain, which ran in parallel with the daylight attacks
on airfields during the Battle of Britain. So began the 'Night
Blitz' that would cause enormous damage and large numbers
of casualties. To counter this, the first-ever large-scale night
bombing campaign, initially the British defences proved woefully
inadequate and the raiders suffered minimal losses. Far more of
the German planes were lost in flying accidents than were shot
down by the defences. In the heat of battle the RAF had to try
to cobble together an effective night air defence system, and by
the end of the campaign it had succeeded.*

The *Luftwaffe* began large-scale night raids on targets in Great
Britain on 28 August 1940, when a force of 160 bombers was
sent to attack Liverpool. The raiders returned to the port in similar
strength on the three nights that followed, and also on the nights of
4, 5 and 6 September.

On 7 September the *Luftwaffe* shifted the focus of its attack to
London, and that afternoon it sent a force of some 350 bombers
escorted by more than 600 fighters to strike at the capital. The raid
started huge fires in the dock areas to the east of the city, which were
still burning that night when 318 bombers delivered a follow-up
attack lasting more than six hours. With their target clearly marked,
the night raiders delivered their high-explosive and incendiary
bombs with devastating accuracy. Soon after midnight there were
nine fires raging that merited the official description of 'conflagra-
tion' (defined as a major fire that was spreading and which required

more than 100 pumps to bring it under control). One such blaze, in the Surrey Docks, grew into the fiercest single fire ever recorded in Britain.

The fire brigades spent the whole of the daylight hours of the 8th in a desperate battle to control the fires, but several resisted their efforts to extinguish them. As a result, there was light aplenty to guide the 207 bombers which returned to the city after dark. The previous fires were fed afresh and new ones were kindled, and by dawn there were twelve conflagrations raging. A further 412 people were killed and 747 seriously injured. The bombers would be back in force on the following night and, with one exception due to bad weather, on every one of the sixty-five nights that followed.

Initially the night bombings could operate at will over Britain and their crews had little to fear from the defences. *Unteroffizier* Horst Goetz, a Heinkel 111 pilot with *Kampfgruppe 100*, recalled:

I have no particular memories of individual operations. They were all quite routine, like running a bus service. The London flak defences put on a great show – at night the exploding shells gave the place the appearance of bubbling pea soup. But very few of our aircraft were hit – I myself never picked up so much as a shell fragment. On rare occasions one of my crew might catch sight of a British night fighter, but it seems they never saw us and we were never attacked. During our return flights the radio operator would often tune in his receiver to a music programme, to provide some relief from the monotony.

The defending anti-aircraft gun and searchlight batteries relied mainly on sound locators to detect the bombers, but these gave only an imprecise indication of the whereabouts of an enemy plane, and if several aircraft were present in the area their engine noises swamped the locators. Few gun batteries had fire-control radar, and in any case this first-generation equipment had a low performance and its reliability was poor. On occasion the searchlights were effective as a means of pointing out targets for guns and night fighters, but they spent most of their time sweeping across the sky looking unsuccessfully for the bombers.

Under strong political pressure to 'do something' about the night raiders, General Frederick Pile, commanding the Army gun and searchlight units, ordered his gunners to maintain a steady fire when night raids were in progress, even if that meant firing off unaimed shells. If the gunners could not provide the substance of an effective defence, at least they would provide the sound of one. Ensconced in their shelters, the capital's citizens had no way of telling the difference. Later Pile would write on this type of engagement:

> The volume of fire which resulted, and which was publicised as a 'barrage', was in fact largely wild and uncontrolled shooting. There were, however, two valuable results from it: the volume of fire had a deterrent effect upon at least some of the German aircrews . . . [and] there was also a marked improvement in civilian morale.

During September 1940 the gunners fired a quarter of a million anti-aircraft shells during the night engagements, most of them into thin air. They shot down less than a dozen enemy planes.

The defending fighter force was no better able to deal with the night raiders. A few twin-engine Blenheim fighters carried airborne interception (AI) radar, but the early equipment was crude and unreliable and the operators had to learn their craft from first principles. Moreover, the Blenheim had little margin of speed over the enemy planes it was supposed to catch. The other types then employed at night, the Spitfire, Hurricane and Defiant single-engine fighters, had the speed to catch the bombers but they lacked the radar necessary to find them.

The night fighter patrols spent many fruitless hours cruising around in the darkness, hoping for a chance sighting of an enemy aircraft. As yet there was no usable system for making controlled interceptions assisted by ground radar. The only help from the ground came from the searchlights which sometimes found their prey. Yet even when the bomber was illuminated in this way, it was still difficult for a fighter crew to engage it. Pilot Officer Dick Haine, a Blenheim night fighter pilot with No 600 Squadron, explained the problem:

> It might seem a simple matter for night fighter crews to see bombers which had been illuminated by searchlights, but this was not the case. If the raiders came on bright moonlight nights, which was usual during this time, the beams from the searchlights were not visible at heights much above 10,000 feet. If the searchlights were actually on the enemy bomber the latter could be seen from some way away, but only if the fighter was underneath the bomber and could see its illuminated underside; if the fighter was higher than the bomber, the latter remained invisible to the fighter pilot. If there was any haze or cloud it tended to diffuse the beams so that there was no clear intersection to be seen, even if two or more searchlights were accurately following the target.

For the future, Fighter Command had great hopes for the twin-engine Bristol Beaufighter that had recently entered service. It was fast and had a good endurance, it carried a heavy armament of four 20mm cannon and six machine guns and it was fitted with the latest Mk IV AI radar. However, the new fighter had been rushed into production and it suffered from its fair share of teething troubles. Some months would elapse before it was operational in sufficient numbers and able to pose a serious threat to the night raiders.

In the meantime, the nightly attacks on London continued. Representative of the heavier attacks on the capital was that on the night of 15/16 October. It was a bright, moonlit night and the raiding force of some 400 bombers approached the city at altitudes above 16,000ft. The vanguard of the raiding force came in from the direction of Holland. Succeeding aircraft came in from Holland and Belgium over the Thames Estuary, and from various points in northern France, crossing the south coast of England between Bognor and Dungeness. The attack commenced at 8.40 p.m. and German crews reported seeing heavy barrage fire over the capital, with shells detonating at altitudes between 13,000 and 20,000ft.

One of those taking part in the raid was Günther Unger, now a *Feldwebel*, in a Do 17 of *Kampfgeschwader 76*. His crew was one of several that flew two sorties that night, one on the evening of the 15th and one on the morning of the 16th. On both occasions their target was in the dock area of the city. Unger's orders were to circle over the target for as long as possible, releasing one bomb every few minutes to cause disruption on the ground over a long period. Untroubled by London's so-called gun 'barrage', Unger spent about twenty-five minutes circling over the target on each sortie.

BRISTOL BLENHEIM Mk IF

Role: Two-seat, long-range fighter and night fighter.
Power: Two Bristol Mercury XV 9-cylinder, air-cooled, radial engines each developing 840hp at take-off.
Armament: Five Browning .303in machine guns firing forwards; one Vickers K .303in machine gun in the dorsal turret.
Performance: Maximum speed 260mph at 12,000ft; maximum cruising speed 220mph at 15,000ft; climb to 15,000ft, 15min.
Normal operational take-off weight: 13,800lb.
Dimensions: Span 56ft 4in; length 42ft 7in; wing area 469 sq ft.
Date of first production Blenheim I: February 1937.
Note: By the summer of 1940, some 30 of these aircraft were operational fitted with AI Mk III radar.

Forty-one Royal Air Force fighters took off to engage the night raiders, but only two made interceptions. A Blenheim made radar contact with one of the bombers, but it lacked the speed to reach a firing position and after a lengthy chase the raider escaped. The other interception, by a Defiant of No 264 Squadron, was more successful. Pilot Officer Desmond Hughes was on patrol to the east of London when he caught sight of the enemy:

It was a bright moonlight night. Suddenly, out the corner of my eye I saw something move across the stars out to my left. If you are scanning the night sky it is normally completely still, so anything that moves attracts the eye. This just had to be another aircraft. I got Fred [Sgt Fred Gash, the gunner] to swing his turret round and we both kept an eye on the black shape. We moved towards it and soon caught sight of a row of exhausts, It was a twin-engined aircraft. I slid alongside, below and to the right of him, and slowly edged in 'under his armpit' while Fred kept his guns trained on the aircraft. Then we saw the distinctive wing and tail shape of a Heinkel – there was no mistaking it. I moved into a firing position, within about 50 yards of his wing tip and slightly below, so that Fred could align his guns for an upward shot at about 20 degrees. Obviously the German crew had not seen us – they continued straight ahead.

Fred fired straight into the starboard engine. One round in six was a tracer, but what told us we were hitting the Heinkel was the glitter of the de Wilde [incendiary] rounds as they ignited on impact. Fred fired, realigned, fired again. He got off two or three bursts. There was no return fire from the bomber

---

BOULTON PAUL DEFIANT Mk I

Role: Two-seat turret fighter.
Power: One Rolls-Royce Merlin III 12-cylinder, liquid-cooled engine developing 990hp at 12,250ft.
Armament: Four Browning .303in machine guns mounted in a Boulton Paul hydraulically operated turret behind the cockpit.
Performance: Maximum speed 304mph at 17,000ft; climb to 15,750ft, 8min 30sec.
Normal operational take-off weight: 8,318lb.
Dimensions: Span 39ft 4in; length 35ft 4in; wing area 250 sq ft.
Date of first production Defiant I: July 1939.
Note: A few Defiants were fitted with AI radar, though these did not become operational until after the events described in this account.

– indeed, I doubt if any guns could have been brought to bear on our position on its beam. The engine burst into flames, then the Heinkel rolled on its back, went down steeply and crashed into a field near Brentwood.

The attack on the capital continued until 4.40 a.m. on the 16th and caused severe damage to the dock area and to the rail system. A bomb blew a large hole in the Fleet sewer, allowing the waters to escape and flood the rail tunnel between Farringdon Street and King's Cross stations. Becton gas works, Battersea Power Station and the BBC headquarters at Portland Place were hit, three large water mains were fractured and there was widespread damage in residential areas. More than 900 fires were reported in the capital, six of which were 'major' and nine 'serious'. London was not the only target that night: twenty Heinkels attacked Birmingham, while eight Dorniers raided.

The Heinkel that Hughes and Gash had shot down belonged to *Kampfgruppe* 126 and was engaged in a minelaying operation over the Thames Estuary. Coincidentally, the only other German loss known to have been caused by the defences came from the same unit: it had been laying mines off the Suffolk coast when it struck a barrage balloon cable and crashed. The other German losses that night were probably the result of flying accidents. A Do 17 crashed on high ground in Wales, probably following a navigational error; another became lost, ran out of fuel and crashed near Wells. A Ju 88 crashed near Bishop's Stortford but its loss does not link with any claim made by the defences. In addition, six German bombers were wrecked in crashes or crash-landings in France and Holland.

As more Beaufighters were delivered to Fighter Command, and as the bugs were gradually ironed out of the aircraft and its equipment, the new fighter began to take an increasing toll of the night bombers. Also, early in 1941, the first ground-controlled interception (GCI) radars went into service. This radar was the first to employ the plan position indicator type of display, with the now-familiar rotating time-base. Using this equipment, a ground controller could see the juxtaposition of the night fighter and the bomber on his screen, and it was relatively easy to direct the former into a position to engage the latter. Gradually night fighting became a structured business, far removed from the hit-or-miss reliance on a chance meeting that Hughes and his gunners had exploited when they shot down their Heinkel.

To demonstrate the method of operation used by RAF night fighters from the spring of 1941, let us observe a typical interception

---

HEINKEL HE IIIP-4

Role: Five-seat medium bomber.
Power: Two Daimler Benz DB 601A 12-cylinder, liquid-cooled
engines each rated at 1,100hp at take-off.
Armament: Normal operational bomb load 3,300lb. (Defensive)
Five Rheinmetall Borsig MG 15 7.9mm machine guns in flexible
mountings, one firing forwards, one firing rearwards above the
fuselage, one firing rearwards below the fuselage from the ventral
position and two firing from the sides of the fuselage from waist
positions; one 7.9mm in a fixed mounting, firing straight ahead.
Performance: Maximum speed 247mph at 16,400ft; normal cruising
speed 190mph at 16,400ft; approximate radius of action (normal
bomb load and operational fuel reserves) 350 miles.
Normal operational take-off weight: 29,760lb.
Dimensions: Span 74ft 1½in; length 53ft 9½in; wing area 943 sq ft.
Date of first production He IIIP: Spring 1939.

---

of that period. At 2 a.m. on the morning of 9 July, *Oberleutnant*
Hansgeorg Bätcher and his crew, flying a Heinkel He III of
Kampfgruppe 100, were cruising over Somerset at 11,500ft, heading
for their target at Birmingham. As the bomber neared the Bristol
Channel it was tracked by the GCI radar station at Huntspill near
Weston-super-Mare. Orbiting near the station, awaiting 'trade', was
a Beaufighter of No 600 Squadron, crewed by Flying Officer R.
Woodward and his radar operator Sergeant A. Lipscombe.

A series of vectors from the ground controller placed Woodward
five miles behind the enemy plane and he was told to go to maximum
speed to catch up. Shortly afterwards Lipscombe, peering at his radar
screens, observed the return from the enemy aircraft just over two
miles away. By then the Beaufighter had accelerated almost to its
maximum speed and was overtaking the enemy plane too rapidly for
a successful interception. Lipscombe told his pilot to throttle back,
but again the speed correction was too great and as the Beaufighter
slowed down the target disappeared off his radar screen. Woodward
requested further help from the ground controller, and was again
guided to within AI range.

By now both planes were north of Cardiff, heading north-east,
with the Beaufighter again gaining slowly on the bomber. Woodward
now takes up the story:

After further vectors ending with 040°, [AI radar] contact was
regained. Bandit [enemy aircraft] was then at 11,500 ft so I
dived to 10,500 ft keeping the Bandit in contact dead ahead:

Our speed then about 160 mph. A visual of a machine's exhausts was obtained about 1,000 ft above and ahead. Having identified the aircraft as Hostile I closed in climbing slowly to 300 feet and fired a three-second burst (with cannon and machine guns). No return fire was experienced. There was a blinding flash and explosion, and bits were seen to fly back. I gave another short burst before the enemy aircraft dived sharply to port with flames and smoke coming from its starboard side.

Hansgeorg Bätcher's recollection of the engagement links with the statements in Woodward's report. The first warning that the German crew had of the presence of the enemy fighter was when the ventral gunner suddenly shouted 'Night fighter . . . ' and the aircraft shuddered under the impact of exploding cannon shells. Bätcher jettisoned the bombs and hurled the aircraft into a diving turn, making for a cloud bank far below. Through the cupola over his position in the Beaufighter, Lipscombe watched the bomber diving away steeply with one engine on fire and disappear into cloud.

The speed of Bätcher's dive extinguished the flames before they took hold, and when he reached the cloud's enveloping folds he levelled out the bomber. As the German pilot took stock of the situation, however, it became clear that the Heinkel was in serious trouble. The ventral gunner was dead and the radio operator was badly wounded. The port engine was stopped and Bätcher feathered the windmilling propeller. The starboard engine had also suffered damage: it was running rough and developing only a fraction of its normal power. A large section of the rudder was shot away and, with the 'live' engine trying to push the Heinkel into a turn to the left, the pilot was unable to hold a straight heading; nor, on the available power, was it possible to maintain altitude. To add to the catalogue of woes, one of the fuel tanks had been punctured and was losing fuel and the main compass system no longer worked.

After some experimenting, Bätcher discovered a novel method of getting the crippled bomber to head in the general direction of France, albeit in a slow descent. Using the remains of the rudder, he held the aircraft on a southerly heading for as long as possible, then, when he could no longer hold it, he reversed the rudder and turned to the left through 300°. As it neared the required heading, he rolled out of the turn and held the required direction for as long as possible, then repeated the process. Using this 'two steps forward, one step back' technique and flying just above stalling speed, the Heinkel headed for France. The navigator tuned the radio compass to a beacon there to provide a heading reference.

BRISTOL BEAUFIGHTER Mk I

Role: Two-seat, long-range fighter and night fighter.
Power: Two Bristol Hercules XI 14-cylinder, air-cooled, radial
  engines each developing 1,590hp at take-off.
Armament: Four Hispano 20mm cannon mounted in the nose; six
  Browning .303in machine guns mounted in the wings.
Performance: Maximum speed 323mph at 15,000ft; maximum
  cruising speed 272mph at 15,000ft; climb to 20,000ft, 14min
  6sec.
Normal operational take-off weight: 20,800lb.
Dimensions: Span 57ft 10in; length 41ft 4in; wing area 503 sq ft.
Date of first production Beaufighter I: July 1940.
Note: During 1940 and 1941, night-fighter versions of the
  Beaufighter were fitted with Mk IV AI radar.

Running the engine from the damaged tank, the latter was soon emptied. As more fuel was consumed the aircraft became progressively lighter, and the rate of sink gradually decreased. In the end Bätcher was able to maintain altitude, though by then the Heinkel was down to 1,200 feet. As yet more fuel was burned, the bomber became progressively easier to handle and the straight runs between the turns became progressively longer. In the end Bätcher was able to maintain the bomber on the desired heading. Shortly after reaching the coast near Cherbourg, the pilot put the battered Heinkel down on one of the landing grounds near the port.

On the basis of his observations, and the report from the ground controller at Huntspill who had seen the 'blip' from the enemy aircraft disappear off his radar screen in the dive, Woodward claimed the Heinkel as destroyed. No wreck could be found that linked with the claim, however, so the Beaufighter crew was credited only with an enemy bomber 'probably destroyed'. *Luftwaffe* records listed the Heinkel as 'damaged beyond repair', however, so Woodward's original claim was correct.

The essentials of radar-assisted night fighting were now in place. Meanwhile, the RAF night bomber force was building up its capability and the climax of the contest between it and the *Luftwaffe* night fighter force would occur in the spring of 1944. We shall observe this in some detail in Chapter 10, 'The Nuremberg Disaster'.

Chapter 6

Battle of the Coral Sea

*The destructive attack by Japanese carrier-borne aircraft on the
US Navy fleet anchorage at Pearl Harbor in December 1941
established the aircraft carrier as the dominant capital ship of
the Pacific war. In the months that followed, the nine Japanese
and five American carriers were at sea for much of the time, yet,
such was the extent of the operational arena, a full half-year
elapsed before carrier battle groups faced each other in action.
That confrontation took place in May 1942, in the area of ocean
between Australia and New Guinea known as the Coral Sea.
It would change the face of naval warfare for all time.*

U p to the spring of 1942 there had been much conjecture, but
little hard evidence, about how carrier battle groups would fare
if they met each other in action. Each of the larger US and Japanese
carriers had a complement of more than 70 aircraft and could launch
an extremely powerful air strike. There were many who argued that
an action of this type would resemble a huge suicide pact: both sides
would locate the other at about the same time and launch an air
strike which would sink or disable the other's carriers. When the
surviving aircraft returned, having no landing strip within range,
they would come down in the sea and be lost. Time and combat
would reveal that, although this 'worst case' scenario never actually
happened, it was not far-fetched.

Of the aircraft types that equipped the front-line carrier squadrons
at the beginning of the Pacific war, those of the Japanese Navy had
the edge over those of the US Navy. The difference was most marked
in the case of torpedo bomber types. The Japanese Nakajima B5N2

NAKAJIMA B5N2 'KATE'

Role: Three-seat, carrier-based torpedo/horizontal bomber.
Power: One Nakajima Sakae 14-cylinder, air-cooled, radial engine developing 1,000hp at take-off.
Armament: (Offensive) One Type 97 torpedo or up to 1,650lb of bombs; (defensive) one Type 92 7.7mm machine gun on a hand-held mounting in the rear cabin.
Performance: Maximum speed 235mph at 9,850ft; cruising speed 164mph; normal attack speed and altitude for release of Type 97 torpedo, 185mph usually below 500ft.
Normal operational take-off weight: 8,360lb.
Dimensions: Span 50ft 11in; length 33ft 10in; wing area 412 sq ft.
Date of first production B5N2: Early 1941.

'Kate' was a fast, versatile and modern aircraft that could serve with equal facility as a torpedo bomber, horizontal bomber or reconnaissance plane. The older American Douglas TBD Devastator was employed in the torpedo- and horizontal-bombing roles, though because of its poor performance it was a good deal less effective than its enemy counterpart. The Japanese superiority in aircraft was compounded by the greater effectiveness of the Type 91 air-launched torpedo compared with the American Bliss Leavitt Mk XIII. One secret of the success of the Japanese weapon was the wooden air tail that stabilized it in flight, allowing it to be released at speeds up to 185mph and from altitudes up to 500ft. The wooden tail broke away when the weapon struck the surface, and in the water the torpedo had a running speed of 42kts. Lacking an air tail, the Bliss Leavitt weapon had a maximum release speed of only 117mph and its maximum release altitude was 100ft. In the water the American torpedo had a running speed of only 33½kts, which meant that, unless the attack were pressed to short range, it was relatively easy for a fast-moving warship to avoid the torpedo.

As regards fighters, the Japanese Zero had a greater maximum speed and a better low-speed manoeuvrability than the American Wildcat, though the latter was the more manoeuvrable in high-speed combat and was a more rugged aircraft that could absorb greater punishment. The Japanese carrier fighter pilots began the Pacific war with the advantage of having had previous combat experience over China. By April 1942 this relative advantage had been eroded slightly, as US Navy pilots gained combat experience. The US Navy fighters had the advantage of a rudimentary system of interception control, using the early-warning radar sets fitted to their carriers.

The Japanese carriers lacked radar and so had no warning of the approach of enemy aircraft until the latter came within visual range.

In terms of dive-bombers, the US Navy was the better off. The Douglas SBD Dauntless was a faster and generally more effective aircraft than the Japanese Aichi Type 99 'Val'. With the bombs removed, the Dauntless could even be used as a makeshift fighter to provide close-in defence for the carrier to ward off attacks by low-flying enemy torpedo bombers.

As April 1942 drew to a close, the Imperial Japanese forces had enjoyed a spell of unbroken victories lasting nearly five months. Large areas of south-east Asia and a swathe of islands in the Pacific were now under their occupation, and forces were poised to launch new amphibious landing operations to expand the area under their control.

A large naval force under Vice-Admiral Shigeyoshi Inoue was about to set out to complete the occupation of New Guinea and seize the Solomon Islands and New Hebrides. A striking force formed around the large carriers *Shokaku* and *Zuikaku* (72 planes each), under the command of Rear-Admiral Chuichi Hara, was to provide distant cover for the operation and prevent the Allied navies from interfering. A separate naval force, including the small carrier *Shoho* (28 planes), was to provide close cover for the Japanese troop transports and their escorting ships.

While the Japanese Navy assembled its forces for the new thrust, US Navy cypher-breakers decoded parts of some signals relating to the operation. It was learned that three Japanese carriers were to take part, and Admiral Chester Nimitz, the US Pacific Fleet commander, saw this as an opportunity to strike a serious blow at the enemy. So long as the large Japanese carriers operated together as a unified force, they could overwhelm any carrier force the US Navy could assemble. Now three carriers had split away from the others to support the thrust into the South-West Pacific area (nothing in the decoded signals suggested that *Shoho* was smaller than the other two). Nimitz saw that if the enemy carriers could be surprised, there was a good chance of reducing the imbalance of naval power in the Pacific. Carefully, he and his staff laid plans for a counter-strike. The US Navy carrier *Yorktown* (72 planes), with three cruisers and six destroyers, was already in the south Pacific area; *Lexington* (71 planes), with two cruisers and five destroyers, was ordered to run from Pearl Harbor to join her. On 1 May the two carriers and their escorts linked up in the eastern part of the Coral Sea, and Rear-Admiral Frank Fletcher in *Yorktown* assumed overall command of the force.

During the night of the 5th/6th, the Japanese strike carrier force passed round the eastern end of the Solomon Islands and into the Coral Sea, moving into position to block any attempt to interfere with the amphibious landings. Throughout 6 May a deep depression lay over the stretch of ocean, giving continuous and dense cloud cover and frequent rain showers. Reconnaissance planes from both sides scoured the area for the opposing warships but, since none of the planes carried radar, almost all were unsuccessful. The sole exception was a Japanese land-based aircraft from Rabaul which found part of Fletcher's force during the morning; but then, because of delays in re-transmitting the report to Hara's flagship, the report would not reach the Japanese commander until the following day.

Both sides realized that the enemy had a strong naval force in the area, though both were ignorant of their opponent's whereabouts and, in the Japanese case, their exact composition. The opposing carrier forces behaved like a couple of short-sighted prize fighters, moving warily around the ring and squinting for some sign of the other, ready to throw a punch. (After the war, the two sides' charts of the action were compared, and it was seen that at one point that day the opposing carrier groups passed within 70 miles of each other without either detecting the other's presence.)

At dawn on 7 May tension in the area was high. By then the Japanese commander knew he was opposed by forces that included at least one enemy carrier and perhaps two. Both sides saw that a clash was imminent and both launched several reconnaissance planes to comb the area for the enemy. Low cloud still made life difficult

---

DOUGLAS TBD DEVASTATOR

Role: Three-seat, carrier-based torpedo/horizontal bomber.
Power: One Pratt & Whitney R-1830-64 Twin Wasp 14-cylinder, air-cooled, radial engine developing 900hp at take-off.
Armament: (Offensive) One Mk XIII Bliss Leavitt torpedo or two 500lb bombs; one Browning .5in or .3in machine gun mounted on the starboard side of the fuselage and synchronized to fire through the airscrew. (Defensive) One Browning .3in machine gun on a hand-held mounting in the rear cabin.
Performance: Maximum speed 206mph at 8,000ft; cruising speed 128mph; maximum attack speed and altitude for release of Mk XIII torpedo, 117mph and 100ft.
Normal operational take-off weight: 9,289lb.
Dimensions: Span 50ft; length 35ft; wing area 422 sq ft.
Date of first production TBD: June 1937.

MITSUBISHI A6M2 MODEL 21 (ZERO)

Role: Single-seat, carrier-based fighter.
Power: One Nakajima Sakae 12 14-cylinder, air-cooled, radial engine developing 950hp at take-off.
Armament: Two Type 99 Model I Mk 4 20mm cannon (German Oerlikon built under licence) mounted in the wings; two Type 89 7.7mm machine guns (near-copies of the WWI British Vickers) mounted above the engine and synchronized to fire through the airscrew; provision to carry two 132lb bombs on underwing racks.
Performance: Maximum speed 331mph at 14,930ft; climb to 19,672ft, 7min 27sec. Normal operational take-off weight: 5,134lb.
Dimensions: Span 39ft 4½in; length 29ft 8½in; wing area 241.5 sq ft.
Date of first production A6M2: February 1941.
Note: Lacking information on the designations of the Japanese aircraft they were meeting in combat, the Western Allies allocated boys' names to fighters and girls' to bombers. Under this system, the Zero was renamed the 'Zeke'; but the old name stuck, and many people continued to refer to the aircraft as the Zero.

for the searchers, however, and led to inaccurate reporting. Early that morning a Japanese scouting plane reported that it had sighted an enemy aircraft carrier in company with a cruiser, at a position 160 miles south of the Japanese striking force. (Because of the poor visibility, the report was quite inaccurate: the ships were in fact the US fleet oiler *Neosho* and the destroyer *Sims*.)

Without waiting for a confirming report from a second plane sent into the area, the Japanese admiral turned to close the distance and launched a striking force comprising 25 B5N ('Kate') horizontal bombers and 36 D3A ('Val') dive-bombers, with an escort of eighteen Zero fighters. Soon after these set out, another Japanese reconnaissance aircraft reported (correctly) the sighting of a enemy carrier and ten other vessels about 280 miles to the *north-west* of the main Japanese carrier force.

The second report raised doubts in Hara's mind, but the distance of the enemy from his force ruled out an immediate air strike from or against his carriers. He decided to let his planes continue with their briefed attack, and when they returned he would prepare a new striking force as soon as possible. Meanwhile Admiral Fletcher, the US carrier commander, had also been misled by an inaccurate reconnaissance report from one of his aircraft. He received a report of two enemy carriers and four heavy cruisers at a position some 225 miles to the *north-west* of his force. (The message should have read 'two heavy cruisers and two destroyers', but there had been an encoding error before transmission; and even the 'correct' message was in error, for in fact the enemy force comprised only two light cruisers and two armed merchant ships.)

Accepting the report at its face value and assuming that it referred to the main Japanese carrier group, Fletcher launched a striking force of 52 dive-bombers and 22 torpedo bombers with an escort of eighteen fighters to attack the enemy 'carriers'. They were airborne when the reconnaissance crew landed on *Yorktown*, and only when they made their verbal report of the mission did the error become clear. To his great chagrin, the US commander learned that he had committed his striking force against what seemed to be a target of relatively minor importance. But, like Hara, Fletcher decided that he had little to gain by ordering the planes to abandon the attack and return.

When the Japanese air striking force reached the area where the enemy 'carrier' and 'cruiser' had been reported, they found only the oiler and the destroyer. With no more lucrative target available, the aircraft vented their spleen on the two ships, sinking *Sims* and leaving *Neosho* ablaze.

As the Japanese planes and their disappointed crews headed back to their carriers, the American air striking force was much more fortunate. By chance, Dauntless bombers scouting ahead of the main attack force chanced upon the Japanese carrier *Shoho*, in an area of clear skies and coincidentally only 35 miles from the position of the erroneously reported carrier. The main striking force was summoned to the scene and the small carrier was overwhelmed by the attack. *Shoho* was soon reduced to a wreck, listing to starboard and burning furiously, but aircraft continued to pound the vessel. Devastators closed to short range to launch torpedoes at the slow-moving target, and under these optimum conditions even the Mk XIII was able to wreak great damage. It is estimated that the light carrier took hits from thirteen bombs and seven torpedoes before she capsized and sank.

Meanwhile, some 300 miles south of the *Shoho* action, the Japanese planes were returning to the two larger carriers after attacking *Sims* and *Neosho*. As soon as all had landed, the deck crews repositioned the aircraft aft and began working furiously to refuel and re-arm those planes earmarked for a next air strike. Rear-Admiral Hara received a radio report of the loss of *Shoho* and, from the number of American aircraft involved, it was clear that his enemy had at least two carriers in the area.

It was late in the afternoon before the Japanese aircraft were ready for launch for their second strike, which meant that the earliest that

---

GRUMMAN F4F-4 WILDCAT

Role: Single-seat, carrier-based fighter.
Power: One Pratt & Whitney R-1830-86 Twin Wasp 14-cylinder,
   air-cooled, radial engine developing 1,200hp at take-off.
Armament: Six Browning .5in machine guns mounted in the wings.
Performance: Maximum speed 320mph at 18,800ft; climb to
   20,000ft, 12min 24sec.
Normal operational take-off weight: 7,975lb.
Dimensions: Span 38ft; length 29ft; wing area 260 sq ft.
Date of first production F4F: Late 1940.

---

they could attack the enemy carriers would be at dusk, and that the
planes would return after dark. Flown by crews chosen for their skill
and experience, twelve D3A dive-bombers and fifteen B5N torpedo
bombers took off from *Zuikaku* and *Shokaku* at 4.30 p.m. and headed
for the position where the American carriers had been reported. The
weather in the area remained poor, however, and the Japanese planes
flew past their intended targets without sighting them. The aircraft
continued on, almost to the limit of their endurance, and carried
out a brief search; then, having found nothing, they jettisoned their
ordnance and turned back for their carriers.

During the return flight, some of the Japanese planes came within
range of the CXAM early-warning radars fitted to *Yorktown* and
Lexington, and Wildcat fighters were vectored into position to intercept them. In the ensuing combats, nine Japanese and two American
planes were shot down.

Darkness came quickly in those latitudes, and the Japanese crews,
many of them near to exhaustion having flown two exacting missions
since dawn, had great difficulty in regaining their carriers. Aircraft
returned individually, and in the gloom five crews mistook *Yorktown*
for one of their own carriers and circled the ship in preparation to
landing. Only when the carrier and her escorts put up a withering
defensive fire, which forced them to break away violently, did the
men realize their error. Those Japanese aircraft that regained their
carriers arrived with their tanks almost empty, and several planes ran
out of fuel and splashed into the sea. Of the 27 aircraft that set out to
attack the American carriers, only six landed safely.

So ended 7 May, the first occasion on which aircraft carriers had
fought against their own kind. Clearly, the day had gone to the US
Navy. *Shoho* had been sunk with all of her planes and, adding these
planes to those lost during the abortive dusk raid, the Japanese force
was now weaker by 49 aircraft. For their part, the American carriers

had lost only six aircraft. The higher Japanese losses left the opposing carrier-borne units almost exactly equal in numerical strength: both now had about 130 aircraft operating from two large carriers.

During the small hours of 8 May both sides again prepared to fight a major fleet action, and all four carriers had striking forces drawn up on their after deck with planes fuelled, armed and ready to launch. Shortly before dawn the carriers dispatched reconnaissance planes to re-scour the ocean for the enemy. Now nothing mattered except for the enemy carriers, and other surface vessels were of importance only in so far as they could influence the carrier-versus-carrier action about to unfold.

Rear-Admiral Hara decided not to wait for the sighting report to come in, and at 8 a.m., he launched 33 dive-bombers, eighteen torpedo bombers and eighteen Zeros and sent them to the area where he expected the enemy to be. In the event, reconnaissance aircraft from both sides located the opposing carriers at about the same time, and their sighting reports reached their respective commanders shortly after 8.30 a.m. The opposing forces were then about 210 miles apart, the Japanese carriers being to the north-north-west of the American ships. Fletcher launched two striking forces comprising 48 Dauntlesses and 21 Devastators with an escort of sixteen Wildcats. The Japanese striking force, already airborne, turned to make for the area where the American carriers had been found.

The opposing striking forces passed in mid-air without either seeing the other. The first to go into action were planes from the *Yorktown*, whose dive-bombers sighted the main Japanese carrier force through a break in the cloud. While the dive-bombers circled,

---

AICHI TYPE 99 'VAL'

Role: Two-seat, carrier-based dive-bomber.
Power: One Mitsubishi Kinsei 44 14-cylinder, air-cooled, radial engine developing 1,070hp at take-off.
Armament: (Offensive) One 550lb bomb under the fuselage; provision for up to four 66lb bombs on underwing racks; two Type 97 7.7mm machine guns mounted above the engine and synchronized to fire through the airscrew. (Defensive) One Type 7.7mm machine gun on a flexible mounting at the rear of the cabin.
Performance: Maximum speed 237mph at 9,845ft; cruising speed 184mph.
Normal operational take-off weight: 8,378lb.
Dimensions: Span 47ft 1¼ in; length 33ft 1¾ in; wing area 376.5 sq ft.
Date of first production Type 99: Late 1940.

DOUGLAS SBD-2 DAUNTLESS

Role: Two-seat, carrier-based dive-bomber and scout aircraft.
Power: One Wright R-1820-52 Cyclone 14-cylinder, air-cooled,
   radial engine developing 1,000hp at take-off.
Armament: (Offensive) Normal load for attacks on warships, one
   1,000lb armour-piercing bomb; two Browning .5in machine guns
   mounted above the engine and synchronized to fire through
   the airscrew. (Defensive) Two Browning .3in machine guns on a
   hand-held mounting in the rear cabin.
Performance: Maximum speed 250mph at 8,000ft; cruising speed
   152mph.
Normal operational take-off weight: 10,400lb.
Dimensions: Span 41ft 6in; length 32ft 8in; wing area 325 sq ft.
Date of first production SBD: June 1940.

---

waiting for the slower torpedo bombers to move into position to attack at low altitude, *Zuikaku* headed into a rain squall and nothing more was seen of her. *Shokaku*, about six miles to the east and in an area of clear skies, turned into the wind preparatory to launching her fighters.

As the American torpedo bombers began their attack runs on *Shokaku*, and with the escorting Wildcats doing their best to hold off the Zeros, *Yorktown*'s 24 Dauntlesses rolled into their attack–dives at 17,000ft and continued down to 2,500ft. Each plane released a single 1,000lb bomb. Although the American crews claimed six certain and three probable hits on the carrier, from Japanese records it is clear that the vessel received only two direct hits. Making good use of cloud cover, the dive-bombers withdrew without loss. Then the nine Devastators from *Yorktown* closed in to launch their torpedoes, under heavy fire from the Japanese carrier and her escorting cruisers. The attack was carried through bravely, but, although the crews claimed three or possibly four hits on the carrier, in fact these weapons caused no damage. The Mk XIII lived down to its reputation that day, and it is clear that the torpedoes either missed the target or, if they hit it, failed to explode (the torpedo had a notoriously unreliable firing system). Arriving ten minutes later, *Lexington*'s air group was less successful and the main force of dive-bombers failed to find a target. Only four Dauntlesses and eleven Devastators found *Shokaku* and attacked her, and they achieved only a single bomb hit.

Although their ship had suffered serious damage from the three bomb hits, the damage control teams on the Japanese carrier soon brought under control the fires started by the explosions. *Shokaku* was

---

IMPERIAL JAPANESE NAVY SHIP *SHOKAKU*

Role: Aircraft carrier.
Displacement: 29,800 tons.
Maximum speed: 34 kts.
Defensive armament: Sixteen 5in guns; forty-two 25mm anti-aircraft guns.
Crew: 1,660.
Flight deck: Length 844ft; beam 85ft 4in.
Complement of aircraft at start of Coral Sea action:
18 Mitsubishi A6M2 Zero fighters; 27 Aichi D3A ('Val') dive-bombers; 27 Nakajima B5N ('Kate') torpedo/ horizontal bombers.
Date of commissioning: Late 1941.

USS *LEXINGTON*

Role: Aircraft carrier.
Displacement: 33,000 tons.
Maximum speed: 34kts.
Defensive armament: Eight 5in guns; 105 20mm and 40mm anti-aircraft guns.
Crew: 3,300.
Flight deck: Length 888ft; beam 105ft.
Complement of aircraft at start of Coral Sea action:
23 F4F-3 Wildcat fighters; 36 SBD Dauntless dive-bombers; 12 TBD Devastator torpedo bombers.
Date of commissioning: 1927.

---

unable to continue operational flying and she left the area under her own steam for the naval base at Truk.

The scene shifts to the two American carriers, which were bracing themselves for a powerful attack from Japanese planes. This time luck was on the side of the latter, whose crews arrived to find clear skies and the large ships visible from 50 miles or more. *Lexington*'s radar operators detected the incoming aircraft from about 75 miles, but the rudimentary equipment provided no indication of height and the fighter controllers failed to position the few available Wildcats effectively. Eight American fighters patrolled at 10,000ft and nine more fighters were launched to join them. To stiffen the defence, a dozen Dauntlesses orbited each carrier three miles away at about 2,000ft. These planes were to pounce on enemy torpedo bombers heading for the carriers (although it was clearly no match for a Zero, a Dauntless without bombs was a formidable opponent for a heavily laden torpedo bomber committed to a long, straight attack run).

As the 'Vals' and 'Kates' delivered their attacks, the American carriers manoeuvred independently to avoid the enemy torpedoes and bombs. *Yorktown* successfully avoided all eight of the torpedoes aimed at her, and all but one of the bombs. The latter struck near the island and penetrated four decks before exploding, causing considerable damage; the ship's flight deck was undamaged, however, and aircraft continued taking off and landing. *Lexington*, larger and less manoeuvrable than *Yorktown*, was less fortunate. She took two torpedo hits on the port side and suffered two bomb hits. Nevertheless, the doughty warship continued to fight back. Within minutes of the end of the attack, her damage control teams had halted the flooding, and her 7-degree list was corrected by moving fuel oil to tanks on the starboard side. Then, about an hour after the attack, as the carrier was recovering aircraft, disaster struck. A huge internal explosion ripped through her vitals, caused by the ignition of petrol fumes leaking from a ruptured aviation fuel tank. The explosion was followed by a series of smaller ones, and within a short time there were fires blazing in several parts of the ship. Those of her aircraft that were still airborne were ordered to land on *Yorktown*. *Lexington*'s crew fought a losing battle to bring the fires under control, but in the end her captain ordered the escorting destroyers to come alongside and take off the crew. Later that evening one of the destroyers finished off the abandoned carrier with a salvo of torpedoes.

By now both sides were down to one usable carrier. Neither commander felt that he was in a position to continue the fight, and both headed away from the area. *Zuikaku* had emerged from the action unscathed, but her air group was reduced to 39 planes. *Yorktown*, having taken on several of *Lexington*'s planes, now had 64 aircraft, but, owing to internal damage from the bomb hit, her operational ability was limited.

So ended the Battle of the Coral Sea. In the short term, it was a victory for the Japanese Navy, for the loss of *Lexington* and the damage to *Yorktown* far outweighed the loss of the smaller *Shoho* and the damage to *Shokaku*. In terms of aircraft losses, including those that went down when their carrier was sunk, the figures were nearly equal – 77 US carrier planes compared with 87 Japanese Navy machines.

In action, the big carriers were found to be relatively easy to damage but extremely difficult to sink. The main lesson of the loss of *Lexington* – the need for improved damage control techniques and a more effective venting system for potentially explosive fumes – would be well learned, and her successors would profit from it. Taking the effect of the battle on the Pacific war as a whole, the Americans were the long-term victors. They had thwarted a full-blooded Japanese invasion attempt and delayed the enemy advance into the south Pacific for several months. The lengthy repairs necessary for *Shokaku*, and the need to reform *Zuikaku*'s depleted air group, kept both of these important carriers out of action during the decisive battle near Midway two months later. *Yorktown*'s damage was rapidly repaired at Pearl Harbor, and she played an important role in the Battle of Midway before she met her end there. In terms of morale, the Battle of the Coral Sea marked a watershed for those trying to stem the Japanese advance through the Pacific: it was the first major action in which Japanese forces had not been victorious and had, moreover, suffered serious losses.

As has been said, the Battle of the Coral Sea was the first naval engagement to be fought solely between carrier-based aircraft. It established the pattern for naval actions in that theatre – a pattern that would continue until the Japanese Navy had no operational aircraft carriers left.

Chapter 7

Battle of the Bay

*'The Bay' was the Bay of Biscay, the area of sea between Brest
on the north-west coast of France and Cape Ortegal on the
north-west coast of Spain. 'The Battle' took place in the strip
of water running from the western edge of the Bay into the
Atlantic. For much of the Second World War this waterway
was of great strategic importance, for U-boats sent to attack the
Allied transatlantic convoys had to pass through it twice on
each sortie as they ran out from and returned to their bases.
The contestants in the campaign were the German U-boats on
the one side and the maritime patrol aircraft of RAF Coastal
Command on the other. The hardest fought phase took place
between June 1942 and October 1943 and saw actions unique
in the history of air warfare. Air crews flew large numbers
of hours but only rarely did they engage their enemy. When
engagements did take place, they were often characterized by
great ferocity and considerable personal bravery. Moreover, to a
degree rarely equalled in other types of air action, there were
continual technological and tactical thrusts and counter-thrusts
as each side sought to gain an advantage, often temporary, over
its adversary.*

Early in 1941, as RAF Coastal Command built up in strength and
its aircraft were fitted with radar and improved anti-submarine
weapons, the air patrols over the Bay of Biscay became progressively more of a threat for the U-boats traversing the waterway. The
German crews found that the easiest way to avoid the air patrols was
to remain submerged during the day and run on the surface at night,
using the diesel engines to recharge the boat's batteries.

At night, the submariners knew, they were safe from air attack on the surface. Although many of the aircraft carried air-to-surface vessel (ASV) Mk II radar, which could detect submarines on the surface, a night attack had little prospect of success. The depth charges had to be released from low level, and when a low-flying aircraft came within about a mile of a U-boat, the latter's echo signals merged into the 'sea clutter' on the radar screen and nothing more was seen of it.

If its aircraft were to deliver successful night attacks on U-boats, Coastal Command desperately needed some means of maintaining contact with the target during the all-important final mile of the attack run. The solution to the problem was a modified naval 24in searchlight that could be lowered under the fuselage of the Wellington bomber, using the installation originally built for the aircraft's retractable ventral gun position. The searchlight put out a narrow but intense beam, which could be trained on to the U-boat and held on it by an operator in the nose of the aircraft using a hydraulic control system. The device was called the 'Leigh Light', after its inventor Squadron Leader Humphrey Leigh. In the spring of 1941 a Leigh Light Wellington carried out a series of mock attacks at night on a Royal Navy submarine, and these demonstrated that the searchlight was of considerable assistance, though it required some modification before it was suitable for operational use. It took some months to perfect the system and put it into production.

Early in 1942 No 172 Squadron was formed to carry out night attacks on U-boats, and the unit received its first Wellington VIII aircraft fitted with a Leigh Light. The crews began a period of intensive training in the difficult and potentially dangerous business of delivering low-level attacks at night. By the beginning of June the Squadron possessed five Leigh Light Wellingtons and several crews proficient in the precise flying necessary to attack targets illuminated by the searchlight.

The Leigh Light was first used in action during the early morning darkness of 4 June, when Squadron Leader Jeff Greswell and his crew attacked the Italian submarine *Luigi Torelli* on the surface as she was heading into the Atlantic. The boat suffered severe damage which forced her to abandon her patrol.

In the course of June, the Squadron attacked five enemy submarines on the surface at night. The first Leigh Light attack to result in the loss of a U-boat was during the night of 5/6 July, when Pilot Officer W. Howell and his crew caught *U502* on her way home after a successful foray in the Caribbean. Just over a week later this crew carried out another successful Leigh Light attack and inflicted serious damage on *U159*.

VICKERS WELLINGTON Mk VIII

Role: Six-seat maritime patrol aircraft.
Power: Two Bristol Pegasus XVIII 14-cylinder, air-cooled, radial engines each developing 1,050hp at take-off.
Armament: Normal operational load eight 250lb depth charges; one hand-held Vickers K .303in machine gun in the nose; two Browning .303in machine guns in the powered rear turret.
Performance: Maximum speed 235mph at 15,500ft; attack speed 172mph at 50ft; normal patrol speed 130mph at 2,000ft; typical radius of action (normal weapon load) 700 miles.
Normal operational take-off weight: 30,000lb.
Dimensions: Span 86ft 2in; length 64ft 7in; wing area 640 sq ft.
Date of first production Wellington VIII: Late 1941.
Note: Aircraft fitted with ASV Mk II radar and Leigh Light in the rear fuselage.

In the initial two months of operations with the Leigh Light, the five modified Wellingtons had an effect on the enemy that went far beyond their achievement of one submarine sunk and two damaged. The U-boat crews had lost the immunity they had previously enjoyed while crossing the Bay at night on the surface: now they were liable to suffer sudden and demoralizing attack from the air without warning. The U-boat crews coined their own epithet for the Leigh Light: *'Das verdammte Licht!'* ('That damned light!').

In July *Admiral* Karl Dönitz, the commander of the U-boat force, reacted to the new situation by ordering his crews to reverse their previous procedure for crossing the Bay: from now on they were to traverse the stretch of water submerged at night and run *on the surface by day*. By day, the argument ran, the boats' lookouts would have a better chance of seeing the aircraft and initiating a crash-dive before an attack developed. The change of tactics gave the Coastal Command daylight air patrols a rare chance to find their enemy, and they seized it eagerly. In August there were 34 sightings of U-boats running on the surface by day in the Bay area, and in September there were 37. Between the beginning of June and the end of September the daylight air patrols sank four U-boats and caused damage to several others, in many cases forcing them to abandon their patrols and return to base.

German naval intelligence officers had long known that the attacking aircraft relied on ASV radar to detect U-boats on the surface, and this device was seen as an essential element of the night attacks. The answer was to fit U-boats with a simple receiver that

---

U966 (TYPE VHC U-BOAT)

Surface displacement: 769 tons.
Armament: (Offensive) Four bow and one stern torpedo tubes
  with fourteen 533mm torpedoes (770lb warheads); (defensive,
  mid-1943) four 20mm cannon in two paired installations and
  one 37mm cannon, mounted on platforms to the rear of the
  conning tower.
Performance: Maximum speed (surface, diesel engines) 17kts,
  (submerged, electric motors) 7kts; endurance (surface) 6,500nm
  at 12kts, (submerged) 80nm at 4kts; minimum time to submerge
  50sec; maximum safe diving depth 650ft.
Dimensions: Length 220ft 3in; beam 20ft 4in.
Date of first Type VIIC U-boat: Early 1941.

---

could pick up the ASV emissions and warn crews of the proximity
of enemy aircraft. The boats could then dive out of harm's way, and
resume their run on the surface when the danger had passed. Named
after the company that built it, the *Metox* warning receiver was introduced in September 1942, and by the end of the year nearly every
operational U-boat carried one. The device restored to the submariners the invulnerability that they had enjoyed when running on the
surface at night: in September the air patrols made only two sightings
of U-boats on the surface in the Bay, and in the following month
there were none.

By the end of 1942, however, the patrol planes were about to
introduce to service two new and advanced types of airborne radar,
the British ASV Mk III and the American SCR-517. The new radars
could locate submarines on the surface at longer ranges and with
greater precision than the earlier equipment. Moreover – and significantly in the light of the German countermeasures – the band of
microwave frequencies in which the new radars operated lay outside
the range of cover of the *Metox*.

Early in 1943 No 172 Squadron re-equipped with the newer
Mk XII Wellington fitted with ASV Mk III radar. For U-boat crews
there was a resumption of the unannounced night attacks which
had devastated morale the previous year. In March and April 1943
the aircraft sank only two U-boats at night, but the crews of several
others returned with hair-raising tales of the narrow escapes.

Pending the introduction of a new warning receiver that would
pick up the signals from microwave radars, at the end of April *Admiral*
Dönitz again issued orders that boats crossing the Bay of Biscay
should remain submerged at night and run on the surface by day.

Also, during their refits between sorties, the boats were fitted with batteries of 20mm cannon, and in some cases 37mm weapons, so that those caught on the surface could drive off their tormentors.

Again, the change in German tactics was immediately obvious to those flying the daylight patrols over the Bay. In the first week in May 1943 these reported sighting U-boats on 71 occasions and attacking them on 43. Air crews reported seventeen occasions when U-boats stayed on the surface and tried to fight off their attackers. During the month aircraft sank six U-boats in the Bay and caused severe damage to six more, for the loss of six aircraft shot down. Such a rate of exchange was overwhelmingly in favour of Coastal Command, for a patrol aircraft cost about one-fifth as much and carried one-eighth as many crew as a U-boat.

By the beginning of June almost every operational U-boat was fitted with anti-aircraft cannon, and *Admiral* Dönitz ordered a further change in tactics. Now the U-boats were to cross the Bay of Biscay on the surface by day in convoy. If an enemy aircraft attempted to attack them, their commanders had strict orders to remain on the surface and use their combined firepower to drive away or shoot down their assailants. After dark the U-boats were to submerge and continue their transit independently; at dawn they were to return to the surface, re-form and continue in convoy until they were clear of the Bay area.

When they were first tried in action, the group-sailing tactics enjoyed some success. A pair of boats reached Brest safely on 7 June after their patrol, as did another pair on the 11th. In the afternoon of the 12th, a patrolling aircraft sighted the first of the large groups to attempt to run the gauntlet – five U-boats on their way to the Atlantic. Darkness fell before an attack could be launched, and the U-boats continued their passage westward submerged. The following evening a Sunderland of No 228 Squadron regained contact with the group. Undeterred by the return fire, the crew carried out an accurate attack on *U564*, but their flying boat suffered mortal damage and shortly afterwards it crashed into the sea. The wounded *U564* was forced to abandon her patrol, and, escorted by one of the other boats, she headed for her base in France. On the following day a Whitley from No 10 Operational Training Unit found the pair and finished off the damaged boat; again the aircraft suffered damage in the encounter, however, and on the way home it was intercepted by German fighters and finished off. While all this was happening, the other three boats in the convoy escaped into the Atlantic.

The next two groups of U-boats which attempted to pass through the Bay on the surface both set sail on 12 June. One group, comprising three boats, crossed the Bay without loss after a running fight with aircraft, during which the German gunners inflicted damage on two of their attackers. The other group, comprising five boats, did not get off so lightly. Their adversaries were Mosquito fighters of No 307 Squadron, which made repeated strafing runs with cannon. One of the British planes was damaged, but the rounds caused so many casualties among the crews of *U68* and *U155* that both boats had to abandon their patrols and return to base.

Having digested the lessons from these actions, *Admiral* Dönitz introduced yet another change of tactics. In the middle of June he ordered his U-boat groups to surface only by day, and then for the minimum time necessary for the boats to recharge their batteries – about four hours in every twenty-four. This reduced the time spent on the surface, making it more difficult for enemy aircraft to find and attack the submarines. As a result of this change, in the final two weeks in June only one U-boat suffered damage from air attack in the Bay area.

The group-sailing tactics now being employed by the U-boats were not unlike those used by Allied merchant ships crossing the Atlantic. The counter-tactics devised by Coastal Command bore a striking resemblance to the 'wolf-pack' methods that the U-boats used with such effect against those Allied convoys. Three times a day, every day, a force of seven assorted patrol aircraft flew on parallel tracks over the transit routes used by the U-boats. If one of the aircraft located a U-boat group, it was to maintain contact out of reach of the return fire and report the position and composition of the enemy force by radio to headquarters. The other planes in the force could assemble over the U-boat group and deliver a concerted attack. The Allied aerial 'wolf-pack' tactics were an immediate success, and July 1943 was the most fruitful month of all for the Bay air patrols: eleven U-boats were sunk and three were seriously damaged, in exchange for six aircraft destroyed.

During this phase of the campaign every action had its unique features and it would be misleading to describe any one of them as 'typical'. However, the action that took place on 30 July was certainly one of the more dramatic and the most successful for the aircraft. That morning a Liberator of No 53 Squadron found a trio of U-boats – *U461* and *U462*, large submarine tankers equipped to refuel attack boats in mid-ocean, in company with *U504* – on the surface and heading west. The aircraft's radio report summoned six other aircraft to the scene – another Liberator, two Halifaxes, two Sunderlands and a Catalina.

A Halifax initiated the attack, making its bombing run from the relatively high altitude of 1,600ft to release three 600lb depth bombs;

these weapons had cases stronger than those of normal depth charges, so that they would not break up on impact when released from higher altitudes. The additional altitude did not save the bomber from the U-boats' return fire, however, and it was forced to break off the action with a damaged elevator. The depth bombs fell wide. The second Halifax then attacked from 3,000ft, where it was relatively safe from the return fire, to release its stick of depth bombs. One of these weapons exploded close to *U462*, causing severe damage. Dark smoke issued from the conning tower, and about a quarter of an hour later the boat lost all speed, slid to a halt and began to settle in the water.

The other two U-boats circled protectively round the drifting craft, providing the opportunity for three of the aircraft to run in for a concerted attack at low altitude. The Liberator that made the initial sighting led the charge, accompanied by a Liberator of No 19 Squadron USAAF. Following some distance behind came a Sunderland from No 461 (Australian) Squadron. The Liberators encountered vigorous return fire, and both suffered damage and were forced to break off their attacks prematurely. But the presence of these planes had kept the German gunners busy long enough for the Sunderland to line up for an accurate attack on the undamaged tanker boat. Only at the last moment did the boat's guns begin traversing to meet the new threat, and by then it was too late. The flying boat's nose gunner loosed off a long and accurate burst which silenced the weapons. Then, his target defenceless, the Sunderland pilot released a stick of seven depth charges from 50ft and they exploded along the length of the boat. The submarine broke in two and sank almost immediately.

Probably rightly, the captain of *U504* decided that he could do nothing further to help his comrades and he took his boat down. The move was too late to save him or his craft, however. Since it had made contact with the enemy force, the Catalina had been directing a Royal Navy submarine hunting team of five sloops to the scene. The vessels arrived in time to dispatch *U462* with gunfire, then they carried out a sonar search for *U504* and sank her too. When the German naval records were examined after the war, it became clear that during the action there had been a remarkable coincidence of numbers: the submarine tanker *U461* had been sunk by Sunderland 'U' of No 461 Squadron.

August began in triumphant vein for the patrol aircraft, with the sinking of four more U-boats in the Bay area during the first two days. Then *Admiral* Dönitz decided that enough was enough. It was clear that the enemy had taken the measure of the group-sailing tactics, and he ordered his crews to cease using them. Those groups of boats that were committed to a transit of the Bay were to split up. The craft were to proceed singly, surfacing to recharge their batteries for as short a time as necessary and only at night. Four boats returning from patrol were told to hug the coast of neutral Spain, also surfacing *only at night* and only long enough to recharge their batteries.

The use of Spanish territorial waters provided the best answer to German submariners' problems, for the clutter of echoes from the land made it difficult to detect boats on radar. Soon afterwards a new type of radar warning receiver began to appear in U-boats, the *Naxos* equipment, which picked up microwave emissions from the ASV HI and SCR-517 radars. The new receiver restored the technical balance in favour of the U-boats. But it had entered service too late, and other influences came to bear to nullify the German advantage.

Following a series of heavy defeats at the hands of the Allied convoy escorts, at the end of August Dönitz decided to suspend large-scale operations in that area. He needed to conserve his trained crews to man the new, high-performance U-boats he planned to introduce into service during the following year. The move reduced the transit of U-boats through the Bay of Biscay to a trickle. Although the air patrols continued with their previous intensity, between the end of the first week in August and the end of the 1943 they sank only five U-boats and damaged only one.

The Battle of the Bay began early in 1941, and the campaign finally ended when Allied ground forces neared the U-boat bases in France in the summer of 1944. The hardest-fought phase was during the fifteen-month period between the introduction of the Leigh Light in June 1942 and the withdrawal of the U-boats from the mid-Atlantic in August 1943. In that time the patrol aircraft sank 33 German and Italian submarines in the area, damaged 30 others and shared the destruction of one with surface ships.

Chapter 8

The Regensburg Strike

During the first seven months of 1943, the heavy bombers of the US Eighth Army Air Force based in England penetrated progressively deeper into Germany to deliver attacks. On 17 August its commander ordered the most ambitious operation so far: a strike on the Messerschmitt aircraft factory at Regensburg in the extreme south of Germany, to be combined with another on the ball-bearing production plant at Schweinfurt. The action that followed would lead to a fundamental change in US strategic bombing policy.

During July 1943 the Messerschmitt aircraft works at Regensburg in Bavaria delivered just under three hundred Bf 109 fighters to the *Luftwaffe*, making it one of the largest of the four plants producing the type. Regensburg had always been high on the list of targets earmarked for precision daylight attack. But the risks involved in such a lengthy incursion into Germany were great: the factory complex lay more than 500 miles from the nearest US bomber base in East Anglia, and 430 miles inside occupied Europe.

When the attack on Regensburg was being planned, that target became linked with another of strategic importance that lay nearby – the ball-bearing production centre at Schweinfurt, about 130 miles to the north-west. It was decided to launch a twin-pronged thrust against both targets. Under the original plan, two raiding forces, with a total of 376 B-17 Flying Fortresses, were to penetrate into Germany together. At a point south of Frankfurt, the two rear divisions were to split away from that in the lead, deliver their attack on Schweinfurt and return to England; the remaining division, comprising 146 B-17s, was to continue on its south-easterly heading for Regensburg. After bombing, this force was to turn on to a south-south-westerly heading over Austria and Italy, then over the Mediterranean to Algeria in North Africa, where the bombers were to land. The purpose of the stratagem was to avoid a long withdrawal flight over north-western Germany, with possible heavy losses. Including formation assembly, the flight would take eleven hours; even for the long-range version of the B-17, that would be close to the limit of the aircraft's endurance.

P-47 Thunderbolt escort fighters were to cover the initial part of the bombers' penetration, and the final part of the withdrawal of the Schweinfurt raiding force. At this stage of the war, the escorts carried insufficient fuel to protect bombers into Germany itself. The Royal Air Force was to contribute twenty squadrons of Spitfires to support the operation, though the radius of action of these aircraft was even more limited than that of the Thunderbolt. The 'bottom line' for the Regensburg attack force was that, in order to reach its target, it would have to fight its way though 300 miles of hostile airspace after the last of the escorting fighters turned for home.

So much for the plan. Early on 17 August a thick layer of cloud lay over eastern England, which was forecast to thin out as the day progressed. Had the raiding forces taken off soon after dawn, as originally scheduled, there would have been a high risk of collision during formation assembly. Because of this, the attack plan was rescheduled. The Regensburg attack force was to take off 1½ hours later than planned (that was the maximum acceptable delay, since the bombers had to reach the unfamiliar airfields in Algeria before dusk). The larger Schweinfurt attack force faced no such constraint and had less far to go, so it was to delay its take-off by five hours to allow time for the skies over East Anglia to clear. Tactically, the change of plan was significant: it meant that the two attack forces were to penetrate into enemy territory separately and that each one in turn would face the full wrath of the German air defences.

At 10.05 a.m. the leading elements of the Regensburg attack force crossed the Dutch coast. Eight bombers had been forced to turn back for various reasons before reaching the coast, and the force now comprised 139 Flying Fortresses in three combat wing formations. Accompanying the bombers during the initial part of the penetration were a couple of dozen Thunderbolts of the 353rd Fighter Group.

As the bombers droned across Holland, three *Luftwaffe Gruppen*, each with about twenty fighters, were moving separately into position to deliver attacks. The bomber formation was spread across twenty miles of sky and the small force of escorts could not cover

---

BOEING B-17F FLYING FORTRESS

Role: Ten-seat, four-engine heavy bomber.
Power: Four Wright R-1820 Cyclone turbo-supercharged, 14-cylinder, air-cooled, radial engines each developing 1,200hp at take-off.
Armament: The bomb load depended on the distance to be flown. During the maximum-range attack on Regensburg, aircraft carried ten 500lb high-explosive bombs or a similar weight of incendiaries. The forward-firing defensive armament depended upon the modification state of the aircraft but comprised at least two Browning .3in machine guns (although some planes carried as many as four Browning .5in machine guns in that position on hand-held mountings). There were two Browning .5in machine guns in each of the powered turrets above and below the fuselage, two on a hand-held mounting in the tail, one in each waist position and one in the radio operator's position firing from above the fuselage.
Performance: Typical formation cruising speed (with bomb load) 180mph at 22,000ft; demonstrated operational range during the Regensburg mission (including aircraft assembling formation, flying in formation, operational fuel reserves and 5,000lb bomb load released near mid-point of flight) 1,500 miles.
Normal operational take-off weight: 48,720lb.
Dimensions: Span 103ft 9½in; length 74ft 8¾in; wing area 1,420 sq ft.
Date of first production B-17F: May 1942.
Note: B-17s taking part in the Regensburg mission were the extended-range version of the aircraft, with additional fuel cells in the outer wings (nicknamed 'Tokyo tanks').

---

every part of it. The Thunderbolts successfully drove off the Focke Wulf 190s of *II Gruppe* of *Jagdgeschwader I*. But while the escorts were thus engaged, the two other *Gruppen*, *I* of *JG 26* with FW 190s and *III* of *JG 26* with Messerschmitt Bf 109s, each delivered a sharp head-on attack on part of the bomber formation.

Lieutenant-Colonel Beirne Lay, a staff officer at Headquarters Eighth Air Force, flew with the raiding force as a co-pilot in a B-17 of the 100th Bomb Group in order to gain first-hand experience of aerial combat. That he would certainly get, for the 100th was at the very rear of the formation in the most exposed position of all. Later Lay wrote a dramatic account of the air action, in which he described the initial encounter with the enemy:

At 1017 hours, near Woensdrecht [in Holland], I saw the first flak blossom in our vicinity, light and inaccurate. A few minutes later two FW 190s appeared at one o'clock level and whizzed through the formation ahead of us in a frontal attack, nicking two B-17s in the wings and breaking away beneath us in half rolls. Smoke immediately trailed from both B-17s but they held their stations. As the fighters passed us at a high rate of closure, the guns of our group went into action. The pungent smell of burnt powder filled our cockpit and the B-17 trembled to the recoil of nose and ball-turret guns. I saw pieces fly off the wing of one of the fighters before they passed from view.

By the end of the encounter, two B-17s had been shot down and several damaged, in some cases so severely that they were forced to break formation and turn for home. Three Messerschmitts were shot down during the engagement.

Soon afterwards the 353rd Fighter Group was relieved by the 56th Fighter Group, and the latter, a more experienced unit, successfully blocked further attacks by enemy fighters on the main formation. The Thunderbolts could do nothing to protect the bombers against enemy flak, however, and two B-17s fell to this cause over Holland and others suffered damage. Unable to reach the main bomber formation, German fighters in the area concentrated their attentions on finishing off a couple of B-17s that had been forced out of formation and were returning to England alone. As the B-17s neared the German frontier, the Thunderbolts reached the limit of their radius of action and had to turn back.

Ahead of the Regensburg attack force lay a flight of more than 300 lonely miles to the target. The *Luftwaffe* fighter units based along the coastal strip had spent their force, however, and their aircraft were making for airfields in the area to refuel and re-arm. For the first time since the bombers crossed the coast, there was relative calm around their formation. Yet few of those on board the American bombers doubted that this was anything other than the lull before the storm.

Trailing the bombers like hungry jackals, taking care to keep outside of range of their guns, were a few Messerschmitt Bf 110 night fighters. The crews of these relatively slow and unwieldy radar-equipped planes had orders not to engage bombers in formation: their role was to finish off stragglers or any others that left the protection of the formation.

One night fighter took on the role of contact aircraft, maintaining a commentary on its position, course, altitude and composition. Beirne Lay had particular memories of that aircraft:

> I noticed an Me 110 sitting out of range on our right. He was to stay with us all the way to the target, apparently reporting our positions to fresh squadrons waiting for us down the road.

Lay's assessment was correct. By now it was clear to the German fighter controllers that the raiding force was heading for a target in the centre or the south of country, though its exact destination remained a matter of conjecture. The only regular day fighter unit in position to meet such a thrust was *Jagdgruppe 50*, the newly formed unit with 25 Bf 109s based at Wiesbaden/Erbenheim. Backing this unit were about a score of Bf 109s and FW 190s flown by instructors from fighter operational training units in the area, and more low-performance Bf 110 night fighters that could finish off stragglers.

The next action opened as the bombers passed Wiesbaden. One of the *Jagdgruppe 50* pilots, *Leutnant* Alfred Grislawski, later commented:

> We climbed and made perfect contact with the Boeings. It was my first view of an American formation. There were so many of them that we were all shaken to the marrow, both our small group of pilots from Russia and the young new pilots – the young ones a bit more than us I think. We started making frontal attacks on the right-hand-side formation; we went in in fours.

Knowing that these B-17s were about to bomb their homeland, the German pilots attacked with great determination. They also knew they had nothing to fear from enemy fighters, so they could afford to take their time positioning themselves for their firing runs and they could expend all of their ammunition against the bombers.

After delivering head-on attacks, the fighters turned around and made further attacks on the bombers from the rear. Much of the action was now concentrated around the embattled 100th Bomb Group at the rear of the formation. Beirne Lay wrote:

> Swinging their yellow noses around in a wide U-turn, a twelve-ship squadron of Me 109s came in from twelve to two o'clock in pairs and in fours, and the main event was on.
>
> A shining silver object sailed over our right wing. I recognised it as a main exit door. Seconds later, a dark object came hurtling through the formation, barely missing several props. It was a man, clasping his knees to his head, revolving like a diver in a triple somersault. I didn't see his chute open.
>
> A B-17 turned gradually out of the formation to the right, maintaining altitude. In a split second the B-17 completely disappeared in a brilliant explosion, from which the only remains were four small balls of fire, the fuel tanks, which were quickly consumed as they fell earthward.

MESSERSCHMITT BF 109G-6

Role: Single-seat day fighter.
Power: One Daimler Benz DB 605 12-cylinder, liquid-cooled, in-line engine developing 1,475hp at take-off.
Armament: (Air defence role) Three Mauser MG 151 cannon, one firing through the propeller boss and one mounted under each wing; two Rheinmetall Borsig MG 131 13mm machine guns mounted above the engine.
Performance: Maximum speed 386mph at 22,650ft; climb to 18,700ft, 6min.
Normal operational take-off weight: 6,940lb.
Dimensions: Span 32ft 6½in; length 29ft 0½in; wing area 174 sq ft.
Date of first production Bf 109G-6: Late 1942.

Our airplane was endangered by falling debris. Emergency hatches, exit doors, prematurely opened parachutes, bodies and assorted fragments of B-17s and Hun fighters breezed past us in the slipstream.

I watched two fighters explode not far beneath, disappearing in sheets of orange flame, B-17s dropping out in every state of distress, from engines on fire to control surfaces shot away, friendly and enemy parachutes floating down and, on the green carpet far beneath us, numerous funeral pyres of smoke from fallen aircraft, marking our trail. The sight was fantastic: it surpassed fiction ...

A B-17 of the Group ahead, with its right Tokyo tanks on fire, dropped back to about 200 feet above our right wing and stayed there while seven of the crew successively bailed out. Four went out of the bomb bay and executed delayed jumps, one bailed from the nose, opened his chute prematurely and nearly fouled the tail. Another went out the left-waist-gun opening, [and] delayed his chute opening for a safe interval. The tail gunner dropped out of his hatch, apparently pulling the ripcord before he was clear of the ship, and jerked him so hard that both his shoes came off. He hung limp in the harness, whereas the others had shown immediate signs of life after their chutes opened, shifting around in the harness. The B-17 then dropped back in a medium spiral and I did not see the pilots leave. I saw it just before it passed from view, several thousand feet below us, with its right wing a sheet of yellow flame.

Seven B-17s were shot down in rapid succession during this phase of the action. Two more suffered damage and were forced out of formation, to be finished off soon afterwards by German fighters. Of those nine bombers, six were from the 100th Bomb Group with which Lay was flying.

As the raiders passed east of Mannheim, the single-engine fighters began to run out of ammunition. One by one they broke away from the fight and the action fizzled out. Of the 139 Flying Fortresses that had crossed the Dutch coast, a total of fourteen had now been shot down, and in the case of several others the crews were struggling to keep their damaged planes in formation.

Few in the raiding force realized it, but in fact the defending fighter force had shot its bolt. The B-17s were now deeper inside Germany than they had ever been before, and had entered an area where there were no regular *Luftwaffe* day fighter units. For the final 25 minutes to the target, the bombers were unmolested, though a few Bf 110 night fighters remained ominously in position on the flanks and behind the raiders.

Because the US daylight bombers had never ventured near Regensburg before, the aircraft plant had only weak defences – a few newly built Bf 109s armed and kept on standby at the works airfield, to be flown by factory test pilots, and three batteries of 88mm anti-aircraft guns.

As the raiders neared Regensburg, they found the weather in the area perfect for an attack, with cloud-free skies and horizontal visibility 25 to 30 miles. At the designated Initial Point for the attack, 25 miles to the west of the target, the leading combat box moved into attack formation. The low and high squadrons moved into trail behind the lead squadron, to reduce the width of the formation for the bomb run. The leading unit, the 96th Bomb Group, arrived unscathed at the IP with all 21 of its B-17s.

Within each Bomb Group formation only four aircraft carried bomb sights, those of the leader, the deputy leader and the leaders of the high and the low squadrons. In the case of the three last, the sights were carried only as a back-up in case of losses. Provided he were still at the head of the formation and his equipment were serviceable, the bombardier in the lead aircraft aimed the bombs of the entire Group. Once the lead B-17 was established on its bomb run, its pilot engaged the autopilot and from then till bomb release the bombardier 'flew' the aircraft. The autopilot was linked electrically to the plane's Norden bomb sight, so that, each time the bombardier adjusted the sight to keep the aiming cross on the target, this fed corrections into the auto-pilot to steer the aircraft on the right path for an accurate attack.

For this raid the bomber crews had been briefed to attack from alti-tudes of between 17,000 and 20,000ft, depending on their position in the formation. That was less than the B-17's maximum attack altitude, to give improved bombing accuracy against this particularly important target. Captain John Latham was the lead bombardier for the 96th Bomb Group at the head of the raiding force. Later he commented:

> As lead bombardier I felt a great sense of responsibility because, if I missed the target, then all of the planes in my formation missed. When you have flown many hours and fought hard and lost many friends from fighters and anti-aircraft fire, it is extremely difficult to condone the failure of the one person upon whom the success of the entire effort depended.

The bombers attacked the target on a due easterly heading and Latham aimed his bombs at a point on the far (eastern) side of the target complex. Regensburg's few anti-aircraft batteries did their best to disrupt the attack, as did the few Messerschmitt fighters that had taken off from the airfield beside the factory. But these weak forces could do little to blunt the force of the bombardment.

When John Latham's B-17 reached the bomb-release point computed by the Norden bomb sight, a pair of electrical contacts snapped closed to release the plane's ten 500lb high-explosive bombs in rapid succession. The rest of the Group held tight formation on the lead aircraft during the bomb run, and when the latter's bombs were seen falling away, the rest of the B-17s in the formation released theirs. Using this method, bombs would be put down in a dense pattern on the ground, running back along a track from the leader's aiming point, the breadth of that pattern being the width of the formation at bomb release.

After bomb release, the pilot of the lead aircraft disengaged the autopilot and commenced a sweeping turn to the right, setting course for Algeria. As his bomber turned away, Latham moved to a side window to observe the results of his handiwork:

> It was just as though we had the conditions made to order and we saw what we hoped to see. Our bombs fell just on the leading edge of the target. It was perfect. We saw the rest of the Group's effort a split second later, moving across the target in a rapid series of bursts. Even from the height we were at, you could see, just momentarily, each bomb hitting the ground, either creating a hole in the ground or sending bricks flying, and then the whitish red of the explosion followed by a cloud of dust growing bigger and bigger and spreading across the target, with the flashes of further bombs continuing to be seen in the smoke and dust.

The lead bombardiers of the first three Bomb Groups to pass over the target were able to see the aiming points easily, and in each case their bomb patterns were extremely accurate. Then, as was so often the case when a large number of bombers attacked the same target, the clouds of dust thrown up by the explosions and smoke rising from the numerous fires began to drift over the aiming points, making them difficult to pick out. The later formations found conditions getting progressively more difficult, and two Bomb Groups, the 94th and the 385th, found visibility so bad that they were unable to release their weapons during their initial bomb runs and had to turn around and make second runs. The 122 bombers that reached the target took 22 minutes to complete their attack, that time being extended by the need for the two Bomb Groups to make second bomb runs.

Despite the problems with failing visibility, the B-17s laid accurate carpets of bombs over the factory complex. The plant area was hit hard and the raid killed about 400 workers and inflicted injuries on a similar number. After leaving the target, the B-17s continued south over the Alps. Two damaged B-17s left the formation and headed for the safety of neutral Switzerland, the first of these aircraft to land there. Describing the 1,000-mile flight from the target to the recovery airfields in Africa, Beirne Lay later wrote:

> The rest of the trip was a marked anticlimax. A few more fighters pecked at us on the way to the Alps. A town in the Brenner Pass tossed up a lone burst of futile flak. We circled over Lake Garda [in northern Italy] long enough to give the cripples [damaged aircraft] a chance to join the family, and we were on our way toward the Mediterranean in a gradual descent. The prospect of ditching as we approached North Africa, short of fuel, and the sight of other B-17s falling into the drink, seemed trivial matters after the vicious nightmare of the long trip across southern Germany. We felt the reaction of men who had not expected to see another sunset.

During the flight from the target a further seven B-17s went down, all of them after having suffered battle damage earlier. In several cases the aircraft had lost fuel from holed tanks and were forced to put down short of their destination.

Of the 146 heavy bombers that had set out from England earlier in the day, 139 had penetrated occupied Europe; and of those, 115 succeeded in landing at airfields in friendly territory. As was often the case in a hard-fought air action of this kind, the losses were not distributed evenly throughout the force. The unit that took the heaviest battering was the 100th Bomb Group, the one with which Beirne Lay flew, in the most exposed position at the rear of the force: of its 21 B-17s, nine were shot down. In contrast, the 96th Bomb Group, which led the raid, suffered no losses at all, and two other units, the 94th and the 388th Bomb Groups, lost only one aircraft each. The air-sea rescue services of both sides turned in an exemplary performance and, miraculously, every man on board the five B-17s of the Regensburg attack force that ditched in the North Sea or the Mediterranean was picked up safely.

In the course of the action, the Regensburg attack force lost 24 B-17s, 16.4 per cent of the force. But that was not the final cost of the raid. A week later 85 of those aircraft took off from Algeria to return to England, attacking an airfield in western France on the way. The rest of the B-17s that landed in Algeria had been damaged too severely to be repaired in time at the poorly equipped landing grounds there. Some of the damaged planes would later be repaired and would return in ones and twos. But in the short term the attack on Regensburg deprived the Eighth Air Force of 61 bombers – uncomfortably close to half of those committed to the venture. During the mission the B-17s' gunners claimed to have destroyed 140 German fighters in air-to-air combat. It was a massive exaggeration, with every fighter that was shot down being claimed several times: from an examination of *Luftwaffe* records, it is clear that fewer than ten German fighters were shot down while engaging the Regensburg attack force.

As has been said, the bombing of the Regensburg aircraft production complex was both accurate and concentrated: it was a fine example of the precision air attack theories then being pushed hard by the US Army Air Forces. Reconnaissance photographs taken after the raid showed a high proportion of the buildings at the plant to be wrecked or burnt-out. Viewing the damage, Allied intelligence officers assessed that production would be halted for several weeks and greatly reduced for several months after that. It was an over-optimistic prognosis.

Once the debris had been cleared away, company officials found that most of machine tools and production jigs at the plant had survived intact. The buildings were repaired or, where this was not possible, the machine tools were quickly re-sited. Production resumed, and in September 1943, the month following the attack, the Regensburg factory delivered nearly eighty Bf 109s to the *Luftwaffe*. In October there were 163 and in November 205. By December, monthly production reached 270, exactly the same as it had been before the attack. The sag in Bf 109 production at the plant amounted to about 400 aircraft, or about 12 per cent of those that would have been built during a four-month period had the raid not taken place. Although the attack administered a heavy blow, it was one from which the *Luftwaffe* would soon recover.

In truth, the 272 tons of bombs that the B-17s laid across the target was insufficient to 'destroy' a factory complex the size of that at Regensburg. Moreover, the 500lb high-explosive bomb, the largest weapon used during the raid, was insufficiently powerful to cause serious damage among machine tools, even if it exploded on the building housing them. As the Allies would learn when they examined the German records after the war, in order to halt production at such a plant, it would be necessary to mount repeated attacks in similar strength at regular intervals.

To round off this account of the attack on Regensburg, we need to look briefly at the fate of the attack on Schweinfurt by 230 Flying Fortresses later on 17 August 1943. These raiders also suffered heavily at the hands of the German fighters, losing 36 bombers. Thus, of the 376 Flying Fortresses that set out from England that day to bomb the two important targets, a total of sixty were destroyed in action.

Both sides learned important lessons from the day's actions. The US Army Air Forces learned that the crossfire from a large formation of heavy bombers could not prevent the latter from suffering unacceptably heavy losses during deep-penetration attacks on Germany. The solution was given a high priority to the production of long-range escort fighter types, notably the P-51B Mustang. When the latter became available in quantity early the following year, it would have a decisive impact on the course of the strategic bombing offensive.

For the German High Command there were other, quite different lessons. The first was the need to pull back more fighter units from the Eastern and the Mediterranean Fronts, to buttress those defending the homeland. This would be done. To allow the formation of more fighter units, the production of these aircraft was stepped up, at the expense of bombers and other types. Moves were made to augment the firepower of home defence fighters, to increase their effectiveness in the bomber-destroyer role. Simultaneously, work began to disperse the production of aircraft and aero-engines among many scores of small factories scattered across the country, instead of concentrating it at a relatively few large plants that were known to the enemy and therefore liable to attack. And, as a long-term solution to defeat the bombers, the *Luftwaffe* poured resources into getting the revolutionary new Messerschmitt Me 262 jet fighter into production and first-line service as rapidly as possible. The degree of success that attended their efforts with the last of these is described in Chapter 12, 'The Jets Get Their Chance'.

Chapter 9

Reconnaissance to Berlin

This chapter looks at an important aspect of air warfare photographic reconnaissance. Flying a long-range reconnaissance mission in wartime requires special skills and a special kind of bravery. In the Second World War, the aircraft operated alone, and usually without armament, at extremes of altitude, speed and often range, penetrating deep into hostile territory to photograph their targets. Once the pictures had been taken, the mission was only half complete, for the finest photographs were of no use unless they could be brought back for processing and interpretation to extract the necessary intelligence.

Harsh experience has shown that, in war, it was usually much easier for reconnaissance aircraft to avoid the enemy defences than attempt to fight their way through them. For that reason, most specialized reconnaissance aircraft are stripped of armament, trading weight and drag for improvements in speed, altitude and range performance. Reconnaissance crews faced a range of foes, quite apart from the fighters and anti-aircraft guns of their human adversary. There was the psychological effect of being alone, deep in enemy territory, with little or no chance of receiving help in an emergency. There was the need to depend on the near-perfect functioning of a flying machine, and the knowledge that even a minor failure could result in death or a long stretch in a prisoner-of-war camp. There was the insidious enemy of boredom which, sometimes assisted by mind-numbing cold at high altitude, could reduce a man's concentration to a point that might be fatal if a sudden attack developed. Also, on maximum-range flights, there was the ever-present danger of running out of fuel if the pilot failed to use this precious commodity frugally or if, to avoid

---

SUPERMARINE SPITFIRE PR Mk XI

Role: Single-seat, long-range, photographic reconnaissance aircraft.
Power: One Rolls-Royce Merlin 63 12-cylinder, liquid-cooled, in-line engine developing 1,760hp at take-off.
Armament: None carried. Military load during the mission described comprised two F.52 cameras (with 36in focal length lenses) fitted in the rear fuselage.
Performance: Maximum speed 417mph at 24,000ft; maximum operational radius of action (carrying a 90-gallon drop tank) 565 miles.
Normal operational take-off weight: 8,519lb.
Dimensions: Span 36ft 10in; length 31ft 1in; wing area 242 sq ft.
Date of first production Spitfire XI: November 1942.

---

enemy fighters, he flew for too long at full throttle. Set against all of this, those that flew reconnaissance missions were regarded as a highly professional elite: they alone were able to play a recognizably important part in war without indulging in the grim business of slaughter.

Aerial reconnaissance missions take several forms. This account describes a post-strike reconnaissance mission, whose purpose was to provide photographs from which intelligence officers determined the damage inflicted on the target. After a strike, an air commander needed to know as soon as possible whether it had been successful, or if a follow-up attack were needed. Because the enemy would often expect the post-strike reconnaissance aircraft to follow a heavy attack, and arrange a suitable reception, this type of mission was potentially the most dangerous of all.

On 6 March 1944 the US Eighth Air Force mounted the first of many large-scale attacks on Berlin. At 1.30 p.m., when the attack was at its climax, Major Walt Weitner eased his Spitfire off the ground at Bradwell Bay near Clacton and turned on to an easterly heading. Weitner commanded the 14th Photo Squadron, 7th Photographic Reconnaissance Group, a Eighth Air Force unit based at Mount Farm near Oxford which operated a mix of Lightnings and Spitfires modified for the long-range photographic-reconnaissance role.

Weitner's aircraft was a Spitfire PR Mk XI appropriately named 'High Lady'. Stripped of its armament, and with a pair of long focal length cameras installed in the rear fuselage, the much-modified fighter was a flying fuel tank. Almost the entire leading edge of both wings had been redesigned to form a large integral tank holding 132 gallons of high-octane petrol. With the 84 gallons in the main tanks in front of the cockpit, and a further 90 in the 'slipper' drop tank mounted under the fuselage, the aircraft carried 306 gallons of fuel. That was more than *three times* the fuel load carried by the early fighter versions of the aircraft.

The flight was planned to last over four hours, most of the time spent at high altitude, and Weitner wore several layers of clothing to keep out the cold. With all of this, plus a parachute, dinghy, life jacket and oxygen mask, the narrow confines of the Spitfire cockpit were no place for the claustrophobic.

Weitner took a direct route to the German capital, heading almost due east over the North Sea towards Holland. Just over half an hour after take-off, he passed his first check-point, The Hague, at 39,000ft. Below him there was five-tenths cloud cover, and he could make out the outline of the Zuider Zee to his left. He later recalled:

> The Spitfire was easy to handle at very high altitude. This one was well trimmed and stayed pretty level. One had always to have hold of the stick, but it needed hardly any pressure. In the reconnaissance business you do not fly straight and level for long: you are continually banking to search the sky all around for enemy fighters and check the navigation.

Outside the cockpit the temperature was around −60F. The thick layers of clothing kept most of his body warm, but nothing could prevent Weitner's extremities, his feet and his hands, from the numbing cold. From time to time he clapped his hands and stamped his feet on the cockpit floor to get the blood circulating again.

The flight at high altitude brought another problem: during its passage through the cold air, the Spitfire left behind a highly visible white condensation trail. Had Weitner wished to draw attention to his presence, there was hardly a better way of doing it, but the realities of the situation forced him to take a calculated risk:

> I could have avoided [the trail] by descending below 22,000 feet, but I did not think that was the thing to do on a deep penetration like this. I thought the best bet was to cruise near to the ceiling of a Messerschmitt 109; then, if I had to go up, I had a little margin of altitude I could use. The Germans must have known I was up there, but nobody was paying any attention to me.

Weitner thought that if enemy fighters climbed to high altitude after him, they too would leave condensation trails, and he would get plenty of warning of their approach.

As the Spitfire passed over Hanover the skies were clear, and Weitner switched on his cameras as he passed over the city. He noticed several condensation trails ahead at about his level, but the aircraft were moving on an easterly heading away from him. The reason for the defenders' present lack of interest in the lone Spitfire was not difficult to fathom: that afternoon almost every available German fighter in the area was battling against the huge force of bombers and their escorts now heading back to England.

As the air battle moved to the west and the Spitfire got closer to Berlin, the *Luftwaffe* finally reacted to the lone intruder. A glance in the rear-view mirrors in the canopy side-blisters revealed three enemy fighters holding formation on the Spitfire, 1,500yds behind and slightly below. All three aircraft were leaving condensation trails.

The arrival of the enemy fighters came at a bad time for the American pilot, forcing him to take another calculated risk. At this time his engine was running on the slipper tank, and from his calculations – which gave only a rough guide – he knew that the tank was nearly empty. If it ran dry, his first indication would be when the engine started to splutter – which might leave him without power at a critical point in the chase. He could switch to one of the internal tanks and release the drop tank, but to complete the mission he needed to use all the fuel that he had. If he released the drop tank, it would mess up his fuel calculations, and he might have to abandon the mission short of the target. Another alternative, to switch to one of the internal tanks, hold on to the slipper tank and use that fuel later, he rejected because the latter might not resume feeding. Weighing up the situation, Weitner decided to try to outrun the enemy fighters using the remaining fuel in the drop tank and hope that it held out long enough. He pushed the throttle as far forward as it would go without selecting emergency power, to pick up speed. Then he eased up the nose and began a shallow climb. As he did so, he kept one hand on the tank selector switch, ready to shift to one of the wing tanks when the engine faltered:

As I climbed through 40,000 feet I could see that the German fighters behind me had split: one went on my right and two on my left, to box me in. And at that moment the engine coughed. I immediately selected internal fuel and the engine caught right away. At 41,500 feet I levelled off and my indicated airspeed increased to 178mph [true airspeed about 360mph]. Gradually the German fighters began to fall back and finally the last slid from view.

Had the enemy planes got closer, Weitner could have pushed his throttle 'through the gate' to get full emergency boost to outrun his pursuers. But that would have increased fuel consumption greatly and he regarded it as a measure of last resort.

The enemy fighters that chased the Spitfire were almost certainly Messerschmitt Bf 109Gs specially fitted with nitrous oxide power-boosting to give an improved performance at high altitude. Probably the pursuers belonged to *I Gruppe* of *Jagdgeschwader 3*, based at Burg to the west of Berlin, one of the units that specialized in such interceptions.

When the enemy fighters passed out of sight, the Spitfire was getting near to the enemy capital. Maintaining a wary eye for other Messerschmitts trying to sneak up on him from behind, Weitner prepared to make his first photographic run over the city. Although he could see clearly the huge expanse of Lake Mueritz, some 50 miles to the north of Berlin, because of the smoke and industrial haze he still could not see the city itself. The Spitfire had no pressurized cabin, and to reduce the risk of decompression sickness Weitner did not want to remain at maximum altitude for longer than necessary. He eased the aircraft into a slow descent to 38,000ft and suddenly he caught sight of the sprawling city laid out beneath him, with the sun glinting off the red brick and tile houses.

Weitner decided to make his first photographic run from almost due north, down wind, to get a good line of photos without drifting off the target. He banked the Spitfire steeply and aligned himself on the string of lakes he was using as a check-point, carefully levelled the aircraft using the artificial horizon and then switched on the cameras.

The Spitfire carried two F52 cameras mounted almost verti-cally in the rear fuselage, each with a 36in focal length lens. The cameras were splayed out sideways, giving a slight overlap in cover. At five-second intervals, the camera shutters opened and closed, to photograph a three-mile wide strip of ground beneath the aircraft. Accurate flying was essential during a photographic run; even a small amount of bank could cause gaps in the cover. During each five-second interval between successive pairs of photographs, Weitner made a painstaking check of his flight path and corrected it where necessary.

His orders were to photograph the targets bombed by the American heavy bombers, and to assist him he had aerial photo-graphs of the city with the targets marked on them. But he could see pillars of smoke rising from other places and decided to photograph those also:

The whole time I kept checking the sky behind my tail, as I expected further interference from the enemy fighters. But none showed up. There was some flak – I could see the smoke bursts mushrooming – but none of it was close. I spent about 25 minutes over Berlin, during which I made runs from different directions and took about 70 photographs. Then a solid layer of cloud began moving over the city from the east, and as fuel was beginning to run low I set a course of 297 degrees for home.

Over Holland on the way home, the Spitfire pilot encountered a further problem with his fuel. The standard procedure was to use the fuel in the drop tank first; then that in the tanks in the wings, changing from one side to the other at fifteen-minute intervals to maintain the lateral trim; then the fuel in the lower main tank; and, last of all, that in the upper main tank. As the Merlin used the last of the fuel in the wing tanks, it coughed briefly, then resumed its even roar as Weitner selected the lower main tank. A glance at the fuel gauge caused the pilot's heart to miss a beat: the needle was jammed hard against the zero mark. If that reading was correct, the tank had been leaking and it would be almost empty, and there was insufficient fuel to regain friendly territory. The more palatable answer was that the tank was full but the fuel gauge had frozen up. Only time would tell which answer was correct.

Weitner made a few quick calculations which proved to his satisfaction that the main tanks had to be full. Any nagging fears were put to rest when the bank of cloud covering the English coast came within gliding distance. He began a slow descent from 38,000ft and soon after he crossed the coast of Essex the fuel gauge jerked into life showing a reading of 20 gallons.

Weitner had intended to land at one of the airfields near to the coast to refuel, but with so much altitude in hand he knew he could fly straight to his base at Mount Farm. Speed was of the essence in delivering the precious films for processing, and by continuing straight to his base he could save nearly an hour in getting the pictures into the hands of the interpreters.

'High Lady' landed at its base after a flight of 4 hours 18 minutes, and ran out of fuel a few yards short of its dispersal point. Walt Weitner pulled on the parking brake, slid back his canopy, undid his straps and climbed stiffly out of the cockpit. For the reconnaissance pilot it had been a successful ending to a rather routine mission.

Chapter 10

The Nuremberg Disaster

In parallel with the American daylight bombing attacks on Germany, the Royal Air Force mounted attacks in strength by night. In the spring of 1944, following the introduction of new electronic detection equipment and a new airborne radar, the German night fighter force reached the peak of its effectiveness. RAF night bombers engaged in deep-penetration attacks against targets in Germany began to suffer increasingly severe losses, until this phase of the battle reached its climax on the night of 30/31 March 1944.

At 9.16 p.m. in the evening of 30 March 1944, the first of 782 Lancaster and Halifax four-engine bombers began taking off from their bases in eastern England. The target for the maximum-effort attack was the city of Nuremberg in southern Germany, an important centre for war production. Within its limits lay the huge Machninenfabrik Augsburg-Nürnberg plant producing diesel engines for tanks and U-boats, the Siemens plant turning out electrical equipment for the Navy and the Zundapp motor works building vehicles for the Army.

After take-off, each aircraft climbed in a spiral to an assigned altitude above 10,000ft, then set course for the force assembly point over the North Sea. Initially the bombers flew with their navigation lights on to lessen the risk of collision, but as they neared the Dutch coast the lights were extinguished and from then on each bomber crew was on its own.

Some accounts have likened the 'bomber stream' tactic employed by RAF night bombers to a loose formation, but such a description is grossly misleading. Crews were briefed to follow the same route and adhere to timing points along it, but the accuracy with which aircraft followed these depended on the skill and good fortune of individual navigators. As a result there was a natural tendency for a force of night bombers to spread itself out over a wide area. During the Nuremberg mission the raiders were divided into six separate waves which were to follow each other, snake-like, through a succession of turning points.

The plan called for the raiding force to pass through the target in a seventeen-minute period, which meant that, at the bombers' 220mph still-air cruising speed, the stream was to occupy a strip of sky 64 miles long and one mile (5,000ft) deep. Given the dispersion that usually occurred during night raids, in good conditions the bomber stream would be about ten miles wide. Even under ideal conditions, however, the density of aircraft within that 640 cubic miles of airspace was extremely low. If the bottom of this page can be taken to represent a distance of one mile, a single heavy bomber to that scale would be roughly the size of this letter 'T' the centre of a well-concentrated bomber stream there would be, on average, just two 'T'-size aircraft within the area represented by this page; if it were less well concentrated, there would be on average only one 'T' flying in that volume of sky.

Despite this relatively low density of aircraft, the bomber-stream tactic caused severe problems for the German night air defences. The bombers would pass any point on the route at an average of 46 per minute. That was sufficient to saturate the defending gun and searchlight defences and present far more targets than they could possibly engage. A concentrated stream was usually difficult for a night fighter crew to locate, though when a night fighter did get into the stream it sometimes caused considerable mayhem.

Shortly before 11 p.m., as the leading raiders were crossing the North Sea, they came into the view of German early-warning radar stations on the coasts of Belgium and Holland. Soon afterwards the first electronic jamming appeared on the radar screens, and this became increasingly severe as the night wore on.

Well before the vanguard of the raiding force reached the Dutch coast, the German fighter controllers had ordered their immediate-readiness aircraft to scramble. From their point of view, it was important to assemble a sizeable force of night fighters over western Germany as soon as possible after the incoming raid was detected. The cruising speed of the Messerschmitt Bf 110 and Junkers Ju 88 night fighters was little faster than that of the bombers they were expected to engage. As yet the raiders' target was unknown, but if it were in the west that could cause problems: the distance from the fighter bases in Denmark or near Berlin to the Ruhr was about the same as that from the bomber bases in Cambridgeshire to the German industrial area.

As the defending night fighters were taking off, the British radio-jamming organization made its presence felt. High-powered transmitters located in England and others carried by the bombers radiated a raucous cacophony on the German fighter radio channels. The *Luftwaffe* night fighter force war diarist noted:

> *Korps* VHF [radio] jammed by bell sounds. RIP traffic hardly possible, jamming of *Korps* HF by quotations from Fuhrer's speeches. *Korps* alternative frequency strongly jammed.

The electronic battle was not to be one-sided, however. The defenders were also well equipped in this regard, and they possessed systems whose existence was unknown to Bomber Command. The *Luftwaffe*'s raid-tracking service had developed to a fine art the technique of plotting the movement of bombers from their electronic emissions. The culprit radars were the H2S ground-mapping equipment and the 'Monica' tail-warning radar, both of which radiated distinctive signals that could be picked up from great ranges. The Germans had established a network of ground direction-finding stations across northern Europe to locate the sources of the emissions by triangulation. *Naxburg* receivers tracked the movements of H2S aircraft and *Korfu* receivers followed those transmitting with 'Monica'; furthermore, *Naxos* and *Flensburg* receivers fitted to some German night fighters enabled them

---

AVRO LANCASTER Mk I

Role: Seven-seat heavy bomber.
Power: Four Rolls-Royce Merlin 24 12-cylinder, liquid-cooled in-line engines each developing 1,640hp at take-off.
Armament: (Offensive) During the attack on Nuremberg, a distant target, these aircraft carried a bomb load of around 9,000lb, the exact weight depending upon the mix of weapons carried; (defensive) eight Browning .303in machine guns, two each in the nose and mid-upper turrets and four in the tail.
Performance: Maximum speed 287mph at 11,500ft; normal cruising speed 220mph at 20,000ft; service ceiling 24,500ft.
Normal operational take-off weight: 68,000lb.
Dimensions: Span 102ft; length 69ft 6in; wing area 1,297 sq ft.
Date of first production Lancaster I: October 1941.

to home on, respectively, the two types of radar emission (the airborne *Naxos* equipment was a variant of the device carried by U-boats, mentioned in Chapter 7).

In the battle now unfolding, the information from the new German devices would be valuable on four counts. First, because the H2S and 'Monica' signals emanated only from RAF aircraft, the sources were obviously and unambiguously hostile (with radar detection, identification was often a problem). Second, the German receivers were unjammable – unless the RAF adopted the irrational course of jamming its own radars. Third, the H2S radiations gave a clear indication of the whereabouts of the Pathfinder aircraft that led each wave of the raiding force to the target. And fourth, because they were passive devices, the receivers emitted no tell-tale radiations that would betray their existence.

The German night fighters carried a further new item of electronic equipment that would have a significant effect on the night's action – the SN-2 airborne interception radar. The earlier *Lichtenstein* set had been rendered virtually useless by the 'Window' metal foil strips dropped by RAF bombers. The SN-2 that replaced it operated on a longer wavelength and was relatively immune to the 'Window' then in use.

Shortly after midnight, the leading bombers crossed the Belgian/German frontier. Their crews found the weather far from ideal for a deep-penetration attack into enemy territory. Instead of the forecast cloud cover during the long approach flight to the target, they found the skies clear at the bombers' altitudes. Moreover, instead of the forecast wind of 60kts from the north-west, on their tails, the actual wind was variable in strength and more from the west. The more skilful navigators discovered the discrepancy relatively quickly and made the necessary corrections, but others took much longer to do so. As a result the force became spread out over a stretch of sky more than 120 miles long and 40 miles wide – more than four times the planned area.

As if that were not bad enough, a further quirk of the weather sealed the fate of many of the bomber crews heading into Germany. After high-octane petrol was burned in the bombers' engines, the residue emerged from the exhausts as steam, which normally dispersed without causing any problem. On this unusually cold night, however, the vapour condensed to form white trails at the raiders' altitudes of around 20,000ft. Lit by the half-full moon, the trails took on a phosphorescent quality that could be seen from great distances. Thus the bombers were shorn of the cloak of invisibility upon which their survival depended.

From his headquarters bunker at Deelen in Holland, *Generalmajor* Walter Grabmann, commanding *Jagddivision 3*, ordered the night-fighters to assemble over radio beacon 'Ida' near Bonn. The usual tactic was to hold the fighters over the beacon until the bombers' route became clear, then have them head out on a set bearing until they made contact with the bomber stream. On this night it soon became obvious to the German commander that no further directions were necessary: many of the bombers in the stream, made diffuse by the wind speed and direction being different from what were forecast, were about to pass over 'Ida'.

Thanks to the *Naxburg* and *Korfu* ground receiving stations, the defenders had no difficulty in distinguishing the RAF feint attack forces from the main body of raiders. The German war diarist noted:

Assembly, leaving England and approach could be followed correctly by *Rotterdam* bearings [*Rotterdam* was the German code-name for H2S]. Feint attacks on Cologne, Frankfurt and Kassel by Mosquitos appeared quite clearly, as the Mosquitos were flying without *Rotterdam*.

As the bombers passed over 'Ida', the radar operators in the orbiting night fighters made contact and guided their pilots on to individual bombers. As they closed on the enemy, the German crews had an important duty to perform before they went into action: they had to broadcast their position and the bombers' heading, to assist the *Luftwaffe* ground controllers to direct yet more fighters into the bomber stream. Soon the ether was thick with *'Pauke!'* calls, followed by position reports and headings. *'Pauke!'*, the *Luftwaffe* equivalent of the RAF's 'Tally Ho!', meant that the fighter had made contact with the enemy and was about to engage.

Thus began a running battle that was to last for more than 200 miles across Germany. As well as the night fighters joining the bomber stream, a small number of Ju 88s from a special illuminating unit released parachute flares to mark its position. The flares were visible from scores of miles away, and from all over Germany night fighters converged on the area like moths to a flame: *Jagddivision 2* came from northern Germany, *Jagddivision 1* arrived from the Berlin area and *Jagddivision 7* came west from Bavaria to meet the raiding force.

It was an ideal night for the free-hunting tactics employed by the German crews, and during the hour that followed they rained retribution on those who were destroying their homeland. *Unteroffizier* Emil Nonenmacher of *III Gruppe* of *Nachtjagdgeschwader 2* based at

Twenthe in Holland, piloting a Ju 88, joined the action shortly after
the initial clash:

> As we climbed out of Twenthe we could see that a great battle
> was already in progress: there were aircraft burning in the air and
> on the ground; there was the occasional explosion in mid-air
> and much firing with tracer rounds. We kept on towards the
> scene of high activity for about five minutes, then suddenly
> we hit the slipstream from one of the bombers. Now we were
> getting close to the bomber stream. It seemed that there was
> activity all around us – here an aircraft on fire, there someone
> firing, somewhere else an explosion on the ground. Yet it was a
> few more minutes before we actually caught sight of a bomber,
> its silhouette passing obliquely over my cockpit.

Now Nonenmacher was in the stream. It was a very clear night
and he could see as many as fifteen bombers around him, all of them
leaving condensation trails. He tried to move into a firing position
behind the first aircraft he had seen, but he misjudged the approach
and had to break away. It did not matter – there were plenty of others:

> With so many targets visible I could take my pick, so I chose
> the nearest one in front of me – a Lancaster – and went after
> him. He was weaving gently. I set myself up for a deflection
> shot, aiming at a point one aircraft length ahead of the bomber.
> I opened fire and saw my rounds striking it. Then I paused, put
> my sight on the bomber again and fired another burst. After
> a few rounds my guns stopped firing – I had exhausted the
> ammunition in the drum magazines on my cannon.

Nonenmacher ordered his flight engineer to replace the ammunition drums, but in the meantime he had to let the bomber escape. As
the crewman wrestled to fit new ammunition drums, Nonenmacher
closed on another Lancaster:

> I moved into a firing position about 100 metres astern and a
> little below it. By then the engineer had one of the cannon
> going so I pressed the firing button and saw my rounds striking
> the left wing. Soon afterwards both engines on that side burst
> into flames. He began to lose height and we could see the crew
> bailing out, it was so clear. The bomber took about six minutes
> to go down; when it reached the ground it blew up with a huge
> explosion.

MESSERSCHMITT BF 110G-4

Role: Three-seat night fighter.
Power: Two Daimler Benz DB 605B 12-cylinder, liquid-cooled, in-line engines each developing 1,475hp at take-off.
Armament: (Offensive) Various weapon mixes carried, but typically two Rheinmetall MK 108 30mm and two Mauser MG 151 20mm cannon mounted in the nose and two Oerlikon MG/FF 20mm cannon in a Schräge Musik installation firing obliquely upwards from the rear cabin; (defensive) two Rheinmetall MG 81 7.9mm machine guns on a hand-held installation in the cabin firing rearwards.
Performance: Maximum speed 342mph at 23,000ft; service ceiling 26,250ft.
Normal operational take-off weight: 20,700lb.
Dimensions: Span 53ft 4½in; length 42ft 9½in; wing area 413 sq ft.
Date of first production Bf 110G-4: June 1942.
Note: From the end of 1943, Bf 110Gs were fitted with SN-2 AI radar as standard equipment and some machines also carried Flensburg homing receivers.

Several night fighters carried the recently introduced *Schräge Musik* installation, a pair of 20mm cannon in a fixed mounting firing obliquely forwards and upwards at an angle of 70 degrees. One pilot who used these weapons to effect was *Oberleutnant* Helmut Schulte, a Bf 110 pilot with *II Gruppe* of *NJG* 5, who later recalled:

Normally our biggest problem was to find the bomber stream, but on this night we had no trouble. I found the enemy at a height of 6,000m [about 20,000ft]. I sighted a Lancaster and got underneath it and opened fire with [*Schräge Musik*]. Unfortunately [the guns] jammed so that only a few shots put out of action the starboard-inner motor. The bomber dived violently and turned to the north, but because of the good visibility we were able to keep him in sight. I now attempted a second attack after he had settled on his course, but because the Lancaster was now very slow, we always came out too far in front. I tried the *Schräge Musik* again, and after another burst the bomber fell in flames.

The effectiveness of the attacks by Nonenmacher, Schulte and their comrades was fully evident to the crews of other bombers. Squadron Leader G. Graham, a Lancaster pilot with No 550 Squadron, recalled:

We went in south of Cologne and were immediately met by the German fighters – I could say hundreds. It was a fantastic sight in the clear moonlight – aircraft going down in flames and exploding everywhere.

Flying Officer George Foley, flying as radar operator in one of the Lancaster Pathfinders, later recalled that he knew that things were beginning to go badly when he heard his pilot say, 'Better put your parachutes on, chaps – I've just seen the forty-second go down.' And the feelings of Lancaster pilot Flight Lieutenant Graham Ross were similar to those of many a bomber captain that night:

I was very shaken at seeing so many aircraft going down in flames. I was scared by that, but still more scared at the thought that my own crew might be scared by it all.

The most successful German pilot during the action was *Oberleutnant* Martin Becker, flying a Bf 110G of *I Gruppe* of *NJG 6*, based at Mainz/Finthen. An experienced pilot, he already had nineteen victories to his credit. Becker had a well-honed technique for bringing down bombers, using his forward-firing cannon. He would approach his victim from slightly below and to one side, to avoid being seen by the rear gunner. When within about 100yds of the bomber, he would edge into position immediately behind and below it, then pull up his nose and rake the bomber with cannon shells as it passed across his gun sight. Becker used these tactics to great effect that night, shooting down a total of seven heavy bombers.

Because of the unusually large area covered by the raiding force, the *Luftwaffe* fighter controllers had great difficulty in determining its intended target. But if there were doubt as to where the raiders were going, there could be none about where they had been. The path of the raiding force running eastward from 'Ida' was clearly marked on the ground by a trail of wrecked and burning aircraft. Not until 1.08 a.m., two minutes before the first bombs were due to fall on Nuremberg, was the city mentioned in the radio broadcasts to night fighters.

As the badly mauled raiding force approached the target, the perfidious weather again took a hand in the proceedings. Instead of the predicted clear skies over the target, the bomber crews found a thick blanket of cloud, When the Pathfinder aircraft released their strings of target-markers, the latter vanished into the murk. The attack that followed was scattered and ineffective, with bombs falling over a wide area. A few bombs fell on the north-eastern part of the city, but the industrial quarter was virtually untouched. That the maximum-effort raid achieved so little illustrates, in the starkest terms, the vulnerability of an air-attack plan to the vagaries of the weather.

As the bombers began their return flights, many crews feared that the savage night fighter attacks would continue. Mercifully for them, this was not the case, however: as the bombers headed west, the night fighters lost contact and there were few engagements during the withdrawal.

Several of the aircraft heading for home bore the scars of earlier encounters with the enemy. One such was a Halifax of No 578 Squadron piloted by Pilot Officer Cyril Barton. On the way to the target the bomber had twice been attacked by night fighters. It had one engine knocked out, the intercom system was shot away, one of the fuel tanks was holed and the hydraulic supply to the three gun turrets had been cut, putting all three out of action. A misinterpreted signal from the pilot had been taken as an order to bail out, and the navigator, bomb-aimer and wireless operator had jumped from the aircraft.

Despite this catalogue of damage, Barton had continued doggedly to the target and dropped his bombs. Then he turned for home, using the North Star to calculate a rough heading. The Halifax made a landfall near Sunderland, well to the north of that intended, on the last of its fuel. Such determination to overcome all odds deserved success, but it was not to be. Shortly afterwards the fuel gave out and Barton had to attempt a crash-landing in the darkness. Suddenly a line of houses appeared in his path, and when he swerved to miss them the bomber stalled and struck the ground heavily, nose-first. The three crew members in the rear fuselage survived, but the gallant pilot was killed. For 'unsurpassed courage and devotion to duty', Cyril Barton later received the posthumous award of the Victoria Cross.

Other bombers limped home with all manner of damage. Flight Sergeant Ronald Reinelt of No 433 (Canadian) Squadron, for example, landed his Halifax at Manston with one engine knocked out and 32 square feet of the skinning of the starboard wing burned away.

Ninety-four of the 782 bombers that set out to attack Nuremberg failed to return. That loss rate, nearly 13 per cent, represented the greatest proportional loss rate ever suffered by so large a force during a single action. Forty-eight bombers returned with major battle damage, in some cases so serious that the aircraft had to be consigned to the scrap heap. As usual during such actions, the German night fighter losses were minimal – five aircraft destroyed and five damaged beyond repair.

Inevitably, an account of an air action leans towards descriptions of aircraft destroyed or damaged. To put the matter into proportion, however, it should be pointed out that of the 782 bombers that set out, more than 500 (over two-thirds) reached the target and returned without damage of any kind.

Following the Nuremberg disaster, there were dark rumours that the raiders had been betrayed – that the defenders had known the target beforehand and had arranged their dispositions accordingly. These rumours were repeated in some post-war accounts. The conspiracy theory finds no support in contemporary *Luftwaffe* records, however, nor in the later recollections of *Luftwaffe* personnel who took part in the action. If the defenders knew the location of the target beforehand, why did the night fighters gain most of their victories along the route to the target, and lose contact with the bombers after it? In truth, during the early months of 1944 the *Luftwaffe* night-fighter force was at the height of its prowess; and, on the night of 30/31 March 1944, almost everything had gone right for the defenders and several things had gone wrong for the raiders.

The *Luftwaffe* night-fighter force would never come close to repeating its success. In April 1944 RAF Bomber Command shifted the focus of its attack to targets in France and Belgium, as part of the softening-up operation preceding the Normandy invasion. These shallow-penetration attacks gave the night fighters little time to find the bomber stream and concentrate forces against it. When the night attacks on Germany resumed, after the invasion, the loss of territory in France allowed raiders attacking targets in the south of Germany to approach over friendly territory. Again, there was no opportunity to set up the sort of long-running fight that was so devastatingly successful during the final night in March 1944.

Chapter 11

Day of the Sturmgruppe

*In the spring of 1944, the US daylight bombing offensive
against Germany entered a new and more devastating phase.
Now with continuous fighter escort all the way to and from
their targets, the heavy bombers were tearing the heart out
of German industry. The Americans were on the point of
establishing air superiority over the German homeland, and
for the time being it seemed that the Luftwaffe could do
little about it. The long-term answer to the problem was the
Messerschmitt Me 262 jet fighter, which alone had the speed
to avoid the American escort fighters and the firepower to
destroy the heavy bombers; its service career will be described
in the next chapter. As a stop-gap until the revolutionary new
fighter became available in quantity, the Luftwaffe formed
a special type of bomber-destroyer unit manned by intrepid
volunteer pilots — the Sturmgruppe.*

By the beginning of 1944 the *Luftwaffe* had pulled back virtually
all of its day fighter units from the battle fronts and redeployed
them to protect the homeland. But still it was not enough. During
actions against the US raiding formations, the defending fighter units
regularly found themselves outnumbered over their own territory
by the hoards of wide-ranging escort fighters. Moreover, the P-51B
Mustang, in service in large numbers, had a performance superior to
that of any of its opponents, and the type was inflicting heavy losses.
By the end of April, the defenders' situation had deteriorated to the
point that *Generalmajor* Adolf Galland, the *Luftwaffe's* Inspector of
Fighters, was moved to report to his superiors:

FOCKE WULF FW 190A-8

(*Details for* Sturmbock *version in parentheses*)

Role: Single-seat, general-purpose day fighter (single-seat bomber-destroyer).

Power: One BMW 801D-2 14-cylinder, air-cooled, radial engine developing 1,770hp at take-off.

Armament: Four MG 151 20mm cannon in the wings; two MG 131 13mm machine guns above the engine. (Two Rheinmetall Borsig MK 108 30mm cannon in place of the two MG 151 20mm cannon mounted mid-way along the wings.)

Performance: Maximum speed 402mph at 18,000ft (about 35mph slower); climb to 19,650ft, 9min 54sec (climbing performance considerably worse).

Normal operational take-off weight: 9,660lb (10,060lb).

Dimensions: Span 34ft 5½in; length 29ft 4½in; wing area 197 sq ft.

Date of first production FW 190A-8: January 1944.

Between January and April 1944 our day fighter arm lost more than 1,000 pilots. They included our best *Staffel, Gruppe* and *Geschwader* commanders . . . The time has come when our force is within sight of collapse.

Even more serious than these losses was the fact that the defending fighter units were not shooting down enough enemy bombers to blunt the American attacks. The situation was completely different from that during the Regensburg raid in August 1943, when *Jagdgruppe 50* had only bombers to contend with and delivered repeated set-piece attacks until its aircraft exhausted their ammunition. Now, if the defending fighters did get through to the bombers, there was usually time for only one or at most two brief firing passes before the escorts arrived in force.

The *Luftwaffe* found itself enmeshed in a vicious 'Catch-22' situation. Its specialized bomber-destroyer types, the twin-engine Messerschmitt Bf 110s and Me 410s, carried hefty batteries of cannon and rockets that were highly effective against the American bombers. But these planes were relatively slow and unwieldy and they often suffered heavy losses at the hands of the escorts. The less heavily armed Bf 109 and FW 190 single-engine fighters had the speed to avoid the escorts and get through to the bombers, but they lacked the firepower to enable pilots of average ability to knock down bombers during the necessarily short firing passes.

In the 'try anything' mood prevalent in the *Luftwaffe*, a new operational concept emerged to counter the enemy bomber formations. The idea centred on the use of a *Gruppe* of about thirty heavily armed FW 190s, fitted with extra armour and flown by volunteer pilots, that would move in en masse behind an enemy bomber formation to engage it from close range. This was the *Sturmgruppe*. The heavyweight FW 190s would be no match for the American escorts in combat, so the *Sturmgruppe* was itself to be escorted into action by two *Gruppen* of lightly armed Bf 109s; the latter were fitted with uprated engines and their task was to hold off the American fighters long enough for the Focke Wulfs to deliver their blow.

A new version of the FW 190, nicknamed the *'Sturmbock'* (battering ram), was produced specially for use with the new tactics. This carried two MK 108 30mm cannon in the wings, powerful-weapons with a rate of fire of 600 rounds a minute. On average, three hits with the 18oz high-explosive/incendiary rounds were sufficient to send a heavy bomber falling out of control. The *Sturmbock* could carry only 55 rounds per gun, enough for just over five seconds' firing. Because the weapon had a relatively low muzzle velocity and was ineffective at long range, the new tactics called for the German pilots to close to within 100yds of a heavy bomber before they opened fire.

As they moved in on their targets, the *Sturmbock* pilots would have to brave the defensive crossfire from the bombers. To give them a reasonable chance of survival, the modified FW 190 carried twice the weight of armour of the standard fighter version. The heavier armament and armour added about 400lb to the aircraft and imposed corresponding reductions in manoeuvrability, maximum speed and climbing performance.

The *Sturmgruppen* were to be élite units. Before a volunteer was accepted, he had to sign a document stating that he was prepared to press home his attacks on enemy bombers to short range and that if the guns failed to destroy the enemy plane he would ram it. Any pilot who signed the affidavit and then failed to carry out its conditions was liable to be court-martialled on a charge of cowardice in the face of the enemy, and those found guilty would face a firing squad. Nobody was forced to sign the affidavit, however, and those who did not wish to do so were not accepted into the *Sturmgruppen*.

By this stage of the war, the American bomber columns were sometimes as much as a hundred miles long. Usually there was a large force of escorts at the head of the force, with small units sweeping the flanks. The German plan was to vector the *Sturmgruppe* into the bomber stream mid-way along its length, where the escort would be at its weakest.

Under the previous tactics, German fighter pilots flew in pairs or in fours to attack the enemy bombers, usually from head-on, and individual pilots decided when to open fire and when to break away. The *Sturmgruppe* pilots were to do things differently, and their tactics were more rigid than any used hitherto. The FW 190s were to fly in nine-aircraft *Staffeln*, with the leader in the middle and the aircraft on each side flying a few yards apart in echelon. Succeeding *Staffeln* would follow close behind that of the leader. The *Sturmgruppe* leader was to manoeuvre his force behind a formation of enemy bombers, then allocate his *Staffeln* to attack different parts of it. Each *Staffel* was to continue firing at the bombers for as long as there was ammunition for the heavy cannon, then the aircraft were to turn away together.

The essence of the *Sturmgruppe* tactics was a short but extremely sharp attack, delivered en masse against a single combat box formation of enemy bombers. Then the Focke Wulfs and their covering Messerschmitts were to leave the scene in high-speed dives, hoping to get well clear before the hoard of vengeful Mustangs and Thunderbolts arrived in the area.

Thus the *Sturmgruppe* differed from other *Luftwaffe* fighter units in three fundamental respects: in the type of aircraft it flew, in the tactics it employed and in the calibre of the men that served in it. The first such unit to be formed, *IV Gruppe* of *Jagdgeschwader 3*, received its complement of aircraft and pilots in May 1944 and began training for the new role immediately. Two other *Jagdgeschwader*, JG 4 and JG 300, were each to convert one *Gruppe* to the new role as and when sufficient *Sturmbock* aircraft became available.

The first full-scale use of the new tactics was on 7 July 1944, against part of a force of 1,129 Flying Fortresses and Liberators attacking industrial targets in the Leipzig area. Fighter ace *Major* Walther Dahl led the attack formation, which comprised the *Sturmgruppe* with two *Gruppen* of Bf 109s providing top cover – about ninety aircraft assembled into one huge formation. The *Luftwaffe* fighter controller guided Dahl into visual contact with a column of bombers, and the latter led his force into the stream behind a formation of Liberators belonging to the 14th Combat Wing. There were no escorts in the area, and, as the *Sturmgruppe* closed in, the *Staffeln* moved into arrow-head formation, preparing to attack. The pilot of each Focke Wulf selected a Liberator and advanced unswervingly towards it. The American gunners put up a vigorous and spectacular return fire, making the sky alive with sparkling tracer rounds. Obeying the strict order to withhold their fire until the *Staffel* leader opened up, the German pilots could only grit our teeth and continue moving forwards. *Leutnant* Walther Hagenah, one of the pilots belonging to *JG 3*'s *Sturmgruppe*, described the mood as he closed in on the enemy bombers:

> It was essential that we held our fire until we were right up close against the bombers. We were to advance like Frederick the Great's infantrymen, holding our fire until we could see 'the whites of the enemies' eyes'.

In fact, the extra armour gave the Focke Wulf pilots considerable protection, and few of the attacks were knocked down by the return fire. The *Sturmbock* slid into firing positions about 100yds behind the enemy bombers and opened a withering barrage. From that range the German pilots could hardly miss, and, as the 3cm explosive rounds struck home, the B-24 formation dissolved in front of them.

That day, the US 2nd Bomb Division lost 28 Liberators, most of them during the *Sturmgruppe* action. The unit hardest hit was the 492nd Bomb Group, which lost a dozen planes in rapid succession. Walther Hagenah was credited with the destruction of one B-24. The *Sturmgruppe* lost nine fighters shot down, and three more crash-landed; five of its pilots were killed. By the standards of the day, it had been a highly successful defensive operation for the *Luftwaffe*. Walther Hagenah was in action with his *Sturmgruppe* on 18 and 20

CONSOLIDATED B-24J LIBERATOR

Role: Ten-seat, four-engine heavy bomber.
Power: Four Pratt & Whitney R-1830 Twin Wasp 14-cylinder, air-cooled, radial engines each developing 1,200hp at take-off.
Armament: (Offensive) The bomb load depended on the radius of action required but was typically 6,000lb; (defensive) ten Browning .5in machine guns, two each in powered turrets in the nose, in the tail and above and below the fuselage and one each in the waist positions.
Performance: Formation cruising speed (with full bomb load) 185mph at 22,000ft; tactical radius of action (flying in formation, with operational fuel reserves and with 6,000lb of bombs) 600 miles.
Normal operational take-off weight: 56,000lb.
Dimensions: Span 110ft; length 67ft 2in; wing area 1,048 sq ft.
Date of first production B-24J: Late 1943.

July, when he destroyed a B-17 on each occasion, and on 3 August, when he shot down a B-24.

Although the pilots had signed affidavits indicating a willingness to ram enemy bombers if other means of destroying them failed, only rarely was it necessary to adopt this course. Once a Focke Wulf reached a firing position, it could usually achieve a kill with its heavy cannon. Of the pilots who did carry out ramming attacks, about half escaped without serious injury. One who did not was *Obergefreiter* Heinz Papenburg of JG 4's *Sturmgruppe*, whose cannon failed at the vital moment during an attack on 27 August. He continued on and destroyed a B-24 by ramming. One wing of the Focke Wulf was torn away during the collision, and as the pilot jumped from the spinning fighter he struck the tail and broke both legs. The unfortunate pilot descended by parachute and had to take the shock of the landing on his shattered limbs.

The American countermeasure to the *Sturmgruppe* tactics was to send large-scale fighter sweeps in front of the bombers and along their flanks, with the aim of breaking up the ponderous German attack formations before they could reach the bombers. Once it had been scattered, there was no way in which an attack formation could reassemble if enemy fighters were about, and the operation had then to be abandoned. Usually, the American countermeasures were successful, though from time to time a *Sturmgruppe* did succeed in getting through to the bombers to deliver an attack. On 2 November 1944 two of these units mounted separate and successful attacks on American heavy-bomber formations. Thirty-nine aircraft of JG 3 attacked the 91st Bomb Group and knocked down thirteen Flying Fortresses, including two by ramming. Later that day, 22 *Sturmbock* fighters of JG 4 attacked the 457th Bomb Group. Sergeant Bernard Sitek witnessed the latter engagement from the ball turret of his B-17:

> Everything, happened pretty fast, as it usually does when the Germans offer any opposition. We had been off the bomb run about ten minutes when vapour trails from fighters started to fill the sky. Friendly or enemy, was the question on everybody's mind. We soon learned the answer. They were FW 190s and Me 109s forming up for one of those wolf-pack attacks. At first it appeared that they were on the same level as our Box, the High Box, but as they came closer they lowered themselves for an attack on the Low and the Lead Boxes.

In the action that followed, the Low and the Lead Boxes of the formation lost nine bombers within just over a minute. In both cases the American escort fighters arrived too late to prevent the attacks, but they were able to exact a heavy price from the *Sturmgruppen* involved. Of the 61 *Sturmbock* aircraft taking part in the actions, 31 were shot down; seventeen German pilots were killed and seven were wounded.

In the weeks that followed, a shortage of fuel – the result of repeated air attacks on German oil refineries – limited the ability of the *Luftwaffe* to retaliate effectively. Successful *Sturmgruppe* actions became fewer and increasingly far between. The last one of note took place on 14 January 1945, when aircraft of *JG 300* delivered a sharp attack on B-17s of the 390th Bomb Group and shot down all eight aircraft in one squadron's formation. During the action five *Sturmgruppe* pilots were killed and two were wounded.

Although the *Sturmgruppen* achieved the occasional spectacular success against individual bomber formations during the autumn and winter of 1944, after an impressive beginning their operations became increasingly difficult and costly. It was not that the tactics were at fault or that the pilots lacked the determination necessary to carry them out: it was simply that no tactical method was likely often to succeed in the face of such overwhelming enemy air superiority.

Chapter 12

The Jets get their Chance

*By mid-1944, the development of the piston-engine fighter
aircraft had reached a dead end. Then, on cue, the jet-propelled
fighter appeared on the scene, offering a huge advance in performance. Faced by numerically superior foes on all fronts and
with the Fatherland under sustained and devastating air attack,
the Luftwaffe channelled enormous resources into bringing the
Messerschmitt Me 262 jet aircraft into mass production. Here,
it seemed, lay the technical innovation that would re-establish
air superiority over Germany and beyond its frontiers. For their
part, the Allies had soon become aware of the existence of the
new aircraft and dreaded the time when it would be introduced
into combat. In the event, both sides underestimated the difficulty of getting the turbojet engine to function reliably, and the
difficulty of mass-producing it.*

By the final year of the Second World War, the performance of
the piston-engine fighter was close to its physical limit. The
problem was fundamental to this form of power unit and there
was no way to circumvent it. The rotational power of the piston
engine was converted into forward thrust by the propeller, but, as
speeds approached 500mph, the efficiency of the propeller decreased
rapidly, and a huge increase in engine power was necessary to give a
small increase in maximum speed.

A few figures will serve to illustrate the point. In round terms,
the Merlin engine powering the Spitfire Mk I developed 1,000hp,
which gave the fighter a maximum speed of about 300mph at sea
level. At that speed, the propeller was about 80 per cent efficient
and the 1,000lb of thrust it produced equalled the drag from the

Spitfire's airframe. Now consider the amount of engine power needed to propel that same Spitfire at twice that speed, 600mph. Drag rises with the square of speed, so doubling the speed meant quadrupling the drag. Thus 1,000lb of drag at 300mph became 4,000lb of drag at 600mph, and to overcome that the aircraft needed 4,000lb of thrust. It can be shown that this was the equivalent of 6,400hp. At 600mph the efficiency of the propeller was only about 53 per cent, however. So to drive the aircraft at that speed the engine needed to develop not 6,400hp but 12,000. In 1945 the best piston engines for fighters produced just over one horsepower for each pound of weight, so a piston engine able to propel the fighter at 600mph would have weighed some 11,000lb – about double the all-up weight of an early production Spitfire.

For flight at high speeds, the turbojet was a fundamentally more efficient form of powerplant. It produced its thrust directly, and that thrust remained nearly constant throughout the aircraft's speed range. The two Jumo turbojets fitted to the Me 262 delivered a total of 3,960lb of thrust for a total weight of only 2,650lb and gave the fighter a maximum level speed of 540mph. No piston engine then in existence or under consideration offered a comparable thrust-to-weight ratio.

So much for the technical rationale for the jet fighter. The business of getting Me 262 into service in the *Luftwaffe* would involve a lengthy and tortuous military-political process. Yet, despite its superb performance, the aircraft would fail utterly to live up to its promise. Some commentators have attributed this to ineptitude on the part of Adolf Hitler for insisting it be used initially as a fighter-bomber. Others have said that the *Luftwaffe* failed to push the development and production of the aircraft with sufficient vigour. It has even been suggested that, had the Me 262 been brought into service more rapidly, the war might have taken a different course. In this chapter we shall examine the facts and the myths concerning this fascinating combat aircraft.

The Me 262 made its first successful flight on jet power in July 1942 and it was soon achieving speeds in excess of 430mph in level flight; as more powerful versions of the Jumo 004 engine became available, its maximum speed rose above the 500mph mark. So long as the power units worked properly, the aircraft had a sparkling performance, but the early turbojets had a poor record of reliability. Flame-outs and turbine failures occurred with disconcerting regularity, and the prototypes spent much of their time on the ground undergoing engine changes.

The turbojet ran at much higher temperatures, and at far greater rotational speeds, than the piston engine. As a result, those who designed the early jet engines had to overcome a host of fundamentally new problems, and in many cases did so from first principles. One of the most intractable problems facing the German engineers was a lack of nickel and chromium. These essential ingredients for the manufacture of high-temperature-resistant steel alloys were in critically short supply in wartime Germany, and neither was available for the jet engine programme. As a result, Junkers technicians had to demonstrate considerable ingenuity in devising substitute materials for the Jumo 004 engine. The combustion chambers, for example, were made from ordinary steel with a spray-coating of aluminium to increase their ability to withstand high temperatures. Such measures were only partially successful, however, and the running life of the early 004s rarely exceeded ten hours before an engine change became necessary.

From the summer of 1943, the *Luftwaffe* was under severe pressure to get the Me 262 into mass production. Although the Jumo 004 was insufficiently reliable to allow the design to be frozen for such, the *Luftwaffe*, anticipating that any problems would soon be solved, ordered the Messerschmitt company to begin tooling up for the mass production of airframes (some of the first jigs were destroyed during the attack on Regensburg, described in Chapter 8). In the months that followed, the need to get the jet fighter into service became steadily greater.

As described in the previous chapter, the fighter units defending Germany were suffering heavy losses and were able to destroy only a small proportion of the attacking bombers. The available day fighter types had either the firepower to destroy the heavy bombers or the performance 'to engage the American escort fighters, but none of them had both. The Me 262 promised to solve this problem at a stroke: it was faster than any Allied fighter, and its armament of four MK 108 30mm cannon was sufficiently powerful to tear apart the structures of heavy bombers.

In the spring of 1944, a test unit was formed at Lechfeld in Bavaria to introduce the Me 262 into service and train a cadre of pilots to fly it. Yet, although the reliability of the Jumo 004 had improved slightly by then, the engine still required skilful handling. Throttle movements had to be made slowly, otherwise there was a risk of the engine overheating or suffering a flame-out. Once he had throttled back and reduced speed on the landing approach, a pilot was committed to landing. If thereafter he advanced the throttles to go round again, the 004's poor acceleration meant that the aircraft was

MESSERSCHMITT ME 262A

Role: Single-seat jet fighter or fighter-bomber.
Power: Two Junkers Juno 004A jet engines each developing 1,980lb of thrust.
Armament: (Fighter role) Four MK 108 30mm cannon; (fighter-bomber role) two 30mm cannon and two 550lb bombs carried externally under the fuselage.
Performance: Maximum speed 540mph at 19,500ft; climb to 19,680ft, 6min 48sec. Normal operational take-off weight: 14,100lb.
Dimensions: Span 40ft 11½in; length 34ft 9½in; wing area 234 sq ft.
Date of first production Me 262A: Spring 1944.

likely to hit the ground before it gained sufficient speed to climb away. Clearly, the aircraft was not yet ready for combat, nor was it a suitable vehicle for fighter pilots of average or below-average ability.

Meanwhile, pressure was being exerted on the Me 262 programme from a quite different source. The most potent threat then facing Adolf Hitler was the expected Anglo-American invasion of north-west Europe. If it succeeded, his forces would have to fight a two-front war against enemies with numerically superior forces. The critical time for such an invasion would be in the hours immediately following the initial landings, as the troops sought to establish defensive positions ashore before German ground forces could mount their counter-attack. If the Allied troops could be subjected to repeated bombing and strafing attacks as they came ashore, they might still be in disarray when the German *Panzer* divisions arrived on the scene. And if that happened, it might be possible to defeat the landing operation with heavy losses.

Given the scale of the Allied fighter cover to be expected over the beach-head, Hitler believed, correctly, that only the Me 262 was fast enough to get through to the landing area and attack with any certainty of success. During discussions, the *Führer* was assured that, if required, the Me 262 could carry a couple of two 550lb bombs, and from then on the aircraft featured prominently in his anti-invasion plans. There can be little doubt that the Me 262 could have performed the task, and that if a landing operation ran into difficulties – as would happen at Omaha Beach on D-Day – such harassment could be decisive. If there were only a few jet aircraft available, they could be used to much greater effect in attacking the troops coming ashore than in battling with the hoards of Allied aircraft in the skies above the landings. *Generalfeldmarschall* Erhard Milch, the *Luftwaffe*

officer responsible for aircraft production, acknowledged the importance of the Me 262 as a fighter-bomber. But he continued to devote
his efforts to getting it into service with the fighter force as quickly
as possible. So far as he was concerned, the fighter-bomber version
could come later.

Matters came to a head on 23 May 1944 when Göring, Milch and
other senior *Luftwaffe* officers were summoned to a conference on
aircraft production at Hitler's headquarters at Berchtesgaden. When
the Me 262 was mentioned, the *Führer* asked, 'I thought the 262 was
coming as a high-speed bomber? How many of the 262s already
manufactured can carry bombs?' Milch replied that to date none had
been modified for this purpose: the aircraft was being manufactured
exclusively as a fighter. There was an awkward silence, then Milch
dug himself further into the pit when he stated that the new aircraft
would not be able to carry bombs unless there were extensive design
changes. Hearing that, Hitler lost his composure and excitedly inter-
rupted his *Generalfeldmarschall*: 'Never mind! I wanted only one
250-kilo [550lb] bomb.'

As the *Führer* realized the implications of what he had been told,
he became increasingly angry. After the assurances he had been
given on the ease with which the Me 262 could be modified to
carry bombs, no preparatory work had been done to enable it to do
so. The Allied invasion might begin at any moment, and it seemed
that the weapon on which he had pinned high hopes had been
snatched from his hands. Hitler delivered a savage denunciation of
the duplicity of the *Luftwaffe* officers present and said that he would
hold Göring personally responsible for ensuring that the Me 262
was introduced into service in the fighter-bomber role as rapidly as
possible.

It must be stressed, however, that, at the time Hitler delivered his
now-famous edict that every Me 262 possible be modified for use
as a fighter-bomber, the continuing unreliability of its 004 engine
precluded the aircraft's operational use in any role. Nothing had
changed two weeks later when, on 6 June, the Allied troops stormed
ashore in Normandy. By the end of that morning the invaders were
firmly established ashore, and the opportunity for Me 262s to achieve
a decisive impact on the landings had passed.

The formation of the first Me 262 jet fighter-bomber unit was
pushed ahead with all speed, and near the end of June the 3rd *Staffel*
of *Kampfgeschwader 51* began to re-equip with these aircraft. On 20
July the jet fighter-bomber unit was declared operational and moved
to Chateaudun near Paris, with nine aircraft each equipped to carry
two 550lb bombs. To reduce losses, and to minimize the risk of one

of the new planes falling into enemy hands, pilots had orders not to descend below 4,000m (13,000ft) over hostile territory. The bombs were released in shallow dives from above that altitude, an inaccurate type of attack which meant that the jet fighter-bombers achieved little against small targets such as bridges or vehicles. Moreover, the short running life of the 004 restricted flying and kept most of the aircraft on the ground.

Also at this time, the fighter ace *Major* Walter Nowotny took command of the Me 262 test unit at Lechfeld and the latter was re-named *Kommando 'Nowotny'*. The unit possessed fifteen early-production machines unsuitable for modification for the fighter-bomber role. The serviceability of these aircraft was poor, and only rarely would it have more than four of the jet fighters available to fly. *Kommando 'Nowotny'* carried out test interceptions using single Me 262s against Allied reconnaissance aircraft, and in the course of August the jet fighter achieved its first kills – two Mosquitos, a Spitfire, a Lightning and a B-17.

In September 1944, following a series of incremental improvements, the running life of the turbojet at last reached the 25-hour mark. That was not a lot by normal standards, but it was sufficient to allow the design to be frozen so that mass production could begin. During that month Hitler rescinded his edict that all Me 262s coming off the production lines be issued only to fighter-bomber units. By then there were more than a hundred Me 262 fighter airframes standing idle awaiting engines, and as the latter became available in quantity these aircraft were completed. During September 91 Me 262 fighters and fighter-bombers were delivered to the *Luftwaffe* – more than in the previous two months put together.

Following the change of policy, *Kommando 'Nowotny'* re-equipped with new-built fighters and had a strength of 23 aircraft at the end of September. The unit was declared ready for operations and moved to Achmer and Hesepe in northwest Germany to operate in the interceptor role. Several accounts on the Me 262 have stated that the *Führer's* edict was responsible for keeping the aircraft out of the hands of German fighter pilots until late in the war. The available documentary evidence makes it clear that this was not the case, however. In fact, Hitler's decree delayed the introduction into combat by the first Me 262 fighter *Gruppe*, with aircraft fitted with production engines, by less than three weeks.

In the event, the operational deployment of *Kommando 'Nowotny'* was a complete failure, and the *Führer's* edict had nothing to do with that. Although the Jumo 004 now gave a slightly longer running life than before, its serviceability remained poor. Furthermore, as with any new type, the airframe of the Me 262 had its share of 'bugs' to be ironed out. One of the most serious problems resulted from the use of low-quality tyres made from synthetic and reclaimed rubber: a heavy landing at the jet fighter's touch-down speed of around 120mph often caused a blow-out, which sometimes led to damage to the undercarriage.

The Allies quickly discovered the Achilles' heel of the jet fighter – its vulnerability to attack while flying at low speed immediately after take-off or on the landing approach. Fighters regularly patrolled over the airfields used by jet fighters, causing almost continual harassment. Moreover, away from the airfields, the horizontal speed advantage of the Me 262 over Allied fighter types was often negated when the latter attacked from above in high-speed dives. These points were illustrated on 7 October when *Kommando 'Nowotny'* scrambled five Me 262s – the largest number of jet fighters yet sent into combat – against formations of American bombers heading for targets in central Germany. Passing over Achmer at 15,000ft, Lieutenant Urban Drew, in a Mustang of the 361st Fighter Group, noticed a pair of jet fighters commence their take-off runs. He waited until the enemy planes were airborne, then rolled into a high-speed dive, followed by his wingman. Drew rapidly caught up with the Me 262s and shot down both before they reached fighting speed. Later that day a third jet fighter was lost during a separate action with escort fighters. Thus the first multi-aircraft action by *Kommando 'Nowotny'* cost the unit three Me 262s destroyed and one pilot killed, in return for three American bombers shot down. In the course of its first full month of operations on the Western Front, *Kommando 'Nowotny'* claimed the destruction of four American heavy bombers, twelve fighters and three reconnaissance aircraft. In achieving this, however, the unit lost six Me 262s in combat and a further seven destroyed and nine damaged in accidents or following technical failures. It was not an auspicious start to the jet fighter's combat career.

Then, on 8 November, the *Kommando* suffered the most grievous blow of all. After getting caught up in a low-level dogfight with Mustangs, Walter Nowotny was shot down and killed. *Generalmajor* Galland happened to be at the Achmer that day, on a visit of inspection to determine why the Me 262 unit had failed to achieve more. Galland saw enough to realize that Nowotny had been given an impossible task. The latter had to introduce a completely new type of fighter into operational service, though many of his pilots had received no proper conversion training. Serviceability was poor, and rarely could the unit fly more than half a dozen sorties per day. As a result, the Allied air forces, which had massive numerical superiority in the area, usually dictated the terms on which the jets had to fight. Galland ordered the Me 262 unit to return to Lechfeld for further training and in order that the aircraft could be modified to overcome some of their defects. He realized that it had been a mistake to commit the jet fighters into combat in such small numbers. If the new fighter were to have a decisive effect, a much larger force would need to be assembled. The formation of the first full *Geschwader* of Me 262 fighters, *JG 7*, had begun, but it would be some time before the unit was fully operational.

Meanwhile, what of the Me 262 as a fighter-bomber? By the latter part of 1944 these aircraft equipped two full *Gruppen*, *I* and *II* of *Kampfgeschwader 51*. Single aircraft delivered attacks on Allied airfields and troop positions in France, Holland and Belgium. Again, due to the small number of aircraft involved and the small tonnage of bombs they carried, these attacks achieved little.

By the beginning of 1945, new Me 262s were coming off the assembly lines at an encouraging rate. Production was running at 36 aircraft a week, and so far about 600 had been delivered to the *Luftwaffe*. Yet the Quartermaster General's records for 10 January 1945 show that only about 60 Me 262s (only 10 per cent of those manufactured so far) were serving with operational units, and none with operational day fighter units, 52 served with *Kampfgeschwader 51* operating in the fighter-bomber role, four were operating as night fighters and five were employed in the short-range reconnaissance role – this some four months after Hitler had rescinded his edict that the Me 262 be employed only in the fighter-bomber role. What had gone wrong?

Although a number of Me 262 fighter *Gruppen* were preparing to go into action, this preliminary work was taking much longer than expected. *III Gruppe* of *Jagdgeschwader 7* had its full complement of aircraft and was working up at airfields in the Berlin area; *I Gruppe* was forming at Kaltenkirchen near Hamburg, as was *II Gruppe* at Brandenburg/Briest. Also at this time, *Kampfgeschwader 54*, a bomber unit, was converting to the Me 262 and its pilots were training to operate the aircraft in the fighter role. The unit was redesignated *KG (Jäger) 54*, and this diversion of Me 262s from 'pure' fighter units has been linked to Hitler's earlier insistence that initially the type be used as a fighter-bomber. But by early 1945 the issues were quite different. Pilots assigned to *Luftwaffe* day fighter units did not receive training in instrument flying, as a move to shorten the training time and save resources. Pilots assigned to bomber, reconnaissance and night-fighter units received training in instrument flying as a matter of course, and *KG(J) 54* was to operate in the bad-weather interception role.

As we have seen, early in January 1945 there were about 60 Me 262s operational with fighter-bomber, night-fighter and reconnaissance units. A further 150 of these aircraft were flying with day fighter units, working up for action or providing pilot conversion training. About 30 Me 262s were serving with the various test centres, and about 150 Me 262s had been destroyed by enemy action in the air or on the ground, or in flying accidents. That accounted for about 400 Me 262s. What had happened to the remaining 200 of these aircraft, about one-third of those built? Many were tied up in the German rail system. After their acceptance test-flights, most of the Me 262s were dismantled and transported to the operational units by rail, in order to save precious aviation fuel. With the German rail network now under systematic attack from Allied strategic bombers, many of the crated jet fighters were destroyed in transit or were stranded in sidings from which they never emerged. Moreover, the attacks on the rail system made it difficult to move fuel and spare parts – including the all-important replacement engines – to the operational airfields.

Adding to the problems of the jet fighter units, their airfields were repeatedly bombed and for much of the time they were patrolled by Allied fighters. This, combined with the poor weather over Germany during the winter of 1944–45, frequently brought jet-flying training to a halt. Even without such impediments, it is difficult enough to introduce a new combat aircraft type into large-scale service. Considering the daunting array of difficulties, it is hardly surprising that the formation of a large and effective jet-fighter force suffered continual slippage.

The Me 262s returned to the day battle on 9 February 1945, when *I Gruppe* of *KG(J) 54* put up about ten aircraft to counter a multi-pronged attack by American heavy bombers against targets in central Germany. The German ex-bomber pilots had received only a sketchy training in air-to-air combat, however, and this was neither the time nor the place to learn its finer points. The escorting Mustangs shot down six Me 262s, while the jet fighters were able to inflict damage on only one B-17. Bomber ace *Oberstleutnant* Volprecht von Riedesel, the *Geschwader* commander, was one of the German pilots killed that day.

Two weeks later, on the 25th, *KG(J) 54* had another bad day when its *II Gruppe* lost no fewer than twelve Me 262s, six in air combat, four during a strafing attack on its airfield and two more in flying accidents. *Major* Hansgeorg Bätcher, a highly experienced bomber pilot, was appointed to command the *Geschwader*. In Bätcher's view, the unit had been sent into operations prematurely, and his first act was to withdraw it from action for further training. Despite the difficulties experienced by the ex-bomber pilots, he felt that, in the circumstances, the decision to use pilots with blind-flying training to fly the Me 262 in the fighter role was correct. It was winter, and on several days the bad weather prevented other jet fighter units from operating.

It was mid-February before *III Gruppe* of *Jagdgeschwader 7* was ready to go into action. On 21 February a force of Mustangs of the 479th Fighter Group, on patrol in the Berlin area, encountered about fifteen Me 262s – by far the largest number yet seen. And, as the American formation leader reported, for the first time these aircraft were handled in an aggressive manner:

> Bounce was directed at Red Flight, as Squadron was making a shallow turn to the left from an easterly direction. Bounce came from 3 o'clock position at our level by four Me 262s flying the usual American combat formation, looking like P-51s with drop tanks. Our Red Flight broke into jets but they crossed in front of our flight up and away: A second flight of four Me 262s flying in American combat formation then made a bounce from the rear, 6 o'clock high. Our flight turned into this second Me 262 flight and the Me 262s broke, climbing up and away. At this time the first flight of Me 262s came back on us again from above and to the rear. We broke into this flight and this kept up for three or four breaks, neither ourselves or Jerry being able to get set or close in for a shot. Each time we would break they would climb straight ahead, outdistancing us. Within the Jerry flight the Number 4 man, while turning, would fall behind and slightly above, so that it was necessary to take on this Number 4 man or he would slice in on our tail if our Flight would take on the rest of the Jerry flight.

The report exemplified the sort of inconclusive action that resulted when well-handled jets confronted well-handled Mustangs. Unless it had the advantage of surprise, the Me 262 was no real threat to the latter.

During the course of February, *Leutnant* Rudolf Rademacher of *III./JG 7* showed what a well-handled Me 262 could achieve. After shooting down a Spitfire reconnaissance aircraft near Brunswick on 1 February, he was credited the destruction of six heavy bombers and a Mustang, to bring his score during that month to eight victories.

Only in March 1945 did Me 262s launch large-scale attacks on American bomber formations. On the 3rd there were 29 Me 262 sorties, mainly by *III./JG 7*, in response to the US attacks on

---

NORTH AMERICAN P-51D MUSTANG

Role: Single-seat, long-range escort fighter and fighter-bomber.
Power: One Rolls-Royce/Packard Merlin V-1650-7 12-cylinder,
liquid-cooled, inline engine developing 1,450hp at take-off.
Armament: Four or six Browning .5in machine guns in the wings;
provision for two 1,000lb bombs or ten 5in rockets under the
wings.
Performance: (Clean) Maximum speed 437mph at 25,000ft; initial
rate of climb 3,475ft/min; operational radius of action (with two
110-gallon drop tanks) 900 miles.
Dimensions: Span 37ft; length 32ft 3in; wing area 233 sq ft.
Date of first production P-51D: Summer 1944.

Magdeburg, Brunswick, Hanover, Chemnitz and other targets. The
jet-fighter units claimed the destruction of six bombers and two
fighters, in return for one Me 262 lost. American records list nine
bombers and eight fighters lost on that day, and mention no Me 262
destroyed.

The Me 262 fighter units saw little action during the next two
weeks, and their next great exertion was on 18 March. On that day
37 of the jets took off to engage a large force of American bombers
making for Berlin. Twenty-eight jet-fighter pilots reported making
contact with the enemy and claimed the destruction of twelve
bombers and one fighter (all except two of the bombers were
claimed by *JG 7*); from American records, it appears likely that only
eight heavy bombers fell to the Me 262s. Two jet fighters were lost
during the action. During each of the following seven days there
were pitched battles between Me 262s and American formations,
with a similar ratio of losses between the two sides.

On the 30th the *Luftwaffe* put up 31 jet fighters to engage US
bomber forces attacking Hamburg, Bremen and Wilhelmshaven. The
jet fighters were at their most vulnerable when taking off or landing,
and Mustang pilot Captain Robert Sargent, of the 330th Fighter
Group, exploited this weakness to the full:

I saw two enemy aircraft taking off from Kaltenkirchen
airfield. I called them in and we split-essed down on them.
Unfortunately due to their camouflage we lost them for a
second and when we got down to their level I was able to pick
up just one of them. From here on it was easy. My air speed
was 430mph and I estimated his as being about 230mph. As we
closed I gave him a long burst and noticed strikes immediately,

the left unit began to pour white smoke and large pieces of
the canopy came off. The pilot baled out. We were at 300 feet
at this time and the plane dove into the ground and exploded,
causing a large oil-like fire which went out almost at once. The
pilot's chute did not open fully and the last I saw of him was
on the ground near the plane with the chute streaming out
behind him. Lt Kunz did a splendid job of covering my tail and
after the encounter we pulled up and looked for the second jet.
But when we sighted him he was going balls-out for central
Germany and we couldn't overtake him.

The Me 262 pilot involved, *Leutnant* Erich Schulte of *I./JG 7*, was
killed. In the course of the fighting that day, the jet fighters claimed
the destruction of three enemy bombers and three fighters, for the
loss of three of their own aircraft.

The US heavy bombers were the main recipients of the Me
262 attacks, but they were not the only ones. By this stage of the
war Royal Air Force Bomber Command was mounting frequent
daylight attacks on targets in Germany, and on the last day of March
460 Lancasters and Halifaxes set out to strike at the U-boat assembly
yards at Hamburg. As they neared the target, Me 262s delivered a sharp
attack which knocked down three Halifaxes and four Lancasters in
rapid succession, before the escorts could drive them away.

At the same time, more than a thousand American heavy bombers
were attacking Zeitz, Brandenburg, Brunswick and Halle, and these
were also engaged by jet fighters. *JG 7* flew 38 sorties that day and,
on the available evidence, it appears that the jets shot down fourteen
enemy bombers and two fighters, for a loss of four of their number.
That was the high-water mark of achievement for the Me 262 units,
and it would never be surpassed. Yet, even on that most successful day,
the losses inflicted by the jets amounted to only 1 per cent of the
huge Allied forces involved. Despite the massive German exertion,
the effect was no more than a pin-prick.

Early in April one further Me 262 fighter unit, *Jagdverband 44*,
commanded by *Generalmajor* Adolf Galland in person, became operational at Munich/Riem. With many of the *Luftwaffe* piston-engine
day-fighter units now grounded for want of fuel, Galland was able
to draw into his unit several ace pilots, including Johannes Steinhoff,
Günther Lützow, Heinz Bär and Gerhard Barkhom. The unit flew
its first interception mission on 5 April, when five fighters were
scrambled and claimed the destruction of two enemy bombers. With
Allied ground forces now advancing deep into Germany, however,
the *Luftwaffe* fighter control organization was on its last legs. Even the

uniquely talented pilots of *JV 44* were unable to achieve much: rarely would the unit fly more than half a dozen sorties or shoot down more than a couple of Allied aircraft in a day. Compared with the huge Allied air activity, this was indeed a puny effort, and the appearance of *JV 44* passed unnoticed by its opponents.

On 7 April the Me 262 fighter force mounted its largest defensive effort, flying a total of 59 sorties. Owing to poor control, they failed to deliver a concentrated attack and they claimed only five Allied aircraft destroyed for the loss of two of their own. On 9 April, the last date for which figures are available, there were about 200 Me 262s on the strength of the various operational units. Of these, 163 were serving in the day-fighter role with *JG 7, KG(J) 54* and *JV 44. KG 51* possessed 21 fighter-bombers, there were about nine operating in the night-fighter role and seven were employed for tactical reconnaissance.

The last major air action involving Me 262s took place on 10 April 1945, when 55 of the jet fighters took off to engage more than 2,000 US heavy bombers and escorts attacking targets in the Berlin area. *Leutnant* Walther Hagenah flew with *III./JG 7* that day from Lärz near Berlin, with an inexperienced *Feldwebel* pilot as wingman:

> Once above cloud at about 5,000m [16,250ft], I could see the bomber formation clearly, at about 6,000m [about 20,000ft]. I was flying at about 550km/h [340mph] in a shallow climb, and turned towards them. Then, as an experienced fighter pilot, I had that old 'tingling on the back of neck' that something was wrong. I scanned the sky and, ahead and high above, I caught sight of six Mustangs passing above from almost head-on. At first I thought they had not seen me, and [I] continued towards the bombers. But to be on the safe side I glanced back, and it was a good thing that I did, because the Mustangs were curving round and diving on the pair of us.

Mustangs in the dive then were considerably faster than the jet fighters in the climb, and the piston-engine fighters soon reached firing range. Tracers flashed disconcertingly close in front of Hagenah's aircraft:

> I lowered my nose slightly, to increase speed and resolved to try to outrun the Mustangs. I did not attempt any manoeuvre to throw off their aim; I knew that the moment I turned, my speed would fall and then they would have me. I told the *Feldwebel* with me to keep going, but obviously he was scared

of the tracers because I saw him weaving from side to side, then he broke away to the left. That was just what the Mustang pilots wanted and in no time they were on to him. His aircraft received several hits and I saw it go down and crash.

Hagenah used his speed advantage to outdistance the Mustangs and he saw the enemy fighters turn away to the west. He had sufficient fuel for a retaliatory attack so he turned after them and quickly caught up. Hagenah opened fire and thought he hit a Mustang, then, maintaining his speed, he broke off the action and dived away to return to base.

That day Me 262s claimed the destruction of ten B-17s and seven escorts. These claims find general support in US records. In their turn, however, the jet fighters suffered their worst losses ever. Twenty-seven Me 262s were destroyed, nearly half of those committed. Far more serious than this loss in aircraft which could be replaced – was the loss of nineteen irreplaceable jet-fighter pilots killed and five wounded.

Now Allied troops were thrusting even more deeply into Germany: on 10 April American troops were nearing Nuremberg and the Red Army was within 60 miles of Berlin. As jet-fighter bases were overrun one by one, the operations by these aircraft underwent a rapid decline, and by the end of the month they had virtually ceased.

In retrospect, it is clear that Hitler's edict regarding the use of the Me 262 as a fighter-bomber caused no appreciable delay in the type's operational introduction in the fighter role. Nor can the *Luftwaffe* reasonably be censured for not rushing the aircraft into production soon enough. Indeed, if anything, production was initiated too soon, for Me 262 airframes started to come off the assembly lines several months before the Jumo 004 engine that powered it was ready for mass production. As we have seen, the failure of the Me 262 in action had much more to do with its unreliable new powerplant, coupled with the direct and indirect pressures imposed by the Allied air attacks, than to shortcomings on the part of the German leadership.

By the beginning of April 1945 the *Luftwaffe* had taken delivery of more than 1,200 Me 262s. Yet there were never more than 200 of these aircraft in service with combat units. During the final months of the war, the *Luftwaffe* faced such intractable problems that its fighter units were quite unable to exploit the superior performance of the Me 262. In combat they suffered heavy losses and achieved little. Given the numerical superiority and the quality of the forces arraigned against them, it could hardly have been otherwise.

Chapter 13

Furball over Hai Duong

*The air war over North Vietnam lasted from August 1964 to
January 1973 and was the first conflict in which surface-to-air
and air-to-air guided missiles played a leading role. With the
advent of the missile-armed supersonic fighter, many people
believed that the dogfight – the close-quarter combat involving
several aircraft – was a thing of the past. In the case of the
great majority of engagements, they were right: given any
choice in the matter, the pilot with the higher performance
fighter and the better weapons system would seek to open the
range and proceed to pick off enemy planes with missiles from
beyond the reach of any return fire. But circumstances can force
pilots to engage in a dogfight whether they want to or not.
That happened over North Vietnam, on one day during the
spring of 1972.*

During the US air campaign against North Vietnam, one air-to-
air action stands out as being the most concentrated of all, in
terms of the number of aircraft involved and the small volume of sky
in which it occurred – that between US carrier planes and North
Vietnamese MiG fighters in the afternoon of 10 May 1972, above the
provincial town of Hai Duong.

At that time the US Navy had three aircraft carriers on station
off the coast of North Vietnam, positioned to deliver air strikes on
targets in that country – *Constellation* and *Kitty Hawk*, each displacing
74,000 tons, and the smaller *Coral Sea*, displacing 49,000 tons. During
the morning of 10 May the carrier planes hit targets around the port
of Haiphong. Shortly before noon, the three carriers launched their
second air strikes of the day, against targets around Hai Duong some

30 miles east of Hanoi. *Constellation's* A-6s and A-7s were to 'hit the railway marshalling yard; those from *Kitty Hawk* and *Coral Sea* were to hit road and rail bridges nearby.

Carrier Air Wing 9 from *Constellation* led the attack, its aircraft comprising six Grumman A-6 Intruders, each carrying sixteen 500lb bombs; ten Vought A-7 Corsairs, each carrying twelve 500lb bombs; eight McDonnell F-4 Phantoms flying as escorts, each carrying four Sparrow (radar guided) and four Sidewinder (infra-red homing) air-to-air missiles; four F-4s configured for both flak-suppression and escort, each carrying six Rockeye cluster bombs, four Sidewinder and two Sparrow air-to-air missiles; two A-7s configured for the 'Iron Hand' missile-suppression role, each carrying two Shrike radar-homing missiles and six cluster bombs; one North American RA-5C Vigilante reconnaissance aircraft to take post-strike photographs of the target; and one Douglas EKA-3B Skywarrior to jam enemy long-range radars (this plane also operated in the tanker role and could provide fuel to other aircraft in the force that required it). The Air Wing flew at 15,000ft and headed for the mouth of the Red River, the other two Air Wings following at ten-minute intervals with a separation of about 60 miles between each.

At 12.54 p.m. *Constellation's* Air Wing crossed the coast of North Vietnam and turned on to a north-westerly heading for Hai Duong. As the formation neared the zone defended by surface-to-air missiles (SAMs), the single EKA-3B Skywarrior climbed to 20,000ft and began flying an oblong orbit pattern. At the briefed time the crew switched on their transmitters to jam the enemy radar frequencies.

In each of the attacking planes the crew methodically scanned the sky around them for the tell-tale muzzle or rocket flash or the glint of sun that might be the first sign of an enemy attack. If the enemy fighters, shells or missiles were to be avoided, it was essential to begin an evasive manoeuvre in good time. The men knew that their lives depended on the efficiency of the search. Radar and radar warning receivers were useful aids, but it would have been foolhardy to place one's trust in those alone.

As it neared the target, the formation split into its component parts, which moved to their allotted places. The two 'Iron Hand' A-7s and their escorting Phantoms headed for positions on either side of the target, ready to engage any enemy SAM control radars that came on the air. The Phantom escorts made for patrol lines to the north, east and west of the target, ready to block the paths of possible incoming MiGs. The A-6s and A-7s headed for separate points to the north of the target, from which they were to roll into their attack dives.

From his Phantom cockpit, Lieutenant Randy Cunningham, part of the flak-suppression force, watched the A-6s and A-7s deliver their attacks on the marshalling yard. Shell-bursts pock-marked the sky, but the American pilot did not notice any muzzle flashes to betray the positions of the guns he was supposed to attack. He and his wingman dropped their cluster bombs on their secondary target, a group of warehouses beside the rail yard. After he had released his bombs, Cunningham pulled out of the dive, and his back-seater Willie Driscoll glanced back at the target. Just above the horizon, to his left, he noticed several black dots in the sky. It took a few seconds to work out that they were planes, then that they were MiG-17s. The sudden arrival of the enemy fighters caught Cunningham off guard, at the time he was in a starboard turn concentrating his attention on seeing where his bombs had landed:

> I shouldn't have been doing that: I wasn't thinking about MiGs. I reversed port and saw two MiG-17s slashing in with guns going, inside gun range. I don't know why they didn't hit me: I could see tracers flying by the canopy.

The MiG was closing in fast and Cunningham could see that its pilot was hauling on the stick to bring his gun sight to bear, so the American turned sharply into the attack and forced the enemy fighter to overshoot. He then reversed his turn and the enemy wingman also shot past him. Now Cunningham could deliver his counter-attack. He reversed course, aligned his sight on one of the MiGs and squeezed the trigger. Trailing smoke, the Sidewinder

---

McDONNELL F-4J PHANTOM

Role: Two-seat, carrier-based, multi-role fighter.
Power: Two General Electric J79-GE-10 turbojet engines each developing 17,900lb of thrust with afterburning.
Armament: (Fighter role) Four AIM-7E Sparrow semi-active radar missiles and four AIM-9G Sidewinder infra-red homing missiles; (air-to-ground role during 10 May 1972 action) ten 500lb Rockeye cluster bombs plus a self-protection armament of two AIM-7E and four AIM-9G missiles.
Performance: Maximum speed (clean) 1,430mph (Mach 2.17) at 36,000ft; maximum rate of climb (clean) 49,800ft/min.
Normal operational take-off weight: 53,000lb.
Dimensions: Span 38ft 4in; length 63ft; wing area 530 sq ft.
Date of first production F-4J: December 1966.

streaked after the North Vietnamese fighter in a shallow left turn, then it smashed into the MiG, which exploded into a ball of fire.

Cunningham had no time to savour the victory, for a quick glance behind revealed yet another MiG-17 trying to close to within firing range. He increased speed and turned to drag the enemy plane in front of his wingman, Brian Grant, to give the latter an easy missile shot. But Grant had problems of his own, with another MiG-17 behind him and shooting when its pilot could bring the gun sight to bear. Taking in the situation, Cunningham saw that the only safe way out was to make use of the Phantom's greatly superior acceleration compared with the Soviet-built enemy fighters. Selecting full afterburner, the two American pilots surged away from their pursuers.

Despite all of the efforts of the escorting Phantoms to drive them off, some of the North Vietnamese fighters succeeded in reaching the A-6s and A-7s now speeding for the coast. Circling over the target at 18,000ft in his Phantom, Lieutenant Matt Connelly observed an A-7 being chased by a couple of enemy fighters. He rolled his aircraft into a diving turn, aligned his nose on one of the MiG-17s and loosed off a Sidewinder. The North Vietnamese pilot saw the missile coming and broke away sharply to avoid it, but in forcing the enemy fighter to abandon its attack on the A-7 the missile had done its job.

As he came away from the target, A-7 pilot Lieutenant Al Junker lost contact with his element leader. He searched the sky around for friendly planes to join up with, and saw what looked like an A-6 heading towards him:

> A few seconds later I looked back again to see how he was coming along and saw red dots coming from each side of his nose. A-6s did not have guns, and even if they did they would not be shooting at me – it was a MiG-17!

Junker pulled into a hard turn to avoid the enemy fire and saw the cannon shells streak past his left wing, so close that he felt their shock waves.

Meanwhile Junker's element leader, Commander Fred Baldwin, had seen that his wingman was in trouble and turned to go to his assistance. Baldwin barrel-rolled into a firing position behind the North Vietnamese fighter. From there he could threaten the enemy plane, but, lacking missiles and with his single 20mm cannon unserviceable, that was all he could do. Of course, the enemy pilot had no way of knowing that the A-7 behind him was unarmed, and each time Baldwin moved into a firing position the MiG broke off its attack.

The high-speed slalom over the paddy fields had been in progress for several miles when another A-7 pilot, Lieutenant George
Goryanec, joined the fight:

> I turned and saw them behind me: they were a lot lower than
> I was. I could see Al Junker with an airplane behind him and
> Fred Baldwin, a couple of thousand feet off to one side, calling
> the turns. What looked like a line of 'grapefruits' was going past
> Al's nose. That made me mad – the guy was trying to shoot Al
> down.

Goryanec's aircraft had a serviceable cannon, and he could play
a more active role in assisting his comrade. He rolled the A-7 on
its back and curved after the MiG, aligning himself for an attack
from above. He fired a long burst at the enemy plane and saw what
looked like a couple of hits near the wing root. Goryanec broke
off his attack, looked back to see what the MiG was doing and
observed that the latter had broken off and was heading north,
away from the fight. Thanks to the timely intervention of the
two A-7s, Al Junker's plane had survived the engagement without
taking any damage.

Matt Connelly joined the mêlée after his spoiling attack on the
MiG-17 and aligned the nose of his Phantom on another of the
enemy fighters. In his headphones he heard a buzz to denote that the
Sidewinder had locked on to the heat source, but the MiG was in
a tight turn and he knew that there was little chance of hitting it. If
the MiG pilot had held his turn he would have escaped, but perhaps
he panicked at the sight of the Phantom bounding towards him. The
North Vietnamese pilot made the tactical blunder of rolling out of
the turn at that point, presenting Connelly with the opportunity of
a snap shot. From about 400yds – almost at minimum range – he
launched a Sidewinder and watched it detonate close to the enemy
fighter's tail. The rear of the plane exploded, and moments later its
pilot ejected.

Having shaken off the MiGs that had been chasing them, Randy
Cunningham and Brian Grant converted their excess speed into altitude and took their Phantoms up to 12,000ft in a fast zoom-climb.
Then both pilots turned to assess the dogfight taking place far below.
Close to the ground they saw no fewer than eight MiG-17s flying
in a loose defensive circle, each covering the tail of the one in front.
The two Phantoms were in a perfect position to attack the enemy
fighters from above, and their pilots entered diving turns to position
themselves to deliver a missile attack.

Matters closer to hand brought an end to this plan, however. Suddenly a Phantom flashed past Cunningham's nose, so close that it nearly collided with him. The aircraft belonged to Commander Dwight Timm, who was under co-ordinated attack from three MiGs. A MiG-17 was about 1,000yds behind him and firing, and a MiG-21 was following him a little further behind, awaiting its chance to engage. Timm was turning tightly to port to avoid their fire, but in the process he failed to see the greatest threat of all – a MiG-17 only 100yds away from him, hidden under his wing and edging into a firing position.

As Timm and his pursuers sped past, Cunningham pulled his aircraft into a tight turn to go to his friend's assistance. He placed his gun sight over the MiG that posed the greatest threat to Timm and prepared to launch a Sidewinder, but he knew that the heat-seeking missile had to be used with great caution in a close-quarter dogfight such as this. The missile could not tell friend from foe: it merely homed on to the strongest heat source within its field of view – which would probably be the jet pipes of Timm's aircraft. Cunningham shouted to Timm to reverse his turn and go starboard, and as the Phantom swung clear he squeezed off the Sidewinder. The missile exploded against the tail of the enemy fighter, which wallowed drunkenly, and its pilot ejected. On seeing that, one MiG broke off its chase and Timm accelerated clear of the other.

Having already knocked down one MiG-17, Matt Connelly was curving into position to engage another. And this North Vietnamese pilot reacted in exactly the same way as Connelly's first victim:

> The guy did the same thing: he saw me coming and started turning. I went behind him, he reversed his turn and I pulled back behind him. I waited till I had a real good tone, but as I squeezed the trigger the tone dropped off.

At first Connelly thought the missile was a dud, but then it appeared to sort itself out and it continued relentlessly after the enemy fighter. The weapon exploded beside the MiG and blew away part of the tail, causing the aircraft to enter a fast roll to the left and the pilot to eject.

Circling in their Phantoms at 14,000ft, Commander Harry Blackburn and his wingman were patrolling some distance away from the main dogfight, positioned to intercept any MiG that attempted to enter or leave the fight. Steve Rudloff, Blackburn's back-seater, made a radar search for MiGs but found none within the set's angle of view. He returned his attention to a search of the

---

MIKOYAN-GUREVICH MiG-17 ('FRESCO')

Role: Single-seat day fighter.
Power: One Klimov VK-1 turbojet developing 7,500lb of thrust with afterburning.
Armament: Three NR-23 23mm cannon.
Performance: Maximum speed 710mph at 10,000ft; maximum rate of climb 12,795ft/min.
Normal operational take-off weight: 14,750lb
Dimensions: Span 31ft 7in; length 36ft 4¼in; wing area 243.3 sq ft.
Date of first production MiG-17: October 1952.

---

sides and rear outside the cockpit, and at that instant several black smoke clouds appeared between him and his wingman – the pair were being engaged by 85mm guns. A moment later Rudloff felt the Phantom shudder as one of the 20lb shells exploded close to its tail. Although he was strapped tightly into his seat, the radar operator was thrown hard against the side of the cockpit. He was in the process of collecting his senses when the instrument panel in front of him suddenly erupted into a mass of smoke and flame. A glance in the rear-view mirrors revealed that the rear of the plane was also on fire.

Then something in front of Rudloff exploded with a dazzling white flash. In a split second his natural reflexes had pressed shut his eyelids, but that was too long. When he next opened his eyes he could see nothing: the flash had blinded him. The plane was obviously beyond saving and Blackburn gave the order to eject. Rudloff yanked the firing handle, there was a deafening roar as the seat fired and he felt a tumbling sensation. Then everything went quiet as his parachute brought him slowly to the ground. Rudloff was taken prisoner immediately after landing, and his sight would return in stages over the next couple of hours. Harry Blackburn, his pilot, also ejected but would later die in captivity.

Meanwhile the air action above Hai Duong continued with unabated fury. Lieutenant Steve Shoemaker aligned his Phantom on another of the enemy fighters and Lieutenant Keith Crenshaw, his back-seater, recalled:

> We came on this MiG-17 to the south-west of the 'furball'. He appeared in front of us; he seemed to be trying to get out of the fight. We didn't make any big turn: we dived on him and I heard 'Shoe' call, 'We got a good [missile] tone', then he fired the Sidewinder.

The Phantom's dive was taking it close to the ground, and the pilot was forced to pull up sharply, with the result that the MiG passed out of sight. Once established in the climb, Shoemaker rolled his fighter on its side and the two Americans observed thick, black, greasy smoke rising from the point on the ground where the enemy fighter had crashed.

By now all of the A-6s and A-7s were safely clear of the target and the Air Group Leader, Commander Gus Eggert, ordered the escorting fighters to break off the action and head back for the carrier. On his way to the coast, Randy Cunningham noticed a plane some distance in front, end-on and apparently stationary. The silhouette increased in size, then the high-set tailplane betrayed it as yet another MiG-17:

> I tried to meet this guy head-on, and all of a sudden he opened fire with tracer. I pulled straight up into the vertical, going up through 15,000 feet, pulled 6Gs going over the top. I looked back, I expected to see him moving straight through and running. But we were canopy to canopy, maybe 400 or 500 feet apart!

Cunningham rolled on his back at the top of the climb and saw his opponent loose off a burst of cannon fire in his direction. Then, as the Phantom dived away, the MiG slid into position behind it – obviously this enemy pilot was no novice at air fighting. Cunningham continued:

> I pitched my nose up, pulled over the top, and rolled in behind his 6 o'clock. As soon as I dropped my nose he pulled straight up into the vertical again. I overshot, he rolled up over the top, pulled through and rolled in behind me.

In turn, each pilot pulled up and rolled into position behind his opponent, to seize a marginal advantage over his opponent. So long as the process continued, neither pilot could get into a firing position, but Cunningham knew he could not let it continue for long. Throughout the low-altitude manoeuvring both planes were losing speed, and in a low-speed fight the MiG 17 could outmanoeuvre the Phantom. During his 'Top Gun' course, Cunningham had practised just the manoeuvre to disentangle him from such a situation:

> The MiG was sitting at my 7 o'clock. When he got his nose just a little too high, I pulled sharply down into him and met

him head on. Then I lit the burners and accelerated away from him. By the time he got his nose on me I was about a mile and a half ahead of him, out of [cannon] firing range and opening.

Cunningham then pulled into another vertical climb to move into a firing position. To his surprise, the MiG again followed him. He had never encountered an enemy pilot who was so aggressive or who had such a grasp of air-fighting tactics. The American pilot broke out of the clinch as before and pulled into yet another zoom-climb, and yet again the MiG followed. This time Cunningham decided to try something different. As the two fighters clawed for altitude, flying almost canopy to canopy, he pulled the throttles to idle and opened the speed brakes. The Phantom decelerated rapidly and the MiG sped out in front. Then Cunningham closed the speed brakes and selected full afterburner:

> I think that caught him by surprise because he shot way out in front of me. But a Phantom on full afterburner at 150 knots with the nose straight up in the air is not really flying, it is standing on 36,000 pounds of thrust. We were hanging behind him but we were not really in a position of advantage. At those speeds a MiG-17 had about 2½ to 3 more Gs available than we had.

As the MiG reached the top of its climb, Cunningham applied full rudder and pulled underneath his opponent. The MiG rolled on to its back, then headed for the ground.

Perhaps the North Vietnamese pilot was running short of fuel and was trying to break out of the fight. Whatever the reason, he made the fundamental error of presenting his tail to Cunningham. The American pilot curved into a firing position, placed the gun sight pipper over the MiG and squeezed the trigger. The Sidewinder's smoke trail reached out to the enemy fighter and detonated a few yards away from it, but caused no apparent damage. The MiG continued its fast-diving turn, making no attempt to pull out, however, and a few moments later it smashed into the ground and exploded.

It was six minutes since Cunningham and Driscoll had first seen the MiGs sweeping in towards Hai Duong, and during the furious action six MiG-17s had been destroyed and one probably damaged; one Phantom had been shot down by ground fire and another was seriously damaged. In time and space the action was the most concentrated ever fought over North Vietnam, and it was not over yet.

Heading for the coast in a climb, Cunningham and his back-seater were elated at having shot down three enemy planes during the short action. During previous weeks they had shot down two MiGs, so their score now stood at five – they had gained the coveted status of fighter aces. Then, suddenly and without warning as the Phantom passed through 16,000ft, a surface-to-air missile exploded within 200yds of the aircraft. The blast hurled the fighter into a steep bank and splinters from the warhead tore into the plane. Cunningham levelled out, looked for signs of obvious damage but saw none. He checked his instruments and, as everything seemed to be in order, continued the climb. The aircraft handled normally and it looked as if it had escaped with a minor shaking.

It had not. Just over a minute later, as the Phantom climbed through 27,000ft, it gave a lurch and the port wing dropped. Again the pilot checked his instruments and this time he saw that the pressure gauge for the main hydraulic system read zero and that for the secondary system was falling. It was clear that the hydraulic system had been ruptured and the precious fluid was seeping away.

The Phantom depended on hydraulic pressure to drive its flying controls, and as the oil pressure dropped away the control systems failed one by one. The first sign of this was when the leading edge of the tailplane edged into the fully down position, forcing the plane's nose up. The text-book answer for pilots in that situation was simple: eject immediately. But the plane was still over North Vietnam: if the men bailed out now they were almost certain to be taken prisoner. Their only hope of avoiding that fate lay in staying with their plane and keeping it in the air just a little longer. If they could reach the coast and parachute into the sea, the chances of rescue would be immeasurably greater.

Cunningham had heard how another pilot in a similar situation had brought his Phantom out of North Vietnam. Following his example, Cunningham now pressed hard on the right rudder pedal to use some of the remaining hydraulic pressure to push the fighter into a yaw to the right. The plane's nose fell and it rolled to the right. As the nose passed through the horizontal, Cunningham pulled back the throttles and extended the speed brakes to prevent the plane from entering a dive. Then the pilot pushed on left rudder, selected full power and retracted the speed brakes. The Phantom continued to roll through 360 degrees until it was the right way up, then the nose pitched up again and Cunningham repeated the process. The Phantom flew a series of extremely clumsy barrel rolls, each one of which carried the stricken aircraft a little closer to the coast and relative safety.

Meanwhile, terrible things were happening at the rear of the fighter. A fire had broken out and the flames rapidly took hold. Then came a small explosion, which deprived Cunningham of the last vestiges of control over the aircraft. The nose pitched up for the last time, then it dropped and the fighter fell into an inverted spin. The doughty pilot was reluctant to leave the crippled fighter, but he was forced to admit defeat. He told Driscoll to eject, then he followed.

In its death throes, the Phantom had performed the final task demanded of it: as the pair dangled from their parachutes they saw plenty of beautiful water below them. Shortly after they splashed into the sea, both men were picked up by rescue helicopters.

Afterwards it was assessed that the twelve Phantoms of *Constellation's* Air Wing had engaged about twenty North Vietnamese fighters – fourteen MiG-17s, two MiG-19s and four MiG-21s. Six MiG-17s had been shot down. During the engagement, ten Sidewinder and three Sparrow air-to-air missiles had been fired, giving an average of just over two missiles fired per aircraft shot down. Air aces are not subject to the law of averages, however, and in his exemplary performance Randy Cunningham had destroyed three enemy fighters for an expenditure of just three Sidewinders. One MiG-17 was assessed as probably damaged by cannon fire from an A-7. During the action two Phantoms had been lost, one to a SAM and one to ground fire, and a Phantom was seriously damaged by ground fire.

Had the Phantoms not had other aircraft to protect, their correct tactic would have been to accelerate away from the MiGs, climb above their adversaries and then deliver a series of long-range attacks with missiles to pick off the enemy planes. But the Phantoms' primary duty was to protect the A-6s and A-7s, and that requirement forced them into the dogfight. On the other hand, Randy Cunningham's close-quarter, manoeuvring fight with the MiG-17 was an aberration. He did not have to enter that fight, and by engaging the more manoeuvrable enemy fighter on its own terms he forfeited the Phantom's advantages of superior speed and superior long-range weaponry. Thanks to the Phantom's better acceleration, however, he knew that he could always break out of the fight whenever he chose. His opponent fought unexpectedly well, but the lower-performance MiG-17 did not allow the option of a safe exit. This proved to be its undoing, and when the North Vietnamese pilot turned away he presented Cunningham with an easy missile shot. The American pilot made the most of the unexpected opportunity. As William Sholto Douglas had stressed more than half a century earlier, if one entered a combat it was valuable to have the means of breaking out of it cleanly if things got too hot.

Chapter 14

Low Level Drama in front of San Carlos

At the start of a conflict, aerial warfare is a 'come-as-you-are' business, in which resourceful men have often to go into action with aircraft that have been designed for a quite different purpose. If the conflict is of brief duration, there will be insufficient time to introduce equipment tailored to their needs. A classic example of this phenomenon occurred in the spring of 1982, when Great Britain and Argentina came into conflict over the possession of the Falkland Islands.

When the British Government decided to send a naval task force to the South Atlantic to retake the Falkland Islands, the fighter protection for the planned amphibious landing operation rested upon what could be achieved by a couple of dozen British Aerospace Sea Harrier aircraft. This short-range, subsonic, VSTOL (vertical and short take-off and landing) machine was a low-cost adaptation of the RAF ground-attack Harrier. The Royal Navy had ordered the aircraft as a general-purpose, carrier-based fighter to support naval operations far out to sea where, it was anticipated, it would be beyond the reach of enemy high-performance, land-based fighters. Although the Sea Harrier was equipped for air-to-air combat, in this role its primary targets were to be the large and relatively slow maritime reconnaissance aircraft used to shadow naval forces and guide in attacking aircraft.

In the context of the Falklands conflict, the Sea Harriers had a much lower maximum speed than the Argentine-operated Mirages and Daggers and the British fighters were outnumbered three to one by these and the enemy Skyhawks and Super Etendards. Set against these drawbacks, however, the Sea Harrier pilots enjoyed three important advantages over their opponents. The first concerned the main air-to-air weapon carried by their aircraft, the AIM-9L Sidewinder. This, the latest variant of the famous infra-red missile, was more reliable, was longer-ranging, had a wider engagement envelope and was generally much more effective than the French and Israeli air-to-air missiles carried by Argentine aircraft. The second advantage concerned the Sea Harrier pilots' level of training. The Fleet Air Arm had the full use of NATO training facilities and its air-fighting doctrines were based on the lessons learned during every previous conflict up to and including that in Vietnam. Prior to the Falklands conflict, the Argentine Air Force and Navy had never engaged in air-to-air combat, and their pilots had no effective tactical doctrine for engaging enemy fighters. The third advantage enjoyed by the British pilots resulted from the unique VSTOL capability of their aircraft. The much-published ability to 'viff' (vector thrust in forward flight) enabled them to tighten turns to a degree impossible for conventional fighter types. Moreover, although it was subsonic in level flight, once it had burned some of its fuel the Sea Harrier had a thrust-to-weight ratio close to unity and its acceleration and climbing performance were vastly better than those of its opponents. The value of these attributes lay in their morale effect on the Argentine pilots: the latter knew of the Sea Harrier's unusual manoeuvring capabilities and were reluctant to enter a close-quarter fight where they could expect to be at a disadvantage. But nor could they engage the Sea Harriers at long range with any prospect of success, because of the latter's superior missile armament.

The air war over the Falklands opened on 1 May 1982. Taking a show of force off the islands by Royal Navy warships as the prelude to the expected landing operation, the Argentine Air Force flew 56 fighter, fighter-bomber and bomber sorties into the area. In the course of the aerial skirmishes that followed, the Sea Harriers shot down a Canberra, a Dagger and a Mirage without loss to themselves. Another Mirage suffered damage and, as it was about to make an emergency landing on Port Stanley airfield, it was shot down by Argentine anti-aircraft gunners.

Following this engagement, the Argentine High Command maintained a limited pressure against the British Task Force, intending to conserve its strength until the real amphibious landings took place. Then there would be plenty of high-value targets off the coast and it would remain to be seen whether the Sea Harriers and their covering warships could prevent attacking aircraft from inflicting heavy casualties.

The British landings on the Falklands began during the early morning darkness of 21 May. Then, following a small reinforcement to make up for losses, the Task Force had 25 Sea Harriers, split between No 800 Squadron in HMS *Hermes* and No 801 Squadron in *Invincible*. The Argentine Air Force and Naval Air units arrayed against them possessed about 75 jet fighters and fighter-bombers.

San Carlos Water, the site chosen for the landings, lies at the north-western tip of East Falkland. The inlet runs north to south, is just over a mile wide and four miles long and is deep enough to accommodate large ships. For ships seeking to avoid air attack, the inlet has the attributes of a slit trench: it is surrounded by hills on all sides except the south-east and the entrance at the north-west. Because of this topography, aircraft engaged in low-altitude attacks would have to make their bombing runs along the north-south axis of the waterway, in one direction or the other.

Although small by Second World War standards, the landing at San Carlos was still a sizeable undertaking. The troops and their equipment were carried to the inlet aboard twelve transports, escorted by a guided missile destroyer and six frigates. Once the transports reached their assigned positions in the inlet, they dropped anchor and began off-loading, with landing craft and helicopters running a shuttle service to the shore. The escorting warships, with the exception of a frigate positioned across the entrance to San Carlos Water, were disposed outside the waterway in readiness to ward off enemy counter-attacks that could not be long in coming.

Soon after dawn the British carriers began sending off pairs of fighters in relays, to protect the landing area. The enemy fighter-bombers were certain to attack at low altitude, below the cover of the British ships' radars and their long-range missiles. Lacking the assistance of airborne early-warning radar, the Sea Harriers' tactics can best be described as 'pre-Battle of Britain'. They mounted standing patrols at two points, one near Pebble Island and the other half way down Falkland Sound, respectively to the north-west and the south-west of the landing area and about 30 miles from it. The Sea Harrier's simple pulsed radar was useless against aircraft flying at low altitude over land, so the pilots had to search visually for the incoming enemy planes.

At thirty-minute intervals a fresh pair of Sea Harriers arrived at one of the patrol areas, and remained in position for 10–15 minutes. It would, of course, have been better if they could have stayed longer, but the Royal Navy carriers were themselves under threat from Super Etendard aircraft carrying Exocet missiles and this forced them to remain at least 200 miles to the east of the Islands. As a means of protecting the landings, the air defence plan was far from watertight. Both in time and in space there were gaps through which low-flying enemy fighter-bombers could penetrate to the landing area. Then it would be up to the ships' own missile and gun defences to deter enemy pilots from making accurate attacks or, if that deterrence failed, shoot them down.

The first Argentine aircraft to approach San Carlos never reached the inlet. Captain Jorge Benitez, flying a twin-engine Pucará light attack aircraft of *Grupo 3* on a routine reconnaissance mission from Goose Green airfield, had the misfortune to pass low over a British Army special forces patrol south of the waterway. One of the men fired a shoulder-launched Stinger infra-red missile at the plane, which homed on an engine exhaust and detonated. The Argentine pilot was forced to eject and the aircraft crashed.

Early that morning the Argentine Army headquarters at Port Stanley received a report that British warships had entered the northern end of Falkland Sound and were bombarding the coastline. This was thought to be yet another diversionary attack. Not until 10 a.m. did another Pucará on reconnaissance get through to observe what was happening at San Carlos. Its pilot reported that there were twelve enemy ships in the inlet, some of which were unloading troops and equipment.

The first air attack on the ships followed a few minutes later, delivered by a Macchi 339 light attack aircraft of the 1st Naval Attack *Escuadrilla*. Lieutenant Owen Crippa, flying on an armed

---

BRITISH AEROSPACE SEA HARRIER
FRS Mk I

Role: Single-seat, carrier-based, general-purpose fighter.
Power: One Rolls-Royce Pegasus 104 vectored-thrust, turbofan engine developing 21,500lb of thrust.
Armament: Two ADEN 30mm cannon; (air-to-air role) two AIM-9L Sidewinder infra-red homing missiles; (air-to-ground role) two 1,000lb bombs or two 640lb BL755 cluster bomb units.
Performance: Maximum speed (clean) 736mph (Mach 0.91) at low altitude; climb to 40,000ft, 2min 23sec.
Normal operational take-off weight: 26,200lb.
Dimensions: Span 25ft 3in; length 47ft 7in; wing area 201.1 sq ft.
Date of first production Sea Harrier: August 1978.

reconnaissance mission from Port Stanley, swept low over the hills surrounding San Carlos Water and suddenly found himself over the beach-head. Braving the return fire, Crippa attacked the frigate *Argonaut* with four 5in rockets and 30mm cannon fire, causing minor damage to the ship and wounding three of the crew.

About half an hour later, at 10.35 a.m., the first fighter-bombers arrived from the mainland. At the head of six Daggers of *Grupo 6*, Major Carlos Martinez was to carry out an armed reconnaissance of the reported landing area. The Daggers swept in from the north, avoiding the Sea Harriers patrolling over Pebble Island. The Argentine pilots caught sight of the three warships in position outside the waterway, and the force split up to attack them. Martinez ran in to bomb HMS *Broadsword*, Captain Rodhe and Lieutenant Bean went for *Argonaut* and Captain Moreno led the second section of three aircraft against HMS *Antrim*. The Daggers attacked with 1,000lb bombs and 30mm cannon and the warships replied with guns of all calibres and air-defence missiles. Bean's aircraft was hit by a Seacat missile, believed to have been fired from the frigate *Plymouth*, and crashed into the sea. The remaining Daggers ran out to the south, hotly pursued by a couple of Sea Harriers. But the Argentine planes, freed of their bombs, rapidly picked up speed and soon outdistanced the slower jump jets.

The only ship to suffer serious damage was the destroyer *Antrim*, struck on the stern by a 1,000lb bomb. The weapon went clean through the missile loading doors, narrowly missing a fully armed Seaslug missile, before coming to rest in a lavatory area. Fortunately for the ship's crew, the weapon failed to explode. The warship also took about forty hits from cannon shells, which left two of the crew seriously wounded. The frigate *Broadsword* was also strafed, and suffered four casualties. Following the attack, *Antrim* moved into San Carlos Water, where a bomb-disposal team defused the bomb and removed it.

Shortly before noon, Major Juan Tomba of *Grupo 3* led a pair of Pucarás from Goose Green to attack the beach-head. A patrol of three Sea Harriers from No 801 Squadron was on the point of returning to *Invincible* when the air controller informed the leader, Lieutenant-Commander 'Sharkey' Ward, of the enemy aircraft flying to the south of San Carlos Water. As the trio passed over the area at 15,000ft, Lieutenant Steve Thomas caught sight of one of the Pucarás. He and Lieutenant-Commander Al Craig dived on the machine, Tomba's, to attack with cannon. The jet fighters' overtaking speed was too great, however, and both pilots overshot the target without scoring hits. While they were thus engaged, the second Pucará escaped. Then Ward ran in to attack Tomba's aircraft with cannon. He scored hits on one of his opponent's wings, before he also overshot the slow Pucará. Having gauged the speed of the enemy plane, Ward lowered his flaps and went in for his second attack much more slowly:

> I opened fire and hit his right engine, which caught fire, and I saw bits falling off the aircraft. On my third pass I got in behind nicely and opened fire and saw his left engine start to burn, part of his canopy fly away, and pieces fall off the fuselage. I pulled away to the left thinking, this is incredible, he hasn't gone down yet! Then I saw the pilot eject. The aircraft continued on, hit the peat, and slid to a halt.

The next attacking force to set out from the mainland ran into difficulties from the outset. The four Skyhawks of *Grupo 5*, led by Captain Pablo Carballo, made their planned rendezvous with the KC-130 Hercules tanker aircraft off the coast of Argentina, but one could not take on fuel and had to turn back. Another went unserviceable and it, too, had to abandon the mission. The remaining two Skyhawks entered Falkland Sound, where they sighted a large merchant ship. It was the *Rio Carcarana*, an Argentine freighter used to supply the garrison on West Falkland, which was still drifting abandoned after being attacked by Sea Harriers five days earlier. Carballo lined up to attack the ship but at the last moment, unsure of its identity, he broke away. His wingman continued with the attack, released his bombs at the freighter and turned for home.

Alone, Carballo continued along the eastern side of Falkland Sound and suddenly came upon one of the British frigates. It was HMS *Ardent*, and her captain, Commander Alan West, later recalled:

> Suddenly somebody on the bridge shouted 'Aircraft closing!' and pointed. We looked in that direction and coming straight towards us from the south-west, over land, was a single Skyhawk about 4,000 yards away and closing very fast. He was right on the bow. I put on full wheel and called for full speed. As he flashed over us we were just beginning to turn, the 4.5-inch [gun] had no time to get on to him and the only thing that could fire was the 20mm. He dropped two bombs, one of which fell short and the other passed over us. He continued past us, banked round and flew down the Sound.

Lieutenant-Commanders Neil Thomas and Mike Blissett of No 800 Squadron had just arrived over Falkland Sound to start their patrol when the air controller ordered them to go after the aircraft that had attacked *Ardent*. The Sea Harriers descended below the puffs of cloud at 1,500ft and headed out over West Falkland. They failed to find Carballo's Skyhawk, but suddenly that became unimportant. As he passed about three miles east of Chartres Settlement, Blissett caught sight of four more Skyhawks in front of him and about 3½ miles away. The enemy planes, belonging to *Grupo 4*, had just crossed the coast on their way in. When their pilots sighted the Sea Harriers, they broke formation and jettisoned their bombs and underwing tanks, pulling hard to the right to avoid the attack. But by then the Sea Harriers were closing rapidly on the enemy planes, as Blissett later described:

> I was in the lead with Neil to my left and about 400 yards astern, with all of us in a tight turn. The Skyhawks were in a long echelon, spread out over about a mile. I locked a Sidewinder on one of the guys in the middle and fired. My first impression was that the missile was going to strike the ground as it fell away – I was only about 200 feet above the ground. But suddenly it started to climb and rocketed towards the target. At that moment my attention was distracted somewhat as a Sidewinder came steaming past my left shoulder – Neil had fired past me, which I found very disconcerting at the time! I watched his 'Winder chase after another of the Skyhawks, which started to climb for a patch of cloud above, then the aircraft disappeared into the cloud with the missile gaining fast.

Blissett regaining his composure in time to see his missile strike the enemy plane, which blew up in a huge fireball. Seconds later another Skyhawk – the one he had last seen vanish into cloud chased by his wingman's Sidewinder – came tumbling from the sky above, out of control and with the fuselage ablaze. The surviving Skyhawks ran out to the west – fast. Lacking the fuel to continue after them, the Sea Harriers broke off the chase.

It was 2.30 p.m., the start of the most dangerous period for the British naval forces in and around San Carlos Water. Until now the Daggers and Skyhawks that reached the area had been engaged in armed reconnaissance missions, searching for the important targets and with time for only a snap attack if they found one. Three and a half hours had elapsed since the first mainland-based aircraft had flown over the area, and the pilots in the next attacking waves would know exactly where their targets lay and how they planned to engage them.

ISRAEL AIRCRAFT INDUSTRIES DAGGER

Role: Single-seat fighter-bomber.
Power: One Atar 9C turbojet engine developing 9,429lb of thrust
  with afterburner.
Armament: Two DEFA 30mm cannon; (air-to-air role) two IAI
  Shafrir infra-red homing missiles; (air-to-surface role over the
  Falklands) two 1,000lb bombs.
Performance: Maximum speed (clean, at low altitude) 830mph,
  (at 40,000ft) 1,460mph (Mach 2.2).
Normal operational take-off weight: 30,200lb.
Dimensions: Span 26ft 11in; length 51ft 0½in; wing area 376.7 sq ft.
Date of first production Dagger: Early 1972.
Note: This aircraft is an unlicensed, Israeli-built copy of the French
  Dassault Mirage V fighter-bomber.

To meet the greater threat, the Sea Harrier patrols had been
increased from two pairs of aircraft an hour to three pairs an hour.
Lieutenant-Commander 'Fred' Frederiksen and Lieutenant Andy
George of No 800 Squadron were on patrol when the next raiding
forces – four Daggers of *Grupo 6*, led by Captain Horacio Gonzalez
– swept in. One of the warships had observed the Argentine planes
on radar before they descended to low altitude, however, and the
controller ordered the Sea Harriers to move over West Falkland to
intercept them. Flying at 2,500ft, Frederiksen caught sight of the
raiders flying low, about three miles away to his right. He ordered his
wingman into trail to watch out for possible escorts, and accelerated
into position behind the left-hand pair of enemy planes. Frederiksen
launched a Sidewinder and saw it home in and explode close to the
tail of one of the Daggers. The fighter-bomber went into an uncon-
trolled roll and its pilot, Lieutenant Hector Luna, ejected just before
it smashed into the ground. Luna's parachute did not open fully
before he landed, and he suffered a dislocated arm and a sprained
knee. Frederiksen loosed off with cannon at another of the Daggers,
but he saw no hits before the enemy fighter-bombers vanished into
the layer of cloud covering the ridge in front of them.

As this was happening, a new force of Skyhawks swung into
Falkland Sound from the north. The six aircraft concentrated their
attack on HMS *Argonaut* and hit her with two 1,000-pounders. One
bomb smashed into her hull and demolished several steam pipes,
causing a boiler to explode, then it went on to wreck part of the ship's
steering gear. The other bomb impacted further forward and ended
up in the forward Seacat magazine, where it caused two missiles to

explode, killing two of the ship's crew. Although both bombs caused secondary explosions, the weapons had been released from too low an altitude for the fuses to function and neither weapon detonated.

Almost immediately afterwards the depleted Dagger formation from *Grupo 6* sped over the coast of West Falkland and lined up to attack HMS *Ardent*. The aircraft were closing in rapidly from astern and Alan West called for full port rudder in a vain attempt to bring the ship's 4.5in gun to bear. For some reason the Seacat missile failed to leave its launcher at the critical time and the ship's only defences comprised a 20mm cannon and a few light machine guns. Running in to bomb the ship at the rear of the attacking force, Captain Robles watched the action begin:

> In front of Captain Gonzalez' plane we could see the tracers flashing towards us. His flight path took him between the masts of the frigate. His bomb hit the sea about 10 metres short of it and lifted a great mass of water which practically enveloped the ship; I believe the bomb skipped and embedded itself in the hull. Then Lieutenant Bernhardt released his bombs, one of which struck the upper part of the ship. Then I arrived at the release point and let go of my bombs.

With no effective defence to distract them, the Dagger pilots were able to press home an accurate attack. Alan West described what it felt like to be on the receiving end of their efforts:

> The first aircraft released two bombs, one of which hit us near the stern and went off. There was an enormous bang; it felt as if someone had got hold of the stern and was banging the ship up and down on the water. With the explosion a column of flash and smoke went up about 100 feet. I looked aft and saw the Seacat launcher about 20 feet in the air where it had been blown, and pieces of metal flying in all directions.

The bomb struck the frigate close to the helicopter hangar, blew off the roof and folded it over the starboard side, wrecking the ship's Lynx helicopter in the process. Several of the ship's crew were killed or injured. Another bomb embedded itself in the stern but failed to detonate.

If a warship has suffered damage in action there are three vital questions that her captain needs to answer: Can she stay afloat? Can she move under control? Can she continue to fight? As West received the damage reports from his First Lieutenant, it was clear that, although *Ardent* could float and move, she could not fight: the Seacat missile launcher had been blown overboard, and damage to the ammunition supply conveyor had put the 4.5in gun out of action too. As the damage-control teams worked to bring the fires under control, West headed for San Carlos Water, where his ship could receive protection from others in the force.

It was 2.45 p.m. and more Argentine planes were streaking over the waterway at low altitude to attack the British ships. HMS *Brilliant* suffered another strafing attack and had some of her crew were injured by flying splinters. Skyhawks entered San Carlos Water to attack the unloading transports, but their pilots found that the high ground surrounding the anchorage complicated the task. Ensign Marcelo Moroni of *Grupo* 5 explained the problem:

> The topography of the island made it difficult to see into the bay because we were too low – we were so close to the hills we could not see over them. As we topped the last hill we saw eight or nine ships in the bay. The moment they saw us, they opened up at us with everything they had. Two of the Skyhawks went for one frigate, another two headed for another ship, and I was last of the five. Suddenly I felt a blow from my right and I thought my aircraft had been hit and damaged by enemy fire. Because of this I took no evasive action but headed straight towards my target; as soon as I dropped my bombs I continued on straight out of the bay.

Apart from one that suffered minor damage from small-arms fire, all the Skyhawks returned safely to Rio Gallegos. Moroni's aircraft was not hit; almost certainly he had run into the slipstream from one of the aircraft in front. No transports were hit.

While this was happening, a sharp engagement was taking place over West Falkland. On their second patrol of the day, 'Sharkey' Ward and Steve Thomas were at the southern end of their orbit when the latter noticed a pair of low-flying Daggers heading east:

> I barrelled in behind them, locked up a missile on the rear guy and fired. The Sidewinder hit the aircraft and took it apart. I didn't see it go in, I was busy trying to get the other one. He went into a climbing turn to starboard to try to get away. I locked up a Sidewinder and fired it. The missile followed him round the corner and went close over his port wing root. There was a bright orange flash close to the aircraft but it didn't blow up or anything.

Ward watched his wingman engage the two Daggers and saw the first one crash, then yet another of the enemy fighter-bombers came speeding past the nose of his aircraft. Estimating that the enemy plane was doing about 500kts (575mph) at 50ft, Ward racked his Sea Harrier into a tight turn to line up for snap attack and launched a Sidewinder. The missile rammed into the Dagger, blowing away part of the tail, and the aircraft dived into the ground, shedding pieces. Then, short of fuel and with only one missile between them, the two Sea Harriers headed back for their carrier.

On the available evidence, Thomas could claim the second machine he attacked only as 'possibly destroyed'. After the war, however, Argentine sources revealed that all three of the Daggers engaged with Sidewinders had been shot down. The three pilots reached the ground with relatively minor injuries – a remarkable testimony to the effectiveness of their ejection seats since all of them had been at ultra-low level when their aircraft were hit.

Also at this time, Lieutenant-Commander Alberto Philippi entered the south end of Falkland Sound, leading three Skyhawks of the 3rd Naval Fighter and Attack *Escuadrilla*. The new attack force sped up the waterway at low altitude, and the first ship they encountered was the already battered *Ardent*. The aircraft moved into line astern and wheeled into their bombing runs. Half a mile from his target, Philippi pulled up to 300ft, aligned his bomb sight on the warship and released his four 500lb, American-made 'Snakeye' bombs. These weapons were specially designed for release from low altitude, and as each left the aircraft four drag-plates opened at the tail to slow the bomb during its fall. The slower rate of fall would allow the aircraft to get clear before the weapons detonated, and would also give the bombs time to become 'live' before they hit the target.

From the bridge of his ship, Alan West watched the first salvo of bombs approach and disappear from view. Then there was a series of huge explosions. The captain was lifted off his feet and struck the deck head, then he fell in a heap on the deck. He got up in time to see the second of the Skyhawks, that piloted by Lieutenant Jose Arca, sweep-low over the ship after releasing its bombs. *Ardent's* machine-gunners maintained a steady fire at the plane, and West saw a row of holes appear across one of the wings. Immediately afterwards yet another bomb exploded against the ship's stern. The third Skyhawk to attack, piloted by Ensign Marcelo Marquez, failed to score any hits. After completing his attack, Philippi remained at low altitude and headed south-west down Falkland Sound, with the other Skyhawks following at two-mile intervals.

DOUGLAS A-4P SKYHAWK

Role: Single-seat, carrier-based attack aircraft.
Power: One Wright J65 W-18 engine developing 8,500lb of thrust.
Armament: Two Mk 12 20mm cannon; up to 2,000lb of bombs.
Performance: Maximum speed (with warload, at low altitude)
    575mph.
Normal operational take-off weight: 22,500lb
Dimensions: Span 27ft 6in; length 40ft 4in; wing area 260 sq ft.
Date of first production A-4B Skyhawk: Late 1956 (A-4P was
    the designation given to A-4Bs exported to Argentina).

Passing over Goose Green at 10,000ft and heading for their patrol line, Lieutenant Clive Morell and Flight Lieutenant John Leeming of No 800 Squadron heard a radio broadcast that *Ardent* was under attack. Looking down, Morell saw the bombs explode on the frigate:

> Having seen the bombs explode, I deduced that the attackers would probably exit going south-west down the Sound. I looked to where I thought they would be and they appeared, lo and behold, below a hole in the clouds.

The Sea Harriers dived at full throttle after the attackers, and Marquez, in the rear Skyhawk, was the first to sense danger. Later Philippi commented:

> A couple of minutes after attacking I thought we had escaped, when a shout from Marquez froze my heart: 'Harrier! Harrier!' I immediately ordered the tanks and bomb racks to be jettisoned in the hope we would be able to reach the safety of cloud ahead of us.

The Sea Harrier that Marquez had seen was Morell's, which was now gaining rapidly on Philippi's Skyhawk. The Royal Navy pilot launched a Sidewinder at the enemy fighter-bomber, and watched it home and explode close to its target. Philippi's first indication that he was being attacked was a powerful explosion at the rear of his aircraft, after which the nose pitched up violently. Unable to control the machine, Philippi ejected and came down in shallow water just off the coast. Clive Morell continued after the remaining Skyhawk in front of him – Arca's. His remaining Sidewinder refused to leave its launcher, so he satisfied himself with emptying his guns in the direction of the fighter-bomber. He saw no hits.

Speeding through the narrows at low altitude, Marquez appeared to be concentrating his attention on the fate of the two Skyhawks in front him. He did not notice John Leeming slide into position for a gun attack from behind on his aircraft. The RAF pilot recalled:

> He was at about zero feet, I was at zero plus 50. Still there was no sign that he had seen me; he was heading out as fast as he could. I fired a couple of tentative bursts, then my third splattered the sea around him. He must have realized what was happening then, because about a second later he rolled hard to starboard. But by then it was too late: I was within about 200 yards. Before he could start to pull round I put my sight on his cockpit, pressed the firing button and, as the first rounds struck, the aircraft exploded. I think the engine must have broken up because the aircraft just disintegrated.

Leeming pulled up sharply to avoid the rapidly growing cloud of debris in front of him, and, as he did so, Morell glanced back and saw the expanding fireball. His first horrified thought was that his wingman might have gone down, but Leeming reassured him with a brief radio call.

All of the events described, from the moment Steve Thomas first sighted the incoming Daggers until John Leeming swerved to avoid the debris from the Skyhawk, had taken place during the ten-minute period between 2.52 and 3.02 p.m.

By now *Ardent* was in dire distress, with a major fire blazing in her aft section. The frigate was taking on water rapidly and her steering gear was out of action.

With a heavy heart, Alan West gave the order to abandon ship and asked the frigate *Yarmouth* came alongside to take off survivors. West himself was the last to leave the ship. Twenty-two of the ship's crew had been killed and more than thirty injured.

None of the three Skyhawks involved in the final attack on *Ardent* survived the encounter. Clive Morell and John Leeming had each shot down one. Philippi ejected, but Marquez was killed. Jose Arca's Skyhawk suffered damage from the ship's return fire or from Morell's cannon shells, or perhaps both. Losing fuel from a punctured tank, Arca knew he could not return to the mainland, so he flew to Port Stanley and ejected.

After Philippi's attack, a second formation of three naval Skyhawks ran in to bomb ships in the landing area. These aircraft suffered no losses, but they also failed to score any hits with their bombs. That was the last attack of the day, and from then on the transports were allowed to continue their unloading operation unmolested.

Just over six hours after Alan West left her, the burning *Ardent* finally slid under the waves. With two unexploded bombs lodged in her hull, *Argonaut* was towed into San Carlos Water, where work began to defuse the weapons and remove them from the ship.

During the action on 21 May, the Argentine Navy and Air Force lost ten of the fifty or so Skyhawks and Daggers sent to attack the landing area – an unsustainable loss rate of 20 per cent; in addition, two Pucarás based on the Falklands were also shot down. Nine of these planes fell to attacks by Sea Harriers, one fell to a ground-launched Stinger missile, one was shot down by a ship-launched missile and one was shot down by a Sea Harrier or small-arms fire from a ship, or both. The Sea Harriers suffered no losses.

The lack of proper air-to-air tactical training for the Argentine fighter-bomber pilots manifested itself throughout the action, and they had little awareness of how aircraft in an attack formation could provide mutual cover for each other using their cannon armament. When engaged by Sea Harriers, the Argentine fighter-bomber pilots never attempted to fight back or assist a comrade under attack.

By placing themselves in positions to draw the Argentine air attacks on themselves, the warships in the 'gun line' saved the vulnerable transport ships from a severe battering. The cost was not light: one frigate had been sunk and a frigate and a destroyer had been seriously damaged. Yet, despite this serious loss in material, the proximity of rescue ships and helicopters kept losses in personnel relatively low: 24 Royal Navy sailors were killed during the series of attacks that day.

The Argentine pilots had pressed home their low-altitude attacks with great bravery and determination. But, although they caused severe damage, they failed in their primary aim of defeating the amphibious landing operation. The unloading was allowed to proceed with little hindrance, and by the end of the day more than 3,000 British paratroops and commandos and nearly 1,000 tons of stores were ashore. Once the beach-head had been thus secured, the opportunity for the Argentine air units to have a decisive impact on the conflict had passed.

Chapter 15

The Epic of 'Bravo November'

In the previous chapter, we observed that, while the posses-
sion of air superiority would not prevent a determined enemy
from carrying out destructive air attacks, the raiding forces
were themselves likely to suffer heavy losses. In this chapter,
we again look at the Falklands conflict for an example of one
type of operation, the free movement of troops and supplies by
air that becomes possible once a measure of air superiority has
been secured. It also shows that a single medium-lift helicopter,
resolutely handled, can exert an enormous influence on a small
land campaign.

To support the planned ground operations on the Falklands
following the initial landings, No 18 Squadron of the RAF sent
four Boeing Chinook medium-lift helicopters to the South Atlantic
in the spring of 1982. The machines were transported as deck cargo on
the container ship *Atlantic Conveyor*, together with a contingent of air
and ground crewmen from the unit. Shortly before the landings, the
container ship joined up with the British Task Force off the islands,
and the Harriers and Sea Harriers she also brought south took off
from her deck and flew to the aircraft carriers waiting to receive them.

Since they had not been intended to operate from ships, the RAF
Chinooks were not fitted with folding rotor blades. Those loaded
on to *Atlantic Conveyor* had their rotor blades removed so that they
could be stowed more easily. On 25 May, in preparation for the
fly-off scheduled for the following day, ground crewmen of No 18
Squadron began refitting the blades to the Chinooks.

Each blade was nearly 30ft long and weighed about 300lb, and there were three to be fitted each to the front and the rear rotor hubs, which were, respectively, 15ft and 18ft above the deck. A fork-lift truck was used to hoist each blade to the required height, the latter being suspended midway along its length from a rope attached to the lifting forks. Further ropes were tied to each end of the blade, their other ends held by men on deck, to guide it into position beside the hub. The men had no previous experience of fitting blades to big helicopters on the deck of a ship rolling in open sea and, in the words of Sergeant Steve Hitchman, it was 'a swine of a job'.

The problem was that, when the lifting truck's forks were raised or lowered, they moved in a series of jerks that caused the blades to flex along their length. The difficulty was further exacerbated by the movement of ship as she pitched and rolled. Hitchman continued: 'We had a man leaning over the rotor head as the blades were manoeuvred into position, ready to push the locking bolt into place. And a couple of times he nearly lost fingers.' During the afternoon of the 25th, the final blade was locked into place on the first of the Chinooks and, after completing engine running checks, Flying Officer John Kennedy took off for a brief air test. Thereafter the helicopter, radio call-sign 'Bravo November', would be used to transfer supplies between ships in the Task Force.

Soon after Kennedy had got airborne, the Task Force came under attack from a pair of Argentine Navy Super Etendard fighter-bombers, each of which launched an Exocet missile. The threat was detected in good time and the warships fired salvos of chaff rockets to seduce the Exocets clear of them. In this they were successful, but *Atlantic Conveyor* happened to be in the wrong place at the wrong time – behind a cloud of chaff that had drawn one of the missiles away. The Exocet emerged from the cloud of metallized strips, 're-acquired' the container ship and aligned itself on the new target. The weapon smashed into the ship's port quarter, where it detonated, starting several fires in the hold. Soon the fires were blazing out of control and *Atlantic Conveyor* was abandoned. Twelve men lost their lives in the incident, though everyone from No 18 Squadron escaped without injury.

The container ship foundered five days later with the charred remains of three Chinooks and several smaller helicopters on her deck. Only 'Bravo November' and one of the smaller helicopters had survived. The orphaned Chinook spent that night on the deck of the aircraft carrier *Hermes*, and the following day she flew to the San Carlos bridgehead.

At San Carlos, Squadron Leader Dick Langworthy took charge of the No 18 Squadron detachment, which comprised the Chinook, two four-man flight crews and nineteen technicians and supporting staff. The rest of the squadron personnel were put on one of the ships heading northwards out of the combat zone, for until the next batch of Chinooks reached the island there was no useful work for them to do.

All of the Chinook spare parts, special tools and servicing manuals intended for the detachment had been lost with *Atlantic Conveyor*, and there was speculation on how long the surviving helicopter could remain in an airworthy condition. 'Everybody thought we would be back on board ship in a couple of days,' recalled Chief Technician Tom Kinsella, in charge of the servicing team. 'The Chinook was bound to go unserviceable and that would be the end of our time ashore.'

For his part, Langworthy resolved to get as many flights as possible out of the Chinook before that happened. With a lifting capacity of 12 tons, it was the largest helicopter available to the British forces on the island; the Sea King, the next largest, could carry only 4 tons. Following the loss of so many helicopters on *Atlantic Conveyor*, the British land forces were desperately short of lifting capacity to sustain the advance on Port Stanley. For as long as she could be kept flying, 'Bravo November' would represent a significant proportion of that capacity.

As an initial task, 'Bravo November' was set to work transferring supplies from the transports moored in San Carlos Water to the storage areas ashore. Then, during the advance on Goose Green, she ferried artillery shells to the forward gun positions, carrying ten tons each time on a pallet slung below her fuselage. After the battle

BOEING CHINOOK HC Mk I (CH-47C)

Role: Medium-lift transport helicopter with a crew of four.
Power: Two Lycoming T55-L-11E turboshaft engines each developing 3,750shp.
Armament: None usually carried, though infantry machine guns can be fired from open windows or from the open rear loading door.
Performance: Maximum speed 184mph; cruising speed 153mph.
Normal operational take-off weight: 46,000lb (maximum weight carried on operations about 27,000lb).
Dimensions: Rotor diameter 60ft; overall length (rotors turning) 99ft.
Date of first production CH-47C: February 1968.

at Goose Green, she ferried Argentine prisoners, 60 at a time, to San Carlos. Describing these operations, Dick Langworthy commented:

> We threw away all the rules, operating the helicopter at its maximum all-up weight as often as we could. The aeroplane [sic] went on day after day with bits going unserviceable. But the engines kept going, the rotors kept turning and she continued to do the job.

After dark on 30 May, 'Bravo November' was sent deep into enemy-held territory, on a mission that was nearly her last. Reconnaissance patrols by the Special Air Service had discovered that the most of the Argentine troops had been withdrawn from Mount Kent, the strategically important strip of high ground ten miles west of Port Stanley. This was now a vacuum waiting to be filled, and three Royal Navy Sea Kings flew into the area and landed a detachment of commandos. Dick Langworthy followed in the Chinook, carrying 22 men and two 105mm guns in the fuselage and a further 105mm gun as an external load beneath the helicopter.

To enable them to navigate close to the ground in the darkness, the crew wore night-vision binoculars clipped to their flying helmets. Throughout much of the 45-mile flight, Langworthy kept the heavily laden Chinook at low altitude as he followed the series of ridge lines towards the objective. Occasionally a snow shower blotted out vision and forced him to climb well above the ground, but when the skies cleared he returned to low altitude.

The first problem arose when the Chinook reached the area where it was to put down the guns. Flight Lieutenant Tom Jones, the loadmaster responsible for the unloading operation, recalled:

> We had been led to believe that the ground on which we were to land would be relatively flat. Only when we arrived did we find it was on a sloping peat bog flanked on either side by stone rivers. We put down the underslung gun, no problem. Then we had to position the other two guns quite accurately in relation to the first. When Dick landed the Chinook, the back end sank into the peat so that we couldn't lower the ramp even with hydraulic pressure.

Langworthy eased the helicopter up a few feet, the ramp was lowered and he landed again. Now the exit was clear, and the gun crews toiled to move the first of the 2½-ton weapons to the opening and wheel it to the ground. They had not got far when a fire-fight broke out nearby between SAS men covering the operation and an Argentine patrol. Then, to add to the gunners' troubles, the red dim-lighting system in the rear of the helicopter failed. The cabin was plunged into darkness except for the shielded beams of hand torches, kept low to avoid drawing enemy fire. In case he needed to make a quick getaway, Langworthy kept the helicopter's engines running and the rotors turning.

Finally, the third and last of the guns was off-loaded, and the Chinook took off to return to Port San Carlos. The crew had no way of knowing it, but the worst was yet to come. The Chinook ran out at low altitude, giving the developing battle a wide berth, and almost immediately it ran into a thick snow shower. Blinded for a few all-important seconds, Langworthy allowed the helicopter to lose altitude and suddenly it shuddered as it struck something hard. Tom Jones, standing in the rear cabin, was thrown to the floor and had his flying helmet torn from his head. Inexplicably, at the time, the structure of the Chinook remained intact.

Only later would the crew learn that the helicopter had flopped down on the water in one of the small creeks to the west of Mount Kent. The wide, flat underside of the Chinook had skidded across the surface like a giant surf-board, throwing up a cloud of spray. Some of the water went into the air intakes and the two Lycoming engines began to lose power. As the engines ran down, there was a loss of hydraulic pressure, the power-assisted flying controls began to lose their effect and the helicopter became considerably heavier to handle. Thinking that a crash was imminent, the co-pilot released the escape door on his side of the cockpit. Dick Langworthy described what happened next:

> I shouted at the co-pilot to come on the controls with me. We both heaved on our collective pitch levers to increase the pitch of the running-down rotor blades, and that did the trick. The helicopter lifted just clear of the water, the spray ceased, and the engines started to wind up again.

With full power restored, Langworthy put the helicopter into a maximum-rate climb to get clear of high ground around him.

Soon afterwards the Chinook landed at San Carlos, and four very subdued men climbed out and made a grateful re-acquaintance with *terra firma*. Remarkably, apart from the loss of the co-pilot's door and minor damage to the rear loading ramp caused during the struggle to get the guns out, the helicopter had suffered little damage. 'After that incident we felt nothing was going to stop the Chinook keeping going for the rest of the war!' commented Tom Kinsella.

In the afternoon of 2 June, an operation by 'Bravo November' was to have far-reaching consequences for the campaign. The British ground-force commander had learned that Argentine troops had evacuated Fitzroy settlement some fifteen miles south-west of Port Stanley. He resolved to seize the area before the enemy commander changed his mind and perhaps re-occupied it.

At Goose Green, 'Bravo November' was 'hijacked' from her planned task and 81 paratroopers in full battle order clambered aboard her. The captain of the Chinook, Flight Lieutenant Dick Grose on this occasion, had only a vague idea of how much weight had been put aboard his helicopter. Standard assumptions regarding the weight of passengers plus their baggage were useless in this case: the battle-hardened troops expected to go into action soon after they landed, and each man carried as much ammunition as he could physically lift. Tom Jones described the conditions inside the helicopter:

> The paras were doing what we euphemistically call 'strap hanging' except that there were no straps to hang from. The seats were folded against the sides of the fuselage; the men were standing up and had to carry their weapons because there was no room to put them on the floor. The troops were packed in so tightly, they could hardly turn around. It was worse than a tube train in the rush hour.

The paratroops accepted their discomfort without complaint – they knew that the alternative to going by helicopter was a 30-mile forced march over difficult and broken country.

Fortunately for those on board, a vertical take-off in a helicopter is a fail-safe operation. If the machine is too heavy to get off the ground, it simply stays where it is. If it is light enough to get airborne, everything that follows works in its favour: as the machine gains forward speed its lifting capacity is increased, and as fuel is consumed the reserve of lifting capacity is increased further. Grose found that he could lift the heavily laden helicopter off the ground without difficulty, and he headed in the direction of Fitzroy. Throughout the flight the weather was poor, with low cloud covering the surrounding hills and visibility about two miles. Near Fitzroy the Chinook linked up with a couple of Army Scout helicopters, which led it to the landing area they had reconnoitred to the west of the settlement. The big helicopter landed, the ramp came down and within a quarter of a minute all the para-troops were outside and flat on their stomachs, weapons levelled ready to return fire. The move had passed unnoticed by the enemy, however, and the men began moving out to establish a defensive perimeter.

Grose returned to Goose Green, collected a further 75 paratroops and flew those to Fitzroy. It had been a bold operation and one that involved a degree of risk – there had been no time to reconnoitre the helicopter's route, and if it had flown over an Argentine position and been shot down there might have been heavy loss of life. It was a gamble, the sort that must sometimes be taken if there is a likelihood of shortening a conflict and preventing even greater losses.

During the days that followed, 'Bravo November' resumed her normal transport duties, flying over friendly territory. As British forces advanced on Port Stanley, the Chinook joined the shuttle service moving artillery shells from Teal Inlet to the gun positions around Mount Kent which were bombarding the Argentine positions. The 30-mile round trip took about 45 minutes, and the Chinook flew up to fifteen such missions each day, her two crews flying on alternate days.

On 7 June there was a break in the routine, when 'Bravo November' was sent to pick up two Navy Sea King helicopters that had suffered damage. Carrying one Sea King at a time as an underslung load, the Chinook transported the helicopters to their operating base near Port San Carlos. And on 8 June 'Bravo November' transported 64 wounded men in a single lift from Fitzroy to the hospital ship *Uganda* lying off the coast.

Of the underslung loads transported by 'Bravo November', the pilots found the pallets of artillery ammunition the easiest to carry: the load was immensely heavy but relatively small, and in flight it was stable in the airflow. Loads that were less dense sometimes developed a will of their own in flight, and were much more difficult to handle. On 14 June Dick Grose was called upon to fly an 8-ton steel girder bridge from Fitzroy, where it had been assembled by Army engineers, to Murrell. Flying Officer Colin Miller, co-pilot on the flight, explained the problems caused by this particular load:

> The girder bridge was quite heavy but it was very flat, and once we started moving with it under the Chinook it generated its own lift. Almost immediately it became unstable, swinging from side to side on its loading chains. We had to slow down to 20 knots to let it stabilize – though at no point was it fully stable – [and] from then on fly the helicopter very slowly and very carefully. That bridge was a bloody awful load!

As the Chinook was in the process of manoeuvring the bridge into position, assisted by Army engineers on the ground, the word came through that the Argentine forces on the islands had surrendered.

The story of 'Bravo November' on the Falklands is a text-book example of how a single aircraft of the right type, in the right place and at the right time, can have considerable influence on the course of a conflict. Now, more than two decades afterwards, that particular Chinook is still in service. One might have expected that she would have pride of place in a military museum, or be sitting as gate guardian at an RAF station to inspire future generations of helicopter crews. In fact, at the time of writing she was at the Boeing Helicopter plant in Philadelphia, undergoing a year-long modification programme to bring her to the latest CH-47D standard. When the work was completed, in the summer of 1993, she returned to the United Kingdom to resume her place in a front-line squadron.

Chapter 16

Precision Attack – By Night

When Iraqi forces invaded Kuwait in August 1990 and sparked off the crisis in the Persian Gulf, the US Air Force's 48th Tactical Fighter Wing was equipped with the General Dynamics F-111F 'Aardvark' swing-wing attack plane. The unit was based at Lakenheath in England and its primary role was that of night attack using precision-guided munitions. This account chronicles the activities of the Wing during the conflict and describes ways in which it exploited the capabilities of its unique equipment.

The development of air-launched guided weapons that are effective against pin-point land targets has been long and arduous. Since 1944 several such weapons have been introduced into service, but most of them failed to live up to their maker's expectations when they were used in combat. Only in the 1970s, with the advent of the laser-guided bomb (LGB), did a weapon exist that could really achieve the accuracy necessary to destroy such targets under combat conditions. Since the mid-1980s, the 48th Tactical Fighter Wing has been equipped with two basic types of precision-guided munition, the LGB and the more accurate (but also more expensive) electro-optically guided bomb (EOGB).

By 1990 the General Dynamics F-111 was what is euphemistically called 'a mature design' – or, in the words of one of the pilots of the 48th TFW, most of the unit's planes were 'old enough to vote'. The 48th was the only unit to be equipped with the F model of the famous aircraft, the final production version which was optimized for the night attack role with precision-guided weapons.

The F model carried a Pave Tack pod under the fuselage, to enable it to laser-designate targets for its LGBs; alternatively, the aircraft could carry a data-link pod for the control of EOGBs in flight. During attacks with these weapons, the plane's WSO (weapon systems officer) observed the target during the final part of the bomb's trajectory on a TV-type screen in the cockpit of the aircraft. These video pictures were taped for later analysis, and every reader will have seen the spectacular video footage of attacks with LGBs and EOGBs during the Gulf War. As well as the two main types of precision-guided munition, the F-111 could carry almost any unguided weapon on the US Air Force inventory.

In August 1990 the US President, George Bush, ordered his armed forces to implement Operation 'Desert Shield', initially with the aim of preventing Iraqi forces from advancing into Saudi Arabia. As part of this move, Colonel Tom Lennon, commander of the 48th TFW, received instructions to deploy part of his force into the crisis area. On the 25th, eighteen F-111Fs took off from Lakenheath and, supported by KC-135 tankers, flew non-stop to the Royal Saudi Air Force base at Taif near Mecca. At the time there were no precision-guided munitions in the new theatre, so each F-111F carried four LGBs or four EOGBs to produce an initial stock of these weapons at the new base. Within 48 hours of the arrival of the first aircraft at Taif, the unit had fully armed planes on ground alert there.

From the start, it was accepted that, if hostilities commenced, the 48th TFW would fly almost all (perhaps all) of its missions by night. Thus assured, the commander ordered his crews to begin an intensive programme of training flights to familiarize themselves with night operations over the desert. Tom Lennon recalled:

Having so long to prepare for combat was great. It allowed us to practise operations with very large packages of aircraft. It allowed us to convince the Saudis that we needed to do business differently on their airfields, with mass night comms-out [radio-silent] launches, mass rejoins on the tankers, things that we don't practise in peace time.

The unit was also able to practise night, low-level operations over the desert, with aircraft flying on the terrain-following radar (TFR), initially at 400ft and later going down to 200ft. The F-111s also practised the difficult and demanding flight profiles necessary to deliver precision-guided munitions from low altitude.

The United Nations Security Council's deadline for the withdrawal of Iraqi troops from Kuwait expired at midnight on 15 January 1991. In the afternoon of the 16th, Coalition operational units received orders to execute Operation 'Desert Storm', the attack on Iraqi forces, during the early hours of the following morning.

The initial wave of air strikes hit numerous targets in Iraq and Kuwait. Tom Lennon explained how his force was used:

It was a maximum effort: we launched 54 F-111Fs out of 64 and 53 of them went into action that night. If I had had 60 planes available, I would have sent all 60.

The aircraft were split into forces of four to six planes and delivered attacks on the chemical weapons storage bunkers at H-3, Salman Pak and Ad Diwaniyah, and on the airfields at Balad and Jalibah in Iraq and Ali Al Salem and Al Jaber in Kuwait. The attacking F-111Fs received fighter and SAM-suppression support at their target areas, but they were on their own while en route to and from their targets. Planes making for the same target flew singly at low altitude in trail, with a spacing of about a minute (about 8½ miles) between each.

Tom Lennon led the deepest penetration by the Wing that night, a six-plane strike on Balad airfield north of Baghdad. The commander and his wing aircraft hit designated buildings in the airfield's maintenance complex with EOGBs, then the remaining F-111Fs laid

---

General Dynamics F-111F

Role: Two-seat, swing-wing, night precision-attack aircraft.
Power: Two Pratt & Whitney TF30-P-100 turbofan engines each rated at 25,100lb of thrust with afterburner.
Armament: On normal operations a bomb load of up to 8,000lb was carried. Typical loads were four 2,000lb LGBs, or four 500lb LGBs, or four 2,000lb EOGBs (in this configuration the aircraft carried a data-transmission pod under the fuselage, to receive video pictures transmitted from the weapons after release and transmit guidance signals to them).
Performance: Maximum speed (clean, at 35,000ft) 1,450mph (Mach 2.2), (clean, at low altitude) 800mph (Mach 1.2)
Maximum gross take-off weight: 100,000lb.
Dimensions: Span (wings fully forward) 63ft, (wings fully swept) 31ft 11½in; length 77ft; wing area (wings fully forward) 525 sq ft.
Date of first production F-111F: August 1971.

area–denial mines across the ends of each of the runways and among the hardened aircraft shelters (HASs). The aim of the attack was to neutralize this important airfield during the critical few hours that followed, by making the movement of Iraqi aircraft on the ground hazardous until the mines could be cleared. In that it was successful.

During the period leading up to the conflict, commanders of air attack units had been told to expect 'worst-case' losses of around 10 per cent of sorties flown during the initial air strikes. On that basis Tom Lennon feared he might lose six planes during his unit's initial wave of attacks. In the event, all the F-111Fs returned safely; two had damage from small-arms fire, but in each case it was minor and repaired easily.

During the second night of the war, the 17th/18th, the unit dispatched 35 F-111s to hit several more targets in Iraq. Four planes carrying EOGBs headed for Saddam Hussein's summer palace at Tikrit, which housed one of the dictator's command centres. On the way to the objective, a MiG-29 'Fulcrum' attempted to engage the raiders, starting an intercept on each one in turn. The Iraqi pilot nibbled down the line and finally slid behind the last F-111 in the trail. His intended victim then folded back its wings and accelerated to maximum speed at low altitude, and the high-speed chase continued for more than 70 miles before the MiG gave up the struggle. In the meantime, the three remaining F-111Fs reached Tikrit and delivered their EOGBs with great precision. The palace was devastated.

Also that night, a six-plane striking force carried out an experimental attack on HASs at Mudaysis airfield. This attack was to have far-reaching consequences. Mudaysis lay outside the main Iraqi SAM-defended area, so the raiders could attack in safety from medium altitude. The F-111Fs released their LGBs from altitudes around 20,000ft and each swing-wing bomber carried out four separate runs, aiming a single 2,000lb weapon at an individual HAS on each run. The aircraft flew in trail, following each other around the same oblong 'race-track' pattern. After guiding its first bomb to impact, the leading F-111F turned and flew round the 'race-track', then turned and made its second bomb run flying the same track as for the first. The F-111Fs repeated the process for as long as they had ordnance remaining. That night the raiders scored hits on 23 hardened shelters, and those that contained planes produced spectacular secondary explosions when they were hit.

The Iraqi air plan, such as it was, depended on the hardened shelters to keep combat planes safe until they were required to go into action against Coalition ground forces. Undoubtedly the ease with which the F-111Fs destroyed the HASs and their contents at Mudaysis came as a nasty shock to the Iraqi High Command, and this played a part in prompting the later decision to fly the most modern combat planes out of the country.

During the initial attacks, the Wing dispatched several small striking forces, each night, aiming to cause damage at as wide a spread of targets as possible. After a few days the tactics changed, with far larger forces of aircraft being sent against far fewer targets. As Tom Lennon explained:

After the first night we didn't do anything with six aircraft. When we went after something, we would go after it big time. We would put 20 to 24 airplanes on one airfield at one time. If we had to hit a target, we hit it with everything we had, all at once, and got out of there.

During the night of 20/21 January, the Wing sent twenty F-111Fs to deliver a set-piece attack on Balad airfield. By then the threat from Iraqi fighters and long-range SAMs was judged to have been contained, and even when passing over the most heavily defended areas the F-111Fs could fly at medium level. These aircraft now attacked from altitudes of between 12,000 and 20,000ft, where they were beyond reach of most of the anti-aircraft artillery (AAA) fire. In a repeat of the tactics used over Mudaysis, the F-111Fs cruised over the enemy airfield, guiding individual 2,000lb LGBs at the strategic points on the runways and taxiways. When released from medium altitude, the LGB proved particularly effective for this purpose: the weapon impacted at a steep angle and penetrated the concrete surface before it detonated to produce a large crater.

Despite the constant harassment at the hands of their American counterparts whenever they got airborne, there were still Iraqi fighter pilots willing to make determined attempts to engage the raiders. As the last F-111F was leaving Balad that night, a MiG-29 closed in to

---

Operation of Pave Tack Attack Pod

When the F-111F reached the area of the target, its Weapon Systems Officer (WSO) operated a small hand controller to steer the Pave Tack head until it was pointing at the target. The head was linked to an infra-red TV camera, whose picture was displayed on a screen in the cockpit. The target was placed under the aiming reticle in the centre of the screen, a process which aligned the laser head on the target. The laser beam was then turned on, the laser-guided bomb or bombs were released and the weapons homed on the laser energy reflected from the target.

attack it and locked on its radar. Captain Jerry Hanna, the WSO in the bomber, recalled that from then on everything happened very quickly indeed:

> We immediately initiated a high-speed combat descent, the pilot got the wings back and we went screaming downhill. Puking chaff, we went from 19,000 to about 4,000 feet in a heartbeat! The adrenalin was really pumping, Jim [the pilot] was busy trying get the plane close to the ground, I was on radio hollering at the AWACS that we had been jumped by a MiG and to get the F-18s coming back in our direction.

Hanna set up the terrain-following radar so that it would take automatic control of the plane as soon as the latter got close to the ground. By following the contours closely at maximum speed, the F-111F made a very difficult target. Before that happened, however, the MiG suddenly broke away. No doubt aware that American fighters were converging on him, the Iraqi pilot probably thought he had done all that honour required.

The large-scale attacks from medium altitude became the main mode of operation by the F-111Fs, and their tactics were continually refined. During attacks on clusters of weapons storage bunkers or HASs, the bombers used the so-called 'Wagon Wheel' tactic, with a number of race-track flight patterns arranged like the spokes of a wheel centred on the target. Lieutenant Bradley Seipel, a WSO on the unit, described what it was like to be part of a multi-aircraft attack of this type on the HASs dotted around an enemy airfield:

> It was awesome. After you released your bomb [from medium altitude] it was in the air for nearly a minute. While you marked your own target with the laser, on the Pave Tack video screen you saw this shelter blow up, then you saw that shelter blow up, then you saw another one blow up. Then the one that you had your laser on blew up.

Using such methods, the Wing fought its own battle to dismember the Iraqi Air Force. And because it could deliver the precision weapons at night, it did so with minimal risk to its aircraft and crews.

Lieutenant-Colonel Tommy Crawford, the Wing's Assistant Deputy Commander for Operations, described the Iraqi SAM and AAA defences at this stage of the war. In his view, against high-flying night raiders, they were ineffective:

> They fired lots of SAMs. At first there were cases of the guys on the ground holding the radar lock-on throughout an engagement. But with the HARM firers [Wild Weasel aircraft firing High Speed Anti-Radiation Missiles at the radars] supporting us they didn't survive long if they did that. Then the SAM batteries changed their tactics. The radar would come on, they would lock on and fire their missile, then shut down the radar. They would send the missile up ballistically and hope that we didn't turn or anything. We could see them coming, so it was pretty easy to avoid them.

Almost all of the AAA was unaimed barrage fire, which could be ignored at altitudes above 15,000ft.

As well as carrying out attacks on airfields, the Wing also struck at munitions production and storage facilities. One of these targets that came in for particular attention was the huge Latifiyah munitions production complex and research centre near Baghdad. The Wing mounted four separate attacks against this target, each with between 20 to 24 aircraft.

On 25 January Iraqi Army engineers opened valves to discharge millions of gallons of crude oil into the waters of the Persian Gulf, producing a huge slick off the coast. The move was intended to make it more difficult for Coalition forces to launch an amphibious landing operation in the area, and it is questionable whether it could have been effective (even if such an operation had been planned). But what is certain is that the act caused a great deal of pollution and posed a severe threat to marine wildlife in the area. President Bush termed it an act of 'environmental terrorism' and asked his military commanders to examine ways of bringing it to a halt. The 48th Wing was given the task of destroying the two pumping stations at Al Ahmadi in Kuwait that were pushing the oil into the sea. Both targets lay close to areas of civilian housing, so an extremely precise attack was required.

The operation against the pumping stations took place during the night of 26/27 January and, because of its political importance, the attackers employed a large measure of 'overkill'. Five F-111Fs (including two reserve aircraft) took off for the mission, each carrying two 2,000lb EOGBs and a data-link pod. One F-111F suffered a technical malfunction and was unable to take part, but the rest of the mission went off without a hitch. Flying supersonic at 20,000ft, one of the planes lobbed an EOGB towards the first pumping station from more than 20 miles away. The plane then entered a sharp diving turn and sped out of the area. A second F-111F, flying parallel to the coast on a north-westerly heading more than 50 miles out to sea and beyond the reach of the defences, then took control of the bomb and guided it throughout the rest of its flight. Bradley Seipel, WSO in the controlling plane, observed the video picture transmitted from the camera in the nose of the missile and steered the weapon in for a direct hit on the first pumping station.

Captain Michael Russell, Seipel's pilot, then turned his aircraft through 180 degrees and then flew south-east, parallel to the coast, as a second F-111F lobbed an EOGB in the direction of the second pumping station. Again Seipel took control of the EOGB in flight and guided the weapon to score a direct hit. The entire attack, from the release of the first bomb to the impact of the second, took about five minutes. Then the five F-111Fs, between them bearing eight unused EOGBs, returned to Taff. The video footage transmitted to the aircraft from the cameras in the missiles later featured in news broadcasts shown all over the world. With both of the offending pumping stations wrecked, the flow of oil into the sea ceased.

On 26 January the Wing's earlier campaign against HASs brought a sudden and quite unexpected bonus for the Coalition as Iraqi combat planes started to flee to neutral Iran. The move continued for several days and more than a hundred Iraqi aircraft made the one-way flight. None of the planes were returned, and since then several have been incorporated into the Iranian Air Force.

During the night of 29/30 January the Wing shifted its attention to the bridges along the Iraqi supply routes into Kuwait. The first such attack was on bridges over the Hawr Al Hammar Lake north-west of Basrah, and in the days that followed the unit mounted a system-atic campaign against bridges over the Tigris and Euphrates rivers.

OPERATION OF ELECTRO-OPTICAL GUIDED BOMB (EOGB)

When it operated with this weapon, the F-111F had a special data-link pod mounted under the rear fuselage. The EOGB was aimed and released in the same way as a normal free-fall bomb, and was controlled only during the final part of its trajectory. The weapon was fitted with a TV-type camera in the nose, whose picture was relayed by radio link to the controlling aircraft (which might or might not be the one that released the weapon). The picture seen from the nose of the bomb was viewed in the cockpit of the controlling aircraft on a screen in front of the WSO, and the latter operated a hand controller to send steering signals to correct the missile's flight path during the final fifteen seconds or so to impact.

Modern steel and concrete bridges are difficult targets for air attack, however, as Lieutenant Dave Giachetti explained:

> With precision-guided munitions, hitting the bridge was not a problem. The problem was hitting it at a weak part, a point where the weapon would cause structural damage and drop a span. If you didn't hit it exactly on the abutment at either end, or where the supports were, the bomb would often go through the pavement, leaving a neat round hole that they could easily repair.

One of the most difficult such targets proved to be the twin highway bridges over the River Tigris near Basrah, which required three separate attacks before they were put out of action.

After a period of trial and error, the Wing evolved the optimum tactics for use against the different types of bridge. One method that proved particularly effective was to have two planes each aiming four 2,000lb EOGBs at the middle support sections of the bridge and two planes each aiming four 2,000lb LGBs at the abutments at each end. During these attacks the aircraft flew race-track patterns and each bomb was guided individually to the required impact point. Where an important bridge had been rendered unusable, Iraqi Army engineers would often erect a pontoon bridge alongside it to keep the traffic moving. These flimsy structures proved easy targets for LGBs, however, and a single hit at either end would shatter the structure, releasing the remaining pontoons to float downstream.

Early in February the Wing was asked to join in the general attack on Iraqi tanks and armoured vehicles in the battle zone, as part of the final preparations for the Coalition ground offensive. Individual vehicles lay in bulldozed scrapes 10ft deep and were covered with sandbags to give added protection. Each vehicle was thus a small pin-point target that was largely invulnerable to air attack unless the latter came from almost vertically above. The Iraqis had no inkling of the effectiveness of the F-111F and its Pave Tack equipment, however. Planes traversing the area on their way to and from other targets brought back infra-red video film of the dug-in vehicles. It was found that the bulldozer scrapes produced a distinctive infra-red signature which showed up clearly on Pave Tack.

Staff officers at the Wing devised a plan to use LGBs against the enemy vehicles, dropped from F-111Fs flying at medium altitude so that the bombs would impact at a steep angle to achieve maximum destructive effect. Each aircraft was to carry four 500lb LGBs and release one at a time and guide it to impact on an individual vehicle, then repeat the process.

During the night of 5/6 February the Wing mounted an operational trial to test out the new tactics. Tom Lennon and Tommy Crawford each took off in an F-111F and attacked a Republican Guard unit deployed in the desert, and the eight LGBs they carried scored hits on seven enemy vehicles. These tactics did not appear in any military text-book, and Crawford later quipped that if he had stood up at Staff College a year earlier and proposed using the F-111F in this way he would have probably been laughed out of the room!

Laughter or not, the tactics proved highly productive. The F-111Fs achieved their greatest success during the night of 13/14 February, when 46 aircraft attacked the dug-in vehicles. The planes were credited with scoring hits on no fewer than 132 tanks and armoured vehicles. Initially there were doubts regarding the ability of the small LGBs to knock out tanks, but this ability was confirmed to the full when Coalition ground troops later occupied the area.

On 27/28 February, the last night of the conflict, two F-111Fs attacked a military command centre buried deep underground at Al Taji near Baghdad. Each plane aircraft carried a 4,700lb 'Bunker-Buster' LGB, a deep-penetration weapon that had been hastily produced specifically for use in attacks on such targets. One of the new bombs hit the bunker and caused a small puff of smoke to blow out of an entrance to the structure. Then, a few seconds later, came a large secondary explosion that was thought to have destroyed the interior of the bunker.

During the conflict in the Gulf, the 48th Tactical Fighter Wing inflicted severe damage on several airfields and munitions production and storage facilities. The F-111Fs destroyed a dozen permanent bridges and caused severe damage to 52 more, and they hit 920 Iraqi tanks and armoured vehicles (one-seventh of all of those destroyed by Coalition forces) and 245 hardened aircraft shelters (two-thirds of the total destroyed). Moreover, in achieving these impressive results, the Wing did not not lose a single aircraft in combat.

Chapter 17

St Valentine's Day Shoot-Down

During its attacks on targets in Iraq, the Royal Air Force lost
six Tornado fighter-bombers in combat. The last fell on the
morning of 14 February 1991 during an attack on Al Taqaddum
airfield near Baghdad, shot down by a couple of SA-3 missiles.
This is the story behind that loss.

It was getting light at Muharraq airfield, Bahrain, as Wing Commander John Broadbent took off at the head of a raiding force comprising eight Tornados and four Buccaneers. Each Tornado carried two 1,000lb laser-guided bombs (LGBs) and each Buccaneer carried a Pave Spike designator pod to laser-mark the targets for the Tornados' bombs. The crews were briefed to carry out yet another attack on the hardened aircraft shelters (HASs) at the important Al Taqaddum airfield near Baghdad.

The attack was planned to commence at 8.40 a.m. and it was to take place in broad daylight (unlike the Pave Tack day/night attack system fitted to the F-111Fs described in the previous chapter, the less-advanced Pave Spike equipment carried by the Buccaneers was a daylight-only system). Taking off at about the same time as the RAF planes were those of the US Air Force defence-suppression package to support the attack – two F-15C Eagle air superiority fighters, two F-4G Wild Weasel aircraft carrying radar-homing missiles and two EF-111 Raven radar jamming aircraft.

The Tornados and Buccaneers arrived over the target at the briefed attack altitudes, around 20,000ft, and the crews found the skies clear of cloud, though there was some haze lower down. Al Taqaddum had been one of the most heavily defended airfields in Iraq, but by this stage of the war the SAM sites in the area had taken a severe battering and had been rendered inactive.

The main raiding force flew in elements of three aircraft, each of which comprised a pair of Tornados and an attendant Buccaneer. After releasing its bombs, each Tornado turned away and headed out of the defended area, while the navigator in the Buccaneer laser-marked the selected HAS until the bombs impacted. A couple of 1,000-pounders striking the roof of a HAS within a few feet of each other and a fraction of a second apart would punch a sizeable hole through the structure, wrecking anything inside.

At the controls of one of the last Tornados to attack, Flight Lieutenant Rupert Clark commenced his bombing run. The attack was progressing more or less normally until he was five seconds short of the bomb-release point, when he noticed a brief burst of signals from an enemy missile control radar on the plane's radar homing and warning receiver (RHWR). Clark opted to continue with the attack, and there was no further indication from the enemy radar until he reached the release point. One bomb left the aircraft cleanly, but from then on things quickly turned sour.

The second LGB remained stubbornly on its rack, defying all efforts by the navigator, Flight Lieutenant Steven Hicks, to get it to release. Shortly after that came a panic radio call that raised the hairs on the back of Clark's neck: 'Double missile launch over the target!' Now the Tornado's RHWR showed clear indications that missile command guidance signals were being beamed in its direction: a missile had been launched and was being guided on to the aircraft! Hicks called 'Break left!' and began releasing chaff. Clark selected full power, lowered the plane's manoeuvring flaps and threw the aircraft into a tight turn. Later he recalled:

We were going through north when there was this huge explosion and I felt the blast wave hit the aircraft. It was obvious what had happened. I shouted to Steve 'You OK?', but there was no reply.

The missile was a Soviet-built SA-3 'Goa' and it had detonated a few feet from the bomber's port side. Scores of high-velocity fragments tore into the plane, causing widespread damage. With a rush of air, the cabin depressurized itself through a 2in diameter hole that suddenly appeared in the left side of the canopy just in front of Clark's head. As the pilot looked around the cockpit to assess the situation, he realized how lucky he had been to escape serious injury. On the warning panel there were too many red lights for him to count. The reflector glass of the head-up display had disappeared altogether. The instrument panel was a shambles with only two dials seemingly intact, but the instruments, hydraulic gauges, both read zero.

Clark had no time to dwell on this catalogue of problems, however, for he had a more immediate threat to deal with. Almost certainly there was a second missile coming his way:

I moved the stick, overbanked the aircraft, and pulled back. Then I saw the second missile coming at me. It was coming up vertically, waggling as it guided on to me. I pulled on the stick as hard as I could, there was nothing else I could do. The missile disappeared from view going behind and to the right of the aircraft. There was another explosion as it went off.

Again Clark shouted to ask how his navigator was, and again there was no reply. Normally he could look round and see Hicks's smiling face. He now looked over each shoulder and, seeing nothing of his friend, began to fear the worst.

Clark found that he was bleeding from several cuts, though none appeared to be serious. Like Randy Cunningham and Willie Driscoll over Vietnam (see Chapter 13), his immediate concern was to put as much distance as possible between himself and the target. He had no wish to be taken prisoner, and he knew that for every minute he

---

Panavia Tornado GR Mk I

Role: Two-seat, swing-wing attack and reconnaissance aircraft.
Power: Two Turbo-Union RB 199 turbofan engines each rated at 15,000lb of thrust with afterburners.
Armament: Maximum load carried on operations comprised two JP233 airfield-denial weapons containers weighing a total of 40,300lb or up to eight 1,000lb bombs (during attacks with laser-guided bombs the aircraft carried two or three 1,000lb LGBs); two Mauser 27mm cannon; two AIM-9L Sidewinder infra-red homing missiles for self-defence.
Performance: Maximum speed (with full warload, at low altitude) 680mph, (clean, at altitude) over 1,450mph (Mach 2.2).
Maximum gross take-off weight: 60,000lb.
Dimensions: Span (wings fully forward) 45ft 7in, (wings fully swept) 28ft 2in; length 54ft 9½in; wing area (wings fully forward) 323 sq ft.
Date of first production Tornado GR.I: June 1979.

held the aircraft in the air he and his crewman would be six or seven miles closer to possible rescue.

A brief scan around the exterior of the Tornado revealed considerable damage. The wings and the external fuel tanks were peppered with holes and, looking back, he could see fuel streaming out and leaving a long white trail behind the aircraft. On the starboard wing, one of the slats had been blasted away from the leading edge and was sticking above the wing like some obscene gesture.

With the hydraulic system wrecked, the Tornado had automatically reverted to the manual flying mode. Clark found that if he pushed hard on the stick the plane would slowly respond. He had no way of telling if either of the engines was working, though from the way the plane handled it was obvious that they were producing little if any thrust. Ever the optimist, Clark went through the emergency procedure to restart the engines after a double flame-out. It made no difference.

A Tornado with no flying instruments makes a lousy glider. Clark raised the plane's nose a couple of times in an attempt to extend its glide, but each time he did so the noise level – and with it the speed – dropped. He had no idea which noise level equated to the stalling speed of the Tornado in that condition, and he had no wish to stall the plane to find out. He lowered the nose until the wind noise sounded about right, and accepted the resultant rate of descent.

As the plane descended below what he judged to be 10,000ft, Clark found the Tornado progressively more difficult to control. He had to apply more and more right stick to hold the wings horizontal, until in the end the stick was almost fully to the right – and still the aircraft wanted to 'lean' to the left. There was no point in hanging on any longer: he wanted to abandon the aircraft before he lost control entirely.

He tried one more time to call his navigator, and when there was still no answer he let go of the stick, placed both hands on the firing handle between his legs and yanked hard. In the Tornado, the ejection seats are interconnected so that, if the pilot pulls his handle, the navigator's seat is fired first and the pilot's seat follows shortly afterwards. Clark heard a loud bang and the cockpit filled with swirling black smoke as the rockets fired to lift off the canopy. Then came another loud bang in the rear cockpit, as the navigator's seat fired. Then it was Clark's turn:

> I got the kick up the backside as my seat fired. I heard or sensed each action in turn: the cartridges firing in my seat, my drogue gun going, and my seat tumbling as I left the aircraft. I was

fully conscious and I remember thinking, when are all these explosions going to stop? Then suddenly there was dead silence, absolutely no noise at all, and I was hanging from my parachute.

After the traumatic events of the previous few minutes – of being hit by the missiles, of trying to keep the plane airborne, of ejecting – that silence was like a sudden and unexpected gift from the gods.

Clark glanced down to observe the final moments of his crippled aircraft. It continued down in a sweeping turn to the left until it plunged into the ground with a hollow-sounding *boomphf.* The wreckage immediately burst into flames, fed by the remaining fuel in the tanks. A cloud of dense black smoke rose quickly to mark the impact point. Next came a succession of loud crackles and bangs as 27mm cannon shells in the plane's ammunition magazines 'cooked off' in the heat. Meanwhile Clark was assessing his direction of drift, trying to gauge where his parachute would deposit him. The predicted landing point looked disconcertingly close to the pile of wreckage now blazing fiercely on the ground. The pilot needed no reminding that, as well as the cannon shells, somewhere in the twisted remains of the aircraft lay a 1,000lb bomb and a couple of Sidewinder missiles. He hauled hard on the rigging lines to steer himself away from the danger. Shortly before Clark touched down, he saw his navigator's parachute land some distance away. The canopy deflated and there was no sign of life, and it seems certain that Steve Hicks never regained consciousness after the detonation of the first missile.

The pilot made a good landing a couple of hundred yards from the funeral pyre of his plane. He released his parachute harness, then his combat survival training took over and he cast an eye over the landscape for somewhere to hide while the rescue operation was set in train. Yet the flat desert landscape extended for more than a thousand yards in every direction. Clark recalled:

You could have put a cricket pitch almost anywhere there and you wouldn't have needed to use the heavy roller. There was nothing at all to hide behind. Just off to the south were what looked like some big sandstone blocks, [and] I thought that was the best place to head. So I picked up the survival pack and started legging it in that direction. The pack was heavy and after about 200 metres I decided to get rid of the dinghy. I started to open the pack, very carefully so as not to inflate the dinghy, when *pssssssss* . . . the bright orange dinghy started to inflate itself!

He dropped the dinghy and continued his long jog in the direction of the outcrop, though in retrospect it is clear that the Iraqis would have had to be deaf and blind not to have noticed his arrival. The wreckage of the Tornado was marked with a pillar of thick black smoke hundreds of feet high, with a series of bangs to draw attention to it. Nearby lay the pilot's discarded parachute. From there a trail of footprints lead to the bright orange dinghy sitting incongruously on the desert floor, and from there a further line of footprints led to the British airman heading away from the scene as fast as his legs could carry him.

Rupert Clark's period of freedom lasted less than a quarter of an hour, before a civilian on a motor cycle and brandishing a rifle came speeding across the desert towards him. Seeing that he had no chance of escape, Clark raised his hands in surrender, to begin a short but extremely unpleasant spell as a 'guest' of the Iraqi Government.

PART 2
Sky Warriors

Introduction

As in the case of the part 1, 'Sky Battles', this section describes in detail several air actions fought during the past eight decades, and uses these to illustrate the multi-faceted nature of air warfare.

The narrative opens in September 1917, when the First World War was in its fourth year and in Europe the opposing armies were locked in the deadly stalemate of trench warfare. Chapter 1, 'By Zeppelin to Africa' describes the epic attempt by Zeppelin *L59* to transport supplies to the German troops cut off in East Africa. In the event, the venture was unsuccessful, but the failure was not due to any shortcoming on the part of the airship or her intrepid crew. Had the Zeppelin arrived at her destination there can be no doubt that the flight would have been hailed as a stunning propaganda *coup*, and quoted later as a shining example of what a single, resolutely handled aircraft could achieve. As it was, the 95-hour flight by the airship established a record for the length of a combat flying mission that has never been broken.

The narrative then moves on to the Second World War. During the 1930s two new areas of technology combined to bring about a revolution in air defence and air fighting tactics: radar and radio telephony. The former enabled ground controllers to gain early warning of the approach of enemy raiding forces and send off large numbers of single-seat fighters in time to meet the threat. The latter made it possible to assemble fighters in unprecedented concentrations and direct them into action against the enemy force. The Battle of Britain in the summer of 1940 was the first occasion when both of these factors came into play in a large-scale air battle. It was also the first decisive military action to be fought solely in the air, without any serious involvement from either ground or naval forces. The action described in detail in Chapter 2, 'Battle of Britain Day' was that fought over London on 15 September 1940 and commemorated each year. Nothing can, nor should, detract from the bravery of the RAF fighter pilots that went into action that day. But it was also a victory for the system of fighter control that Air Chief Marshal Dowding had painstakingly built up from first principles. The *Luftwaffe* mounted two attacks on London that day. To meet the first, Fighter Command scrambled twenty-three squadrons of Spitfires and Hurricanes and all except one made contact with the enemy. To meet the second attack Fighter Command scrambled twenty-eight squadrons, and every one of them went into action. No conceivable system of fighter control could have done better than that.

Not only was the Second World War the first conflict to see the assembly of really large forces of combat planes to deliver a co-ordinated attack, it was also the first in which an air arm could deliver a sufficiently large weight of high explosive to cause major destruction to targets. The combination of the two made the pre-emptive air strike an attractive option to any regime ruthless enough to employ it. In such an attack the transition from peace to war came like 'a bolt out of the blue', with devastating air strikes hitting simultaneously at a spread of targets. Usually these were followed by powerful armoured thrusts by ground forces. The technique had been pioneered in Poland, Belgium, Holland and Yugoslavia. Chapter 3, 'Pre-Emptive Strike' describes the largest and the most effective of them all, that on Sunday 22 June 1941 when Adolf Hitler unleashed his *Blitzkrieg* offensive against the Soviet Union. The day was certainly one for the aviation record books. In an eighteen-hour period between 3.15 a.m. and sunset the Soviet Air Force lost about 1,800 combat planes, most of them destroyed on the ground. It was by far the largest number of aircraft wrecked in a single day's fighting and it represented the most comprehensive defeat ever inflicted by one air force on another. More than 300 Soviet aircraft fell in air-to-air combat, the largest number ever shot down in a one-day period.

The advancing German troops quickly overran every one of the airfields that the *Luftwaffe* had attacked on the first day. This added to the losses already suffered by the Soviet Air Force, for any damaged or unserviceable planes that could not be flown out before their airfields were captured were lost. Moreover, the capture of the airfields enabled the *Luftwaffe* to move to bases closer to targets in the Soviet hinterland. As a means of securing air superiority, the capture of enemy airfields is a highly effective method that is sometimes omitted from such calculations.

Despite the enormous material losses suffered by the Soviet Air Force during the early days of the war, however, the effect on that service was crippling only in the short and the medium term. Very few air crew were lost when the airfields were attacked and later captured, so as new aircraft became available there was no shortage of trained personnel to put them into action. Furthermore, the Soviet Air Force was on the point of re-equipping its front-line units with more modern fighter and bomber planes; most of the aircraft lost during the initial onslaught were obsolescent types that were about to be replaced anyway.

Chapter 6, 'Hard Fight to "The Big B"' describes the first large-scale US Army Air Force attack on Berlin, on 6 March 1944. These deep-penetration attacks became a feasible proposition only when long-range escort fighters, and in particular the superb P-51B Mustang, were available in large numbers to protect the bombers. On that day the Eighth Air Force lost 69 bombers and eleven fighters; it was a heavy loss, but there were sufficient replacement crews and aircraft to fill the gaps in the ranks of the front-line units. During the action the *Luftwaffe* lost 66 fighters and 46 pilots killed or wounded, and while the losses on planes were easily made good, the crews were almost irreplaceable. Following that attack, no target in Germany was beyond the reach of American heavy bombers protected by the escorts. The *Luftwaffe* was inexorably losing control of the skies over its homeland, and would never regain it.

During the final months of the Second World War night raiders were also being escorted to and from their targets, not only by long-range Mosquito night fighters but also by special jamming aircraft carrying equipment to neutralize or spoof defending radars. These operations were the work of No 100 Group of the Royal Air Force, and they are described in Chapter 10, 'Confound and Destroy'.

As we have observed, a well-executed air attack can inflict enormous damage on an adversary. By the same token, however, an air attack that is ill-conceived or badly carried out can result in heavier losses for the attackers than for the attacked. Two clear examples of the latter are described in Chapter 7, 'The Great Marianas Turkey Shoot' and Chapter 11, 'New Year's Day Party'. In the first of these the Japanese Navy launched a massive carrier air strike against a US

Navy carrier task force. Had the Japanese Navy possessed a better fighter at that time than the aging A6M5 Zeke 52, and had its air crews received a level of training comparable with those sent into action earlier in the war, the battle might have ended as a resounding victory for that service. As it was, the Japanese attack forces were massacred by defending American Hellcat fighters which, together with the ships' guns, shot down 181 of the attackers in a morning for a loss of only seven US fighters.

Chapter 11, 'New Year's Day Party' describes the *Luftwaffe* attack on Allied forward airfields in Europe on 1 January 1945, when that service attempted to repeat the success it achieved against the Soviet Air Force in June 1941. But the Allied Air Force units based in France, Holland and Belgium were a good deal better prepared to meet such an attack than the *Luftwaffe's* earlier victim had been. Moveover, by the beginning of 1945 the *Luftwaffe* was a good deal less able to deliver an effective blow than it had been in 1941. As a result, the attack failed at several points and the *Luftwaffe* lost rather more aircraft in the action than the Allied air forces. Even worse, the *Luftwaffe* lost 237 pilots killed, wounded, missing or taken prisoner that day and these included several experienced fighter commanders who were quite irreplaceable. Allied pilot losses during the action were minimal – probably less than twenty. The German fighter force never recovered from the blow that it suffered that day.

At the beginning of the Second World War the range of offensive weapons available to air forces was strictly limited. Often crews faced appalling risks in order to deliver their bombs on the assigned targets when, with hindsight, it is clear that those weapons had little chance of achieving a worthwhile degree of damage. For example, during its valiant efforts to stem the Germany advance through Holland, Belgium and France in May 1940, the Royal Air Force sent obsolescent Blenheims and Battles armed with 250lb general-purpose bombs to attack bridges. This weapon was insufficiently powerful to destroy a steel or masonry bridge even if several of them scored direct hits on the structure. The bombers suffered horrifying losses and, predictably, they achieved no tangible results. During the war each of the major belligerent air forces had to learn the same lesson, and in the hardest possible school of all – that of combat. The Royal Air Force went on to develop a range of specialized aerial weapons that were highly effective against their intended target. In Chapter 9, 'Bombers against the *Tirpitz'* we look at two types of specialized weapon that were employed in attacks on the mighty German battleship – the ingenious 'Johnny Walker' underwater walking mine and the 'brute force' 12,000lb 'Tallboy' bomb. To attack the *Tirpitz* was a man-size job, and certainly the 'Tallboy' was a man-size weapon with which to do it.

The Second World War also saw the introduction into service of the first air-launched guided weapons. Such a weapon can be defined as 'a missile whose path can be corrected during its travel, either automatically or by remote control, to bring it into contact with the target'. If that definition is accepted, the reader will note that it makes no mention of the medium through which the weapon passes, nor of its speed. While most guided weapons travel through the air at high speed, the first such air-launched weapon did not: it was in fact an anti-submarine homing torpedo, and its maximum speed when running underwater was 12kts. Developed in the United States, the homing torpedo was code-named the 'Mark 24 Mine' to conceal its true purpose. Its operational career is described in Chapter 4, 'Guided Missiles Make Their Mark (1)'. In the course of the Second World War these homing torpedoes were credited with the destruction of 38 German and Japanese submarines, and with inflicting damage to a further 33.

During the Second World War Germany fought two of the world's largest maritime powers, Great Britain and the United States, each of which possessed a navy that was far larger than her own. To redress this imbalance the *Luftwaffe* accorded the highest priority to the development of specialized weapons for use against enemy shipping. Two types of radio command-guided missiles resulted, the Henschel Hs 293 glider bomb and the Ruhrstahl Fritz-X guided bomb, and their operational careers are described in Chapter 5, 'Guided Missiles Make Their Mark (2)'. During August and September 1943 these weapons scored a string of successes. Fritz-X bombs sank the Italian battleship *Roma* and inflicted severe damage on her sister ship *Italia*, the Royal Navy's HMS *Warspite* and several Allied cruisers. The Hs 293 sank a number of smaller warships. The Allies quickly discovered the secrets of the missiles' radio guidance system, however, and introduced a special type of transmitter designed to jam the guidance signals. The result was that, from the spring of 1944, the two German guided missiles achieved little.

To take the story of specialized weapons into the jet age, in Chapter 12, 'Target Hanoi', we examine the first use of laser-guided and electro-optically guided 4,000lb bombs against a target in North Vietnam. The attack described is that on the famous Paul Doumer Bridge, in May 1972. Even a score of these powerful weapons, aimed with unprecedented accuracy at vulnerable points on the structure, failed to drop a span during the first attack. But they rendered the bridge unusable to wheeled traffic, and on the next day a follow-up attack, in which these weapons were aimed into the previously weakened area, did drop one of the spans. The narrative gives an insight into the force-package type of operation, showing the fighter escort and defence-suppression techniques that had evolved in the quarter-century since the end of the Second World War. From cockpit voice-recording tapes made in the aircraft at the time of the action, the reader can get a sense of the drama of modern air combat.

Airfield runways, like bridges, are small, hard targets that are very difficult to attack effectively unless specialized weaponry is used. Yet in Chapter 13, 'The First "Black Buck"', we see a Vulcan bomber having to do the job in with a stick of twenty-one 1,000lb 'dumb', general-purpose bombs for want of anything better. For the sheer determination of the crew to succeed in the face of atrocious weather conditions and mind-blowing distances, that raid takes a lot of beating. But the attack produced only one bomb crater in the runway at Port Stanley. The effort expended in making the attack was out of all proportion to the physical damage that it inflicted. Yet, as is often the case in aerial warfare, the psychological effect of the raid on the enemy was also out of all proportion to the physical damage that had been caused. The attack convinced the Argentine Air Force that Vulcans might strike at targets on the Argentine mainland at any time, and it withdrew its only specialized Mirage interceptor squadron to bases further north. The unit played little further part in the air fighting over the Falklands, and its withdrawal conceded air superiority in the skies over the islands to the Royal Navy Sea Harriers. That was the 'bottom-line' result of that first 'Black Buck' mission.

Reconnaissance is a vitally important aspect of air power and one that is sometimes neglected in accounts written on this subject. Yet the intelligence from a single photograph can have a major influence on the conduct of a land or an aerial bombing campaign. In Chapter 8, 'Reconnaissance over Normandy', we see how one Arado Ar 234 jet aircraft might have achieved decisive results had it gone into action just a couple of months earlier. In Chapter 15, 'Tornado Spyplanes Go to War' we see the state of the art of aerial reconnaissance as carried out during the recent war in the Persian Gulf. These aircraft carry no conventional film cameras. Instead, they use electro-optical, infra-red cameras similar to the camcorder to record the scene passing below the aircraft. The system is entirely passive and it works even on the darkest night. No longer is the main product of aerial reconnaissance the glossy photograph; now the buzz-word is 'electro-optical imagery'.

Chapter 14, 'Countdown to "Desert Storm"' brings together many of the lines of thought developed in previous chapters, to show the high-tech world of modern air warfare. The reader will see how the various disparate elements of the Coalition attack force came together during the first night's action in Operation 'Desert Storm'. The highly elaborate plan to neutralize parts of the enemy air defence system employed a spread of weapons ranging from armed helicopters, via cruise missiles, to F-117A stealth bombers. Scores of decoy drones were launched to bring the enemy missile batteries into action, then salvos of radiation-homing missiles were launched to knock out the missile guidance radars. In this chapter we also see the latest fighter escort techniques, in which powerful F-15 fighters were guided on to Iraqi fighters by E-3A AWACS planes orbiting far outside the battle area. That night teams of Royal Air Force Tornado fighter-bombers ran in at ultra-low altitudes to hit the runways and taxiways at Iraqi airfields with the purpose-built JP.233 airfield-denial weapons. At the same time F-111s and A-6s attacked pin-point targets with the laser-guided and electro-optically guided bombs.

I have assembled this series of accounts in order to provide readers with as wide-ranging as possible an overview of the nature of aerial warfare. If after reading the accounts the reader feels that he or she has a better insight into the true nature of this complex subject, I shall consider that my efforts have succeeded.

Alfred Price
Uppingham, Rutland

Chapter 18

By Zeppelin to Africa

The huge airlift of troops and equipment to support the recent
conflict in the Persian Gulf made unprecedented demands on
Western military air transport fleets. But at least the crews
knew where they expected to land before they took off, and
they could be confident that they would not be called upon
to fight as infantrymen when they reached their destination.
It was quite different for those who set out for the first-ever
intercontinental military airlift mission, almost three quarters
of a century earlier . . .

In September 1917, the First World War was in its fourth year. In France and on the Eastern Front the opposing armies were locked in the deadly stalemate of trench warfare. Far away from all of this, in the German Protectorate of East Africa (now Tanzania), German and German-African troops were fighting a classic guerrilla-type war in the south-eastern highlands against overwhelmingly superior Allied forces. The German commander, *General* Paul von Lettow-Vorbeck, mounted occasional but sharp attacks then withdrew into the bush to avoid the larger forces sent in pursuit.

Thanks to the Allied naval blockade, the German troops in East Africa were desperately short of ammunition, weapons, medical supplies and every type of equipment. At the Colonial Office in Berlin one of the officials drafted an imaginative proposal for a method of circumventing the blockade and getting supplies through to the beleaguered force – by Zeppelin.

The idea was passed to the Imperial German Naval Airship Division for consideration, and when its staff officers investigated it they found that there were several major obstacles. First, the nearest

German airship base to East Africa was at Jamboli (now Yambol) in Bulgaria, 3,600 miles away by the most direct route. No airship in existence could carry a useful load over so great a distance, though it might be possible to modify one of the craft under construction to do so. Second, since the Germans had no air base in Africa where the airship could refuel and replenish its supply of hydrogen, the flight would be a one-way mission. Third, this was a venture into unknown territory in more senses than one. No airship had ever attempted to fly so far over desert or tropical areas. It would encounter temperature variations between the hottest part of the day and the coldest part of the night that would be much greater than any previously experienced. These would induce large differences between the temperature of the hydrogen in the gas cells and that of the outside air, which could give rise handling problems not encountered before. Fourth, the maps of the interior of Africa were unreliable and accurate navigation would be difficult. And fifth, and not least, the Allies had several air bases in north Africa and in East Africa, which meant that the Zeppelin could come under attack from hostile aircraft.

Certainly the operation was a high-risk venture, but the risks were far outweighed by the physical and moral gains if the scheme succeeded. *Fregattenkapitän* (Captain) Peter Strasser, Chief of the Imperial Naval Airship Division, fervently endorsed the undertaking and commented:

> Completion of the operation will not only provide immediate assistance for the brave Protectorate troops, but will be an event which will once more enthuse the German people and arouse admiration throughout the world.

Admiral von Holtzendorff, Chief of Imperial Naval Staff, was equally enthusiastic and so was the German Kaiser when the proposals were submitted to him for final approval. Detailed planning for the operation, code-named 'China Matter', went ahead rapidly and under the strictest secrecy.

Had this been a normal operation, the Navy would have placed an experienced airship commander in charge of it. But if things went according to plan neither the airship nor any member of its crew would return in the foreseeable future, and when they reached their destination the crew of the Zeppelin would join the German ground forces in Africa and continue the fight as infantrymen. Always short of experienced commanders, the Naval Airship Service could not afford to lose one of them in such a venture. As a result, a relatively junior and inexperienced Zeppelin commander,

Kapitänleutnant (Lieutenant-Commander) Ludwig Bockholt, was chosen to take command of the 'China Matter'.

Zeppelin *L57*, whose construction was about to begin at Friedrichshafen, was chosen for the mission. To provide the extra lift necessary to carry the greater payload, the hull was lengthened by 99ft to make room for two additional gas cells. With a hydrogen capacity of 2,418,000 cu ft she was to be the largest airship yet built.

Several other changes were made to the Zeppelin to suit it for its unique mission. When it arrived in East Africa it was expected that the crew would deflate the craft and strip away everything that might be of use to the German forces. The radio transmitter and receiver, one of the engines, a dynamo and tanks containing the remaining petrol and lubricating oil were all to be removed and reassembled into a transportable ground radio station. Light alloy girders unbolted from the hull would support the aerials. Other girders would be removed and reassembled into a framework to support large areas of cotton fabric removed from the outer covering, to provide lightweight portable shelters for men and equipment. *L57* even had walkways around the hull made of leather – which could be unstitched and made into boots for the soldiers.

The much-modified airship made her maiden flight on 26 September 1917, but fate decreed that she would never leave Germany. Early the following month, following her fourth flight at the airship base at Jterbog near Berlin, a wind squall caught the Zeppelin and slammed her into the ground. Her back was broken and shortly afterwards the hydrogen exploded into flames. The crumpled structure sank to the ground and burned out. Fortunately for the crew, they had all scrambled clear of the airship before she caught fire.

Bockholt accepted the blame for the loss. He had been under pressure to complete the flight trials of the airship as quickly as possible, and in doing so he had ordered the flight to proceed despite an adverse weather forecast. A more experienced commander might have acted differently, but, as we have noted, a more experienced commander was not available. Moves to replace Bockholt were overruled at the highest level, and the young officer remained in command of 'China Matter'.

Meanwhile, in German East Africa events had also taken a turn for the worse. During September British troops cornered parts of von Lettow-Vorbeck's force and in the bitter fighting that followed both sides suffered serious losses. Radio communications between the German force and the homeland were poor, and the main source of information on the action available to Berlin came from intercepted enemy reports which spoke of an important British victory.

ZEPPELIN *L59*

Role: Transport airship; crew of 22.
Powerplant: Five Maybach HSLu petrol engines, each developing 240hp. One was mounted aft of the forward car, two were mounted in the rear car driving a single propeller via clutch mechanisms, and two were carried in the two separate engine cars suspended from the hull.
Armament: Several rifle-calibre machine guns were carried.
Performance: Maximum speed (all engines running) 64mph; cruising speed (one engine stopped for maintenance) 40mph.
Gas capacity: 2,418,700 cu ft held in 16 gas cells. This gave a gross lifting capability of 174,000lb under standard atmospheric conditions and a usable lifting capability of 114,400lb after the 59,600lb unladen weight of the airship structure and engines had been subtracted.
Dimensions: Length 743ft; diameter 78ft 5in.

Cargo carried by L59 during Africa operation (lb)

Small-arms ammunition, 381,000 rounds	21,777
20 machine guns and spare barrels	2,550
Medical supplies	5,790
Mail; miscellaneous items	770
Total	30,887

Consumables carried by L59 during Africa operation (lb)

Petrol	47,800
Lubricating oil	3,360
Water ballast	20,200
Total	71,360

If 'China Matter' were to reap any of its sought-after benefits, it had to be undertaken quickly. Within two days of the loss of *L57*, the Naval Airship Service reassigned its next airship to be laid down, *L59*, to the Africa mission. Workers at the Staaken factory toiled round the clock to prepare the Zeppelin in a similar fashion to her sister-ship, and *L59* was completed in the remarkably short period of sixteen days. She made her maiden flight on 25 October, and successfully completed her trials. Then she was loaded with the 13¾ tons of supplies to be delivered to Africa, and she flew to her jumping-off base in Bulgaria on 4 November.

Still there was a dearth of information on the whereabouts of the main body of von Lettow-Vorbeck's troops. Unless he received further instructions by radio, Bockholt's orders were to make for the area between Lake Nyasa and the Indian Ocean (close to the present-day border between Tanzania and Mozambique) and search for his countrymen there. If he found what looked like a body of friendly troops, he was to remain outside the range of small-arms fire while a petty officer volunteer jumped by parachute and made contact with the troops. If the man signalled confirmation that the troops were friendly, the airship was to descend.

After a couple of false starts, *L59* commenced her unique mission shortly after dawn on 21 November. At Jamboli the weather was almost perfect for the launch, with a northerly breeze of about 5mph and a ground temperature close to freezing point (the higher the temperature of the hydrogen in the cells compared with the ambient air, the greater the craft's lift). Each gas cell was filled to 95 per cent capacity, to allow room for the hydrogen to expand when the airship reached her cruising altitude. Fully loaded and ballasted, the airship was 'weighed off' with her lift and weight exactly balanced. On the order 'Airship out of the hangar – March!' the 400-strong ground handling party shuffled forwards, dragging the Zeppelin into the open like a gigantic broadsword being withdrawn from its scabbard.

Once the airship was clear of the shed the ground party halted, holding the craft stationary as her five engines stuttered into life. While they were warmed up, the big, 14ft diameter, two-blade propellers remained stationary in the horizontal position, their shafts declutched from the engines.

At 8.30 a.m., satisfied that all was ready, Bockholt barked the order 'Up ship'. At intervals along the length of the ship the command was repeated, and the ground party released its collective hold. At the pull of a toggle in the control car, 550lb of water cascaded from ballast bags to restore the Zeppelin to its lighter-than-air state. The craft drifted sluggishly upwards and once she was well clear of the ground the commander ordered the propellers to be engaged. There was a clanking of telegraphs in the engine cars, and the propellers started to turn. Slowly gaining speed and altitude, *L59* edged round gently until she was pointing almost due south. The great adventure had begun.

For readers who are not familiar with the large rigid airship and its method of operation, a brief description of the craft might be appropriate at this point. From nose to tail the *L59* measured 743ft – more than three times the length of a Boeing 747 jumbo jet – and her 91ft girth was more than four times that of the modern airliner. In addition to the 13¾ tons of supplies, the Zeppelin carried 21 tons of petrol, 1½ tons of lubricating oil and 9 tons of water ballast. With the crew of 22 living in spartan accommodation and supplied with food for ten days, in the fully loaded state the airship's gross weight was just over 77¼ tons.

CREW COMPOSITION OF L59

For the flight to Africa the airship carried a crew of 22:
Commanding Officer
Second-in-Command
Rudder operator: One rating plus relief.
Elevator operator: One rating plus relief. This crewman was also
responsible for operating the gas valves and releasing ballast.
Navigator: one warrant officer.
Radio operator: One petty officer plus relief.
Senior Engineer: One warrant officer.
Engine room mechanics: One rating stationed at each of the
five engines, plus five reliefs.
One sailmaker to make repairs on the gas cells and outer covering.
One medical doctor (not part of the normal crew of a Zeppelin).

The crew was divided into two watches. Those not on duty served
as additional lookouts, or rested in hammocks strung across the
main gangway that ran the length of the airship's hull.

Note: The big rigid airships were controlled in the manner of
sea-going ships rather than aeroplanes. The officer of the watch
stood on the bridge and made the flying control decisions, which
were carried out by the two ratings who operated the craft's
rudders and elevators. Control of the engines was ordered via
telegraph indicators similar to those fitted to a ship, and carried out
by mechanics in the engine cars.

Four gondolas hung below the hull of the airship, arranged in
diamond fashion. The front gondola, or control car, housed the captain,
the second-in-command, the radio operator, one rating to operate
the rudders and another to operate the elevators. At the rear of the
car was a hefty 6-cylinder Maybach HSLu petrol engine developing
240hp, driving a two-blade pusher propeller via a reduction gear. The
two side gondolas each accommodated one of these engines driving
a pusher propeller; and the rear gondola housed two such engines,
which were clutched to the same shaft and drove a single pusher
propeller. During normal operations each engine had a mechanic in
constant attendance. One of the problems of the rigid airships was that
they were seriously underpowered, and with a total of only 1,200hp
the heavily laden *L59* suffered from this affliction more than most.

Assisted by the moderate tail wind, the first twelve hours of the
Zeppelin's flight were relatively uneventful. For two hours in every
ten, each engine was shut down in turn for maintenance. Once the

craft had left behind the mountainous area of eastern Turkey, the crew established her in the cruise at altitudes of about 2,000ft, maintaining an airspeed of about 40mph on the four running engines. A major difficulty facing Bockholt was the lack of any advanced meteorological information on conditions along the route. He was ignorant of the existence of difficult conditions until he ran into them, literally. Don Layton, an airship skipper who amassed some 4,000 flying hours aboard US Navy blimps between 1947 and 1957, described the problem:

> It would have made all the difference if the crew could have received meteorological information by radio along the route. That would not have solved the problem of the head winds, but the crew could have mitigated their effect by re-routing or climbing or descending to avoid the worst of them. The crew could also have avoided areas where there were extremes of temperature, by routing around those places if they knew where they were. But they didn't have ground stations that could tell them if there was a hot spot ahead.

The lack of information soon made itself felt. On the first evening, as the airship headed over the Mediterranean, the weather suddenly deteriorated into an electrical storm. The wind rose, and to avoid the worst of the turbulence and the headwind Bockholt descended to 1,000ft. Rain and hail lashed the hull, then a sudden panic cry from the upper look-out station chilled the blood of all who heard it: 'The ship is on fire!' In fact it was only St Elmo's Fire, the shimmering, fluorescent blue glow caused by the build-up of static electricity. Large areas of the upper part of the hull were bathed in the strange light. It was the inexperienced lookout's first sight of the spectacle – which, despite its terrifying appearance, was quite harmless.

Shortly after dawn on the 22nd, the Zeppelin crossed the Egyptian coast near Sollum. The British possessed air bases in the Nile Delta, and to avoid these Bockholt kept well to the west. Once the ship was over the desert, identifiable ground features were few and far between, and the maps showing their positions were unreliable. The crew kept track of their movement southwards by a series of position lines from sun shots taken from, the upper platform. The airship's drift and ground speed were calculated (with remarkable accuracy) by using a stopwatch to measure the time it took for its shadow to pass a point on the ground.

As the day progressed the crew encountered a set of problems quite different from those experienced when flying the airship over

Europe. The hot sun playing on the hull heated the hydrogen, until that in some of the gas cells was 10°C warmer than the surrounding air. The phenomenon, known as 'superheating', caused the gas to expand and generate extra lift. In these circumstances the additional lift was an embarrassment, however. If the airship drifted above 2,500ft the pressure of the gas in the cells would exceed that outside the hull, and the automatic pressure release valves would then open and vent off some of the hydrogen. Like a miser hoarding gold, Bockholt had to minimize losses of the vital lifting gas. When the temperature fell, as it inevitably would that night, he would need all of his hydrogen.

To generate the negative dynamic lift to counter the unwanted lift, *L59* flew nose-down over the desert. Don Layton described the problems of maintaining an airship in that flying attitude:

> *L59* was 743 feet long, and if her nose went up or down a couple of degrees she produced a tremendous amount of drag. Then she would lose a lot of speed. If the nose of the craft was pushed down too far, it was easy to lose control. Something I used to enjoy doing with the pressure airships, if you are 'light' and flying nose down to prevent her gaining altitude and you are going too slowly, the airship would stall and drift upwards. It is the only vehicle I know where you can stall, and go up!

The manoeuvre that provided amusement for Layton during training flights would have cost Bockholt more hydrogen than he could afford.

Quite apart from that of maintaining the Zeppelin at the desired altitude, her crew had to contend with other problems. The hot air rising from the shimmering desert sands caused the craft to rise and fall gently but continually, like a cradle rocked by some giant invisible hand. The unfamiliar motion affected several crew members, and reduced even veteran seamen to the indignity of airsickness. In addition, the lookouts suffered blinding headaches from gazing for too long at the bright reflections off the sand.

During the afternoon the forward Maybach engine began to vibrate and had to be shut down. On opening the casing the mechanics found that the reduction gears had developed cracks that could not be repaired in flight. The motor could not be used again. With one 'good' engine always stopped for maintenance, the airship was to continue the flight on three engines. As luck would have it, the 'lost' engine drove the dynamo that supplied power to the airship's radio transmitter, which meant that the latter could not be used either.

Still the airship continued determinedly southwards, and late that night she passed over the Nile at Wadi Haifa. By midnight *L59* was well into the Sudan and approaching the latitude of Khartoum. Since leaving Jamboli she had covered 2,800 miles and was more than half way to her destination. Despite the baking heat of the day, followed by sub-zero temperatures at night, the crew made light of their physical discomfort The prospects of success increased with each hour that passed and they knew that their triumphant arrival would give new heart to the Fatherland and its allies, and cause dismay to their foes.

Yet circumstances now conspired to defeat the best efforts of the doughty crew. Intercepted British radio reports reaching Berlin painted a disturbing picture of Allied troops thrusting into parts of German East Africa that had, previously been considered secure. This, coupled with the lack of information on the location of von Lettow-Vorbeck's forces, gave little chance of the Zeppelin making a successful rendezvous. Reluctantly, the Imperial Naval Staff gave orders for the recall signal to be broadcast to *L59*:

> Break off the operation, return. The enemy has captured the greater part of the Makonde Highlands, also Kitangari. The Portuguese are attacking the Protectorate from the south.

The Zeppelin's radio operator picked up the message but, lacking power for his transmitter, he could not acknowledge its receipt. The plaintive signal would be repeated at regular intervals during the days to follow, while in Berlin there were mounting fears for the safety of *L59* and her crew.

Aboard the Zeppelin, the recall signal caused shock and dismay. The crew had risked so much and achieved so much, for nothing. No longer buoyed by the adrenalin of impending glory, several men succumbed to the discomforts and developed symptoms of nervous tension and feverishness. Worse followed, and soon. As the airship headed back for Europe, a problem that had been building up since nightfall neared crisis proportions. After sunset the temperature of the hydrogen fell rapidly, giving rise to 'supercooling', the reverse of what had happened during the day. As the hydrogen slowly cooled, its volume contracted, and gradually the Zeppelin ceased to be a 'lighter-than-air' craft.

To maintain the 3,000ft altitude necessary to clear high ground in the area, Bockholt ordered the helmsman to hold the craft in a 4-degree nose-up attitude, with all four usable engines running at full power. The release of 4,400lb of water ballast eased the problem

Zeppelin L.59 being hauled out of its shed for a proving flight, during her preparation for the flight to Africa.

The 22-man crew of L.59 pictured after their return from the epic flight to Africa in November 1917. The captain of the airship, *Kapitänleutnant* Ludwig Bockholt, is in the centre of the rear row wearing the dark hat and dark leather coat.

Junkers Ju 87 Stuka dive bombers of *Sturzkampfgeschwader* 5 returning from an attack on a target in Russia.

View over the nose of a Stuka in its near-vertical attack dive, which enabled it to deliver its bomb with great accuracy.

If enemy fighters caught up with Stukas, the latter often suffered losses. This dive bomber of *StG 77* was one of several shot down near Chichester on 18 August 1940.

Krydziai airfield in Lithuania pictured on the morning of 22 June 1941. This photograph was taken shortly before it came under attack from Junkers Ju 88s of *Kampfgeschwader 76*.

This enlargement of Krydziai airfield shows the airfield's Tupolev SB-2 twin-engined light bombers lined up as if for inspection, indicating that the attackers had achieved complete surprise.

A Heinkel He 111 bomber seen getting airborne with two 2,200 pound bombs mounted under the fuselage.

The Bristol Beaufighter, the first effective night fighter type to enter service in the RAF, came close to shooting down Hans Georg Baetcher during the early morning darkness on 9 July 1941.

The Mitsubishi B5N 'Kate' with a Type 91 torpedo under the fuselage taking off from a Japanese carrier. The Type 91 was considerably more effective that its US counterpart, and it played an important part in assisting the Japanese expansion in the Pacific during the early months of the war.

The Grumman F-4F Wildcat was the only effective fighter type operated by the US Navy when the Pacific War began.

The Japanese light carrier *Shoho* under heavy attack and taking a torpedo hit amidships, shortly before she capsized and sank.

The US Navy carrier *Lexington*, abandoned, on fire and listing after. After the action, fumes had leaked from a damaged aviation fuel tank, and when they ignited they caused a major explosion.

A Vickers Wellington maritime patrol aircraft with the Leigh Light extended beneath the rear fuselage, and a radome for the ASV Mark III radar under the nose.

A British submarine illuminated by a Leigh Light during the trials with the device.

To protect themselves against attack from the air, U-boats were fitted with batteries of anti-aircraft weapons. This was the installation on U-802, with three mountings carrying a total of eight 20mm cannon.

Despite this armament, Allied aircraft continued to press home attacks on U-boats caught on the surface, as in this case of a US Navy Liberator.

Colonel 'Hub' Zemke led the P-47 Thunderbolts of the 56th Fighter Group escorting the bombers part of the way to Berlin on 6 March 1944. During the action he shot down a Fw 190 trying to close in and engage the bombers.

The pilot of the German fighter was *Leutnant* Wolfgang Kretchmer of *Jagdgeschwader 1*, who suffered moderate burns from which he has since recovered. After the war he met Zemke and they became firm friends.

An Arado Ar234 prototype gets airborne using the unusual take-off trolley.

Photograph taken during Eric Sommer's historic jet reconnaissance flight over Normandy on 2 August 1944, showing the Allied 'Mulberry' artificial harbour off the coast of Asnelles-sur-Mer.

Focke Wulf Fw 190 *Sturmbock* aircraft fitted with a powerful Mk 180 30mm cannon in each outer wing position, for attacks on US bomber formations from short range.

Feldwebel Hans Schaefer of *Jagdgeschwader 3*, wearing a leather flying jacket bearing the 'whites of the eyes' badge signifying his *Sturmgruppe* status.

Sturmbock aircraft of *Jagdgeschwader 300* being prepared for action.

A B-24 Liberator in serious trouble after taking several hits from 30mm rounds during a *Sturmgruppe* attack.

F-4D Phantom of the 8th Tactical Fighter Wing that took part in the attack on the Paul Doumer Bridge at Hanoi on 10 May 1972. The attack was the first to employ laser guided 2,000 pound bombs over North Vietnam. One of these weapons is seen on the port outer bomb station, with the Pave Knife laser marking pod on the port inner station.

The North Vietnamese MiG 21 MF force was heavily committed during the action on 10 May 1972.

Above: Sea Harriers of No 801 Squadron aboard HMS *Invincible*, loaded with Sidewinder missiles, about to take off for an air defence mission.

Left: Chinook 'Bravo November' delivering supplies between ships in the British task force.

Below: Low-level attack: a Dagger fighter bomber of *Gruppo 6* of the Argentine Air Force delivering an attack on supply ships in San Carlos Water.

General Dynamics F-111F of the 48th Tactical Fighter Wing, carrying its standard load of two 2,200 pound laser-guided bombs during attacks in Iraq.

Panavia Tornado GR1s each carrying two P233 airfield-denial weapons under the fuselage, on a training flight before the war began.

RAF Armourers loading a JP.233 canister on to a Tornado.

of maintaining altitude, but not for long. The process of 'super-cooling' continued, until in some cells the hydrogen was 6°C lower than the surrounding air. Never before had an airship encountered so great a swing in temperature in such a short time.

Matters came to a head shortly before 3 a.m. that morning. Without the crew realizing it, the airship ran into a layer of relatively warm air, which further decreased the lift from the hydrogen. When the helmsman increased the nose-up attitude to hold the required 3,000ft altitude, the Zeppelin suddenly stalled and began to fall out of control. She came down relatively slowly, at about 150ft a minute, but the situation was no less serious for that. Don Layton outlined the problem:

> An airship has a lot of area when viewed from below. When it was coming down under those conditions it was like a huge inflated 'parachute'. It did everything slowly, but you had no control over it. Once you'd lost the airflow over the fins you didn't have any rudder control and elevator control was sloppy. Although the airship was going down relatively slowly, unless something was done she wasn't going to stop. Once she started going down, she had an awful lot of momentum.

The knee-jerk reaction would have been a panic release of ballast to lighten the airship, but her commander had to be much more circumspect. Layton described a flight in a free balloon as part of his training as an airship pilot, when he went down out of control:

> You start coming down so you throw out ballast. You still go down so you throw out more. And still you go down. I threw out the rest of the ballast, then the instrument panel, then our flight jackets. I thought it was never going to stop going down until it hit the ground. Finally it did stop. But by then we had thrown out too much, and the balloon started going up again! That was what happened if you got behind what the craft was doing. It would have been even worse for a big craft like the *L59*, particularly if she was coming down nose first or tail first.

Bockholt took the appropriate stall recovery action for an airship, ordering the release of some ballast and having the propellers declutched from the engines until he had recovered control. When these measures failed to arrest the descent, he jettisoned part of the cargo. Only after the airship had been lightened by 6,600lb, having narrowly missed smashing into the side of a hill on the way, was its

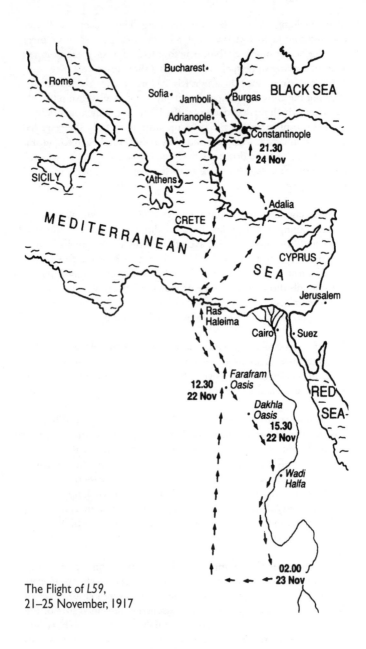

The Flight of *L59*,
21–25 November, 1917

downward drift halted. When *L59* bottomed out she was uncomfortably close to the ground, in a ravine with steep-sided and craggy ridges on either side. As she began to float upwards, her commander ordered the propellers to be engaged and as the craft slowly picked up speed he gingerly manoeuvred her away from the danger. It had been a mouth-drying experience for all on board.

L59 retraced her earlier path across Egypt and left the coast early in the afternoon of the 24th. She crossed the Mediterranean without incident, and darkness had fallen when she began to re-cross the mountains of eastern Turkey. And there the crew had another brush with death. The Zeppelin suffered a re-run of the near-catastrophe over the Sudan, and for much the same reason: flying 'heavy' at night, relying on dynamic lift to maintain altitude, she caught a down-draught and started to descend out of control. Only after the release of 3 tons of ballast and ammunition was control restored.

The airship arrived at Jamboli at 4.30 a.m. in the morning of the 25th. Nobody there had anticipated that she would return and, since her radio transmitter was out of action, she appeared unannounced. *L59* had to circle the base for a couple of hours until the necessary landing party was assembled, and not until 7.40 a.m. was she finally settled into the hands of the ground crew. Mentally and physically exhausted, the captain and crew climbed slowly from the craft that had brought them back safely but unexpectedly.

The attempt to transport supplies to the German troops in East Africa had failed, but that was no fault of *L59* or her crew. The men had done all that had been asked of them, and they could indeed be proud of their achievement: in a flight lasting 95 hours 5 minutes, just under four days, they had covered a distance of 4,200 miles – about as far as from London to Miami. That distance would have easily taken them to any rendezvous with von Lettow-Vorbeck, if he could have been found. The flight had broken every distance record by a wide margin, with a cargo heavier than any previously transported by air. And the crew could have gone a long way further had they been required to do so: the 2,760 Imp gallons of petrol remaining in the Zeppelin's tanks when she landed at Jamboli could have kept her engines running for a further 2½ days.

In time of peace Ludwig Bockholt and his men would have been fêted as national heroes, but this was wartime and other long-distance missions were being considered for the modified Zeppelin. Her flight remained shrouded in secrecy and would not be revealed until after the war. In East Africa the German commander succeeded in rallying his forces after the hard fought-battles during the autumn, and they continued to mount occasional attacks until the end of the war. There was no attempt to resurrect the idea of supplying the troops by Zeppelin, however.

Neither *L59* nor most of her intrepid crew would long outlive their return from Africa. The airship reverted to normal bombing operations and on 7 April 1918 she set out from Jamboli for an attack on the Royal Navy base at Valletta, Malta. On the way to the target the Zeppelin suddenly burst into flames and plunged into the sea. There were no survivors. No Allied forces in the area reported any engagement that can be linked to the incident. A subsequent German investigation concluded that '*L59* was probably lost to accidental causes, possibly as a result of leaking petrol catching fire and igniting the hydrogen'.

In summing up the flight of *L59* to Africa and the performance of her crew, Don Layton commented:

> I think the flight was one of the great epics of aviation. In terms of hours flown it was the longest operational flight, ever. That would have imposed considerable stress on the crew over a very long period. On the way out everybody was buoyed up, full of adrenalin and ready to go. But I think that on the return flight their morale must have been very low. Another point to consider is that Bockholt was an inexperienced airship commander, and his second-in-command was even less experienced. It is likely that the captain had to stay close to the controls throughout almost the entire four-day flight. I take my hat off to Bockholt; I think they ought to put up a monument to him some place.

Chapter 19

Battle of Britain Day: 15 September 1940

In August 1940 the Royal Air Force attacked targets in Germany,
in retaliation for bombs that had fallen on London. The move
enraged Hitler, who ordered a massive bombardment to be
unleashed against London by way of reprisal. The new phase
in the Battle of Britain opened on 7 September, when several
hundred bombers attacked the dock areas to the east of the city,
causing severe damage and several large fires. In the week that
followed there were three further daylight attacks on the capital.
For the fifth action in the series, to take place on Sunday 15
September, the Luftwaffe *planned to deliver two separate attacks*
on the city, both with a strong escort of fighters. The resultant
action would mark the climax of the Battle of Britain.

During the first four German daylight attacks on London, on
each occasion a large proportion of the defending fighters had
failed to come to grips with the raiding formations. The initial attack
had surprised the defenders and the fighters had been positioned
to meet yet another attack on their airfields. During the next three
daylight attacks on the capital, banks of cloud hindered the tracking
of aircraft over southern England by ground observers; the result was
a series of scrappy actions with relatively light losses on both sides.

Luftwaffe intelligence officers ascribed a quite different reason to
the lack of a ferocious fighter reaction that characterized several of
the actions in August: they thought it was a symptom of the long-
predicted collapse of RAF Fighter Command. If the latter assessment were accurate, the correct German strategy was to mount

further large-scale attacks on London that would force the surviving British fighters into battle to suffer further losses from the escorting Messerschmitts.

Seeking to follow up its apparent advantage, the *Luftwaffe* planned to mount two separate attacks on the British capital for 15 September, one against an important part of the rail system and the other against the docks. Every Messerschmitt Bf 109 unit in *Luftwaffe 2* was to be employed in supporting these attacks, several flying double sorties.

In fact, in the second week in September Fighter Command was numerically as strong as it had been when the Battle began. German intelligence officers had underestimated British fighter production, and also the ability of the repair organization to get damaged fighters back into action. Moreover, although Fighter Command had lost several of its experienced pilots, there had been a steady infusion of these from other commands and also from the air forces of countries under German occupation. The force had also gained considerable combat experience in the course of the Battle. The action about to take place would be no 'walk-over' for the *Luftwaffe*.

The first attack on the capital was to take place during the late morning, with a raiding force comprising twenty-one Messerschmitt Bf 109 fighter-bombers of *Lehrgeschwader 2* and twenty-seven Dornier 17s of *Kampfgeschwader 76*. Providing open and close-cover escort for the bombers were about 180 Bf 109s. The fighter-bombers were to hit rail targets, then the Dorniers were to deliver a precision bombing attack on the important swathe of railway lines and viaducts running through the borough of Battersea.

Soon after the first of the German bombers got airborne, however, this part of the day's operation started to go awry. As the Dorniers climbed away from their base airfields heading for the Pas de Calais to link up with the fighter escort, the aircraft ran into a layer of cloud that was considerably thicker than forecast. *Feldwebel* Theodor Rehm, a navigator in one of the bombers, described what happened next:

> In cloud the visibility was so bad one could see only the flight leader's plane a few metres away. In our bomber four pairs of eyes strained to keep the aircraft in sight as its ghostly shape disappeared and reappeared in the alternating darkness and light. One moment it was clearly visible, menacingly large and near; then suddenly it would disappear from view, in the same place but shrouded in billowing vapour. At the same time we also scanned the sky around for other aircraft, ready to bellow a warning if there were a risk of collision. After several anxious minutes that felt like an eternity, we emerged from cloud at about 3,500 metres [11,000ft]. Around

us were the familiar shapes of Dorniers spread over a large area in ones, twos and threes. Our attack formation had been shattered.

Major Alois Lindmayr, the German formation leader, flew a series of wide orbits to allow the others to re-form behind him. Two of the bombers failed to rejoin the formation and returned to base.

Ten minutes late, the remaining bombers reached the Pas de Calais and picked up their escorts, then swung on to a north-westerly heading for London. The Messerschmitts of the close-cover and open-cover forces held position around the bombers, while those assigned to the free-hunting patrols sped out in front of the force. Now for a second time the weather intervened in the proceedings to the raiders' disadvantage, for at the bombers' altitude of 16,000ft there was a fierce 90mph headwind.

Running in at altitudes around 23,000ft, the Bf 109 fighter-bombers reached London unchallenged by the defenders. As intended, the high-flying Messerschmitts looked like any other German free-hunting patrol, and, given the choice, RAF pilots preferred to leave those well alone. Only one of the defending pilots' reports, that from Pilot Officer P. Gunning of No 46 Squadron, can be linked to this incursion. He reported seeing a force of Messerschmitt 109s pass over him, but these aircraft '. . . did not appear to attempt to attack anyone below.' Certainly the German fighter-bomber pilots had no intention of becoming embroiled with enemy fighters unless they were directly threatened. It was one of those confrontations in which both sides were quite happy to leave the other unmolested.

The fighter-bombers reached the city and their leader, *Hauptmann* Otto Weiss, banked his aircraft steeply and picked out one of the smaller urban railway stations. Then, with his two wing-men maintaining close formation on either side, he pushed his Messerschmitt

SUPERMARINE SPITFIRE Mk I

Role: Single-seat fighter.
Powerplant: One Rolls-Royce Merlin III 12-cylinder, liquid-cooled engine developing 1,030hp at 16,250ft.
Armament: Eight Browning .303in machine guns mounted in the wings.
Performance: Maximum speed 353mph at 20,000ft; climb to 20,000ft, 7min 42sec.
Normal operational take-off weight: 6,050lb.
Dimensions: Span 36ft 10in; length 29ft 11in; wing area 242 sq ft.
Date of first production Spitfire I: May 1938.

into a 45-degree dive and lined up on the target. After a descent of just over 3,000ft, Weiss released his 550lb bomb and his wing-men released theirs, then all three planes pulled out of their dives. The other Messerschmitts in the force delivered their attacks in a similar manner. It was an inaccurate method of aiming, however, and most of the bombs fell across residential areas in the boroughs of Lambeth, Streatham, Dulwich and Penge. The raiders caused little damage and few casualties, then withdrew without loss.

While this was happening, the Dorniers and their escorting Messerschmitts fought their way across Kent to get to the capital. Throughout this time the British fighter controllers fed eleven squadrons of Spitfires and Hurricanes into the action in ones and twos, to set up a series of skirmishing actions around the raiding force. The Messerschmitts responded energetically to each attempt to break through to their charges, however, and the bombers reached the eastern outskirts of London without suffering a single loss.

Now, however, the delay the Dorniers had incurred when they reassembled their formation over France, coupled with the powerful headwind experienced over Kent, meant that the bombers arrived in the target area more than half an hour late. The twin-engine aircraft carried sufficient fuel to cope with such an eventuality, but the Messerschmitts did not. For the latter, even under optimum conditions, the British capital lay close to the limit of their effective operational radius of action when flying from bases in France. Now they were running low on fuel, and the escorts were forced to break away from their charges and turn for home. As the Dorniers lined up for their bombing run on Battersea, the last of the escorts departed.

In the No 11 Group command bunker at Uxbridge, Air Vice-Marshal Keith Park had no way of knowing his enemy's predicament. He had already decided to fight his main action over the eastern outskirts of the capital, however, and had directed seven squadrons of Spitfires and Hurricanes to that area to engage the raiding force. In addition, from No 12 Group to the north, Squadron Leader Douglas Bader was making for the capital at the head of a 'Big Wing' with five further squadrons of fighters.

The main action began shortly after mid-day, 16,000ft above Brixton. Holding his Dornier straight and level for the bomb run, *Feldwebel* Wilhelm Raab noticed what looked like a swarm of small flies emerge from behind cloud ahead of him:

> Of course they weren't flies. It was yet more British fighters, far in the distance but closing rapidly. I counted ten before I had to give up and concentrate on holding formation.

The pilot of the nearest 'small fly', Squadron Leader John Sample, was leading twenty Hurricanes of Nos 504 and 257 Squadrons in for the attack. Ahead of him he could see the Dorniers clearly, silhouetted against the tops of the clouds:

> As we converged I saw that there were about twenty of them and it looked as though it was going to be a nice party, for the other squadrons of Hurricanes and Spitfires also turned to join in. By the time we reached a position near the bombers we were over London. We had gained a little height on them, too, so when I gave the order to attack we were able to dive on them from their right.

To Raab and many of those in the Dorniers, it looked as if the enemy fighter pilots had waited until the Messerschmitts turned away before they delivered their main attack. The truth was more prosaic: Sample and the other British squadron commanders were ignorant of the Dornier crews' problems and were merely following the intercept instructions from their ground controllers. The fact that there were no escorts in the area was a lucky break for the RAF pilots, but from better experience they knew that the Messerschmitts had a nasty habit of turning up at the most inconvenient time. Everyone maintained a careful lookout.

Despite the sudden disappearance of the fighters that should have been escorting his Dorniers, Alois Lindmayr held his heading for the target. John Sample and his pilots picked out individual bombers in the formation and closed on them swiftly, firing long bursts. As they

---

DORNIER Do 17Z

Role: Four-seat bomber.
Powerplant: Two Bramo 323 Fafnir 9-cylinder, air-cooled radial engines each developing 1,000hp at take-off.
Armament: Normal operational bomb load 2,200lb. Defensive armament of six Rhienmetall Borsig MG 15 7.9mm machine guns in flexible mountings, two firing forwards, two firing rearwards and one firing from each side of the cabin.
Performance: Maximum speed 255mph at 13,120ft; normal formation cruising speed at 16,000ft, 180mph; radius of action with normal bomb load, 205 miles.
Normal operational take-off weight: 18,930lb.
Dimensions: Span 59ft 0¼in; length 51ft 9½in; wing area 592 sq ft.
Date of first production Do 17Z: Early 1939.

broke away, the Hurricanes of No 257 Squadron delivered their attack. Then the fighters split up into twos and threes and curved tightly to get behind the bombers for further attacks.

The Dornier crews held tight formation and traded blows with their tormentors, until the inevitable happened: one of the bombers suffered engine damage and was forced to drop behind the formation. The straggler immediately came under attack from several fighters and was badly shot up. Three of the crew, including the pilot, bailed out.

Things were going badly for *Kampfgeschwader 76* and they were about to get worse, for now Douglas Bader's 'Big Wing' arrived over the capital with its fifty-five fighters. The size of the force would later swell with the telling, and the official *Luftwaffe* report on the action noted: 'Over the target large formations of fighters (with up to 80 aircraft) intercepted.' For bomber crews who had been confidently assured a few hours earlier that Fighter Command was in its death throes, it was a devastating sight.

As Bader closed on the enemy force, the Dorniers were in the final seconds of their bombing run. Wilhelm Raab observed:

> With the British fighters whizzing through our formation, the leading aircraft began releasing their bombs. My navigator shouted *'Ziel!'* and released ours.

Each bomber in the formation disgorged a stick of twenty 110-pounders, then, lighter by about a ton, it began a sweeping curve to the left.

Flying on autopilot with two dead or dying crewmen on board, the Dornier that had left the formation continued on its north-westerly course across the capital. Four Hurricanes and a Spitfire from three different squadrons engaged the bomber, then John Sample ran in to deliver a further attack. Later he wrote:

> I found myself below another Dornier which had white smoke coming from it. It was being attacked by two Hurricanes and a Spitfire, and was travelling north and turning slightly to the right. As I could not see anything else to attack at that moment I climbed above him and did a diving attack. Coming in to the attack, I noticed what appeared to be a red light shining in the rear gunner's cockpit, but when I got closer I realised I was looking right through the gunner's cockpit into the pilot's and observer's cockpit beyond. The 'red light' was a fire. I gave it a quick burst and as I passed him on the right I looked in through the big glass nose of the Dornier. It was like a furnace inside.

Finally the lone Dornier was finished off in unconventional fashion by another member of Sample's squadron. Sergeant Ray Holmes ran in to deliver a head-on attack, but after a short burst his Hurricane's guns fell silent – he was out of ammunition. The fighter pilot made the snap decision to continue on and ram the enemy plane, and a split second later his port wing struck the rear fuselage of the Dornier. The collision sliced off the bomber's entire tail and, deprived of the balancing force provided by that vital appendage, the plane's nose dropped violently. The forward momentum maintained the aircraft on its previous flight path, however, imposing tremendous forces on the wing and causing the structure to fail. Both outer wing sections sheared away just outboard of the engines and the doomed bomber entered a violent spin.

The incident took place three miles high, almost exactly over Buckingham Palace. The Dornier still carried its bomb load, and the savage *g* forces now imposed further unsustainable stresses on the plane's already weakened structure. Two 110lb bombs and a container of incendiary bombs tore away from their mountings, smashed their way out of the aircraft and fell into space. One 110-pounder plunged into the roof of the Palace and passed through a couple of floors before coming to rest in the bathroom of one of the Royal Apartments. The other 110-pounder, and the container with sixteen incendiary bombs, landed in the Palace grounds. The high-explosive bombs failed to detonate but some of the incendiary bombs ignited on impact. The main part of the Dornier came down on the forecourt of Victoria Station, while the severed tail unit fell on a house in Vauxhall Bridge Road nearby. Borne on the strong northwesterly wind, the outer wing sections fluttered down slowly and covered more than a mile before they landed south of the Thames in Vauxhall. Ray Holmes's Hurricane did not emerge from the collision unscathed either. The port wing suffered severe damage and the fighter went out of control, and with some difficulty the pilot struggled out of his cockpit. The fighter plummeted into a road junction in Chelsea and Holmes landed by parachute in Pimlico.

Remarkably, considering that the bombs and the wreckage of both aircraft came down on built-up areas, nobody was injured on the ground and there was relatively little damage to property. The incendiary bombs starting small grass fires in the grounds of Buckingham Palace, but these were quickly extinguished by Palace staff. No member of the Royal Family was in the Palace at the time. Two of the crewmen who bailed out of the Dornier were taken into captivity soon after landing. The third man, the pilot, was less fortunate. He landed by parachute beside The Oval Underground station in Kennington, but before troops could reach him he was attacked by angry civilians and suffered fatal injuries.

As the formation of Dorniers withdrew from the capital it was under sustained attack from more than a dozen squadrons of fighters. Nine bombers suffered damage and were forced out of formation, and five of them were finished off shortly afterwards by fighters. Near Maidstone the Bf 109s assigned to cover the bombers' withdrawal linked up with them and shepherded the survivors home, assisted by the same 90mph wind that had impeded the raiding force on its way in.

Kampfgeschwader 76 had suffered a fearful mauling. Of the twenty-five bombers that had crossed the coast of England less than 50 minutes earlier, six had been shot down and four had been seriously damaged and only just made it back to France. Most of the fifteen Dorniers that stayed in formation had also taken lesser amounts of battle damage. Yet, considering the absence of escorts over the target and the overwhelming concentration of RAF fighters present, it is perhaps surprising that any of the Dorniers survived. The fact that three-quarters of the bombers managed to return to France is testimony to the tactical leadership of Alois Lindmayr and the flying skill and discipline of his crews. It is also testimony to the ruggedness of the Dornier 17's structure and its ability to withstand heavy punishment.

In contrast to Fighter Command's reaction to previous attacks on the capital, the system of fighter control that morning had functioned brilliantly: twenty-three squadrons with a total of 254 Spitfires and Hurricanes had been scrambled, and every squadron except one had made contact with the enemy.

As the survivors of the first attack on London crossed the coast of France, the bombers assigned to the second attack on the capital were airborne and heading for the Pas de Calais to rendezvous with their escorts. Far larger than the previous raiding force, this one comprised 114 Dorniers and Heinkel 111s. Their targets were in the Port of London to the east of the city the Royal Victoria, the West India and the Surrey Commercial Docks. About 360 German fighters were to support the incursion.

As soon as the incoming German force appeared on his plotting table, Air Vice-Marshal Keith Park initiated his riposte. Eight squadrons of Spitfires and Hurricanes were ordered to scramble and patrol in pairs over Sheerness, Chelmsford, Hornchurch and Kenley. During the ensuing minutes other squadrons followed them into the air.

After crossing the coast at Dungeness, the attack force wheeled on to a north-north-westerly heading, making for the capital. The raiders were arrayed in five separate *Gruppe*-sized formations, the smallest with eighteen and the largest with 29 bombers. The three leading formations flew in line abreast, three miles apart; the other two flew three miles behind the left and the right leading formations.

Soon after the bombers crossed the coast, three of the forward-deployed Spitfire units, Nos 41, 92 and 222 Squadrons, with a total of twenty-seven fighters, went into action. The escorting Messerschmitts moved into position to block the attacks and one of the German pilots, *Hauptmann* Fritz Losigkeit of *JG 26*, later recalled:

> After we crossed the coast the British fighters came in from a great height, going very fast. They broke through to the He 111s ahead of us and below, to attack the rear of the formation. During the dive some of the Spitfires became detached from the others. Using full throttle, my *Staffel* was able to catch up with them and I get into an attacking position. I fired a long burst and pieces broke away from the Spitfire's wing and fuselage. The pilot slid back the canopy and jumped from the cockpit. Overtaking rapidly, I pulled to the left of the Spitfire and saw his parachute open.

Probably the Spitfire that Losigkeit hit was that flown by Pilot Officer Bob Holland of No 92 Squadron. The latter suffered minor injuries on landing.

As the first of his fighters went into action, the last of Keith Park's day fighter units were taking off. No 11 Group had twenty-one squadrons of Spitfires and Hurricanes and everyone was now airborne. From No 12 Group in the north, Squadron Leader Douglas Bader was again on his way south at the head of the five-squadron 'Big Wing'. From No 10 Group in the west, three squadrons were on their way to meet the raiders. Fighter Command had now committed all 276 of the Spitfires and Hurricanes based close enough to the capital to assist with its defence. Winston Churchill was at Park's underground operations bunker at Uxbridge that day and he watched as the No 11 Group commander committed his entire force. Later the Prime Minister wrote:

> I became conscious of the anxiety of the Commander, who now stood still behind his subordinate's chair. Hitherto I had watched in silence. I now asked: 'What other reserves have we?' 'There are none,' said Air Vice-Marshal Park. In an account which he wrote about it afterwards he said that at this

I 'looked grave'. Well I might. What losses should we not suffer if our refuelling planes were caught on the ground by further raids of '40 plus' or '50 plus'! The odds were great; our margins small; the stakes infinite.

In this action the British fighters were outnumbered by more than two to one by the raiders; in terms of single-seat fighters, there were three Bf 109s airborne over southern England for every two Spitfires and Hurricanes. Keith Park's tactics during the afternoon engagement were the same as those he had employed in the morning. As the raiders tracked across Kent he again fed fighter squadrons into actions in pairs. In one of these encounters Nos 213 and 607 Squadrons, with twenty-three Hurricanes, delivered a head-on attack on the Dorniers of *Kampfgeschwader 3*. During this action there was another case of deliberate ramming, as Pilot Officer Paddy Stephenson of No 607 Squadron recalled:

> Our squadron was flying in four vics, in stepped-down formation. The bombers were flying in stepped-up formation. In a head-on attack each vic was supposed to pass above the aircraft being attacked, and immediately below the following bomber. To do this there needed to be a proper spacing between the vics in our squadron. My vic had moved too far forward and to break away upwards would have involved me in a crash with a Hurricane in the leading vic of our formation.

Stephenson made a quick decision: if there had to be a collision, it was far better to hit a foe rather than a friend. He held his heading towards the bomber and the Hurricane's starboard wing smashed into the starboard wing of one of the Dorniers, shattering both. *Feldwebel* Horst Schultz, one of the German bomber pilots, watched the approaching Hurricanes with wings blinking as they opened fire.

> The next moment there was an explosion in front of me, then pieces of planes were falling out of the sky like confetti. I didn't know whether a British fighter had collided with one of our planes, or if it had suffered a direct hit from flak. There was no time to brood about it: I had my own job to do.

The rammed Dornier immediately entered a vicious spin, the savage *g* forces pinning the terrified crew in the cabin until the bomber plunged into a wood near Kilndown. Deprived of a large section of one wing, Stephenson's Hurricane rolled on to its back, then went down in a steep inverted dive. After a lengthy struggle the British pilot fought his way out of the cockpit and jumped clear of the stricken aircraft.

After their initial firing pass, the Hurricanes split into sections and curved round to attempt follow-up attacks on the bombers from their flanks and from astern. Repeatedly the escorting Messerschmitts dived on the would-be assailants to break up their attacks. For the German fighters assigned to the close escort force it was a frustrating business. They could not pursue the enemy fighters to the kill, for to do so would have meant leaving their charges, and that was strictly forbidden. Again and again the Messerschmitts had to break off the chase and return to their bombers, only to see the British fighters return. Then the whole process had to be repeated.

As the raiders neared Gravesend the British fighter attacks slackened off, and ahead the bomber crews could see the distant smudge of London on the horizon. But now the raiders faced a new hazard. Defending the south and west of Chatham was a concentration of twenty 4.5in and eight 3.7in guns which now opened up a heavy cannonade. *Oberleutnant* Peter Schierning, the navigator in a Heinkel of *Kampfgeschwader 53*, saw a series of black lumps suddenly appear in the sky around him. They came from exploding anti-aircraft shells, some of them so close that their blast rocked the bomber. Within seconds the smoke puffs had been left behind, but by then the damage had been done. Schierning recalled:

> One of the first salvos knocked out our right motor. We felt no shock, but the motor slowly wound down. The pilot shouted 'Get rid of the bombs! Get rid of the bombs! I can't hold it!' I jettisoned the bombs over farmland.

Unable to keep up with the formation, the bomber entered a steep diving turn, making for the protection of a bank of cloud. Another German bomber suffered a fate similar and it too was forced out of its formation and made a dash for the cloud bank.

As during the earlier action, Keith Park again concentrated the bulk of his fighters immediately in front of London for the main engagement. No fewer than nineteen squadrons of fighters, with 185 Spitfires and Hurricanes, were now moving into blocking positions to the south and the east of the city.

As Douglas Bader's 'Big Wing' reached the capital it came under attack from free-hunting Bf 109s diving from above. The three Hurricane squadrons split up to fight off their tormentors and, in a reversal of their usual role, Bader ordered the two Spitfire squadrons to try to get through to the bombers alone. Yet although the 'Big Wing' was unable to deliver the intended massed attack on the enemy bombers, by its presence it kept the enemy's free-hunting patrols occupied and made it easier for other British squadrons to reach the bombers.

The No 11 Group squadrons waiting in front of the capital went into action as the bombers came into sight. Flying Officer Tom Neil of No 249 Squadron took part in the attack on one of the formations of Dorniers and in his book *Gun Button to Fire* later wrote:

> Closing, I fired immediately and the whole of the port side of the German aircraft was engulfed in my tracer. The effect was instantaneous; there was a splash of something like water being struck with the back of a spoon. Beside myself with excitement, I fired again, a longish burst, and finding that I was too close, fell back a little but kept my position. Then, astonishingly, before I was ready to renew my assault, two large objects detached themselves from the fuselage and came in my direction, so quickly, in fact, that I had no time to evade. Comprehension barely keeping pace with events, I suddenly recognised spreadeagled arms and legs as two bodies flew past my head, heavy with the bulges that were undeveloped parachutes. The crew! Baling out! I veered away, shocked by what I had just achieved.

Almost certainly the bomber that Neil hit was that carrying the *Kampfgeschwader 3* formation leader, *Hauptmann* Ernst Püttmann, and the aircraft crashed into the Thames.

During this series of attacks three other Dorniers were knocked out of Püttmann's formation. *Oberleutnant* Hans Schmoller-Haldy of *Jagdgeschwader 54*, flying as close escort with the formation of Heinkels coming up behind, watched the planes go down:

> There were parachutes all over the place. Several British fighters were buzzing around the Dorniers. I thought 'Oh, those poor men . . .' But we couldn't do anything to help; we had to stay with our Heinkels.

On the way to the target four German bombers had been shot down, and seven were forced out of formation and heading for home alone. All five of the bomber formations reached London intact, however, and now they were prepared to commence their bombing runs on their assigned dock targets.

Throughout the morning and the early afternoon, cloud had gradually been thickening over southern England. Now most of the capital lay under nine-tenths cumulus and strato-cumulus cloud, with the base at about 2,000ft and tops extending to 12,000ft. And, as luck would have it, none of the targets the German crews had been briefed to attack was visible. West Ham was one of the few parts of the metropolis clear of cloud, and two formations of Heinkels and one of Dorniers re-aligned their attack runs to hit the borough and the nearby gasworks at Bromley-by-Bow. Their bombs caused widespread damage throughout the area.

On the southern flank of the German force, the two formations of Dorniers from *Kampfgeschwader 2*, briefed to attack the Surrey Commercial Docks, arrived to find no part of the complex discernible. The raiders turned away without bombing, much to the surprise and delight of the three squadrons of Hurricanes that had been battling with the Dorniers and their escorts. Many of the RAF pilots thought that by their presence they had scared the enemy into making the U-turn, and this version would be given wide prominence later in press reports. In fact both Dornier formations arrived over the capital intact, having lost only one aircraft on the way in; they could easily have attacked their briefed targets if their crews could only have seen them. On their way home the raiders bombed on 'targets of opportunity', causing scattered damage in the boroughs of Penge, Bexley, Crayford, Dartford and Orpington.

Those German bombers that had been forced out of formations engaged in a deadly game of hide-and-seek, as they tried to pick their way through the banks of cloud over Kent to avoid the defending fighters. Peter Schierning's Heinkel was one of those bombers, limping home with one engine wrecked by flak:

> By the engine, part of the skin of the wing had been blown away and I could see the structure inside. I remember thinking what a marvellous aircraft the Heinkel was, being able to stay airborne with that sort of damage.

Then, suddenly, both the cloud and the bomber crew's luck ran out. Surrounded by clear skies, almost at once the Heinkel came under attack from a couple of Hurricanes and a Spitfire. Schierning recalled:

> They attacked from the rear and the sides, and I saw their tracers coming past the nose of the Heinkel. Early on, the intercom

was shot away and I had no idea what was happening in the rear of the aircraft; I had no opportunity to use my nose gun.

The Hurricane pilots, from No.229 Squadron, were Squadron Leader A. Banham and Flight Lieutenant E. Smith. The latter reported that with his commander he went after a lone Heinkel that was also being engaged by a Spitfire:

> I attacked from dead astern with a 6-second burst from 200 yards, closing to 150 yards. I saw bullets entering the fuselage and hitting the mainplane. The port engine was smoking and brown oil from the E/A splashed over my windscreen.

When Smith last saw the bomber it was diving for a patch of cloud. Schierning heard his pilot shout that the port engine had also been hit and was losing power, there was a fire in the vicinity of the right engine and he was taking the bomber down for a crash landing. One of the gunners was killed and the radio operator was wounded. The Heinkel crash-landed near Staplehurst and slithered to a halt in a cloud of dust.

Despite the presence of cloud, which made the plotting of aircraft difficult over land, during the afternoon action the RAF system of fighter control surpassed even the morning's fine performance. Twenty-eight squadrons, with 276 Spitfires and Hurricanes, had been scrambled to meet the afternoon attack. Every one of those squadrons went into action.

Although the main attacks of the day were against London, the city was not the only target. In the expectation that Fighter Command would concentrate all of its remaining strength for the defence of the capital, twenty-seven Heinkels of *Kampfgeschwader 55* were sent to make an unescorted attack on the Royal Navy base at Portland. Only a lapse by the British fighter controllers saved the raiders from heavy losses. The strength of the attack force was underestimated, and just one half-squadron of Spitfires was sent to intercept it. Only one bomber was shot down, although another suffered damage. The bombing of the naval installation was inaccurate and it caused no significant damage.

Later in the afternoon ten Messerschmitt Bf 110s and three Bf 109s of the fighter-bomber unit *Erprobungsgruppe 210* ran in at low altitude to attack the Supermarine aircraft works at Southampton, then building Spitfires. Although the raiders reached the port without interference, they failed to find their intended target and the weight of their attack fell on a residential area a few hundred yards to the east. During their withdrawal the fighter-bombers fought a brief skirmish with Hurricanes of No 607 Squadron, but there were no losses on either side.

In the course of the hard-fought series of actions on 15 September 1940, the *Luftwaffe* lost a total of 56 fighters and bombers. RAF Fighter Command lost 29 aircraft. At the time the defenders claimed the destruction of 185 German planes, the largest of many huge overclaims that were made during the Battle of Britain.

A close analysis of the day's actions puts Douglas Bader's 'Big Wing' tactics in a new light. During the Battle of Britain the five-squadron fighting unit from No 12 Group made contact with a large force of enemy aircraft on three occasions, and two of those were on 15 September. At noon on that day the 'Big Wing' went into action on the most favourable terms imaginable, when its 56 fighters engaged a formation of 25 Dorniers with no escorts. An air combat that involves large numbers of aircraft is likely to give rise to large overclaims in the number of enemy planes destroyed. Furthermore, by definition, if the 'Big Wing' took part, then a large number of aircraft were involved. During the noon action the 'Big Wing' claimed 26 German aircraft destroyed, including twenty bombers, for no loss to itself. From German records and interviews with surviving bomber crewmen it is clear that only six bombers were lost during the entire action. It appears likely that fighters of the 'Big Wing' shared in the destruction of five, possibly all six, of the Dorniers shot down; but every one of those bombers was also attacked by fighters of No 11 Group.

During the afternoon action German fighters broke up the 'Big Wing' before it could get close to the bombers. The Wing split into small units and its pilots claimed the destruction of 26 enemy aircraft, including seventeen bombers. From German records it is clear that only 21 bombers were lost during the entire engagement and again, from British records, it is clear that most of those were attacked by fighters of No 11 Group.

The 'Big Wing' actions on September 15 resulted in huge over-claims of the number of German aircraft destroyed, which produced an exaggerated assessment of the effectiveness of these tactics. During the noon action there were cases of fighters getting in each others' way, and attacks had to be broken off to avoid collisions. In terms of enemy aircraft destroyed, the 'Big Wing' was less effective than five squadrons of fighters sent into action in ones and twos.

The failure of the 'Big Wing' to shoot down many bombers was more than counter-balanced, however, by the resounding success that it had in another area – its devastating impact on the morale of the German bomber crews. During their briefings in the morning of 15 September, the raiders had been told that Fighter Command was a spent force that need no longer be feared. The repeated attacks by Spitfires and Hurricanes on the way to the capital cast doubts on the accuracy of that intelligence. But then, as they arrived over London, the raiders were confronted by more than fifty Royal Air Force fighters approaching in parade formation. That display, mounted twice during the day, demonstrated beyond possible doubt that the Fighter Command was far from beaten. By impressing that unpalatable fact on the *Luftwaffe*, the 'Big Wing' was well worth the effort involved.

Because of the huge victory claim, which we now know to be exaggerated, 15 September has come to be commemorated as 'Battle of Britain Day'. In fact that date did mark the decisive point in the Battle, though for a different reason. The strength of Fighter Command's reaction during the two actions around London convinced Hitler that the *Luftwaffe* could not gain air superiority before the weather broke that autumn. On 17 September he ordered that Operation 'Sealion', the planned invasion of southern England, be postponed 'indefinitely'. The ships and barges assembled for the enterprise at ports along the Channel coast began to slip away to resume their normal tasks. With each week that passed the threat of invasion lessened, never to return. Although it was chosen for the wrong reason, the date commemorated by the British public for the deliverance of the nation was the correct one.

Chapter 20

Pre-emptive Strike

On 22 June 1941, without warning or prior declaration of war, German forces launched a massive attack on the Soviet Union. During the first day one of the primary objectives of the Luftwaffe *was the destruction of the Soviet Air Force. The latter was quite unprepared to meet the blow and, as a result, it suffered the heaviest defeat ever experienced by an air arm.*

Despite the non-aggression pact signed between the governments of Germany and the Soviet Union in 1939, there was little trust between the two. The treaty gave the Soviet government a free hand in the east. Its army occupied Latvia, Estonia and Lithuania and parts of Poland, Rumania and Finland, and the additional territories were incorporated into the Soviet Union. Moreover, between the summer of 1939 and May 1941 the Soviet Army increased in strength from 69 to 158 divisions, the majority of them positioned along the nation's western frontiers. During the same period the Soviet Air Force also expanded and, significantly, at the end of it many units were about to re-equip with the high-performance new bomber and fighter types then coming off the production lines. Adolf Hitler believed that, sooner or later, Germany would find herself at war with the powerful communist state to the east, and he resolved to get his blow in first.

During the spring of 1941, while the night blitz on Great Britain was in full swing, *Luftwaffe* combat units in western Europe secretly moved to bases in eastern Germany and Poland. The transfer was painstakingly planned to keep its true intent a secret for as long as possible. *Leutnant* Dieter Lukesch, a Junkers Ju 88 pilot who served as technical officer with *III Gruppe* of *Kampfgeschwader 76* based at

Cormeilles-en-Vexin near Paris, described the elaborate subterfuge. The first indication he had that something strange was afoot was when his unit was ordered to remove the temporary black distemper applied to the aircraft for night operations and repaint the upper surfaces in light brown camouflage. That suggested daylight operations in a desert area, but where? Half way through the work the order was countermanded, then a new order arrived to the effect that the planes were to be restored to their original temperate colour scheme, with the topsides camouflaged in two shades of green. When this was done, the bulk of the unit's technical personnel suddenly departed for an undisclosed destination, leaving behind a few men to look after the aircraft.

Rumour followed counter-rumour, and a few days later the mystery deepened, as Lukesch explained:

The air crew were summoned to a meeting in the middle of the airfield, well clear of everyone else. There the *Gruppe* commander, Major Lindmayr, solemnly opened an envelope that contained our sealed orders. What followed only served to heighten our curiosity. Our planes were fuelled up. We were told to load our personal kit on the aircraft, then take off and form up by *Staffeln* behind Lindmayr, who was to lead us to our still-secret destination. We took off from Cormeilles and flew over Holland and Germany before landing at Anklam [a *Luftwaffe* airfield on the Baltic coast]. After we taxied in and shut down the planes, we were driven to a barrack block where we were kept in isolation. Everything there had been prepared for us, our beds were made, the tables had been laid and a meal was ready.

The following morning there was a near-repeat of the previous performance. Again there was the briefing on the airfield, the brown envelope was solemnly opened and again the crews were told to take off and follow Lindmayr to the undisclosed destination. Lukesch continued:

This time, after a flight of two hours, we landed at Schippanbei just south of Konigsberg. When we arrived we found that our technical people were already there; they marshalled us into prepared camouflaged dispersal points around the airfield. The aircraft were then carefully concealed under camouflage netting and branches cut from trees. Then the planes were refuelled and bombed up, but still we did not know where we were going.

For *II Gruppe* of *Kampfgeschwader 3* it was a similar story, though this unit started its move from Oldenburg in Germany, where it had been converting from Dornier Do 17s to Ju 88s. The *Gruppe* moved to Podlotowka near Brest-Litovsk in Poland, and one of the pilots, *Feldwebel* Horst Schulz, recalled:

When we arrived at Podlotowka we saw a lot of army units there, infantry, artillery and tanks. Rumours were rife and the most popular was that the Russians were going to let a German force of two or three divisions with air support through their territory to attack the British oil fields and pipelines in Iran.

During the afternoon and evening of 21 June the men finally learned whom they were to attack, and when. The new enemy was the Soviet Union, and the war would begin with a series of co-ordinated land and air attacks, to commence simultaneously before dawn the following morning. The men were assembled and each commander read out an personal order of the day from Adolf Hitler that began 'Soldiers of the Eastern Front .' The missive stated that, despite the treaty of friendship between the two nations, German intelligence had discovered that Soviet forces were massing for a treacherous onslaught against Germany. As a result, the *Führer* had reluctantly ordered the counter-stroke in order to blunt the force of the planned attack before it could begin.

At 3.00 a.m. Central European Time on 22 June the German Army opened its offensive with a massive artillery bombardment all along the front, in true *Blitzkrieg* style. Then the spearhead units began moving forwards. Between the Baltic and the Black Sea, 117 German divisions, of which 48 were armoured, plus fourteen Rumanian divisions and a Hungarian army corps, swung into action. Facing them in the immediate battle area were 132 Soviet Army divisions, of which 34 were armoured. A total of 7¾ million men were thus committed in one of the greatest armed clashes in history.

On the first day of the campaign the *Luftwaffe* had a total of 1,954 combat aircraft deployed to support the attack on the Soviet Union, of which just over two-thirds were serviceable: 510 twin-engine bombers, 290 dive-bombers, 440 single-engine fighters, 40 twin-engine fighters and 120 reconnaissance planes. The earliest that the *Luftwaffe* could attack targets in force was about half an hour after sunrise, or 4.20 a.m. This would enable aircraft to take off and assemble into formation in the morning twilight and reach their targets to strike with greatest effect. German Army commanders decreed that the earlier starting time was necessary, so that their own attacks could achieve surprise, however. The best that the air force could do was to send small numbers of Heinkel He 111s, Dornier Do 17s and Ju 88s flown by picked crews, in three-plane units with each machine flying independently in the darkness, to attack some of the more important Soviet fighter airfields. These attacks took place simultaneously at 3.15 a.m., fifteen minutes after zero hour. Their purpose was to disrupt operations at the airfields, and in particular to delay the dispersal of aircraft on the ground until the arrival of the large-scale air attacks after dawn.

As the daylight attack units soon discovered, however, the state of readiness of the Soviet units was so poor that, even at airfields that had not been attacked, no measures had been taken to meet such a possibility. Long conditioned to obey those above without question, the Soviet airfield commanders were afraid to do anything until they received orders. Had they actually wanted to make things easy for their attackers, it is difficult to see what more the Soviets could have done to assist in the destruction of their planes. Scores of fighters, bombers and reconnaissance aircraft sat on the ground in neat rows at their airfields. Putting the planes close together meant that a single bomb could damage two or more, and putting them in a line meant that a strafing fighter or bomber could fly down the line at low altitude and fire at each one in turn. Even the simple precaution of dispersing the aircraft around the perimeter of each airfield, with a hundred yards or so between each, would have made the raiders' task

---

JUNKERS Ju 88A-4

Role: Four-seat medium bomber.

Powerplant: Two Junkers Jumo 211J in-line engines each developing 1,340hp at take-off.

Armament: Normal operational bomb load 3,320lb; typical combat load four 550lb and ten 110lb high-explosive bombs, or 360 SD fragmentation bombs. Defensive armament of seven MG 15 7.9mm machine guns in flexible mountings, one firing forwards, two firing rearwards from the cabin, one on either side of the cabin and one firing downwards and rearwards from the ventral gun position. Performance: Maximum speed 292mph at 17,400ft; normal formation cruising speed at 16,000ft, 180mph; radius of action with 2,200lb bomb load, 550 miles.

Normal operational takeoff weight: 26,690lb.

Dimensions: Span 65ft 7½in; length 47ft 2½in; wing area 587 sq ft.

Date of first production Ju 88A-4: Summer 1940.

MESSERSCHMITT Bf 109F-4

Role: Single-seat fighter.

Powerplant: One Daimler Benz DB 601E 12-cylinder, liquid-cooled, inline engine developing 1,350hp at take-off.

Armament: One MG 151 20mm cannon firing through the propeller boss; two MG 17 7.9mm cannon mounted above the engine and synchronized to fire through the propeller.

Performance: Maximum speed 334mph at sea level, 388mph at 21,300ft; initial rate of climb 4,290ft/min.

Normal operational take-off weight: 6,390lb.

Dimensions: Span 32ft 5¾in; length 29ft 0½in; wing area 174 sq ft.

Date of first production Bf 109F4: Spring 1941.

---

more difficult and their attack less effective. Taxying the planes a short distance off the airfield and applying simple camouflage would have made things more difficult still. And a few anti-aircraft guns around each airfield would have served to distract the attackers at the critical time and make their bombing runs less accurate. But, so confident were the Soviet leaders that no attack was in the offing, none of these things was done. The Soviet Air Force was to suffer accordingly.

It was light when Dieter Lukesch and his *Gruppe* took off to attack the airfield at Krudziai south of Riga in Lithuania. Although he already had flown several combat missions against Great Britain, this was one he would never forget:

> The skies were beautifully clear, with visibility almost unlimited. Soon after we took off we could see the front line quite clearly, marked by fires and the smoke from bursting shells. Once we had passed the front, however, there was no flak. We did not have, nor did we expect to need, an escort for the first attack. As we passed other airfields we saw Russian fighters taking off, but they climbed somewhat slower than our cruising speed so we soon left them behind.

The Ju 88s cruised at 10,000ft, each carrying the standard load of four 550lb and ten 110lb general-purpose bombs. Five miles short of the target the planes dropped their noses and began shallow-dive attacks to plant their bombs with the greatest possible accuracy. The attack opened at 6 a.m., but although it was some hours after the opening bombardment more than a score of the Tupolev SB-2 bombers were drawn up in line along one side of the airfield. Lukesch continued:

There was no flak, and even though the war had been in progress for about three hours it seems that we had achieved surprise. As we approached for the first attack we could see ground crewmen standing on the wings refuelling the aircraft, looking up in curiosity as we ran in. As the bombs started to explode they made hasty retreats into the nearby forest. Our bombers attacked in a long line but there was some jockeying for position. As I was about to release my bombs I saw another aircraft converging on me from the right and releasing its bombs. I had to break away, make a circuit and attack at the end of the force. I ran in as the last aircraft in the *Gruppe* to attack. By then several aircraft on the ground were burning and there was quite a lot of smoke, but the line of trees behind the aircraft helped me to line up on some planes that had not been hit before. During the attack my observer fired at the enemy planes with his machine gun. As we were pulled away after the attack some Russian fighters appeared on the scene, Ratas and Gulls [Polikarpov I-16s and I-15s]. Although they got close they did not fire at us; perhaps they did not have any ammunition. With my greater speed I soon left them behind.

That morning some *Luftwaffe* units employed a new weapon in action for the first time: the 4½lb SD-2 fragmentation bomb (sometimes called the 'Butterfly bomb'), carried in special containers fixed to the attacking planes. After release, the casing of the SD-2 opened up to form a pair of 'wings' and the weapon spun to the ground like a sycamore seed. The 7oz explosive charge detonated on impact, hurling high-velocity fragments in all directions with sufficient force to cause serious damage to aircraft up to 40ft away. Dropped in large numbers during low-flying attacks on Soviet airfields, the SD-2s proved highly effective against aircraft and other 'soft' targets. *II Gruppe* of *Jagdgeschwader 27* was one of the units to employ the new weapon, its Bf 109E fighters each carrying 96 of the small bombs. That morning it sent 31 fighters to deliver a low-altitude bombing and strafing attack on Wizna airfield. By the end of this attack and one by fifteen dive-bombers, a total of 31 Soviet aircraft had been destroyed. The two raiding forces then went on to attack Lomza-South airfield, where they destroyed another 40 planes. All of the fighters from *JG 27* returned safely.

Kampfgeschwader 51 had a much less happy experience with the new weapon. That morning the *Geschwader* dispatched all 91 serviceable Ju 88s in attacks on six major Soviet airfields on the southern part of the front, each plane carrying 360 SD-2s.

POLIKARPOV I-16 TYPE 24

Role: Single-seat fighter.
Powerplant: One Shvetsov M-62 9-cylinder, air-cooled, radial engine developing 1,000hp for take-off.
Armament: Two ShVAK 20mm cannon; two ShKAS 7.62mm machine guns.
Performance: Maximum speed 326mph at sea level, 286mph at 14,750ft; climb to 16,400ft, 5min 48sec.
Normal operational take-off weight: 4,215lb.
Dimensions: Span 29ft 6½in; length 20ft 1¼in; wing area 161 sq ft.
Date of first production I-16 Type 24: Summer 1939.

The bombing and strafing attack on Stryj airfield, by eighteen Ju 88s, caused the destruction of twenty Soviet bombers; the raiders then continued to Lemberg airfield, where they destroyed fifteen fighters. After the attack crews learned that the new fragmentation bombs could also be extremely dangerous companions, however. Bombs were liable to jam in the container, and the plane's crew had no way of knowing of the 'hang-up'. Because of a design fault, the bomb's fuse could become live in flight and thereafter the slightest shock might set off the charge with disastrous results for the aircraft; alternatively, on landing, a jammed SD-2 was liable to jolt free, fall to the ground and explode. On the first day of the campaign KG 51 lost fifteen bombers to enemy action or to accidents with SD-2s – nearly half the number of aircraft lost by the entire *Luftwaffe* on that day – and the SD-2s immediately gained the grim nickname 'Devil's Eggs'.

While the attacks were in progress against Soviet airfields, other *Luftwaffe* units attacked targets in support of advancing German ground troops. Dive-bombers attacked fortified positions, headquarters, artillery parks and barracks. Horst Schultz's *Gruppe*, *II* of *KG 3*, sent out several Ju 88s on single-plane armed reconnaissance missions along roads in the Soviet rear areas leading to the battle front. He recalled:

We went free hunting on our first mission [over the USSR], flying at 1,200m [about 3,800ft] looking for enemy road traffic. We dropped our bombs on a road filled with troops and artillery, and on a bridge over which troops were passing.

Simultaneously, packs of German fighters ranged over the battle area hunting for any Soviet planes that had got into the air. Again, it was a one-sided battle. Close to the ground the Polikarpov I-16 Type 24, the main Soviet fighter type, was almost as fast as the Bf 109F that equipped the majority of *Luftwaffe* fighter units. But the Type 24's radial engine was optimized for low-altitude operations, and as height increased its performance fell away steadily: at 20,000ft the I-16 was about 100mph slower than the German fighter. The Soviet fighters were more manoeuvrable than their adversaries, but in a fighter-versus-fighter combat this advantage did no more than allow a pilot to avoid being shot down, provided he saw his attacker in good time. The faster fighter always held the initiative, and its pilot dictated the terms of the engagement and could attack or break off the combat at will. For their part, the Soviet fighter pilots had to dance to their enemies' tune.

Typical of the scrappy actions taking place that morning was one near Brest-Litovsk, described by *Unteroffizier* Reibel of *I Gruppe* of *Jagdgeschwader 53*:

> I was flying as wing man to *Lt* Zellot. We flew in the direction of Brest from Labinka. As my leader ordered a turn about, I saw two biplanes in front of us. I immediately reported them and we brought them under attack. When we were about 200m from them they both pulled into a tight turn to the right. We pulled up high and then began a new attack, but though we both opened fire it was without success. Soon there were about ten other [enemy] machines in the area. My leader ran in to attack one of the planes while I remained high in order to cover him. Then an I-15 became separated from the others. I immediately prepared to attack it, but I had to break away when another enemy machine, which I had not seen, suddenly appeared 50 metres in front of me. I opened fire with machine guns and the cannon and it burst into flames and spun out of control. Apparently the pilot had bailed out. Then I had to turn away, as I had two [enemy] machines behind me.

Using their superior speed, the German fighter pilots easily pulled clear of their pursuers:

JG 27 lost its commander, *Major* Wolfgang Schellmann, near Grodno when he pressed home an attack on an I-16 to short range. Following an accurate burst the Soviet fighter exploded and debris from the aircraft struck Schellmann's fighter. He was forced to bail out and was taken prisoner. It appears that he was shot soon afterwards by his captors.

TUPOLEV SB-2bis

Role: Three-seat medium bomber.
Powerplant: Two M-103 inline engines each developing 960hp at take-off.
Armament: Normal operational bomb load 2,200lb. Defensive armament of five 7.62mm machine guns, two in the fuselage gun turret, two on a flexible mounting in the nose and one firing downwards and rearwards from the ventral gun position.
Performance: Maximum speed 280mph at 12,900ft; radius of action with 2,200lb bomb load, 200 miles.
Normal operational take-off weight: 10,500lb.
Dimensions: Span 66ft 8½in; length 41ft 2½in; wing area 610 sq ft.
Date of first production SB-2bis: 1937.

German twin-engine bombers and dive-bombers had flown a total of 637 sorties by 10 a.m. that morning, striking at 31 airfields as well as military positions and supply routes. The success of the attacks on the Soviet Air Force that morning is confirmed by the official Soviet postwar publication *History of the Great Patriotic War of the Soviet Union* (not a source likely to exaggerate German successes):

> During the first days of the war enemy bomber formations launched massive attacks on sixty-six airfields in the frontier region, and in particular those where the new Soviet fighter types were based. The result of these raids and the violent air-to-air battles was a loss to us, as at noon on 22nd June, of some 1,200 aircraft, including more than 800 destroyed on the ground.

From mid-day small forces of Soviet bombers attempted to deliver retaliatory attacks on airfields used by the *Luftwaffe*, but with little success. About a dozen Tupolev SB-2s carried out a high-level bombing attack on the airfield at Biala-Podlaska just inside German-held Poland, home of the Junkers Ju 87 dive-bombers of *I Gruppe* of *Sturzkampfgeschwader 77*. The Stukas were being refuelled and re-armed after their initial mission but, in contrast to those of their enemy earlier in the day, the German planes were dispersed around the airfield and camouflaged. A flak battery positioned nearby went into action against the raiders, and although some of the bombs burst across the airfield, no Stukas were damaged.

Summoned to the scene by the flak bursts, German fighters were soon converging on the Tupolevs from several directions. One Bf 109F pilot who took part in the action, *Oberleutnant* Ohly of

I Gruppe of *JG 53*, later reported that he had scrambled with four fighters at 12.18 following a report of enemy planes in the Brest-Litovsk area heading west:

> About [8,000ft] over Biala Polkaska, I saw flak bursts and a formation of about a dozen multi-engined monoplanes that turned out to be SB-2s. During the climb I lost contact with the two other pilots, so I headed towards the SB-2s with just our pair. These [enemy] aircraft had already been engaged by other fighters and were heading towards the Bug [river]. I engaged three SB-2s flying in vic formation, and fired at the machine on the right with my cannon and machine guns from a range of between 150 and 75 metres. My speed was too great and I had to pull up [to avoid colliding with] the SB-2, and as I flew past it my aircraft received hits in the radiator and the fuselage. I made a left turn to check that my aircraft responded to the controls, during which the machine I had attacked passed out of view. I turned through 360 degrees and the SB-2s again came into view. I watched my wing-man and another fighter shoot down three SB-2s. At the same time several SB-2s that had been attacked by other fighters were also going down. I cannot say if the one that I had hit was shot down.

The Soviet bomber formation lost about three quarters of its aircraft during the series of attacks by German fighters. As a footnote to the day's air fighting, there were five cases reported in which Soviet fighters deliberately rammed enemy planes. This practice often resulted in the death of all of those aboard both planes, and it was a grisly portent of what lay in store for the *Luftwaffe* when the fast-moving *Blitzkrieg* campaign drifted into a long war of attrition.

By the end of the first day of its campaign against the Soviet Union the *Luftwaffe* had flown a total of 1,766 sorties by single-engine and twin-engine bombers and 506 by fighters. In the course of these operations it lost thirty-five aircraft. Official German sources claimed the destruction of 322 Soviet planes in air-to-air combat or by flak, and 1,489 destroyed on the ground. Given the size of the aircraft losses admitted by the Soviets up to noon on that fateful day, the German claims undoubtedly have a ring of truth. Certainly the day was one for the aviation record books. In the course of an eighteen-hour period between 3.15 a.m. and sunset the Soviet Air Force losses represented by far the greatest number of aircraft ever destroyed in a single day's fighting. It was also the most comprehensive defeat to be inflicted by one air force on another, in the long history of air warfare. Although five-sixths of the Soviet aircraft were destroyed on the ground, one-sixth, or 322 machines, fell in air-to-air combat; this was the largest number of planes ever to be shot down in a single day.

During the days that followed, the German armoured units thrust rapidly into the Soviet Union, overrunning every one of the airfields that the *Luftwaffe* had attacked on the first day. This compounded the effect of the earlier losses, for aircraft that were not flyable because of battle damage or other types of unserviceability either had to be destroyed by the retreating forces or were left behind to be captured. Having one's ground forces capture enemy airfields is a most effective means of reducing the capability of an enemy air force and one that is often neglected when considering this aspect of warfare.

Yet, despite the enormity of the material losses suffered by the Soviet Air Force during the early days of the war, their effect was crippling only in the short and medium terms. In June 1941 the programme to re-equip the Soviet front-line units with modern aircraft had scarcely begun, with the result that the great majority of the aircraft lost were obsolescent types that were scheduled to be replaced in the near future. Moreover, very few Soviet air crew were lost in the attacks on the airfields or when the latter were captured, so as the modern planes came off the production lines there was no shortage of trained personnel to put them into action. Despite the ferocity of their initial onslaught, the German forces were unable to secure victory in the Eastern Front within the expected five months; at the end of that time they had to face the much improved Soviet ground forces and a revitalized Soviet Air Force. It was not going to be a short war.

Chapter 21

Guided Missiles Make Their Mark (1)

The term 'guided missile' can be defined as 'a missile whose path can be corrected during its travel, either automatically or by remote control, to bring it into contact with the target'. Note that this definition makes no mention of the medium through which the weapon usually passes, nor of its speed. To be sure, most such weapons travel through the air at speeds of several hundreds of miles per hour. But the first air-launched guided missile to be used in action was a quite different animal – an anti-submarine torpedo with an underwater running speed of 12kts. During the Second World War the weapon was a closely guarded secret, as were its successes.

During 1942 scientists and technicians in the United States, Britain and Canada worked on several detection and location devices, and weapons, to counter the U-boats. One weapon that resulted from the US Navy's work in this field was the first air-dropped anti-submarine homing torpedo, a weapon so secret that it was given the deliberately misleading code-name 'Mark 24 Mine'. Although the weapon had a running speed of only 12kts, within most definitions of the term it was a self-homing guided missile.

The diameter of the weapon, 19in, was about the same as that of the standard anti-ship torpedo; however, its 7ft length was less than half that of the standard weapon, and this gave the Mark 24 Mine a disproportionately dumpy appearance. Intended for use against U-boats that were running underwater or that had recently crash-dived, the homing torpedo weighed 640lb, of which 92lb was the high-explosive warhead with an impact fuse in the nose.

The method of operation of the Mark 24 Mine was as follows. Aimed at the diving swirl left by the boat when it disappeared under the waves, or on the most accurate datum point available on the location of the submarine, the weapon was released from an altitude of about 250ft. On entering the water the electric motor started and the torpedo began its search pattern, running round the circumference of a circle about 4,000yds in diameter. The acoustic homing head was tuned to listen for distinctive sounds produced by cavitation, the noise of the popping of bubbles caused when a propeller rotates in water at high speed. When it picked up these sounds, the homing head assessed the bearing and elevation of their source and steered the weapon in that direction until it impacted. If for any reason the acoustic head ceased to pick up sounds on which it could home, the torpedo resumed its search pattern: The weapon had a maximum running time of ten minutes, after which it sank to the bottom of the sea to prevent its capture.

At the end of 1942 the Mark 24 Mine entered series production, and thus became the first self-homing guided missile in the world to achieve this status. Tests revealed that under ideal conditions, with a calm sea and the submarine running at speed just under the surface, the weapon could home on its target from a distance of three-quarters of a mile. However, after a crash-dive it was likely that a boat would be running at speed, because the commander would want to get clear of the telltale diving swirl as rapidly as possible. Thus while the homing torpedo promised to be highly effective against an unsuspecting foe, the weakness of its concept would be obvious to an enemy who knew its method of operation. The acoustic head could home only on a *cavitating* propeller, so the submarine would be safe if its commander overcame his instincts and slowed the boat to below cavitation speed as soon as it had submerged. If the existence of the homing torpedo became known to the enemy it would be useless, so exaggerated security precautions surrounded every aspect of the weapon. To reduce the possibility of capture, it was not to be used close to enemy-held shores; furthermore, it was not to be used in areas where an attack might be observed by the enemy and its method of operation deduced.

An old adage assures us that 'It is almost impossible to make a system completely foolproof, because fools are so resourceful', and the Mark 24 Mine nearly fell foul of this logic a few months before it was ready for action. In February 1943 an early-production homing torpedo was transported to Great Britain aboard the liner *Empress of Scotland*. Group Captain Jeaff Greswell, returning from a liaison visit to the United States, was the custodian of the top-secret weapon, and he described the elaborate security precautions attending the move:

The homing torpedo arrived at the quay at New York in a US Navy lorry escorted by armed guards; there seemed to be guns all over the place. The weapon was packed in three large boxes: one contained the nose, one the centre section and one the tail. These the sailors brought on to the ship, they formally handed them over to me and I signed for them. Then I witnessed the placing of the boxes in the captain's safe, and he gave me a receipt. At Liverpool it was the same thing in reverse. There we were met by an RAF lorry, again with armed guards. I received the boxes from the Captain and signed for them, then I handed them over to the RAF officer and obtained his receipt. The demands of security had been observed to the letter. Now my part in the operation was over and I went off for a few days' leave. I had been at home for a couple of days when I received a buff-coloured envelope with OHMS across the top, by ordinary post. Inside was a letter from His Majesty's Customs; they wanted to know why I had imported into the United Kingdom 'packing cases containing what is believed to be some form of aerial homing torpedo for use against submarines'. Why had I failed to declare them?

Greswell passed the letter with a secret covering note to Air Chief Marshal Sir Philip Joubert, Commander-in-Chief of Coastal Command, with a frantic appeal: 'For heaven's sake do something about this one.' The Group Captain heard no more from the bureaucrats.

By May the homing torpedo was ready to go into action. Among the first units to receive it were US Navy Patrol Squadron VP-84, equipped with Catalina amphibians based in Iceland, and two Royal Air Force Liberator units, No 86 Squadron based at Aldergrove in Northern Ireland and No 120 Squadron based at Reykjavik in Iceland. All three squadrons were engaged in flying anti-U-boat patrols in support of convoys in mid-Atlantic.

Early in May the twin eastbound convoys HX.237 and SC.129 set sail from Newfoundland bound for Liverpool, and from 'Ultra' decoded signals Royal Navy Intelligence officers learned that a German wolfpack with no fewer than 36 U-boats was moving into position to engage the merchantmen. By the morning of the 12th the U-boats were closing on their prey and three Liberators from No 86 Squadron were sent to patrol ahead of the convoys, with

---

CONSOLIDATED LIBERATOR III (Modified B-24D)

Role: Eight-seat maritime patrol and anti-submarine aircraft.

Powerplant: Four Pratt & Whitney R-1830 14-cylinder, air-cooled, radial engines each developing 1,200hp at take-off.

Armament: Offensive weapon load varied with the type of operation being flown; in the anti-submarine role it was typically four or six 250lb depth charges and two Mark 24 Mine homing torpedoes. Defensive armament also varied, but was typically four .303in machine guns in the powered tail turret and one .5in gun on a hand-held mounting in the nose and in each of the waist positions on either side of the fuselage.

Performance: Typical speed and altitude for attack with Mark 24 Mine, 200mph at 250ft; depth charges released at between 50 and 150ft. Typical cruising speed 145mph at 5,000ft. With a maximum fuel capacity of 2,500 Imp. gallons, including the tank in the bomb bay, these aircraft could spend three hours on patrol at a distance of 1,100 miles from base. Maximum endurance 16 hours, with operational fuel reserves.

Normal maximum take-off weight: 64,000lb.

Dimensions: Span 110ft; length 66ft 4in; wing area 1,048 sq ft.

Date of first production B-24D: Late 1941.

Note: The Royal Air Force 'de-modification' process to render the strategic bomber suitable for the maritime patrol role included the removal of the self-sealing liners of the fuel tanks, of the turbo-superchargers from the engines, of the top and ball turrets and of much of the armour protection for the crew. Additional fuel tanks were fitted in the wings.

---

the aim of driving the U-boats underwater to prevent them from reaching their attack positions. Each of these aircraft was loaded with four 250lb depth charges and two Mark 24 Mines. If an aircraft found a U-boat and it remained on the surface, they were to attack it with depth charges; if the boat submerged, the crew would attack it with a homing torpedo.

The honour of being the first to use a guided missile in action goes to Flight Lieutenant J. Wright and his Liberator crew. They located *U456* on the surface, and as they closed in to deliver their attack the boat obligingly dived. Wright took the aircraft low over the diving swirl and released a homing torpedo, together with a smoke float to mark the point of entry. Then he swung the aircraft round in a wide circle, while he and his crew waited for some indication that the new weapon had been effective. For two long minutes nothing happened then, about 900yds from the point where the torpedo had entered the water, there was a small upheaval as though a depth charge had exploded with less than its normal force (the homing torpedo's warhead contained less than half the explosive charge of an air-dropped depth charge). Shortly afterwards the damaged U-boat re-surfaced, but by then the Liberator was close to the limit of its endurance and Wright was forced to head for base. From German records it is known that the U-boat reported by radio that it had suffered damage in an air attack and was unable to dive, and it requested assistance. The boat survived the night, but the next day a couple of the convoy escorts finished her off.

The action around the two convoys continued, and on the 14th aircraft delivered attacks with homing torpedoes on two occasions. In separate actions against two U-boats that had dived as aircraft approached, a Liberator of No 86 Squadron and a Catalina of VP-84 each released a homing torpedo beside the diving swirl. In each case, more than a minute later, a mushroom-like disturbance appeared in the water some distance from the entry point. No other results were observed, but from German records it is known that *U226* and *U657* disappeared without trace in positions which corresponded to these attacks and the homing torpedo is credited with their destruction. On the 19th, a Liberator of No 120 Squadron used one of the new weapons to dispatch *U954*.

From then on the Mark 24 Mine, affectionately nicknamed 'Wandering Annie' by those who used it, took an increasing toll of the German submarines. During the early summer of 1943 the US Navy escort carrier *Santee* took part in a series of actions off the Azores, and developed an effective technique against U-boats that stayed on the surface and used their anti-aircraft weapons to try to fight off their assailants. The carrier dispatched pairs of aircraft during U-boat hunts, a Grumman F4F Wildcat fighter teamed with a Grumman TBF Avenger bomber. The Avenger used its radar to locate the U-boat running on the surface and directed the Wildcat into position to deliver a strafing attack to force the submarine to dive. Then the Avenger planted a homing torpedo beside the diving swirl. Using these tactics *Santee's* aircraft sank three U-boats during July 1943.

During 1944 the Coastal Command Tactical Development Unit put together a elaborate procedure for using the Mark 24 Mine to attack U-boats that had been submerged for some time or those whose diving swirl was not visible (i.e. in poor weather or at night). First the aircraft laid out a pattern of five sonobuoys, each with a smoke marker (at night a flame float) to mark its position. By listening to the underwater sounds transmitted from each buoy in turn, an operator in the aircraft made a 'guesstimate' of the U-boat's position. Then the aircraft ran in and released one or more homing torpedoes at the position thus found. The tactics pushed the early non-directional sonobuoys and the Mark 24 Mine to the limits of their capabilities, and to succeed they required a high degree of skill and teamwork from the crew of the aircraft, plus a measure of luck.

The technique brought its first success on 20 March. 1945. 'Ultra' decrypts had indicated that a U-boat on the way to its patrol area would pass close to the Orkney Islands that evening, and a Liberator of No 86 Squadron was dispatched to hunt for it. It was nearly dark when Flight Lieutenant N. Smith and his crew began their search, and soon afterwards the plane's radar operator reported a suspicious contact at a range of three miles. Smith turned towards the object, but as the Liberator closed to within half a mile the object disappeared into sea clutter. In the darkness the plane's look-outs saw nothing of the contact and at this stage it did not justify the expenditure of expensive weapons: the object might have been nothing more significant than a piece of flotsam.

Smith's suspicions had been aroused, however, and he decided to put down a pattern of sonobuoys to see if there was something less innocuous there. The first sonobuoy was released at the point where the object had been seen on radar, to serve as the centre of the pattern. This was followed by four more buoys, laid out in a square with each one at a distance of 214 miles from the central buoy. A flame float was released with each sonobuoy, to mark its position.

Laying out a sonobuoy pattern was a complicated process requiring very precise flying, and it took the crew thirteen minutes to position all five buoys in the water. But when the first sonobuoy came on the air they immediately had their reward: the operator heard the unmistakable *swish* of a cavitating propeller rotating at 114rpm – a submerged U-boat. One by one the other sonobuoys began transmitting, and the operator was able to narrow the position of the, boat to one part of the pattern. As he was doing so, the radar operator caught another short glimpse of the object he had first seen. It was now clear that the mystery object was the *Schnorkel* head of a submarine that was running just below the surface. With the target identified and located sufficiently for his purpose, Smith took the Liberator to the opposite side of the pattern and began his attack run. As the aircraft passed over the flame float in the centre of the pattern, the navigator began counting off the seconds for a timed run along the bearing where the U-boat was thought to be. When the aircraft reached the boat's computed position Smith released one homing torpedo and, after a measured interval, a second.

The painstaking aerial activity over that patch of water had lasted for more than 20 minutes, during which the unsuspecting U-boat crew continued towards their operating area. It took a further six minutes for one of the homing torpedoes to catch up with the boat, then the sonobuoy operator in the Liberator heard a long, reverberating sound in his phones followed only by sea noises. At the time that was the sole evidence of a successful attack, but from German records it is clear that *U905* had disappeared in that area at about the time of Smith's attack.

Between May 1943 and the end of the war a total of 346 Mark 24 Mines were dropped in action, and the weapon was credited with the destruction of 38 submarines and with causing damage to a further 33. The first air-launched guided missile to be used in action, it was also the most successful weapon of this type to be used during the Second World War: under operational conditions about 20 per cent of the weapons used scored hits on targets.

Chapter 22

Guided Missiles Make Their Mark (2)

*In the previous chapter we observed the development and
use of the first 'guided missile' to go into action. Within a
few months two other types of guided missile saw combat,
weapons that were quite different from each other and from
the one employed previously. This chapter describes the*
Luftwaffe *operations against Allied shipping using its new
guided weapons.*

During the Second World War at sea Germany faced two of
the world's largest maritime powers, each of which possessed
a fleet much larger than her own. In order to redress this imbalance in naval forces, much would depend on the ability of the
Luftwaffe to deliver effective attacks on naval targets. During the
early part of the war Allied ships had weak anti-aircraft defences
and, as a result, aircraft could deliver accurate attacks from low
altitude using conventional high-explosive bombs. That phase soon
passed, however, and air crews learned that if they were to survive
they had to employ less risky modes of attack. High-level bombing
was generally ineffective against warships manoeuvring at speed in
open water. Dive-bombing was effective against such targets, but it
required clear skies to 10,000ft and the short radius of action of the
Junkers Ju 87 Stuka precluded it from attacking targets far from the
coast. German torpedo bombers scored some successes, but regular
training was necessary to keep crews proficient, the force could not
be employed on other types of war mission and its opportunities to
go into action were few and far between.

HENSCHEL Hs 293A

Role: Air-launched guided missile, designed primarily for use against shipping.

Powerplant: One Walter HWK 109-507 liquid-fuel rocket developing 1,300lb of thrust for 12 seconds.

Warhead: 1,100lb high-explosive warhead mounted in the nose.

Performance: Maximum speed at end of rocket burn about 375mph, after which the missile coasted on to its target; effective range under operational conditions depended on launch altitude, but was typically about 5 miles; minimum operational launch range about 2½ miles, governed by the time required to take the missile under control and move it on to the line-of-sight with the target.

Weight at launch: 1,990lb.

Dimensions: Span 10ft 3½in; length 11ft 3¼in.

Method of guidance: Radio command-to-line-of-sight.

Date first used in action: August 1943.

Because of these limitations, the *Luftwaffe* accorded the highest priority to the development of more effective weapons for use against enemy shipping. In November 1941, over the Baltic, flight trials began of a completely new radio-controlled guided weapon, the Henschel Hs 293 glider bomb. Intended for attacks on unarmoured warships or transports, the Hs 293 resembled a small winged aircraft and carried a 1,100lb warhead in the nose. Following its release from the launching aircraft, a rocket motor accelerated the weapon to a maximum speed of about 375mph. After a burning time of twelve seconds the rocket cut out and the missile then coasted on towards the target, steered by an observer in the nose of the launching aircraft operating a joystick controller linked to a radio transmitter. A flare in the tail of the weapon assisted tracking, and the observer's task was to superimpose the flare on the target and hold it there until the weapon impacted. To allow a number of aircraft to deliver simultaneous glider-bomb attacks without causing interference with the others' guidance signals, each Hs 293 was pre-set to use one of eighteen separate radio channels.

Early in 1942 a second type of radio-controlled guided missile began flight tests, the Ruhrstahl Fritz-X. This was an unpowered free-fall bomb weighing 3,100lb, with fixed cruciform wings mid-way along the body to give stability and movable control spoilers in the tail to allow it to be steered in flight. After release, the weapon could be steered on to the target using a similar radio guidance system to that fitted to the Hs 293. The Fritz-X was designed for use against armoured warships and, provided it was released from altitudes above 20,000 feet, it achieved an impact velocity that was sufficient to penetrate the deck armour of a battleship.

After a period of development and testing lasting over a year, the two new weapons entered series production in the spring of 1943. Two *Gruppen* of *Kampfgeschwader 100* were re-equipped with versions of the Dornier Do 217 specially modified to carry each of the missiles: *II Gruppe* received the E-5 variant able to carry one Hs 293 under each outer wing section; and *III Gruppe* re-equipped with the K-2 variant which could carry one Fritz-X bomb under each inner wing between the engine and the fuselage. The K-2 had a larger wing with a span 19ft greater than that of other variants of the bomber, to enable it to haul the Fritz-X bombs above 20,000ft so that they could achieve the required velocity during their fall to penetrate heavily armoured targets. Both *Gruppen* underwent a period of intensive training with their new aircraft, operating over the Baltic.

Early in July *III Gruppe* moved to its operational base at Marseilles/Istres in the south of France. The unit began flying combat missions soon afterwards, but initially the performance of the Fritz-X was disappointing. At dusk on the 21st, three aircraft attacked Allied ships in the port of Augusta in Sicily. No hits were scored. An attack on ships off Syracuse two days later was no more successful, nor were those against ships off Palermo and Syracuse on 1 and 10 August respectively. More seriously, the last two missions cost the *Gruppe* three Dorniers and their crews.

Meanwhile *II Gruppe* had moved to its operational base at Cognac in the west of France. The unit first went into action with its glider bombs on 25 August, when *Hauptmann* Heinz Molinnus led twelve Dorniers in an attack on a Royal Navy submarine-hunting group off the north-western tip of Spain. Each aircraft carried an Hs 293 only under the starboard wing, and a 66-gallon drop tank under the port wing. This attack was little more successful than the previous ones with the Fritz-X, and only the destroyer HMS *Landguard* suffered damage from a near-miss.

During a follow-up attack two days later, *II Gruppe* was much more successful. A force of eighteen Dorniers attacked another submarine-hunting group and this time a glider bomb scored a direct hit on the sloop HMS *Egret*. The explosion started a fierce fire that detonated the ammunition in the ship's after magazine. The ship broke up and sank with heavy loss of life. During the same action the destroyer HMCS *Athabaskan* suffered blast and splinter damage when a missile exploded in the water close to her, but again most of the glider bombs missed their targets.

RUHRSTAHL FRITZ-X

Role: Air-launched guided missile, designed primarily for use against heavily armoured warships.

Powerplant: None.

Warhead: 3,100lb armour-piercing bomb containing 660lb of high explosive.

Performance: The weapon fell under gravity and its impact speed depended upon the altitude at which it was released. If released from 22,000ft it reached an impact speed of about 750mph.

Dimensions: Span (over cruciform fins) 4ft 3in; length 10ft 3¼in.

Method of guidance: Radio command-to-line-of sight.

Date first used in action: August 1943.

It was clear that a disconcertingly large proportion of the missiles were failing to guide properly after launch, and a technical investigation was ordered. This quickly unearthed evidence of sabotage to the aircraft. *Feldwebel* Fritz Trenkle, a technician working on the radio systems associated with the missile, explained how it was done:

> The command guidance signals from the aircraft transmitter were carried to the antenna via a coaxial cable, and somebody had cut the central conducting wire half way along its length and then reassembled the cable. It was very clever, and obviously done by an expert. When we tested the transmitters on the ground with the aircraft engines stopped, the central conducting wire made a good enough contact and the signals were radiated properly. But when the engines were running the vibration caused the gap in the wire to open and close so that for long periods the guidance signals never reached the antenna. Once we had discovered the reason for the failure we checked all the Henschel 293-carrying aircraft and found that about half had been 'doctored' in this way.

The German security service carried out exhaustive inquiries in an effort to find the culprit, but without success. We shall never know how many Allied sailors owe their lives to the stealth and skill of the nameless saboteur. Once the reason for the failures was known, the faults were quickly cleared, and suddenly the new guided missiles began to demonstrate an awesome destructive power.

On 9 September the Italian government announced that it was making peace with the Allies. Under the terms of the armistice the Italian battle fleet was to sail to Malta to surrender. *Major* Bernhard

---

DORNIER Do 217K-2

Role: Four-seat bomber and missile carrier.
Powerplant: Two BMW 801D 14-cylinder, air-cooled, radial
engines each developing 1,700hp at take-off.
Armament: Normal operational bomb load about 4,900lb (up
to 2,000lb more could be carried for short-range attacks); or
one or (for short-range attacks) two Fritz-X guided bombs each
weighing 3,100lb and carried on external racks on the wing
between each engine and the fuselage. Defensive armament of
one MG 151 15mm machine gun in top turret, two MG 131
13mm machine guns and three MG 81 paired 7.9mm guns on
flexible mountings, firing forwards, rearwards and from either
side of the cabin.
Performance: Maximum speed 313mph at 12,600ft; maximum
cruising speed 280mph at 12,600ft; normal attack speed with
Fritz-X missile, 290mph at 21,000ft; radius of action with one
Fritz-X bomb with normal operational reserves, 820 miles.
Normal operational take-off weight: 36,625lb.
Dimensions: Span 80ft 4½in; length 55ft 9¼in; wing area 721 sq ft.
Date of first production Do 217K-2: Spring 1943.

Jope, the commander of *III Gruppe*, had been briefed on such a
possibility a week earlier (German cryptographers had been able to
read the Italian naval cyphers for much of the war). Thus for several
days, while Germany and Italy were nominally fighting on the same
side, Jope had aircraft standing by at Istres ready to attack warships
of his 'ally'.

As the armada of three battleships, six cruisers and eight destroyers
neared the Strait of Bonifacio between Corsica and Sardinia, Jope
at the head of twelve Dorniers caught up with the vessels. Each
aircraft carried one Fritz-X and, concentrating on the battleships, the
bombers ran in to deliver attacks from altitudes of around 22,000ft.
Despite violent evasive action by the ships and a vigorous anti-
aircraft defence, one of the missiles scored a direct hit on the Italian
flagship, the modern battleship *Roma*. Impacting at a speed of about
750mph, the weapon struck amidships and punched clean through
the hull before detonating immediately under the ship. The powerful
explosion wrecked the steam turbines on the starboard side of the
warship, causing her to lose speed. A few minutes later *Roma* took
a second hit just forward of the bridge, which put the rest of her
machinery out of action. The warship lost speed rapidly, with fierce
fires raging inside the hull. Part of the blaze reached the forward

magazine and touched off the ammunition stored there, causing a huge explosion. Her hull already weakened by the first bomb, the ship broke into two and sank with most of her crew. During the same action *Italia*, a sister-ship of *Roma* and formerly named *Littorio*, was hit by one Fritz-X. She took on 800 tons of water but was able to continue to Malta at a slightly reduced speed. The missiles also inflicted damage on two destroyers.

On the same day Allied troops landed at Salerno in southern Italy, and in the days that followed the concentration of shipping off the coast came under repeated attack from the missile-carrying Dorniers. On 11 September a Fritz-X hit the cruiser USS *Savannah* on the forward gun turret and detonated in the ammunition handling room, killing or injuring 270 of the crew. The force of the explosion punched a hole in the ship's bottom, opening a seam that allowed in sea water that extinguished the ship's boilers. Only prompt action by the damage control teams saved the ship. Two days later a similar attack on the Royal Navy cruiser HMS *Uganda* caused severe damage which required repairs lasting more than a year.

On 16 September the Royal Navy battleship *Warspite*, operating close inshore to provide bombardment support for the ground troops, came under attack from three Fritz-Xs. One struck amidships near the funnel and penetrated six decks to explode on, and blow a hole though, her double bottom. The other two bombs scored near-misses that tore gashes in her starboard side compartments. The ship lost steam and could not be steered, her radar and armament systems ceased to function and she took on 5,000 tons of water. The battleship was towed to Malta for repairs but was out of action for nearly a year.

II Gruppe was also in action during this period, but in several cases it is difficult to determine which type of guided missile caused the loss of a particular ship that was sunk. During the six weeks following the Salerno landings the missile-carrying Dorniers caused serious damage to four other warships and sank four small vessels. As the Allied bridgehead became established the fighter defences in the area stiffened markedly, and during the 42-day period the two *Gruppen* lost twelve crews in action. For the remainder of the year the missile-carrying Dorniers went into action from time to time against Allied convoys passing through the Mediterranean. In one such engagement, against a convoy off Oran on 11 November, sixteen Do 217s of *II Gruppe* took part in a co-ordinated attack together with forty He 111 and Ju 88 torpedo bombers from *Kampfgeschwader 26*. Three large freighters and a tanker were sunk, for the loss of one Dornier and six of the torpedo bombers.

With only incomplete information on the working of the German missiles, the US Naval Research Laboratory at Annapolis turned out a small batch of makeshift jamming transmitters. Two of these were installed in the destroyers USS *Davies* and *Jones*, which were sent to the Mediterranean.

In November 1943 a third *Luftwaffe* unit became operational with Hs 293s, *II Gruppe* of *Kampfgeschwader 40*, equipped with Heinkel He 177 heavy bombers. The first action by the *Gruppe* using glider bombs, on the 21st against a convoy passing to the west of the Bay of Biscay, resulted in one merchant ship being sunk and another damaged.

On the 26th the Heinkel 177s were in action again, when Major Rudolf Mons led twenty-one of them, each loaded with two glider bombs, to attack a convoy near Algiers. The destroyers *Davies* and *Jones* formed part of the convoy escort and they began jamming as soon as the missile guidance transmissions were picked up. As would later become clear, however, the jamming modulation was ineffective and it is doubtful whether it deflected any of the missiles. Glider bombs scored hits on the large troopship *Rohna* and she sank with heavy loss of life. Then Allied fighters arrived on the scene, and their vigorous counter-attack forced the Heinkels to abandon their missiles in flight or jettison those remaining. Six of the big bombers were shot down and others suffered damage. Rudolf Mons, one of the most successful German anti-shipping pilots, was among those killed.

The next major Allied landing operation in the Mediterranean was at Anzio, on 21 January 1944. The Dorniers of *II./KG 100* were again in action but by now the Allies had learned the crucial importance of providing strong fighter cover and establishing powerful anti-aircraft gun defences ashore as soon as possible after the landings. As a result there were few easy pickings for the missile-carrying bombers. During the 3½ weeks following the landings glider bombs sank the cruiser HMS *Spartan*, two destroyers and at least four transports, for a loss of seven crews from the *Gruppe*.

Representative of the attacks during this period by *II Gruppe* was that on the evening of 15 February. Nine of its Do 217s, each carrying two glider bombs, set out from Bergamo near Milan to attack shipping off the beach-head. It was almost dark when the bombers, flying singly, arrived at the target. *Oberfeldwebel* Paul Balke, flight engineer in one of the Dorniers, described the action from his viewpoint:

> When we arrived the attack was already in progress. We did not see any other Dorniers, but from the ferocity of the flak it

was obvious they were in the area. The ships put up a terrific barrage, as did the batteries on land; also some of the warships began laying smoke screens. We climbed to about 2,500 metres [8,000ft] and circled the target, then picked out a ship and headed towards it. *Hauptmann* Schacke, the observer, released the left bomb at a range of 7km [about 4 miles], which meant the missile had a flight time of about 50 seconds. After launch we could see the red flare in the tail of the missile clearly as Schacke guided it towards the ship. From where I saw it, the flare seemed almost stationary; each time it moved slightly off the target, Schacke guided it back on again. As the range increased the flare gradually became fainter and fainter, then there was a white explosion as it struck the ship almost amidships.

The Dornier turned and sped out of the defended area, then turned for a second attack and the crew lined up on another ship. Soon after the second glider bomb was launched, however, several of the ships concentrated their fire on the bomber. In the resultant profusion of converging tracer rounds Schacke lost sight of the missile's tracking flare and had to abandon it.

That evening glider bombs sank the 7,000-ton transport *Elihu Yale* and a tank landing craft. Despite the ferocity of the defences, all the Dorniers returned safely to Bergamo; usually they were not so fortunate.

By now the Allies had captured an intact example of the Hs 293 guidance receiver, and it quickly surrendered its secrets. Once its exact method of operation had been discovered, the Naval Research Laboratory developed the high-powered MAS jammer to counter the German guided missiles. The weakness of the missiles' guidance system was that it employed tone modulations on 1, 1.5, 8 and 12KHz to carry the appropriate up, down, left or right command to the weapon in flight. The MAS jammer concentrated all of its power on just one of the tone modulation frequencies, thus making the most efficient use of the available power. During tests against the captured receiver the MAS equipment demonstrated its effectiveness, and the jammer was ordered into production. Fifty of these transmitters were built and installed in escort vessels.

The *Luftwaffe* confidently expected that Hs 293 and Fritz-X missiles would be able to inflict severe losses when the Allies launched their long-awaited invasion of northern Europe. The specialized antishipping units were grouped together in *Fliegerkorps X*, based in the south of France under the command of *Generalleutnant* Alexander Holle. Previous attacks using the guided missiles had been made with forces of 25 aircraft or fewer: By careful husbanding of resources, by the end of May 1944 Holle had assembled a formidable force of missile carriers – four *Gruppen* with a total of 136 Heinkel He 177, Dornier Do 217 and Focke Wulf FW 200 aircraft. Supplementing these were four *Gruppen* with 136 Junkers Ju 88 torpedo bombers.

After dark on the evening of D-Day, 6 June 1944, *Fliegerkorps X* launched about forty missile-carriers and torpedo bombers to attack the concentrations of Allied shipping off the beach-head. When the bombers arrived in the invasion area they encountered a violent reception from the ships' gunners, while escort vessels added to their problems by laying smokescreens and radiating jamming on the missiles' radio-guidance channels.

Quite apart from these distractions, night attacks with the missiles proved much more difficult than by day. In the case of the Hs 293 there was a 2½-mile minimum launch range, and under operational conditions it was necessary to acquire the target initially at twice that distance to give time to align the aircraft on the target before missile launch. Unless there were clear moonlight conditions it was necessary to have other planes drop flares to illuminate the targets. With so many ships in the invasion area, it was difficult to co-ordinate the activities of the flare-droppers and the attack planes. As a result, the ships illuminated were often too far away from the missile-carriers; and by the time the latter had manoeuvred into position to deliver their attacks the flares had burned out. Because of the strength of the defences, the attacks had usually to be carried out in great haste, and with the combination of darkness, the jamming from the MAS transmitters and the smokescreens, the effectiveness of the glider bombs was greatly reduced.

A few aircraft attempted to deliver attacks with Fritz-X missiles but in order to score hits these weapons required the target to be visible from at least 15,000ft. Clear skies were thus an essential prerequisite for a successful attack, and such conditions were not often met over the English Channel.

In the weeks following D-Day, *Fliegerkorps X* smashed itself against the powerful defences protecting the concentrations of Allied shipping. There were few successes to show for its efforts: during the two weeks following the invasion only two Allied ships were sunk and seven damaged as a result of air attacks using conventional bombs or guided missiles,

Throughout most of their operational career the glider bombs and guided bombs had been restricted to attacks on naval targets, to reduce the likelihood of an example of either weapon falling into Allied hands (an embargo that continued long after the Allies had captured sufficient parts of both types of weapon to deduce their methods of operation). However, at the end of July 1944 US forces seized intact the bridges over the See and Sélune rivers at the southern end of the Cherbourg Peninsula, and several divisions streamed over the bridges before fanning out into the undefended countryside beyond. In the desperate attempts to slow the advance, the *Luftwaffe* received clearance to employ the Hs 293 against land targets for the first time. Do 217s of *III Gruppe* of *KG 100* attacked the bridges on the nights of 2, 4, 5 and 6 August, losing six aircraft and crews in the process. One of the bridges was hit, but the damage was not serious and after makeshift repairs by US Army engineers it continued in use.

Following the withdrawal of the remnants of *Fliegerkorps X* from France in August 1944, the Fritz-X was not used in action again and the Hs 293 saw little further use. The last recorded attack with the glider bombs was on 12 April 1945, when a dozen Do 217s flown by crews of *Kampfgeschwader 200* launched these weapons at bridges over the Oder river that had been captured intact by Soviet forces and over which forces were streaming westwards. Although the attackers claimed some hits, most of the bridges remained in use and the relentless Soviet advance continued.

The successes achieved by the Hs 293 and the Fritz-X fully justified the effort that was put into their development and production. Nearly all of those successes took place within a couple of months of the operational introduction of these weapons, however, and from then on their effectiveness deteriorated steadily. There were two reasons for this. First, it should always be borne in mind that an air-launched weapon is not one jot better than the ability of the carrying aircraft to bring it to within range of the target and, in the case of each of the two German weapons, to guide it throughout its flight until it impacted. Once the Allies knew of the existence of the new weapons, only rarely would a lucrative maritime targets appear within range of the German bombers without strong fighter protection. If the missile was in flight and the launching plane had to manoeuvre to avoid fighter attack, further guidance was made impossible. The second point is that if a new weapon is used in action, it is almost inevitable that examples will fall into enemy hands intact. When it does, the weaknesses of the system will be discovered and the enemy will exploit these in developing suitable countermeasures. In the case of the German guided missiles, the Achilles' heel was the tone-modulated guidance system that was vulnerable to the MAS jamming transmissions. Once the new jammer had been deployed aboard Allied naval escort vessels, the German weapons were able to achieve little.

Chapter 23

Hard Fight to 'The Big B'

The US bomber offensive against Germany sparked off some of the largest air actions in history. On 6 March 1944 the Eighth Air Force fought its hardest battle against the Luftwaffe, and suffered its heaviest losses, in the course of the first maximum-effort daylight attack to 'The Big B' – Berlin. This chapter tells the story of that engagement.

By the beginning of March 1944 the US Eighth Air Force considered itself sufficiently strong to take on the ultimate challenge – a daylight maximum-effort strike on Berlin, the most heavily defended target in Ge rmany. After a couple of false starts, the attack took place on 6 March.

A total of 563 B-17 Flying Fortresses and 249 B-24 Liberators were assigned to the Berlin mission. The 1st Bomb Division, with 301 B-17s in five Wing formations, was to attack the VKF ball-bearing factory at Erkner, the third largest plant of its kind in Germany. The 2nd Bomb Division, with 249 B-24 Liberators in three Wing formations, was to bomb the Daimler-Benz works at Genshagen, then turning out more than a thousand aero engines per month. The 3rd Bomb Division, with 262 B-17s in six Wing formations, was to strike at the Bosch factory at Klein Machnow, which manufactured electrical equipment for aircraft and military vehicles.

For such a lengthy penetration of enemy airspace – 800 miles from the Dutch coast to Berlin and back – much would depend on the ability of the escorting fighters to ward off the inevitable attacks by German fighters. Fifteen Groups of P-38 Lightnings, P-47 Thunderbolts and P-51 Mustangs of the Eighth Air Force, four Groups of Thunderbolts and Mustangs of the Ninth Air Force and three squadrons of RAF Mustangs – a total of 691 fighters – were to support the operation. After they had covered the bombers' initial penetration, the plan called for 130 Thunderbolts to return to the base, refuel and re-arm, then return to eastern Holland to cover the final part of the bombers' withdrawal.

Numerically, the escorting force was formidable, but two factors imposed limits on the number of escorts in position to protect the bombers if they came under attack from German fighters. The first constraint was the limited radius of action of the escorts: with drop tanks the fighters could penetrate deep into Germany, but only if they flew in a straight line. When accompanying bombers the escorts had to maintain fighting speed while matching their rate of advance with that of their slower charges. To do that they had to fly a zig-zag path, which added greatly to the distance flown. Furthermore, the escorts needed to retain a reserve of fuel in case they went into combat. These factors limited the time a fighter Group spent with the bombers over Germany to about half an hour, or 100 miles of the bombers' penetration. Then, it was hoped, another Group of fighters would relieve it. Thus the escort of a deep-penetration attack resembled a relay race, with some fighter units moving out to join the bombers, some with the bombers and others returning after completing their time with the bombers. At any one time there would be only about 140 Allied fighters flying with the bombers, less than one-sixth of the number of sorties they would fly that day.

The second serious constraint on the escorts was the great length of the bomber stream: 94 miles during that attack on Berlin. Had the 140 escorts been spread out evenly throughout that distance, there would have been just three fighters to cover every two miles of the bomber stream. Tactically that would have been a useless distribution. The solution was to concentrate about half the escorts around the one or two Combat Bomb Wings at the head of the bomber stream, for that part of the formation was the most likely to come under attack from German fighters. The remaining escorts were split into eight-plane flights that patrolled the flanks of the rest of the bomber stream. The arrangement meant that at any one time most of the bomber Wing formations had no escorts in a position to respond immediately if they came under attack from German fighters. Until help arrived, the bombers would have to rely on their own defensive firepower to hold off their attackers.

Starting at 7.50 a.m., the bombers of the Eighth Air Force began taking off from their bases in eastern England. Once airborne, they assembled into Group formations, then the Groups joined up to form Combat Bomb Wings. As the Bomb Wings crossed the coast of England at designated places and times, they slotted into position to form Divisions. At 10.53 a.m. the vanguard of leading Bomb Division, the 1st, crossed the Dutch coast a little over three hours after the first plane had taken off.

As they assembled into formation, the bombers were under the attentive gaze of the *Mammut* and *Wassermann* long-range early-warning radar stations in Holland and Belgium. Their reports were passed to the fighter-control bunkers from which the air defence of German homeland was managed. The action about to open would be controlled from Headquarters 3rd Fighter Division near Arnhem in Holland, that of 2nd Fighter Division at Stade near Hamburg and Headquarters 1st Fighter Division at Doberitz near Berlin.

With the three Bomb Divisions in line astern, the 1st and the 3rd with Flying Fortresses, then the 2nd with Liberators, the bombers thundered eastward over Holland at three miles per minute and at altitudes of about 20,000ft. The armada took half an hour to pass a given point on the ground, presenting an awesomely impressive spectacle of military might to those watching.

Some commentators have likened the US heavy bomber actions over Germany to those fought by the *Luftwaffe* over England during the Battle of Britain in the summer of 1940. Both led to large-scale daylight combats in which a numerically inferior defending force strove to protect its homeland against attacks by enemy bombers with strong fighter escorts. To be sure, there were similarities between the two campaigns, but the far greater distances to the targets in Germany meant that the defenders had time to assemble forces and deliver a more measured response than had been possible for their British counterparts. During the Battle of Britain the German raiding forces took half an hour to reach London, one of their more distant targets, from the south coast. In 1944, the US bombers often had to spend four times as long over hostile territory to reach their targets in Germany. In contrast to the hectic British fighter scrambles of 1940, the German fighter controllers usually had ample time to prepare their response and direct their fighters into position. Certainly, that would be the case on 6 March 1944.

At airfields throughout Germany, Holland, Belgium and northern France, fighter units were brought through the different stages of alert until the pilots were at cockpit-readiness, awaiting the order to take off. As the raiding force headed due east across Holland, the German fighter controllers could see that it was probably heading for a target in northern Germany.

On this day the *Luftwaffe* had just over 900 serviceable fighters available for the defence of the Reich. Eighty were twin-engine Messerschmitt Bf 110s and Me 410s, specialized bomber destroyers

---

BOEING B-17G FLYING FORTRESS

Role: Four-engine heavy bomber.

Powerplant: Four Wright R-1820 turbo-supercharged, 14-cylinder, air-cooled, radial engines each developing 1,200hp at take-off.

Armament: The bomb load carried depended upon the distance to be flown. During the attack on Berlin these aircraft carried ten 500lb high-explosive bombs. The defensive armament comprised two Browning .5in machine guns in powered turrets in the nose, above and below the fuselage and in the tail, and one on a hand-held mounting in each waist gun position and in the radio operator's firing position above the fuselage.

Performance: Typical formation cruising speed with bomb load, 180mph at 22,000ft; demonstrated operational radius of action during the Berlin mission, 550 miles (this included fuel consumed in assembly into formation, additional fuel consumed flying in formation, operational fuel reserves and the carriage of a 5,000lb bomb load released near the mid-point of the flight).

Normal operational take-off weight: 55,000lb.

Dimensions: Span 103ft 9½in; length 74ft 4in; wing area 1,420 sq ft.

Date of first production B-17G: September 1943.

---

armed with batteries of heavy cannon and launchers for 21cm rockets. There were nearly 600 Messerschmitt 109 and Focke Wulf 190 single-engine fighters. Backing these were more than 200 night fighters, Messerschmitt Bf 110s and Junkers Ju 88s, that could also be used by day.

Just as there were operational constraints to limit the proportion of the escorting fighters available to protect US bombers at any one time, so there were other constraints that limited the proportion of the defending fighter force that could be put into action against them. The tyranny of distance imposed its will on attacker and defender alike, and the defending fighters had to be disposed to protect targets in France, Holland and Belgium as well as almost the whole of Germany. To bring into action those units based far from the bombers' route, for example in eastern France or southern Germany, would require considerable prescience on the part of the fighter controllers and not a little luck. Moreover, although the bomber-destroyers had the range to reach any part of Germany, these large and unwieldy machines were liable to suffer heavy losses if they were caught by the escorts. Because of this, the twin-engine fighters were limited to engagements east of the line Bremen–Kassel–Frankfurt. The night fighters, slowed by the weight of their radar equipment and the drag from its complex aerial arrays, were suitable only for picking off stragglers.

MESSERSCHMITT Me 410A

Role: Two-seat bomber-destroyer.
Powerplant: Two Daimler Benz DB 603A 12-cylinder, inline
   engines each developing 1,750hp at take-off.
Armament: Offensive armament of six MG 151 20mm cannon
   mounted in the nose; four launchers for 21cm Wgr rockets
   under the outer wings. Defensive armament of two MG 131
   13mm machine guns fitted in two remotely controlled barbettes
   firing rearwards and to either side.
Performance: Maximum speed 350mph at 22,000ft.
Normal operational take-off weight: 21,275lb.
Dimensions: Span 53ft 7¾in; length 40ft 11½in; wing area 390 sq ft.
Date of first production Me 410A: March 1943.

The risk that escorts would be accompanying the bombers, and the heavy defensive armament of the latter, presented further problems for the German fighter pilots. In order to overwhelm the escort, the defenders needed to deliver their attack en masse, and it took some time to assemble the units into one large formation. To reduce the effectiveness of the bombers' return fire, the fighters were to deliver their attack head-on, and that required careful direction from the ground controllers and skilful tactical handling from the formation leader.

At 11 a.m., seven minutes after the leading bombers crossed the Dutch coast, the first of the German fighter units began taking off in order to contest the incursion – 107 Bf 109s and FW 190s drawn from *I* and *II Gruppen* of *Jagdgeschwader 1*; *I*, *II* and *III Gruppen* of *JG 11*; and *III Gruppe* of *JG 54*. Once airborne, the fighters assembled into *Gruppe* formations then climbed to altitude. As they did so they converged on the distinctive oblong outline of Lake Steinhuder near Hannover, the designated assembly point for the battle formation. Although this 'Big Wing' was twice as large as any that Douglas Bader had led during the Battle of Britain, it would not suffer the same shortcomings of the earlier tactic. For one thing the American bomber formations occupied a much larger volume of airspace than their *Luftwaffe* counterparts in 1940. Furthermore, the head-on attack offered time for only a short firing pass. These factors ensured that fighters would rarely get into each other's way during the actual attack.

Escorting the bombers during the initial part of their penetration into Germany were 140 Thunderbolts from the 56th, 78th and 353rd Fighter Groups. Although the escorts outnumbered the German fighters now preparing to engage the bombers, the arithmetic of

---

FOCKE-WULF FW 190A-8

Role: Single-seat general-purpose day fighter.
Powerplant: One BMW 801D-2 14-cylinder, air-cooled, radial
   engine developing 1,770hp at take-off.
Armament: Four MG 151 20mm cannon in the wings and two
   MG 131 13mm machine guns above the engine.
Performance: Maximum speed 402mph at 18,000ft; climb to
   19,650ft, 9min 54sec.
Normal operational take-off weight: 9,660lb.
Dimensions: Span 34ft 5½in; length 29ft 4½in; wing area 197 sq ft.
Date of first production FW 190A-8: January 1944.

---

the ensuing engagement was not on their side. The German fighter
pilots would focus their attack on one Combat Bomb Wing formation, but until the last minute the escorts would be ignorant of
where the blow would fall and so they had to divide their forces
among several Wing formations.

Soon after the vanguard of the attacking force crossed the Dutch
coast, the pathfinder B-17 at the head of the attack force suffered
a radar failure. As a result, it flew a heading that took it a slightly
south of the planned route. The rest of the bombers in the 1st Bomb
Division followed it, as did those at the head of the 3rd Division.
Before the leader had deviated 20 miles from the planned track the
error was discovered, and the pathfinder edged on to a more northerly heading to regain the planned route. But by then the damage
had been done. The 13th Wing, situated mid-way along the bomber
stream, was a couple of minutes late at the Dutch coast and it had
lost visual contact with the 4th Wing ahead of it. Ignorant of the
deviation from the briefed route by the bombers ahead of it, the 13th
adhered to the flight plan. The Wing would soon pay a terrible price
for this accumulation of relatively minor errors.

At 11.55 *Hauptmann* Rolf Hermichen, at the head of the German
battle formation, sighted the swarm of black specks in front of him.
He had seen this many times before: it was a formation of US heavy
bombers, a long way away. The specks appeared almost stationary in
his windscreen – the two forces were closing almost exactly head-
on. The German ground controllers had done their work well. From
that distance Hermichen knew that any escorts with these bombers
would be too small to see; he hoped there would be none, but he was
enough of a realist not to depend on it.

It was sheer bad luck for the American bomber crews involved
that the formation now under threat was not that leading the

bomber stream, where more than half of the escorting Thunderbolts were concentrated: it was the 13th Wing, that heading the detached second half of the bomber stream, and it was almost devoid of such protection. Lieutenant Robert Johnson of the 56th Fighter Group was to one side of the Wing when he suddenly noticed Hermichen's force closing in fast:

> I was on the left side of the bombers and going 180 degrees to them when I noticed a large box of planes coming at us at the same level. There were about forty or fifty to a box, and I saw two boxes at our level and one box at 27,000 or 28,000 feet. I called in to watch them, and then that they were FW 190s. There were only eight of us . . .'

The Thunderbolts attempted to disrupt the attack but the German pilots simply ignored them as they streaked for the bombers. The opposing forces met at noon, 21,000ft above the small German town of Haselünne, close to the Dutch border.

A head-on attack on a bomber required a high degree of skill from the fighter pilot if it was to succeed. Closing at a rate of 200yds a second, there was time only for a brief half-second burst from 500yds before he had to ease up on the stick to avoid colliding with his target. For experienced pilots like *Hauptmann* Anton Hackl, the fighter ace leading the Focke Wulfs of *III Gruppe* of *Jagdgeschwader 11* that day, that was quite sufficient:

> One accurate half-second burst from head-on [on a four-engine bomber] and a kill was guaranteed. Guaranteed!

Feldwebel Friedrich Ungar of *Jagdgeschwader 54*, flying a Bf 109, saw his rounds exploding against the engine of one of the bombers and pieces flying off it:

> There was no time for jubilation. The next thing I was inside the enemy formation trying to get through without ramming anyone. Nobody fired at me then, they were too concerned about hitting each other. When we emerged from the formation things got really hot; we had the tail gunners of some thirty bombers letting fly at us with everything they had. Together with part of our *Gruppe* I pulled sharply to the left and high, out to one side. Glancing back I saw the Fortress I had hit tip up and go down to the right, smoking strongly.

Sergeant Van Pinner, a top-turret gunner with the 100th Bomb Group, recalled that he had far more targets than he could possibly fire at:

There were fighters everywhere. They seemed to come past in fours. I would engage the first three but then the fourth would be on to me before I could get my guns on him. I knew our aircraft was being hit real bad – we lost the ball turret gunner early in the fight . . .

The initial head-on attack was over in much less than a minute and then, almost in slow motion, a succession of mortally wounded Fortresses began to slide out of formation. The 13th Wing comprised A and B formations flying almost in line abreast with a mile between them. The B formation comprised 38 Flying Fortresses from the 100th and 390th Bomb Groups and its Low Box, with sixteen B-17s at the start of the action, suffered the worst. All six bombers of its High Squadron were shot down, as were two of the six in its Lead Squadron and two of the four in its Low Squadron.

Lieutenant John Harrison of the 100th Bomb Group, Captain of one of the bombers, gazed in disbelief as planes began to go down around him:

The engine of one Fort burst into flames and soon the entire ship was afire. Another was burning from waist to tail. It seemed [that] both the pilot and co-pilot of another ship had been killed. It started towards us out of control. I moved the squadron over. Still it came. Again we moved. This time the stricken Fortress stalled, went up on its tail, then slid down.

Following the initial firing pass, the German fighters split into twos and fours and curved around to deliver fresh attacks on the same formation. Some overtook the bombers and sped ahead of them preparatory to moving into position for further head-on attacks. Other German fighters attacked the bomber formation from behind, and yet others dived after damaged B-17s that had been forced to leave the formation and were trying to escape to the west.

Lieutenant Lowell Watts, Captain of a bomber in the next formation in the stream, was an unwilling spectator to the unequal battle:

About two or three miles ahead of us was the 13th Combat Wing. Their formation had tightened up since I last looked at it. Little dots that were German fighters were diving into those formation, circling, and attacking again. Out of one High Squadron a B-17 slowly climbed away from its formation, the entire right wing a mass of flames. I looked again a second later. There was a flash – then nothing but little specks drifting, tumbling down. Seconds later another bomber tipped up on a wing, rolled over and dove straight for the ground. Little white puffs of parachutes began to float beneath us, then fall behind as we flew toward our target.

From the moment the German fighters had first been sighted, the 13th Wing put out frantic radio calls to summon assistance from the escorts. Colonel Hub Zemke, commander of the 56th Fighter Group and heading an eight-plane flight of Thunderbolts, arrived at the beleaguered unit just as *Oberleutnant* Wolfgang Kretschmer of *JG 1* was lining up for another firing pass. Zemke spotted the lone Focke Wulf below him and ordered one section of four aircraft to remain at high altitude to cover him, while he led his section down to attack.

Before opening fire at the bomber he had selected as a target, Kretschmer glanced over his own tail to check that the sky was clear. It was not. The German pilot was horrified to see Zemke's Thunderbolt closing in rapidly on him, followed by three others. Kretschmer hauled the Focke Wulf into a tight turn to the left get out of the way, but it was too late. By then Zemke was in a firing position and .5in rounds from his accurate burst thudded into the wings and fuselage of the German fighter. As Zemke pulled up to regain altitude he glanced back and saw the enemy fighter falling out of the sky enveloped in flames. Kretschmer extricated himself from the cockpit of his blazing aircraft and jumped clear. He landed by parachute with moderate burns to his hands and face and splinters embedded in his thigh.

The main part of the initial action lasted about ten minutes. Then, as the German fighters exhausted their ammunition, they dived away from the fight, trying to avoid the rampaging escorts. However, even as the initial action petered to its close, a second German battle formation was already moving into position to engage the raiders. In their bunker at Döberitz the controllers of the 1st Fighter Division had assembled every available fighter in that part of Germany. The core of the battle formation comprised the bomber-destroyers, 42 Messerschmitt Bf 110s and Me 410s from *II* and *III Gruppen* of *Zerstörer-geschwader 26* and *I* and *II* of *ZG 76*. Providing cover for these, though they were also expected to engage the bombers, were

70 Bf 109s and FW 190s from *I, II* and *IV Gruppen* of *Jagdgeschwader 3, I* of *JG 302* and *Sturmstaffel 1*. Leading the formation was *Major* Hans Kogler, the commander of *III./ZG 26*, flying a Bf 110.

Again, a large force of German fighters charged head-on into a pair of formations of Fortresses flying in line abreast: the 1st Combat Wing comprised 51 aircraft drawn from the 91st and 381st Bomb Groups; and the 94th Combat Wing, with 61 Flying Fortresses from the 401st and 457th Bomb Groups, flew a couple of miles to the right of it. But these two Wings were in the vanguard of the bomber stream and were protected by a large proportion of the available escorts – 80 Mustangs from the 4th and 354th Fighter Groups. This time the escorts were in the right place, at the right time and in sufficient numbers to blunt the German attack. Lieutenant Nicholas Megura of the 4th Fighter Group described the approach of the defending formation:

> Twelve-plus smoke-trails were seen coming from twelve o'clock and high, thirty miles ahead. 'Upper' [the Group leader] positioned the Group up-sun, below condensation height, and waited. Trails finally positioned themselves at nine o'clock to bombers and started to close. Six thousand feet below the trails were twenty-plus single-engine fighters line abreast, sweeping area for twenty-plus twin-engine rocket-carrying aircraft. 'Upper' led Group head-on into front wave of enemy aircraft.

The Mustangs' spoiling tactics forced several German fighters to abandon their attack, but others continued doggedly on to launch their hefty 21cm-calibre rockets head-on into the bomber formations.

Accidentally or deliberately, an Me 410 collided with, or rammed head-on into, a Flying Fortress of the 457th Bomb Group and tore away a large section of the bomber's tail. The stricken bomber, which had been flying on the right side of the High Squadron, went out of control and entered a steep, diving turn to the left. After narrowly missing several bombers in the formation, it smashed into the aircraft on the far left of the Low Squadron. Only one man survived from the three crews involved in the incident, the tail gunner from the last aircraft to be struck. As the bomber-destroyers emerged from the rear of the bomber formation, other Mustangs pounced on them and the nimble single-seaters did great execution; fourteen of the twin-engine fighters were shot down.

Hard on the heels of the heavy fighters came the main body of the attack formation – 70 single-seat Messerschmitts and Focke Wulfs.

One of the attacking pilots was *Leutnant* Hans Iffland of *Jagdgeschwader 3*, flying a Messerschmitt Bf 109:

> During the firing run everything happened very quickly, with the closing speed of about 800 kilometres per hour [500mph]. After firing my short burst at one of the B-17s I pulled up over it; I had attacked from slightly above, allowing a slight deflection angle and aiming at the nose. I saw my rounds exploding around the wing root and tracers rounds from the bombers flashing past me. As I pulled up over the bomber I dropped my left wing, to see the results of my attack and also to give the smallest possible target at which their gunners could aim. Pieces broke off the bomber and it began to slide out of the formation.

The action around the leading formations lasted little over ten minutes and, thanks to the efforts of the Mustangs, the bombers' losses were much lighter than during the earlier attack: seven had been either destroyed or damaged so seriously that they had been forced out of formation and finished off as stragglers.

Now, shortly after 1 p.m., the raiding units were moving into position to begin their bomb runs. Defending Berlin was the 1st Flak Division, commanded by *Generalmajor* Max Schaller and comprising the 22nd, 53rd, 126th and 172nd Flak Regiments with more than 400 8.8cm, 10.5cm, and 12.8cm guns. German fighter pilots were unwilling to pursue the raiders into the inferno of flak that would soon be put up over the capital, and they broke off the action.

As they approached their targets, the bombers split into their three divisions and lined up for their bombing runs. The first to feel the gunners' wrath were the Flying Fortresses of the 1st Bomb Division. Captain Ed Curry, a bombardier with the 401st Bomb Group, never forgot that cannonade:

> I'd been to Oschersleben and the Ruhr, but I'd never seen flak as heavy as that they had over Berlin. It wasn't just the odd black puff, it was completely dense; not just at one altitude, but high and low. There was a saying that you see the smoke only after the explosion; but that day we actually saw the red of the explosions. One shell burst near us, and we had chunks of shell tear through the radio room and the bomb bay.

Now, however, the weather protected the primary targets more effectively than the German defences ever could. At first it seemed that the bombardiers would be able to make visual bomb runs on the targets through breaks in the clouds, but at the critical moment the aiming points were obscured. None of the planes hit the 1st Division's primary target at Erkner, and the attackers released their bombs on the Köpenick and Weissensee districts of the city.

It was a similar story for the 3rd Bomb Division, whose Flying Fortresses missed the primary target at Klein Machnow and bombed the Steglitz and Zehlendorf districts instead. Lowell Watts was on his bomb run when the gunners zeroed in on his formation:

> They didn't start out with wild shots and work in closer. The first salvo they sent up was right on us. We could hear the metal of our plane rend and tear as each volley exploded. The hits weren't direct. They were just far enough away so they didn't take off a wing, the tail or blow the plane up; they would just tear a ship half apart without completely knocking it out. Big ragged holes appeared in the wings and the fuselage. Kennedy, the co-pilot, was watching nothing but the instruments, waiting for the tell-tale indication of a damaged or ruined engine. But they kept up their steady roar, even as the ship rocked from the nearness of the flak bursts . . . The flak was coming up as close as ever, increasing in intensity. Above and to the right of us a string of bombs trailed out from our lead ship. Simultaneously our ship jumped upwards, relieved of its explosive load as the call 'Bombs away!' came over the interphone. Our left wing ship, one engine feathered, dropped behind the formation. That left only four of us in the Low Squadron. A few minutes later the flak stopped. We had come through it and all four engines were still purring away.

Only a few Liberators of the 2nd Bomb Division, the last to attack, put their bombs on their primary target, the Daimler-Benz aero-engine works at Genshagen; the rest of the attack also fell on secondary targets in and around the capital.

The vicious bombardment knocked down only four bombers, but it caused sufficient damage to several others to force them to leave formation. Moreover, nearly half the bombers that reached Berlin collected flak damage of some sort.

As the bombers emerged from the flak zones, a few German single-seat fighters tried to a press home attacks, while fourteen Messerschmitt 110 night fighters from *Nachtjagdgeschwader 5* closed in to finish off stragglers. The escorts quickly took charge of the situation, however. The defending single-seaters were chased away and the night fighters, too slow to escape from their pursuers, lost ten of their number within the space of a few minutes. For the time being the German fighters had spent their force, and during the next half-hour there was a lull in the fighting.

Relieved by fresh squadrons of Thunderbolts, the Mustangs peeled away from the bombers and headed for home. As they were running out past Bremen, a section of Mustangs of the 357th Fighter Group came upon a lone Bf 109 and Lieutenants Howell and Carder shot it down. *Oberleutnant* Gerhard Loos of *Jagdgeschwader 54*, a leading *Experte* credited with 92 victories, was killed.

The air action around the bombers resumed at 2.40 p.m., with attacks by Bf 109s and FW 190s that had landed to refuel and re-arm after taking part in the noon action near Haselünne. Other fighters came from units based in France and Belgium that had missed the raiders on their way in.

The formation hardest hit during this engagement was the 45th Combat Bomb Wing. Once again Lowell Watts of the 388th Bomb Group takes up the story:

> The interphone snapped to life: 'Focke Wulfs at 3 o'clock level!' Yes, there they were – what seemed at a hurried count to be about 30 fighters flying along just out of range beside us. They pulled ahead of us, turned across our flight path and attacked from ahead and slightly below us. Turrets swung forward throughout the formation and began spitting out their .50-calibre challenge. Some Focke Wulfs pulled above us and hit us from behind while most dived in from the front, coming in from 11 to 1 o'clock to level, so close that only every second or third plane could be sighted on by the gunners. Still they came, rolling, firing and diving away, then attacking again.

He watched two bombers fall out of the formation, then his own aircraft came under attack:

> Brassfield called from the tail position, 'I've got one, I've got one!' Then, almost with the same breath, 'I've been hit!' No sooner had the interphone cleared from that message when an even more ominous one cracked into the headsets: 'We're on fire!' Looking forwards I saw a Focke Wulf coming at us from dead level at 12 o'clock. The fire from our top and chin turrets shook the B-17. At the same instant his wings lit up with fire from his guns. The 20mm rounds crashed through our nose and exploded beneath my feet amongst the oxygen tanks. At the same time they slashed through some of the gasoline cross-feed lines. The flames which

started here, fed by the pure oxygen and the gasoline, almost exploded through the front of the ship. The companionway to the nose, the cockpit and the bomb bays was a solid mass of flame.

Watts struggled to hold the bomber level while his crew abandoned the machine. The flames prevented him from seeing ahead and he could not know that his aircraft was edging ever closer to another formation. With a crash of tortured metal the bombers smashed together, then broke apart and, shedding pieces, they began their long fall to earth.

Unaware that there had been a collision, Watts knew that the bomber was no longer under his control. Moreover, seemingly for no good reason, almost the whole of the cabin roof above his head had suddenly vanished:

It was a wild ride from that point. I could tell we had rolled upside down. My safety belt had been unbuckled. I fell away from the seat, but held myself in with the grasp I had on the control wheel. After a few weird sensations I was pinned to the seat, unable to move or even raise my hand to pull off the throttles or try to cut the gas to the inboard engines. My left foot had fallen off the rudder bars while we were on our back. I couldn't even slide it across the floor to get it back on the pedal. Flames now swept past my face, between my legs and past my arms as though sucked by a giant vacuum. Unable to see, I could tell only that we were spinning and diving at a terrific rate. That wild eerie ride down the corridors of the sky in a flaming bomber still haunts my memory. But it wasn't just the terror of death, it was the unending confusion and pain of a hopeless fight and the worry for the nine other men that were my responsibility. Contrary to the usual stories, my past life failed to flash in review through my mind. I was too busy fighting to keep that life.

The next thing Watts knew, he was hurtling through space and well clear of the blazing bomber. He opened his parachute and landed safely, as did five others from his crew. Six men from the other bomber involved in the collision also parachuted to safety.

During this sharp engagement the 388th Bomb Group lost a total of seven aircraft. The losses were not all on one side, however. *Hauptmann* Hugo Frey of *Jagdgeschwader 11*, an ace pilot credited with the destruction of 26 US heavy bombers, was killed when his FW 190 was shot down by return fire from the bombers.

On 6 March a total of 812 Flying Fortresses and Liberators had set out from England, 672 of which had attacked primary or secondary targets in the Berlin area. Sixty-nine B-17s and B-24s failed to return to England, including four damaged machines that came down in Sweden. Sixty bombers returned with severe damage and 336 had lesser amounts of damage. Of the 691 fighters taking part in the operation, eleven were destroyed and eight returned with severe damage. In a concentrated fighter-versus-bomber action of this type, the heavy losses were confined to a few unfortunate units; as luck would have it, all of them flew Flying Fortresses. The hardest hit, the 100th Bomb Group, lost fifteen of the 36 aircraft that had crossed the Dutch coast; most of these fell during the initial clash near Haselünne. The 95th Bomb Group, which with the 100th made up the 13B Wing formation, lost eight bombers. The 91st Bomb Group lost six during the attack in front of Berlin, and the 388th Bomb Group lost seven planes during the sharp action over western Germany on the way home.

The losses suffered by these four Groups accounted for more than half the heavy bombers that failed to return. By its nature, an account such as this will tend to concentrate on the areas of heaviest fighting and the units that took the heaviest losses. To put things into perspective, it should be pointed out that the remaining 33 bomber losses were shared almost evenly between nineteen Bomb Groups; and the remaining six Bomb Groups flew the mission without suffering a single loss between them.

That day the *Luftwaffe* flew 528 fighter sorties, of which 369 probably made contact with the raiders. Sixty-two German fighters, 16 per cent of those that made contact, were destroyed and thirteen damaged. The twin-engine fighter units took the heaviest losses. *Nachtjagdgeschwader 5* lost ten of the fourteen Messerschmitt Bf 110 night fighters sent up, while *Zerstörergeschwader 26* lost eleven of its eighteen Messerschmitt Bf 110 and Me 410 bomber-destroyers. Altogether the *Luftwaffe* lost 44 air crew killed, including two leading aces, and 23 wounded. The aircraft losses could be made good, but the experienced fighter pilots were irreplaceable.

With the attack on Berlin on 6 March 1944 the Eighth Air Force bombing campaign passed another important milestone. Thenceforth no target in Germany, no matter how far from England nor how strong its defences, was immune from daylight precision attack.

Chapter 24

The Great Marianas Turkey Shoot

The Battle of the Philippine Sea in June 1944, involving fifteen US and nine Japanese aircraft carriers with full supporting forces, was the largest carrier-versus-carrier action of all time . . .

On 6 June 1944, as Allied troops fought to secure a foothold on the Normandy beaches, half a world away another large invasion force was making its opening moves. Comprising more than 600 ships bearing 127,000 assault troops, its objective was the Pacific island of Saipan in the strategically placed Marianas group.

The cutting edge of the US Pacific Fleet was Vice-Admiral Marc Mitscher's fast carrier striking force, Task Force 58. This comprised seven large aircraft carriers and eight smaller ones, with 467 Hellcat fighters. In addition there were 425 attack planes – Dauntless and Helldiver dive-bombers and Avenger multi-purpose bombers that could attack with bombs or torpedoes. The US carrier air groups were highly trained and proficient and most of their crews had several months' combat experience. They functioned as well-knit teams, confident in their equipment and in their ability to defeat their opponents.

In addition to its front-line force, Task Force 58 was well provided with reserves for the forthcoming battle. Since the action was planned to take place about a thousand miles away from the nearest US support base, at Eniwetok Atoll, the size of the force deployed against the enemy was limited to that which the available fleet logistics train could support. Because of this, no fewer than five escort carriers with a total of 135 aircraft were held in reserve off Eniwetok, ready to move into the combat zone to replace any carrier put out of action; and some 100 combat aircraft of all types, with crews, were at sea aboard the replenishment carriers sailing with the logistic support ships, available to replace losses. Operating separately from the fast carrier force were eight more escort carriers, with 114 Wildcat fighters and 82 Avenger bombers, earmarked to protect the transports and landing craft and provide air support for the troops as they went into action ashore.

Since its disastrous defeat during the Battle of Midway in June 1942, when the Japanese Navy lost four large carriers together with most of their air groups in a single day, that service had spared no effort to rebuild its aircraft carrier fleet. By the spring of 1944 it was once again a force to be reckoned with, with three large and six smaller carriers operating a total of 430 combat aircraft. In addition there were nearly 500 combat aircraft of all types based at airfields in the Marianas, and a further 100 in the Caroline Islands within range to intervene in the action about to begin.

On 11 June Task Force 58 arrived within attack range of the Marianas and began a programme of offensive strikes aimed at establishing air superiority over Guam, Saipan and Tinian. Two days later a force of battleships and their attendant cruisers and destroyers arrived off Saipan, to bombard coastal positions and provide cover for the mine-sweepers moving inshore to check that the approaches to the invasion beaches were clear of mines and other obstacles.

The importance of Saipan, and the deterioration to Japan's war situation if that island were lost, was all too clear to the Japanese High Command. The island lay within 1,500 miles of Japan itself, and therefore within B-29 heavy bomber range of the home islands. If the Marianas fell, Tokyo and every other Japanese city faced the menace of sustained aerial bombardment. The threat could not be ignored, and the Japanese Navy was prepared to stake everything it had to deliver an effective counterstroke.

On 13 June the Japanese carrier force, commanded by Vice-Admiral Jisaburo Ozawa, set sail from Tawi Tawi in Borneo and headed for the Marianas. On the way other groups of warships joined the force, and the Japanese Commander-in-Chief, Admiral Soemu Toyoda, repeated to each ship the famous signal that Admiral Togo had sent before the decisive Battle of Tsushima that had seen the defeat of the Imperial Russian Navy 38 years earlier: 'The fate of the Empire rests on this one battle. Every man is expected to do his utmost.'

To win the forthcoming engagement the Japanese sailors and airmen would certainly need courage and resourcefulness of a very high order. Their carrier planes were outnumbered more than two to one by those of Task Force 58 alone, and that was only one of their predicaments.

YOKOSUKA D4YI ('JUDY')

Role: Two-seat, carrier-borne dive-bomber/reconnaissance aircraft.
Powerplant: One Aichi Atsuta liquid-cooled, 12-cylinder, inline
engine developing 1,200hp for take-off.
Armament: One 1,100lb bomb carried in an internal bomb bay;
two sychronized Type 97 7.7mm machine guns firing through the
propeller disc and one hand-held Type 1 7.92mm machine gun
firing rearwards.
Performance: Maximum speed 332mph at 17,225ft.
Normal operational take-off weight: 8,276lb.
Dimensions: Span 37ft 8¾in; length 33ft 6½in; wing area 254 sq ft.
Date of first production D4YI: October 1942.

The most serious problem was the general lack of combat experience,
compounded in many cases by the incomplete operational training, of
the Japanese air crews. The hastily reassembled Japanese carrier force
had reached its present size only by the careful husbanding of resources
and by keeping most of the flying units out of action. The air crews
aboard the three larger carriers had six months' operational training and
were considered proficient in their respective roles (though their level
of training was considerably less than that received by their US Navy
counterparts). Aboard the six smaller Japanese carriers the average level
of training was much lower and many of the crews had not reached
even the minimum Japanese operational training standard.

The unevenness in the quality of the Japanese air crews was
matched by that of the aircraft they flew. The best Japanese attack
planes, the B6N ('Jill') and the D4YI ('Judy') that equipped the
torpedo and dive-bomber units respectively on the three larger
Japanese carriers were first-rate fighting aircraft with a good turn
of speed and a radius of action superior to that of their American
counterparts. On the six smaller Japanese carriers it was a different
matter. Their decks were too small to operate the high performance
'Jills' and 'Judys', and their attack units were equipped with the obsolete B5N ('Kate') torpedo bombers and D3A1('Val') dive-bombers
that dated from the beginning of the Pacific war. These small carriers
also operated units equipped with the elderly A6M2 Model 21 Zero
fighter modified as a dive-bomber with a rack to carry a single 550lb
bomb under the fuselage. The modified Zeros lacking dive brakes,
however, and they were limited to medium- or shallow-dive attacks
that were less accurate against moving ships than steep-dive attacks.

The most serious equipment weakness faced by the Japanese
carrier air groups was the relative obsolescence of their standard

---

NAKAJIMA B6N2 ('JILL')

Role: Three-seat, carrier-borne torpedo bomber.
Powerplant: One Mitsubishi Kasei 25 14-cylinder, air-cooled,
radial engine developing 1,825hp at take-off.
Armament: One 1,760lb torpedo, or an equivalent weight of
bombs; one sychronized Type 97 7.7mm machine gun firing
forwards through the propeller disc, one firing rearwards from
the cabin and one firing rearwards and below the aircraft from
the ventral hatch.
Performance: Maximum speed 318mph at 19,500ft.
Normal operational take-off weight: 12,070lb.
Dimensions: Span 49ft; length 36ft 1in; wing area 395 sq ft.
Date of first production B6N2: October 1943.

---

fleet air defence fighter type, the Mitsubishi A6M5 Type 52 (Allied
code-name 'Zeke 52'). Developed from the earlier Zero, it was only
slightly more effective, with a maximum speed increased by a paltry
20mph. Compared with the standard US Navy carrier fighter type,
the Grumman F6F Hellcat, the Type 52 was inferior in almost every
aspect of performance that mattered in air combat. Flights trials in
which a captured A6M5 Model 52 was pitted in mock combats
against Hellcats revealed huge discrepancies in the performance of
the two aircraft. The report on the trials stated:

> In maximum speed, the F6F ranged from 25 mph faster at sea
> level to 75 mph faster at 25,000 feet. In the climb the Model
> 52 was superior below 14,000 feet, at altitudes above that the
> F6F was superior. Below 230 mph the rate of roll of the two
> fighters was similar, above that speed the F6F-5 was much the
> better. Below 200 mph the Model 52 was far more manoeu-
> vrable than the F6F, while above 230 mph the F6F was the
> more manoeuvrable.

Hellcat pilots engaging the Zeke 52 were urged to exploit to the
full their superior speed and altitude performance. On no account
were they to allow themselves to be drawn into dogfights with the
more nimble but slower Japanese fighter. An effective tactic, when
the Japanese fighters were sighted, was to increase speed to 300mph
then enter a zoom climb, converting speed into altitude to get
well above and out of reach of their opponents. Once there the
American pilots had the initiative and could dictate the terms of
the engagement, delivering high-speed slashing attacks on the Zekes
followed by a zoom climb back to altitude to allow no opportunity

for retaliation. Under such conditions the Japanese fighter's superior low-speed manoeuvrability would be an unusable asset.

On 15 June US Marines stormed ashore on Saipan, and by nightfall they had established two beach-heads. This development gave added urgency to the Japanese fleet now approaching the island. During the initial phase of the battle Admiral Toyoda enjoyed three important advantages over the US fleet commander, Admiral Raymond Spruance. The first advantage was freedom of action: Toyoda could deploy his carriers as the tactical situation demanded, whereas Spruance had to keep his force of fast carriers close to Saipan to protect the landing operation and the vulnerable transport ships off the coast. Toyoda's second advantage was that his long-range aerial reconnaissance was much the more effective, and planes flying from the Marianas were already shadowing the various groups of US ships. For their part the Japanese carriers were still beyond the 350-mile radius of action of the US carrier reconnaissance planes, so Spruance had to rely on the fleeting and often misleading sighting reports from submarines for information on the whereabouts of his opponents. The third great advantage enjoyed by the Japanese commander was that the attack radius of action of his carrier planes, 300 miles; was a full 100 miles greater than that of the US planes that were burdened with greater armour protection and self-sealing fuel tanks.

Toyoda had regular reports on the movements and approximate compositions of the US Navy task groups, while Spruance had only a vague idea of the location of the Japanese carriers. So long as that situation continued, it was inevitable that the Japanese would be the first to launch an air strike and that the US ships would have to brace themselves to fight a defensive battle.

The first attacks on the US ships came not from the Japanese carrier planes, nor from those based in the Marianas, but from

---

MITSUBISHI A6M5 MODEL 52 ('ZEKE 52')

Role: Single-seat, carrier-borne fighter.
Powerplant: One Nakajima Sakae 21 14-cylinder, air-cooled, radial engine developing 1,130hp for take-off.
Armament: Two Type 99 20mm cannon and two Type 97 7.7mm machine guns.
Performance: Maximum speed 358mph at 22,000ft.
Normal operational take-off weight: 6,050lb.
Dimensions: Span 36ft 1in; length 29ft 8½in; wing area 239 sq ft.
Date of first production A6M5: Autumn 1943.

GRUMMAN F6F-3 HELLCAT

Role: Single-seat, carrier-borne fighter.
Powerplant: One Pratt & Whitney R-2800-10 Double Wasp
   18-cylinder, air-cooled, radial engine developing 2,000hp for takeoff.
Armament: Six Browning .5in machine guns mounted in the wings.
Performance: Maximum speed 373mph at 23,700ft; climb to
   15,000ft, 7min 42sec.
Normal operational take-off weight: 12,186lb.
Dimensions: Span 42ft 10in; length 33ft 4in; wing area 334 sq ft.
Date of first production F6F-3: October 1942.

aircraft based at Yap in the Caroline Islands. In the afternoon of the 17th, a force of B5N 'Kate' torpedo bombers sank a Landing Craft (Infantry). That evening seventeen D4Y 'Judy' dive-bombers and two P1Y1 'Frances' torpedo bombers with a strong fighter escort attacked the transports and escort carriers off the beach-head and damaged one of the small carriers so seriously that she had to be withdrawn from the operation. In further air attacks the next day a fleet oiler was damaged.

Before dawn on the 19th Admiral Ozawa's carriers reached a position from which they could launch a massive air strike against the Task Force 58. Japanese reconnaissance planes increased their shadowing activity around the US task groups, an essential operation before the attack but also a costly one: of about 60 carrier and land-based aircraft assigned to the task, no fewer than 35 were shot down by the Hellcats.

Early that morning the Japanese carriers turned into the wind and began launching their planes. The operation did not take place unhindered, however, for the submarine USS *Albacore* was able to sneak past the escorting destroyers and loose off a spread of torpedoes at the large Japanese carrier *Taiho*. One of the weapons struck the warship, but it caused only minor damage to her hull and after a short delay *Taiho* resumed launching her planes.

The first of the incoming attack forces, comprising 43 Zero dive-bombers and seven B6N ('Jill') torpedo bombers with an escort of fourteen 'Zeke 52s', was detected on radar while still 150 miles from the US carriers. Any possible doubts regarding the force's intentions were dispelled soon afterwards when the Japanese air group commander delivered a radio briefing to his crews that was overheard by a monitor on board one of the US warships.

The US carriers immediately began to clear their decks for action. The Hellcats assembled into flights and climbed to the west to meet the threat while the attack planes headed east to keep out of harm's way until it was safe to return. When the Japanese force was detected there were 59 Hellcats airborne on combat air patrol to defend the task force, and now they were joined by a further 140 fighters.

The cloud-free skies and the ample flow of radar information on the raiders' approach provided ideal conditions for the defending fighters, and the latter made the most of their advantage. The first to go into action were eight Hellcats of the USS *Essex*, which intercepted the Japanese force when it was still 70 miles from the American carriers. With a 6,000ft altitude advantage, Commander C. Brewster led a diving attack on the Zero dive-bombers that accounted for two of them, then the escorting 'Zekes' intervened and a wild mêlée developed. Soon afterwards twenty Hellcats from *Hornet* and *Princeton* pitched into the fight, followed by a further fourteen from *Cowpens* and *Monterey*. Other fighters, having recently taken off from their carriers, joined the action as the Japanese force closed on the US carriers. Subjected to a series of savage onslaughts from above, the raiding force took heavy losses. Some of the Japanese attack formations lost cohesion but their pilots refused to countenance retreat and pressed on grimly towards their targets. Despite the heavy odds against them, about twenty Japanese attack planes broke through the fighter screens and lined up to deliver attacks on the US warships.

It requires a large amount of training and practice to deliver an accurate dive-bombing or torpedo attack on a warship manoeuvring in open water, and the abilities of the Japanese crews did not match the iron determination they had displayed in getting through to their targets. Their sole hit was a bomb that struck the battleship *South Dakota*, causing localized damage and some fifty casualties, but did not prevent the warship continuing in action. Forty-two of the 64 attacking planes were shot down, for the loss of three Hellcats.

Hard on the heels of the first Japanese striking force came the second. Launched from the three largest Japanese aircraft carriers, this comprised 53 D4Y1 ('Judy') dive-bombers and 27 B6N ('Jill') torpedo bombers with an escort of 48 'Zeke 52' fighters. These were the most modern of the Japanese carrier attack aircraft and they were flown by the best-trained of the available crews. Again the striking force was detected on radar when it was more than 100 miles from the American carriers, and again a monitor eavesdropped on the airborne radio briefing given by the Japanese attack commander. Since the earlier launch there had been time to range more Hellcats on the decks of the US carriers. In addition to the fighters sent aloft to engage the first raid, many of which had fuel and ammunition to continue the fight, more than 160 fresh fighters were scrambled to buttress the defence.

The second action was a near-repeat of the first. Once more the raiders suffered heavy losses on the way in, but again about twenty broke through the defences. And once again the resultant attack highlighted the Japanese crews' poor training and lack of combat experience. The aircraft carriers *Wasp* and *Bunker Hill* suffered minor damage and some casualties from bombs exploding nearby, while other ships were narrowly missed by torpedoes. A 'Jill' crashed into the battleship *Indiana*, but the latter's armoured belt took the force of the explosion and the warship continued in operation. As before, the defending fighters did great execution, and of the 128 planes in the attack wave, 94 were shot down for a loss of four Hellcats.

Owing to an inaccurate report on the position of the target, most of the 49 aircraft in the third Japanese attack wave failed to reach the US task force. Only the escorting force of sixteen 'Zeke 52s' went into action, and the Hellcats shot down seven of the Japanese fighters for the loss of one of their own.

The fourth attack wave, comprising 46 'Judy', 'Val' and Zero dive-bombers, six 'Jill' torpedo bombers and an escort of thirty 'Zeke 52s', did no better than the first two. A few Japanese planes did break through the fighter screens and to deliver attacks to the US carriers, but none of them scored hits. Thirty-eight of the planes in this force were shot down, either in the vicinity of the US carriers or when they were caught by Hellcats as they were on the landing approach to Orote airfield on Guam.

During the series of air combats, four Japanese carrier-borne attack forces with a total of 323 aircraft had been hurled into action against Task Force 58. Of those aircraft, 181 were shot down – a crushing 60 per cent of the raiding force. Seven Hellcats had been lost in the swirling air combats, but none of the ships had suffered serious damage and all were able to continue operating.

Meanwhile the US submarines continued to nip at the heels of the Japanese carrier groups far to the west. Shortly after the survivors from the four attack waves returned to their ships, the USS *Cavalla* scored three torpedo hits on the large carrier *Shokaku*. In spite of desperate efforts by the latter's crew to contain the fires, these were soon blazing out of control and, following a large explosion, the vessel went to the bottom. Soon afterwards *Taiho* followed her; although the single torpedo hit earlier in the day had caused relatively little structural damage, fumes from a ruptured aviation fuel tank had leaked into the hull. A chance spark ignited these, leading to a series of explosions of increasing severity until finally the carrier sank. Twenty-two planes went down with the two Japanese carriers.

By dawn on 20 June the Japanese carrier air groups were reduced to a shadow of their former strength: they were left with just 68 'Zeke 52s' and Zeros, three D4Y 'Judy' dive-bombers and 29 B5N 'Kate' and B6N 'Jill' torpedo bombers. Ozawa had no alternative but to order his seven surviving carriers to withdraw to the west. On Guam the Japanese air strength was almost exhausted too, following the loss of 110 planes in the air and on the ground and many more damaged during the US attacks on airfields.

Despite the best efforts of the US carrier reconnaissance planes, it was mid-afternoon on the 20th before Admiral Mitscher received the first clear reports on the location of the Japanese carrier groups. At last, Task Force 58 could deliver its counterstroke. The striking force comprised 77 Helldiver and Dauntless dive-bombers, 54 Avenger torpedo bombers and an escort of 85 Hellcats. The attack was to be mounted at maximum range, and soon after the force set out there was an unexpected change of plan. Lieutenant-Commander James Ramage, leading the Dauntlesses of VB-10 Squadron from *Enterprise*, recalled:

> The *Enterprise* and Air Group 10 had been waiting a long time for an opportunity to resume action against the Japanese fleet. We particularly wanted to get at their carriers. One rather dismaying event occurred after take-off and rendezvous of my strike group when we received word from the *Enterprise* that the position of the Japanese fleet given to us in our briefing was one degree off in longitude. That meant that the fleet was about 60 miles farther to the west than we had anticipated.

Nonplussed by the sudden addition of 120 miles to their round trip, the raiding forces continued determinedly after their quarry. In front of the Japanese carriers about 40 'Zeke 52s' mounted a spirited air defence in which they shot down six Hellcats and fourteen attack planes for the loss of 25 of their number. The remaining US planes then delivered their attack, in which Avengers torpedoed and sank the small carrier *Hiyo*. Dive-bombers caused damage to the large carrier *Zuikaku* and the small carriers *Chiyoda* and *Ryuho*.

It was dark when the US planes, in many cases flying on the last of their fuel, reached the area where their carriers and escorts were waiting to receive them. To assist the returning crews the warships were ordered to turn on their lights and fire starshell, but the move was not as helpful as it might have been. James Ramage recalled:

> The idea was good, but it was incorrectly executed. Had the order been to turn on lights only on the aircraft carriers, it

would have been a great help to us. As it was, it added greatly to the confusion. Every ship was illuminated and it was quite impossible to tell the carriers from other surface ships until one was close aboard. Nevertheless I managed to bring the *Enterprise* group back, augmented by some 30 to 40 stragglers that we had picked up en route, and broke my formation over the *Enterprise* for landing. I made my first pass at the *Enterprise*, but she had a foul deck from a crash landing by another ship's aircraft, so I proceeded to the *Yorktown* and made a very uneventful night landing with only a cupful of fuel remaining.

In the general confusion 80 of the returning planes ran out of fuel and were forced to ditch. Thanks to the warm seas in the area and an effective rescue operation mounted the following day, however, more than three-quarters of the 209 US airmen who came down in the water were picked up alive.

The Battle of the Philippine Sea, or 'The Great Marianas Turkey Shoot' as it came to be nicknamed, was as big a disaster for the Japanese carrier fleet as that suffered at Midway. Of the three large carriers – the only ones that could operate the new Japanese high-performance attack planes – two had been sunk and one had been damaged. One of the smaller Japanese carriers had been sunk and two had suffered damage. And, to crown it all, despite the loss of about three-quarters of their aircraft and crews, the Japanese carrier air groups had inflicted no significant damage on the opposing naval force.

To be successful, carrier-launched air strikes require a particularly high degree of crew training and operational experience. During the action off the Marianas the US Navy air groups possessed those qualities in good measure, while their opponents did not. That, plus the superb performance of the Grumman Hellcat and its presence in large numbers, simply smothered the Japanese attacks. The air action around Task Force 58 off Saipan on the morning of 19 June 1944 was one of the most intensive air actions ever fought. More than 700 carrier planes took part in the fighting, and, of those, 188, or just over a quarter, were destroyed. As has been mentioned, 181 of the losses in the one-sided action came from the Japanese Navy, and these represented 60 per cent of the force it sent into action. The great majority of the losses were inflicted by US fighters, though ships' guns also accounted for a few.

The brilliant defensive action by Task Force 58 inflicted a defeat on the Japanese carrier air groups from which the latter never recovered. The Pacific war would run for another fourteen months, but the Japanese aircraft carriers would play little further part in it.

Chapter 25

Reconnaissance over Normandy

From the start of the D-Day invasion of Normandy in June 1944, Allied army commanders received frequent and comprehensive aerial reconnaissance of the enemy-held areas in front of them. In contrast, throughout the initial phase of the land battle their German counterparts received only glimpses of what was happening in parts of the beach-head area. Often the first indication they had of an Allied attack was the preparatory artillery bombardment or when the spearhead units came within view of German forward positions. In an effort to redress this critical deficiency, the Luftwaffe *pressed into service a new and completely unproven type of aircraft.*

It was not that the *Luftwaffe* was short of reconnaissance planes. On D-Day *Luftflotte 3* in France possessed four long-range reconnaissance *Gruppen* with a total of 60 aircraft, for the most part Junkers Ju 88s, Ju 188s and Messerschmitt Me 410s. There was also a tactical reconnaissance *Gruppe* with 42 Messerschmitt Bf 109s with reduced armament and modified to carry cameras. The problem was that the German twin-engine reconnaissance aircraft lacked the performance to operate in the face of the Allied day-fighter patrols and so had to resort to night photographic missions using flares – but night photographs gave far less information than those taken by day.

The Bf 109 reconnaissance fighters flew low-altitude photographic missions over Allied positions by day, but their incursions usually ended with a high-speed dash for home, pursued by defending fighters, and produced nothing like comprehensive cover. These

---

ARADO Ar 234A

Role: Single-seat reconnaissance aircraft.
Powerplant: Two Junkers Jumo 004A jet engines each developing 1,980lb of thrust; two Walter HWK 500A liquid-fuel booster rockets in pods under the outer wings, each developing 1,100lb of thrust for 30sec (once the fuel was exhausted, these pods were jettisoned and fell by parachute, and after landing they were collected for re-use).
Armament: None. The military load carried during the missions described comprised two Rb 50/30 cameras with 50cm focal length lenses, fitted in the rear fuselage.
Performance: Maximum speed 485mph at 19,700ft. Typical speed and height for high-altitude operational photographic run, 460mph at 34,200ft.
Normal operational take-off weight: 17,640lb.
Dimensions: Span 46ft 3½in; length 41ft 5½in; wing area 284 sq ft.
Date of first flight of Ar 234A: August 1943. This version of the aircraft did not enter series production.

---

reconnaissance missions were flown at great cost in both aircraft and crews, and produced only a fragmentary picture of the Allied dispositions. The lack of effective aerial reconnaissance brought its inevitable consequences at the end of July 1944, when American troops broke out of the western side of the lodgement area in force and advanced rapidly down the western side of the Cherbourg Peninsula. By the time German field commanders realized what was afoot, it was too late to stop the move or even begin to contain it.

Shortly after the invasion began, *Oberleutnant* Horst Götz was appointed commander of a new air reconnaissance unit that was to operate under the direct control of the *Luftwaffe* High Command (*Versuchstaffel der Oberkommando der Luftwaffe*). Forming at Oranienburg near Berlin, the unit took delivery of the fifth and seventh prototypes of the new single-seat, twin jet Arado Ar 234A reconnaissance bomber. The aircraft were each fitted with a pair of 50cm focal length reconnaissance cameras in the rear fuselage, arranged to look down and slightly away from each other so as to give overlapping cover on the ground beneath the aircraft. The Arado could fly at 30,000ft at speeds in excess of 450mph, and it was confidently expected that it could penetrate the Allied fighter defences with ease.

Having possession of a couple of advanced aircraft was one thing; getting them, their crews and their supporting personnel to the point from which the unit could fly operational missions over enemy territory was quite another. Spare parts were a constant problem, for the aircraft were hand-made prototypes and these could come only from the makers. There were no proper technical manuals for the Arados and the ground crews had to learn the engineering foibles of the new plane as they went along. Götz and his second-in-command, *Leutnant* Erich Sommer, had to teach themselves to fly the new aircraft (there was no two-seat trainer version) as well as the rudiments of handling its temperamental early-production Jumo 004 jet engines.

Quite apart from the turbojet powerplants, the aircraft had a number of other novel features. To provide the necessary accelera-tion for it to take-off when carrying a full fuel load, the Ar 234 was fitted with two rocket pods under the wings, each of which devel-oped 1,100lb of thrust for 30 seconds. Once the fuel was exhausted, the pods were jettisoned and fell slowly to earth by parachute. They were then retrieved for re-use.

To meet the stringent range requirement in the *Luftwaffe* specifi-cation for the jet aircraft, the Arado design team had been forced to dispense with the conventional-type undercarriage to make space available for extra fuel tanks. The aircraft took off from a wheeled trolley that was released on lift-off and remained on the ground. At the end of the flight the Arado landed on sprung skids that were extended below the fuselage and engine nacelles. The use of the releasable trolley helped to give the Ar 234A a sparkling perfor-mance, but at a considerable cost in flexibility of operation. The aircraft could operate only from an airfield that had a trolley avail-able and, in the case of the prototypes, only one trolley had been built for each of them and because of minor differences between the planes their trolleys were not interchangeable. The full significance of this limitation would become clear when the time came to bring the new planes into action.

Ideally Götz should have had at least three months to prepare his unit for action, but the rapid deterioration of the military situation in France ruled that out. On 25 July the two Ar 234As took off from Oranienburg and headed for their operational base at Juvincourt near Reims. On the way Götz's plane suffered an engine failure and he had to fly to the only place where there were both spare engines and a landing trolley – back to Oranienburg.

Erich Sommer reached the French airfield without incident and, after he had landed, the Arado was hoisted on to a low-loader and driven into a hangar to shield it from prying Allied reconnaissance planes. And there, despite the desperate need for its services, the world's most advanced reconnaissance aircraft remained for more than a week (during which the American troops assembled unobserved for their break-out operation). Because of the risk from marauding Allied fighters, the all-important take-off trolley, the rocket pods and other essential items of equipment could not be flown in by transport plane. Instead they were sent to Juvincourt by rail, and despite being accorded the highest priority they took more than a week to get there via the battered French rail network.

Not until the morning of 2 August was the Ar 234 ready for its first combat mission. Perched on its trolley, the strange-looking aircraft was towed to the down-wind end of the airfield. Juvincourt had come under air attack several times, but the bomb craters in the operating surface had been filled in and rolled flat. Sommer climbed into the small cockpit and strapped in. He completed his checks and started the two jet engines, then, when the temperatures had settled down, he released the brakes and eased forward the throttles. Slowly the Arado gained speed as it bumped across the grass surface, then, satisfied that the aircraft was handling properly, the pilot pushed the button to ignite the booster rockets. Sommer felt a reassuring push in the back as the rockets developed full thrust, and its rate of acceleration increased markedly. When the plane reached 100mph he could feel the nose lifting off the ground and the aircraft trying to get airborne, so he pulled the mechanical release for the take-off trolley. Freed of its weight and drag, the aircraft lifted cleanly away. Shortly afterwards the booster rockets exhausted their fuel and the acceleration ceased. The pilot released the two pods and they tumbled clear of the wings. The first-ever jet reconnaissance mission was on its way.

After establishing the aircraft in the climb at 250mph and ascending at 2,500ft/min, Sommer eased the nose round until it was pointing towards the port of Cherbourg. It took the sleek jet twenty minutes to reach its operational altitude of 34,000ft. The view rearwards from the cockpit of the Arado was poor, and from time to time the pilot dropped a wing and turned first to one side then to the other, to glance past his tail to check that there were no enemy fighters in pursuit. Sommer also needed to ensure that the Arado was leaving behind it no telltale condensation trail that would have betrayed his position to the enemy. He found that there were no problems on either count.

Once over Cherbourg, Sommer pulled the Arado round on to an easterly heading, eased down the nose until the speed built up to 460mph, then levelled the plane out at 32,300ft. At the flick of a switch the shutters of the plane's two cameras began to click open at 11-second intervals, taking in a swathe of ground just over six miles wide. The day was clear and sunny, and there was scarcely a wisp of cloud to hinder photography as the invasion beaches slid beneath the aircraft. From his vantage point more than six miles high, Sommer could see no sign of the life-and-death struggle taking place on the ground below. If an Allied fighter did attempt to catch the high-flying intruder, it never got close enough for Sommer to see it. The initial photographic run lasted about ten minutes and took in the coastal strip. Then Sommer turned starboard through a semi-circle and flew a second run six miles inland and parallel to the first. Ten minutes after that he began his third run, heading east on a track six miles further inland. Just before he reached the end of the third run the film in the cameras' magazines ran out.

Sommer had finished the most difficult part of the mission but, like any reconnaissance pilot, he knew that the sortie was not completed until he had returned to base with the precious film. As he approached Juvincourt flares were lit to assist him to find the airfield. Keeping a wary eye open for Allied fighters, he made a high-speed descent, extended the skids and plunked the Arado on the grass. Sommer later recalled that on its skids the plane made a very smooth landing on the grass, much smoother than with a conventional wheeled undercarriage on a runway. No sooner had the machine slid to a halt than men began running towards it from several directions. The camera hatch above the rear fuselage was unlocked and opened, then the film magazines were unclipped, lifted out and whisked away for developing, Next, the Arado was hoisted on to its take-off trolley and towed back to the hangar.

In the course of that single flight of about 90 minutes Erich Sommer achieved 'more than the entire *Luftwaffe* reconnaissance force in the West throughout the previous eight weeks. The 380 photographs he brought back caused an enormous stir, for together they took in almost every part of the Allied lodgement area in Normandy. From Allied records we know that by that date more than 1½ million men and 300,000 vehicles had been put ashore in France. The twelve-man team of *Luftwaffe* photo-interpreters at Juvincourt took more than two days to produce an initial analysis of the photographs, and detailed examination of the prints took weeks.

Soon after Sommer had landed after his epic flight, Horst Götz reached Juvincourt with the other Arado. During the following three weeks the two jet planes flew thirteen further missions, ranging at will over France to photograph their required targets. At last the German field commanders received regular reconnaissance information on what was happening in the beach-head area and on the progress of the American troops advancing deep into France, By 17 August the latter had entered Chartres and Orléans, and were threatening to encircle in the entire German Army Group in Normandy. Under severe pressure, the German troops were forced to withdraw, but then their resistance collapsed and they were plunged into headlong retreat. The time when the Arado's photographs might have a decisive impact on the land battle was past, and now they did little more than provide a detailed picture of a battle that was already lost. On 28 August, with American tanks advancing on Juvincourt, Götz received orders to withdraw his unit to Chievres in Belgium.

During the Battle of France Allied fighters never interfered with the high-flying Arados, and it would seem that the operations of the latter went undetected. Despite a careful search of Allied records this author has found no mention of German jet reconnaissance missions during this period, nor does there appear to have been any reference to them in 'Ultra' decrypted signals. For Erich Sommer and Horst Götz, the continued Allied ignorance of their operations was the greatest compliment that could possibly be paid to the skilful way in which they performed their duties. The task of the reconnaissance pilot was (and, indeed, still is) to penetrate to the target, take the required photographs and return to base with the precious intelligence with as little fuss as possible. If they could do so without the enemy even realizing what had happened, so much the better.

Early in September the first of the new Arado Ar 234B reconnaissance aircraft was delivered to Götz's unit. This version was fitted with a normal tricycle undercarriage, which made for much greater-flexibility of operation and allowed the plane to operate from almost any airfield. The new version was 24mph slower than prototypes and its radius of action was somewhat less, but despite these drawbacks the new Arados ranged far and wide over Allied territory with little interference for the remainder of the war.

Had the Arado Ar 234As been available to fly reconnaissance missions a couple of months earlier, in time for D-Day, there is little doubt that with their photographs German field commanders would have deployed their forces much more effectively than was the case. And, goodness knows, even without their help the German Army put up an extremely hard fight in Normandy. As an old military adage assures us, 'Time spent on reconnaissance is seldom, if ever, wasted.'

Chapter 26

Bombers against the *Tirpitz*

The final generation of battleships made extremely difficult targets for air attack. Although they were large and difficult to hide, they were also very well armed and had strong armour protection. If these vessels were in port or at an anchorage they usually enjoyed the additional protection of smoke generating units, anti-torpedo nets, anti-aircraft guns and, usually, shore-based fighters. To stand a reasonable chance of destroying such a target it was necessary to use either a very large number of planes carrying conventional armour-piercing bombs, or a small number of planes equipped with more specialized types of weapon. During its final series of attacks leading to the destruction of the battleship Tirpitz, *the Royal Air Force adopted the latter course . . .*

The German battleship *Tirpitz* spent almost her entire life holed up in the Norwegian fjords. Too powerful to be ignored, she was a constant menace to the Allied convoys carrying supplies and equipment around the north of Norway to assist the Soviet Union's war effort. *Tirpitz* rarely put to sea, and when she did she saw relatively little action. But by her very presence she tied down a large number of Allied warships, including battleships that could have been better used elsewhere.

Tirpitz, sister-ship of the famous *Bismarck*, was one of the most powerful warships of her time. With a displacement of 42,900 tons, she was 7,900 tons heavier than the *King George V* class battleships, the nearest equivalent in the Royal Navy. Much of the difference in weight

BATTLESHIP TIRPITZ

Surface displacement: 42,900 tons.
Armament: Eight 15in (38cm) guns main armament; twelve 5.9in
  (15cm) guns secondary armament; sixteen 4.1in (10.5cm) high-
  angle anti-aircraft guns; sixteen 37mm and fifty-eight 20mm short-
  range automatic anti-aircraft guns; eight 21in torpedo tubes.
Performance: Maximum speed 30kts; range 9,000 miles at 19kts.
Dimensions: Length overall 822ft; beam 118ft.
Complement: 2,400.
Date operational: January 1942.

was accounted for by the German ship's extra armour. To give protection against naval gunfire and torpedoes, *Tirpitz* had a vertical belt of
side armour 12.6in thick that extended from 8ft below the waterline
to a similar distance above it, above that belt extending to deck level
was a vertical belt of armour 5.7in thick. To keep out aerial bombs, the
vessel carried a layer of horizontal armour just over 3in thick to protect
the machinery spaces, increasing to nearly 4in above the ammunition
magazines. Where the deck armour met the side armour, the former
was inclined at an angle to keep out plunging shot. The German
battleship had an abnormally wide beam of 118ft, giving her a greater
degree of initial stability than any comparable ship in the British or US
Navies (battleships built for the latter had to be narrow enough to pass
through the locks of the Panama Canal, but for obvious reasons that
was not a design requirement for German warships).

British air and naval forces made numerous attacks on *Tirpitz*.
The first, when she was located at sea off Norway on 9 March 1942,
was by a dozen Albacore torpedo bombers launched from HMS
Victorious. The German battleship headed into the wind at maximum
speed, and the slow biplanes lacked the necessary speed advantage
to carry out a co-ordinated attack on her. Several torpedoes were
aimed at the rapidly manoeuvring warship but none of them hit.
The night attacks by Royal Air Force bombers on 31 March and 28
and 29 April of that year, when the ship was in Fötten Fjord near
Trondheim, were no more successful.

On 22 September 1943 midget submarines of the Royal Navy
crept into her anchorage, then in Kaa Fjord at the north of Norway,
and planted four 2-ton mines on the sea bed beneath the vessel.
The detonation of two of the weapons caused widespread internal
damage which required repairs lasting several months. Such an attack
depended on its novelty to have any chance of success, and could be
mounted only once.

On 3 April 1944 a large force of Fleet Air Arm Barracudas dive-bombed the battleship and obtained twelve hits. Most of the bombs were released from too low an altitude, however, and they failed to gain sufficient velocity to penetrate the ship's armoured deck. Although some damage was caused to the superstructure, the battle-ship was ready for sea again within a month. The smokescreens around *Tirpitz* nullified similar attacks by the Fleet Air Arm on 17 July and 22 August, limited that on 24 August to two hits which caused relatively little damage, and ruined the attempt on 29 August.

In September 1944 it was again the turn of the Royal Air Force to pit its strength against *Tirpitz*. A force of thirty-eight Lancasters from Nos 9 and 617 Squadrons deployed to Archangel in northern Russia for the attack, equipped with two novel types of weapon: the 12,000lb 'Tallboy' bomb and the 500lb 'Johnny Walker' underwater 'walking' mine.

Designed by famous inventor Barnes Wallis, the 'Tallboy' had first been used in action less than four months earlier. It was 20ft long and 3ft in diameter, and it took up the whole of the Lancaster's bomb bay. The weapon contained 5,100lb of Torpex explosive and was designed to penetrate deep into the ground before exploding, aiming to cause an 'earthquake' that would literally shake the target to pieces. The four fins at the rear of the weapon were angled at 5 degrees to the airflow, to cause the bomb to rotate about its longitu-dinal axis during its fall. This rotation provided spin stabilization to hold the bomb straight as its velocity approached the speed of sound. The 'Tallboy' had not been designed for use against warship targets, but nobody doubted that a direct hit or a near-miss from one of these weapons would inflict serious damage on *Tirpitz*.

The 'Johnny Walker' or 'JW' mine was purpose-designed for use against ships at anchor. The weapon weighed approximately 400lb and, before use, lead was added to adjust its weight so that it would have neutral buoyancy in the area of sea in which it was to be dropped. The small size of the 'JW' (6ft long, 15¼in in diameter) meant that the Lancaster's bomb bay could accommodate a dozen of these weapons. In both its appearance and its concept, the 'JW' could scarcely have been more different from 'Tallboy'. Whereas the latter depended on sheer brute force to smash its way through the armoured deck and into the vitals of the ship from above, the 'JW' employed more subtle methods. The latter was designed to attack *from the vulnerable underside* where, in the case of *Tirpitz*, the plating was only two-thirds of an inch thick.

The method of operation of the 'JW' was as follows. After its release from the aircraft, the mine descended on a 4ft-diameter drogue para-chute. If it struck a solid surface (i.e. the ground or the superstructure

---

AVRO LANCASTER I

Role: Seven-seat heavy bomber.
Powerplant: Four Rolls-Royce Merlin 24 12-cylinder, liquid-
cooled, inline engines each developing 1,640hp at take-off.
Armament: (Offensive, during the attack on Tirpitz on 15
September 1944) One 12,000lb 'Tallboy' bomb or twelve 'Johnny
Walker' mines; (defensive) eight Browning .303in machine guns, two
each in the nose and mid-upper turrets and four in the tail turret.
Performance: Maximum speed 287mph at 11,500ft; normal
cruising speed 220mph at 20,000ft; service ceiling 24,500ft.
Normal operational take-off weight: 68,000lb.
Dimensions: Span 102ft; length 69ft 6in; wing area 1,297 sq ft.
Date of first production Lancaster I: October 1941.

---

of a ship), an impact fuse detonated the warhead. If the mine entered
water, the drogue was released and the weapon sank. When the mine
reached a depth of 60ft, during its descent, a hydrostatic valve released
a flow of hydrogen from a high-pressure container in the rear of
the weapon and passed it, via a pressure-reducing valve, to eject the
water out of the buoyancy chamber in the nose. The weapon became
lighter than the surrounding water, its descent ceased and it started to
rise nose-first. The fins on the sides of the weapon were so arranged
that when the 'JW' ascended or descended through water it travelled
at an angle of about 30 degrees to the vertical, thus giving a horizontal displacement of about 30ft during each such move. When the
nose of the weapon was uppermost, the nose fuse was made live so
that if the weapon struck anything hard anything during its ascent
(i.e. the bottom of a ship) the warhead would detonate.

The 'JW' warhead contained 100lb of Torpex/aluminium formed
into a shaped charge, with a concave area at the front lined with
soft metal. The explosive was detonated from the rear, so the force
of the explosion was focused on the metal liner. The latter would
dissolve into a slug of molten metal that was hurled forwards from
the warhead at very high velocity. This slug had enormous penetrative
power and, once inside the bowels of the ship, it could cause severe
local damage. That effect would be compounded by the ingress of
water through the hole made by slug. Powerful though these effects
were, they were only part of the damage mechanism the weapon was
designed to produce. The inclusion of powdered aluminium in the
explosive charge meant that when it detonated large amounts of gas
were generated. The huge bubble thus formed was capable of lifting
the ship suddenly at the point of detonation. Then, an instant later, the

bubble collapsed, causing that part of the ship to drop several feet. The sudden up and down movement imposed severe forces on the hull of a vessel and could break its back (sea mines produce a similar effect).

If the 'JW' reached a depth of 15–20ft in its ascent it had obviously missed its target (the bottom of *Tirpitz* was about 34ft below the surface). At that depth the hydrostatic valve stopped the flow of hydrogen and a port opened to release the gas in the buoyancy chamber. Water flooded into the chamber and the mine, now heavier than the surrounding water, turned over and began to descend nose-first at an angle, of 30 degrees. During the descent the nose fuse automatically became 'safe', so that if the weapon struck the sea bed it would not detonate. When the mine approached a depth of 60ft the hydrostatic valve turned on the supply of hydrogen again, the water was forced out of the buoyancy chamber and the cycle was repeated. The container in the rear of the weapon had sufficient hydrogen for the 'walking cycles' to continue for up to an hour. If at the end of that time the 'AV' had not found a target, the self-destruct mechanism set off the warhead to prevent the secret weapon falling into enemy hands.

The attack on *Tirpitz* was launched on 15 September, when 27 Lancasters took off from Archangel. Twenty of the aircraft were each loaded with a single 'Tallboy', six planes carried twelve 'JW' mines each, and the remaining Lancaster was to film the attack for later analysis.

Wing Commander J. Tait, the CO of No 617 Squadron, had drawn up the attack plan. The 'Tallboy' aircraft were to bomb first, running in from the south. As is usually the case, the attack plan had to take into account a number of sometimes conflicting factors. The time of flight of the 'Tallboy', from the planned release altitude of 11,000ft to impact, was about 26 seconds, and when it detonated it would hurl debris and water high into the sky. The explosions from several such bombs, and smoke from any resultant fires, might conceal the target from any aircraft still running in to bomb. This, and the need to prevent German anti-aircraft gunners concentrating their fire on individual planes to disrupt their bombing runs, required a concentrated attack if possible with the last aircraft releasing its bomb within 26 seconds of the leader. On the other hand, the bomb-aimers were all trying to hit the same aiming point, the middle of the battleship, so during the final part of their bomb run there would be several planes flying on the same or on converging headings. If the aircraft bunched together too tightly there would be a risk of collisions, or of the bomb run being disrupted, if aircraft flew into the turbulent slipstream from those in front.

Tait's plan was for the aircraft to attack in four V-shaped waves each of five aircraft. Waves of bombers were to follow each other at intervals of about 800yds; thus the entire formation was 1½ miles long and at its attack speed of 230mph would take about 22 seconds to pass over the target. This ensured that the last Lancaster would have released its bomb several seconds before that from the leader detonated, giving all the aircraft an unobscured target at which to aim. It also meant that the German gunners could not afford to concentrate their fire on individual planes and allow others in the force to bomb unhindered. To keep the aircraft out of each other's way during the bombing runs, there was a 50ft altitude separation between adjacent bombers in each wave. Furthermore, succeeding waves were stepped up by 1,000ft to keep each out of the slipstream of the one ahead of it. During this attack the lowest aircraft in the first wave released its bomb from 11,350ft and the highest in the final wave released from 17,500ft.

The six 'JW' aircraft attacked a few minutes later, running across the fjord in two waves from south-east to north-west and releasing their loads from altitudes between 10,000 and 12,000ft. This order of attack was necessary because it was essential that the mines enter the water after the last 'Tallboy' detonated, or the blast from the latter was likely to cause 'countermining'.

By the time the Lancasters reached the Kaa Fjord the German smokescreen was well developed, however, and, as a result, the Lancasters' bomb-aimers had to aim their 'Tallboys' at where they thought the battleship lay, or at the muzzle flashes visible through the smoke. Some of the bombers failed to release on their first run and made a second attack run; fortunately for these crews, the smoke-screens that hid the battleship from the Lancasters also hid the Lancasters from the anti-aircraft gunners. No German fighters attempted to interfere with the attack, and none of the raiders suffered any damage.

There can be little doubt that the smokescreens saved *Tirpitz* from annihilation that day. Only one 'Tallboy' struck the battleship a glancing blow, yet its effect was devastating. The bomb hit the starboard side of the foredeck between the bow and the forward gun turret, passed through the flare of the ship's side and detonated in the water a few feet below and to one side of the ship. The explosion blew out a large area of bow plating below the waterline, to a distance of about 55ft. There was extensive flooding throughout almost the entire bow area and, with the admission of about 1,500 tons of water during a counter-flooding operation to restore the ship to an even keel, the draught of *Tirpitz* was increased by more than 8ft. The shock of this and several other near-misses affected equipment throughout the vessel; for example, the severe vibration caused damage to the main engines, and most of the optical range-finding instruments were put out of action. Although still afloat, the battleship was barely seaworthy, and she was certainly in no condition to fight.

The 'brute force' method of attack with the 'Tallboy' had obviously been a success. But what of that by the more sophisticated 'Johnny Walker' mines? Had one of these detonated against the battleship's hull, the weapon would have been accorded the fame given to the bouncing bomb that broke the German dams. But it was not to be. During the next hour the 'JW' mines wandered aimlessly and silently up and down the Fjord. Then, as the last of the hydrogen gave out, one by one they blew themselves up harmlessly. The completeness of their failure had but one redeeming factor: it preserved the secrecy of the operation of the weapon, leaving the German Navy with no inkling of what had been attempted.

After the attack German Navy engineers estimated that to restore *Tirpitz* to her full operational capability would require the rebuilding of much of the bow section. That would take a minimum of nine months' uninterrupted repair work in a fully equipped dock, which meant taking her back to Germany. In the current war situation this was not considered feasible, and it was decided to carry out make-shift repairs and move the ship to Tromsø Fjord some 200 miles to the south. There the battleship was to serve as a floating gun battery to stiffen the land defences of the area. The German Navy went to great pains to conceal the true extent of the damage to *Tirpitz*, recognizing that so long as she was perceived as a threat, the battle-ship would continue to tie down substantial Allied naval forces. It took several weeks for information on the damage to filter through to Royal Navy Intelligence, and in the meantime the battleship remained a high priority target.

The move to Tromsø Fjord took place in mid-October. It was to seal the fate of the battleship, for the new location lay just within the radius of action of Lancasters operating from bases in Scotland. A number of these aircraft were fitted with overload tanks to bring their fuel load to 2,406 Imp. gallons, and with more powerful engines. To compensate for the extra weight, the mid-upper turrets and the guns and ammunition from the front turrets were removed from the aircraft, as were all items of equipment not considered essential for the mission.

By the final week in October these modifications were complete, and on the 29th a force of 37 Lancasters took off from Lossiemouth for another attack on the battleship. Now the vessel was moored in water too shallow for the 'JW' mine to operate, so all the aircraft carried 'Tallboys'. The German Navy had not had time to move the smoke-generating equipment to Tromsø, but on this occasion it did not matter. The aircraft arrived over the target to find the warship enshrouded in cloud. Thirty-two crews aimed their bombs into the area where the *Tirpitz* was thought to be, but no hits were claimed. In fact one weapon detonated about 8oft from the ship's port side, causing damage to a propeller shaft and a rudder, but that was all.

Soon after the attack Royal Air Force Intelligence learned that the *Luftwaffe* had moved a *Staffel* of FW 190 fighters to the airfield at Bardufoss, 40 miles from Tromsø, from where they might interfere with an attack on *Tirpitz*. The battleship was still a high-priority target and, if the next attack were to succeed, it was essential that the RAF retain the element of surprise for as long as possible before the force reached the target. As part of the general effort to follow the continual changes in the German radar chain, elint (electronic intelligence) planes had plotted the locations and arcs of cover of the stations along the coast of Norway. These were positioned to give warning of aircraft approaching any part of the coast at altitudes of 5,000ft or above. But if a raiding force remained at 1,500ft or below, there was a chink in the curtain mid-way up the coast through which the planes might pass unseen. It was planned that during the next attack the bombers would fly through the hole in the radar cover at 1,500ft and continue heading east and climb over the mountains into neutral Sweden. The planes were then to head north-east, keeping the mountain barrier between themselves and the German radar stations, until they began the climb to enter their bombing runs.

On 12 November a force of 29 Lancasters took off to attack the battleship, following the route as planned. Some of the bombers were detected crossing the coast, however, and the report was flashed to *Tirpitz* that yet another attack might be in the offing. What the RAF planners had not known was that the fighters at Bardufoss posed no real threat to the attackers. The unit had traded its worn-out Messerschmitt Bf 109s for Focke Wulf 190s only a few days earlier and its pilots, many of whom were straight from training and had little flying experience, needed a period of conversion before they were proficient on their new mounts. The remit of the *Staffel* commander, *Oberleutnant* Werner Gayko, was that, except in an emergency, his unit was responsible only for the defence of the airfield and the immediate area surrounding it. So far as Gayko was concerned no emergency existed, for he had received no request to go to the assistance of the battleship.

As they passed over the distinctive shape of Lake Torneträsk, the stretch of water 1,125ft high in northern Sweden, the bombers moved into attack formation and their pilots pushed on full throttle to commence the climb to attack altitude.

The *Tirpitz* Raid

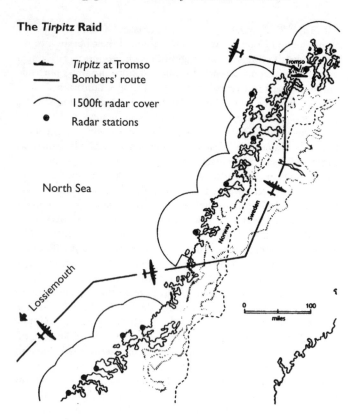

At 9.05 a.m. the formation of bombers hove into view of the look-outs on *Tirpitz*. By then the battleship was fully closed up for action, her watertight doors shut and her weapons loaded and pointing skywards. Even the four 15in guns in the two forward turrets were ready for action, their barrels raised to maximum elevation and aligned on the raiders. As the Lancasters came within range of the big guns, 13 miles, the weapons hurled their one-ton shells in the direction of the planes. The deafening crashes of the guns echoed and re-echoed from the mountain walls surrounding the fjord, then the barrels began lowering smoothly to the horizontal for re-loading. In succession four large clouds of black smoke appeared in the sky near to the bombers, but not so near as to harm any of them. As the range closed, the battleship's 10.5cm guns joined in the action, followed soon afterwards by the 3.7cm automatic weapons' strings of red or green tracers.

Tait's tactics for this attack were the same as those used during the previous two, with planes attacking in closely spaced waves stepped up in altitude. And this time, as luck would have it, there was neither cloud nor a smokescreen to hinder the attackers. The first wave of Lancasters reached the bomb-release point and in unison the five aircraft disgorged their 'Tallboys'. Falling slowly at first but rapidly gathering speed, the salvo of huge bombs bore down on the battleship. Seven seconds later the second wave bombed, then the third, then the fourth wave.

Three 'Tallboys' scored direct hits on the ship. Surprisingly, one of the bombs failed to cause serious damage; it ricochetted off the armoured deck near to 'B' turret and, breaking up and spilling burning charge, it skidded away. The nose of the weapon was later found on a mud bank 200yds from the impact point. The catastrophic damage was caused by the other two weapons, which smashed into the ship within 20yds of each other on the port side, amidships. These penetrated the hull of the ship, whereupon they detonated. In combination with one or more near-misses at about the same time, the explosions tore a huge hole about 200ft long in the port side.

Hundreds of tons of water flooded into the battleship and, despite counter-flooding to correct the list to port, the latter increased steadily until it reached 20 degrees. There the ship steadied for a while, with one bilge keel jammed hard against a bank of mud on the sea bed, before the list slowly resumed. Below decks severe fires were raging. One of them reached a magazine which exploded, lifting the hefty 'C' turret off its mounting and hurling it over the side. The list continued relentlessly until the ship ended up with her superstructure embedded in the mud on the bottom of the fjord and with part of her hull showing above the surface. From the beginning of the attack until the ship came to rest, it had taken about ten minutes. Of the 1,500 sailors on board the warship at the time, about half had been killed.

In the Royal Air Force there was considerable jubilation at the destruction of the German Navy's last remaining modern battleship by air attack. The action proved that no warship, no matter how large, how well armoured or how well protected by anti-torpedo nets, could survive the punishment that could be delivered from the air. The triumph was in no way muted by a carping comment from a senior Royal Navy officer, who tried to denigrate the junior Service's success by pointing out the literal but quite irrelevant fact that *Tirpitz* had not been sunk because part of her hull (the bottom) was still protruding from the water. The aviators could afford to laugh off the crass remark. Given the greater truth that the big bomber was now the master of the battleship, it mattered not one jot if any part of the latter remained above water at the end of the attack.

Chapter 27

Confound and Destroy

*At the end of 1943 Royal Air Force Bomber Command gained
a new capability to assist its night raiders: No 100 Group, a
force with the task of reducing the effectiveness of the German
air defences. The Group's commander, Air Vice-Marshal Edward
Addison, planned a two-pronged attack on the defences. First,
by jamming and spoofing the German radar systems and
blocking the radio channels, he would make it more difficult
for night fighters and anti-aircraft gunners to find and engage
the bombers. Second, by sending long-range night fighters to
seek out their German counterparts and attack their airfields,
the Group would impose constraints on the operations of the
defending night fighter force. In recognition of the dual-nature of
its role, the Group's official motto was 'Confound and Destroy',*

During the autumn of 1944 No 100 Group began to make its presence felt during the night attacks on targets in Germany. The role
of the formation was termed 'bomber support' (what is now called
'defence suppression'). No 100 Group's jamming force comprised four
squadrons of converted heavy bombers: No 171 with Halifaxes, No
199 with Stirlings (later it would convert to Halifaxes), No 214 with
Flying Fortresses and No 233 with Liberators (later it would convert
to Flying Fortresses). These aircraft were modified to carry a menagerie
of specialized electronic jamming equipment: 'Mandrel' and 'Carpet' to
jam the Germans' ground radars, 'Piperack' to jam their night fighters'
airborne interception radars and 'Jostle' to jam their communications
radio channels. In addition, several of the aircraft were modified to
carry large quantities of 'Window' metal foil to create thousands of false
targets on the enemy radar screens to distract and confuse the defenders.

The Group's destroying element comprised seven squadrons of Mosquito night fighters. In addition to their normal airborne interception radar, some of these aircraft carried the 'Serrate' or 'Perfectos' homing devices. 'Serrate' picked up the transmissions from the German night-fighter radars and gave a bearing that enabled the Mosquito crews to home on their source. 'Perfectos' was even cleverer: it radiated signals to trigger the IFF identification equipment of any German aircraft within a range of about fifteen miles, and the latter's coded reply signal betrayed its exact whereabouts. 'Perfectos' provided the three pieces of information necessary for a successful interception: it gave relative bearing and distance, as well as providing a positive hostile identification of the aircraft under observation. The last of these was particularly valuable, since the Mosquitos were too deep in enemy territory where there might be a few German night fighters in an area of sky filled with several hundred friendly bombers. No longer could *Luftwaffe* night fighters cruise over their homeland concerned only with finding and shooting down bombers: now these hunters were liable at any time to become the hunted.

As well as seeking out German night fighters in the air, two of the Mosquito units, Nos 23 and 515 Squadrons, specialized in flying night intruder missions against the enemy night-fighter bases. These aircraft would orbit over the enemy airfields for hours on end, and bomb or strafe any movement seen on the ground.

To provide elint support for these operations the Group had its own 'Ferret' squadron, No 192, with Halifaxes, Wellingtons and Mosquitos fitted with special equipment to collect signals from the various German radar systems.

No 100 Group's jamming element flew four general types of mission in support of the night bombers: the 'Mandrel' screen, the 'Window Spoof', the Jamming Escort and the Target Support operation. The 'Mandrel' screen usually involved between ten and sixteen aircraft orbiting in pairs along a line just clear of enemy territory, with an interval of fifteen miles between pairs. Each aircraft carried several 'Mandrel' transmitters, and the purpose of the operation was to produce a wall of jamming about 100 miles long, to prevent the German early-warning radar operators from seeing aircraft movements behind the screen. Usually the 'Mandrel' screen was employed to conceal the approach of a raiding force, but when no raid was planned it was erected to cause the enemy controllers to think that a raid was in the offing and so force them to scramble night fighters to waste their dwindling supplies of aviation fuel.

The 'Window Spoof' comprised up to twenty-four aircraft in two formations of twelve aircraft flying in line abreast, with 2¼ miles

---

CONSOLIDATED LIBERATOR B.VI (B-24H)

Role: Ten-seat jamming support aircraft.
Powerplant: Four Pratt & Whitney R-1830 14-cylinder, air-cooled, radial engines each developing 1,200hp at take-off.
Armament: Defensive armament comprised four Browning .5in machine guns, two each in powered turrets in the tail and above the fuselage. Sometimes the aircraft carried a small number of target-indicator bombs to give realism to their feint attacks. They carried several items of radar and radio jamming equipment and a large quantity of 'Window' was required for some types of operation.
Performance: Maximum continuous cruising speed 278mph at 25,000ft.
Normal operational take-off weight: 56,000lb.
Dimensions: Span 110ft; length 67ft 2in; wing area 1,048 sq ft.
Date of first production B-24H: June 1943.

---

between the aircraft and the second line some 30 miles behind the first. Each aircraft released 'Window' at a rate of thirty bundles a minute, one every two seconds. In this way the formation could produce on enemy radar the illusion of a bomber stream of some 500 aircraft. The aim of the tactic was to lure night fighters away from the real raiding forces (each real bomber stream also dropped 'Window', though at a lower rate, so that it was impossible to tell the real attacks from the feints).

The Jamming Escort role involved Fortresses and Liberators of No 100 Group flying above the main bomber stream and jamming with 'Jostle' and 'Piperack' transmitters to blot out, respectively, the German night fighters' radio channels and their airborne interception radars. When the Jamming Escort aircraft arrived at the target they often assumed the Target Support role, in which they orbited in the area and operated their 'Carpet' transmitters to jam the frequencies used by the German flak control radars.

Sergeant Kenneth Stone, an air gunner of No 233 Squadron flying Liberators, described his impressions of the types of operations his unit flew:

'Window Spoof' aids were carried out by a few aircraft dropping the metal foil to simulate a large force of aircraft on the enemy radar. The operation was very precisely worked out; there would be a rendezvous point in a safe area and timing was critical to within two minutes. If a crew arrived later than this it had to abort the mission because one aircraft late was a sure give-away on radar. All aircraft had to go in together and dispense 'Window' at a regular pace. The aircraft flew a 'corkscrew' course to disperse the 'Window' more effectively and give the illusion of a larger force than was actually present. Generally six spoofers would show up on radar as 300-plus plots. A spoof target was generally selected which either committed the defences in that area and left the genuine target free, or at worst split the defences and rendered a proportion of them useless. There were two methods of ending this type of spoof. Either we continued to the spoof target and dropped target markers there; or we stopped 'Windowing' short of the target and dived away at a great rate of knots. There is no doubt that the 'Window Spoofs' were highly successful in achieving their purpose, by fooling the defences and diverting their effort. The casualty rate for spoofing aircraft was not so high as might have been expected, because the enemy night fighters would be tied up with the paper-chase and could not winkle out the real aircraft.

In Stone's view the Target Support operation was the most dangerous of those flown by his unit, and in recognition of the hazards these missions were shared out amongst the crews in strict rotation:

The general principle was to cover the target from five minutes before the initial marking began until five minutes after the bombing stopped. The big hazard was having to hang around while the bomber boys ran in, bombed, and got the hell out of it! Fifteen minutes seemed a long, long time suspended over the inferno below. The support aircraft generally flew some 2,000 to 4,000 feet above the bomber stream and jammed the flak and searchlight radars, the night-fighter R/T frequencies, the night fighter radars, etc. – in other words diverting the defensive forces away from the bombers during the most critical period.

The reader may gain an impression of the way in which No 100 Group's tactics dovetailed with those of the rest of Bomber Command from a more or less typical operation of the late war period, that on the night of 20/21 March 1945. The targets were the oil refineries at Bohlen near Leipzig and at Hemmingstedt near Hamburg; the former was to be attacked by 235 heavy bombers, the latter by 166.

The first action by Bomber Command that night was a large-scale nuisance raid on Berlin by 35 Mosquitos, beginning at 9.14 p.m. The

---

DE HAVILLAND MOSQUITO NF.30

Role: Two-seat night fighter.
Powerplant: Two Rolls-Royce Merlin 76 V12, liquid-cooled, inline engines each developing 1,535hp at take-off.
Armament: Four Hispano 20mm cannon mounted in the lower part of the nose.
Performance: Maximum speed 407mph at 28,000ft; climb to 15,000ft, 7min 30sec.
Normal operational takeoff weight: 20,000lb
Dimensions: Span 54ft 23in; length 49ft 10¾in; wing area 454 sq ft.
Date of first production Mosquito NF.30: March 1944.

Mosquitos, flying fast and high, required no support from No 100 Group's jamming force. As the raiding force moved in, night-fighter Mosquitos of Nos 23 and 515 Squadrons fanned out over Germany making for the enemy night-fighter bases likely to become active that night. When the intruders reached their objectives they orbited, waiting to pounce on any aircraft seen taking off or landing.

Just after 1 a.m. the main raiding force bound for Bohlen crossed the French coast and headed south-east towards southern Germany. Also heading across France, on a track almost parallel to that of the Bohlen attack force but a little further south, was a feint attack force of 64 Lancasters and Halifaxes. These aircraft belonged to operational conversion units and were flown by crews in the final stages of their training.

No 100 Group's electronic trickery began at 2.05 a.m. on the morning of the 21st. Established in a line 80 miles long over France and just inside Allied-held territory, seven pairs of Halifaxes of Nos 171 and 199 Squadrons turned on their 'Mandrel' equipment to provide a wall of jamming to conceal the approach of the Bohlen attack force, which by then had split into two separate parts.

Running across France outside the cover of the 'Mandrel' screen, the feint attack flown by trainee crews continued heading east in full view of the enemy radars. German night fighters moved into position to block the threatened incursion but, at 2.55 a.m., when the bombers were just short of the German border, the feint attackers turned round and went home. A few minutes later, well to the north, the two Bohlen attack forces burst through the 'Mandrel' jamming screen and crossed the Rhine into German-held territory. Twenty miles ahead of the bombers flew four Halifaxes of No 171 Squadron and seven Liberators of No 223 Squadron dropping 'Window' to conceal the strength of the attacking forces. Flying ahead and on the

```
┌─────────────────────────────────────────────────────────┐
│                    JUNKERS Ju 88G-6                       │
│                                                           │
│  Role: Three-seat night fighter.                          │
│  Powerplant: Two Junkers Jumo 211J inline engines each    │
│    developing 1,410hp at take-off.                        │
│  Armament: Four MG 151 20mm cannon mounted under the      │
│    fuselage; some aircraft carried two further MG 151     │
│    cannon in an oblique installation firing upwards and   │
│    forwards.                                              │
│  Performance: Maximum speed 389mph at 30,000ft; initial   │
│    rate of climb 1,655ft/min.                             │
│  Dimensions: Span 65ft 10½in; length 52ft 1½in; wing      │
│    area 587 sq ft.                                        │
│  Date of first production Ju 88G-6: Summer 1944.          │
└─────────────────────────────────────────────────────────┘
```

flanks of each of the bomber streams, 33 Mosquito night fighters of No 100 Group began their deadly game of hide-and-seek with their enemy counterparts.

Shortly before 3 a.m. a Mosquito of No 85 Squadron, with pilot Flight Lieutenant Chapman and radar operator Flight Sergeant Stockley, picked up IFF identification signals on 'Perfectos' from an enemy aircraft at a range of 12 miles. Chapman afterwards reported:

At 0255 hours just after passing Hamm on the way in to escort the bomber stream we got a 'Perfectos' contact at 12 miles' range – height 12,000 feet. Range was closed to 1 mile but no AI [radar] contact was obtained and the range started to increase again, so deciding that the contact must be below we did a hard diving turn to port down to 9,000 feet and finally D/F'd [took a bearing] on to the target's course at 7 miles' range. We closed to 6 miles' range on a course of 120° and an AI contact was obtained . . . The target was still climbing straight ahead and was identified with the night glasses as an Me 110. I closed in to 600 feet and pulled up to dead astern when the Hun started to turn to port. I gave it ½ ring deflection with a three-second burst whereupon the E/A [enemy aircraft] exploded in the port engine in a most satisfying manner with debris flying back. It exploded on the ground at 0305 hours, position 25–30 miles NW of Kassel.

From start to finish the engagement lasted ten minutes and, as can be seen, this type of operation tended to involve the Mosquito crew in a lengthy chase before they reached a firing position.

The spoof tactics that night were successful. The German fighter controller seriously underestimated the strength of the two raiding

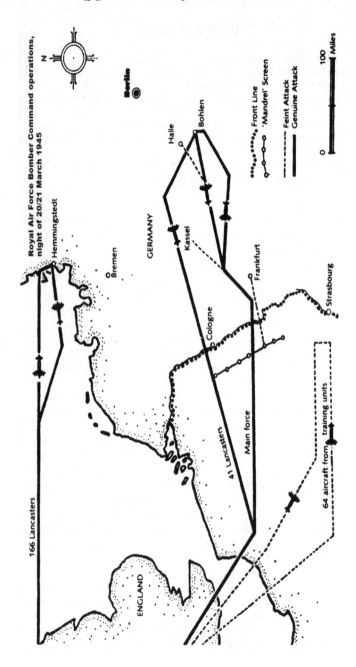

forces heading for Bohlen; he estimated their strengths as about 30 aircraft each and thought they might even be 'Window' feints. Only after the raiders had crossed the Rhine and reports had started to come in from German ground observers did it become clear that the southerly force was far larger than had been thought: no amount of electronic jamming could conceal the roar of 800 aircraft engines.

By now 89 German night fighters were airborne and orbiting over their holding beacons, waiting for their controller to clarify the air situation and direct them against the bombers.

That night the intention of the No 100 Group operation was to create the impression that the raiders' main objective was Kassel, and soon after the main raiding force had crossed into German-held territory it turned north-east towards the city. The German fighter controller swallowed the bait and ordered almost all of his night-fighters to head for radio beacons *Silberfuchs*, Weirner and *Kormoran* in the vicinity of Kassel. He ordered the rest of his force, a single *Gruppe* of Ju 88s, to move to radio beacon *Otto* near Frankfurt to cover a possible threat to that city. Soon afterwards there came reports from Kassel that the city was under imminent threat of attack, as Pathfinder flares blossomed overhead and a few bombs detonated.

German night fighters were ordered to move on the city, but this was no full-scale onslaught, merely a feint by Mosquito bombers backed by No 100 Group Liberators and Halifaxes dropping 'Window'. During the course of this spoof a German night fighter shot down a Liberator of No 233 Squadron; only one member of the crew survived.

Meanwhile, some 25 miles south of Kassel, the main raiding force had turned away from that city and was heading for Bohlen. The Liberator crewmen had not sacrificed their lives in vain, however, for the feint against Kassel kept most of the German night fighters uselessly in that area for nearly half an hour. Not until 3 a.m. did the German fighter controller realize that he had been tricked and order his force to head east in pursuit of the raiders. Six minutes after that he gave the probable target as Leipzig, the city nearest Bohlen, but by then the vanguard of the raiding force was within thirty miles – eight minutes' flying time – of the target.

Still No 100 Group had not exhausted its repertoire of tricks. Just short of Bohlen six Flying Fortresses and Halifaxes broke away from the main raiding force and ran a 'Window' trail to the important oil refinery complex at Leuna which lay twenty miles to the north-west. Twelve Lancaster bombers accompanied the jamming aircraft to give substance to the spoof. When the feint attackers arrived over the complex they dropped further target markers and the Lancasters put down their loads of bombs. Leuna lay directly in the path of the German night fighters streaming to the east, and the spoof attack delayed their arrival at the real target still further. One Lancaster crew paid the supreme price for the precious minutes of additional delay inflicted on the defending night fighters in reaching the main target.

The 211 Lancasters assigned to the Bohlen raid reached their objective and carried out a concentrated eleven-minute attack. The five Flying Fortresses and the Liberator that had provided Jamming Escort Support along the route to the target now orbited over the refinery in the Target Support role throughout the period of the attack. Not until 4.10 a.m., as the last raiders were leaving Bohlen, did the first of the German night fighters arrive in the area. Their radar operators encountered severe jamming and they had great difficulty picking out their prey amongst the large numbers of 'Window' returns. To add to the defenders' confusion, as the Bohlen attack force withdrew to the west, the No 100 Group Halifaxes that had operated in the 'Mandrel' screen role had a further part to play. They now ran a further 'Window Spoof' 'attack' on Frankfurt, and dropped target markers to simulate the opening of a large-scale raid on that city.

As the Bohlen attack force crossed the Rhine to safety, Bomber Command's operations for the night were only half complete. While the defenders' attention had been concentrated over central Germany, the raiding force of 166 Lancasters bound for Hemmingstedt ran in at low altitude, maintaining strict radio silence. Shortly before reaching their target the bombers rose above the radar horizon and began climbing to their attack altitude of 15,000ft. Each aircraft released large amounts of 'Window' to give the impression on radar that this was yet another feint attack. At 4.23 a.m. the attack on the refinery began, supported by jamming from a Fortress and a Liberator of No 100 Group. Because of the low-altitude approach and the clever use of 'Window', the German raid tracking organization failed to appreciate the strength of this force and the bombers were well on their way home before the first radar plots on 'weak formations' were reported in the target area. Night fighters were scrambled to engage the force but there were few interceptions and only one of the bombers was shot down.

During the two raids the oil refineries at Bohlen and Hemmingstedt were both hit hard and neither would resume production before the war ended. The night's action cost Bomber Command thirteen aircraft, including a Liberator and a Fortress of No 100 Group. Eight of the losses were attributed to attacks from night fighters and one to flak, two bombers were lost in a mid-air collision and the cause of the remaining two losses could not be established.

That night No 100 Group's Mosquitos had several skirmishes with German night fighters but only two of the latter were shot down – and both fell to Chapman and Stockley. The bombers' gunners claimed the destruction of two more enemy night fighters. German records indicate that the *Luftwaffe* lost seven night fighters that night, however. The fates of the other three aircraft will probably never be known but it is not difficult to speculate: a tired pilot, trying to land quickly on a dimly lit airfield patrolled by Mosquitos, might misjudge his approach and crash; a crew flying at low altitude to avoid being intercepted by a Mosquito might run into a hillside; a night fighter crew would switch off their IFF equipment to avoid betraying their position on 'Perfectos' and be shot down by 'friendly' anti-aircraft guns. Such losses, which were frequent, were the result of No 100 Group's efforts as surely as were those brought about by its night fighters. By this stage of the war the wide-ranging Mosquitos had became the bane of the German night fighter crews' existence.

When the war in Europe ended in May 1945, No 100 Group had honed its tactical stills to fine edge. Many of the electronic warfare techniques that it had pioneered for supporting bomber attacks would prove useful nearly more than forty-five years later, in the skies over Iraq.

Chapter 28

New Year's Day Party

*Operation 'Baseplate', the massed attack by Luftwaffe fighters on
Allied airfields in France, Holland and Belgium, was originally
intended to neutralize the Allied air forces when the German
Army launched its all-out counter-offensive in the Ardennes
in December 1944 aimed at recapturing the important port of
Antwerp. In the event the attack on the airfields took place a
couple of weeks after the offensive began, and its results were quite
different from those that the Luftwaffe planners had sought . . .*

During the late autumn of 1944 German Army staff officers laid
elaborate plans for Operation 'Watch on the Rhine' (*'Wacct am
Rhein'*), a large-scale counter-offensive in the west. The attacking
force of 200,000 men, including seven *Panzer* divisions, was to smash
through the weakly held Ardennes sector of the US front and thrust
towards the port of Antwerp.

The *Luftwaffe* was assigned three main roles in the forthcoming
operation. First and most important, on the morning of the offensive
it was to mount large-scale strafing attacks on Allied forward airfields
with the intention of destroying as many planes as possible; second, it
was to seal off the battle area to prevent Allied aircraft from attacking
German troops and supply vehicles; and third, it was to fly ground-
attack missions in support of the advancing German troops.

Adolf Hitler had overseen the planning for 'Watch on the Rhine'
and *Luftwaffe* staff officers had been brought in only at a relatively
late stage when detailed planning was required for the air operations
to support the venture. The bulk of the aircraft to be sent against the
Allied forward airfields under Operation 'Baseplate' (*'Bodenplatte'*)
were to come from Reich air defence day-fighter units.

When he heard of the plan *Generalleutnant* Adolf Galland, the Inspector of Fighters, was horrified and he said so in no uncertain terms. In his view it represented a gross misuse of the air defence units. He pointed out that ground attack was a specialized task and one beyond many of his pilots, certainly the newer ones whose limited training and flying experience had been orientated towards the air defence role. Moreover, the majority of the fighter *Geschwader*, *Gruppe* and *Staffel* leaders lacked the necessary training to lead formations attacking ground targets from low altitude. Galland argued that such an attack might achieve little and that there was a serious risk that the attackers themselves would suffer the heavier losses. The fighter ace's injunctions fell on deaf ears, however.

During December the fighter and ground-attack units assigned to Operation 'Baseplate' moved to airfields in western Germany. To preserve the secrecy of the move, the aircraft flew to their new bases at low altitude to remain below the cover of Allied radars, and they maintained strict radio silence. Each unit left behind radio operators at its previous airfield with orders to maintain the previous pattern of radio traffic by means of spoof transmissions.

On 14 December the commanders of the fighter and ground-attack Gruppen *assigned* to 'Baseplate' were summoned to the headquarters of *Jagdkorps II* at Altenkirchen, where they received a top-secret briefing on the planned operation. *Generalmajor* Dietrich Peltz, in command of the attacking force, informed his surprised audience that they were to prepare their units to take part in a series of near-simultaneous attacks on eighteen forward airfields used by the Allied air forces in France, Holland and Belgium. More than a thousand German aircraft were to take part in the operation, which was intended to suppress Allied air opposition during the opening stages of the ground offensive.

Two days later, before dawn on 16 December, a massive artillery bombardment heralded the opening of 'Watch on the Rhine'. Assault units moved forward and rapidly overwhelmed the defences at several points. The code-words that would have initiated Operation 'Baseplate' were not transmitted, however, and the units earmarked for the attack stayed on the ground. The land offensive was launched on that date on the basis of favourable weather forecasts, which predicted several days of low cloud and poor visibility over the battle area. For German Army commanders that offered a heaven-sent opportunity, for they knew that such weather would be more effective in keeping the Allied air forces 'off their backs' than anything the *Luftwaffe* could do.

During the two weeks following the Altenkirchen briefing, the units assigned to 'Baseplate' flew air defence and ground-attack missions in support of the offensive, though at low intensity on account of the poor weather. Since their commanders had heard nothing more about the attack on the Allied airfields, most of them assumed that the operation had been shelved. All the greater was their surprise when, on the afternoon of 31 December, the preliminary warning signal was issued informing them that the attack was to take place soon after first light the following morning.

That evening the German pilots were briefed on 'Baseplate' and on the part that each unit was to play in it. Then they were ordered to bed to 'try to get a good night's sleep. The launching of the operation on New Year's Day had been prompted by a forecast of clear skies over Allied airfields the following morning. But if the previous evening's celebrations left many of those at the target airfields with hangovers that impaired their ability to fight back, so much the better.

Shortly after midnight on New Year's Day, four Arado Ar 234 bombers from *Kampfgeschwader 76* carried out the world's first-ever jet night bombing mission. The aircraft flew a circular route over Rotterdam and Antwerp, then they flew over Brussels and Liege, where they released their bombs at random. In fact the bombs were merely a diversion to allay Allied suspicions if the aircraft were tracked on radar; the true purpose of their mission was to provide a final check on weather conditions over the targets to confirm that 'Baseplate' could go ahead. The jet bomber pilots reported that the skies over Holland and Belgium were clear of cloud.

During the early-morning darkness the pilots assigned to 'Baseplate' were roused for their final briefings, and soon after dawn

---

MESSERSCHMITT Bf 109K-4

Role: Single-seat, high-altitude day fighter.

Powerplant: One Daimler Benz DB 605 ASCM 12-cylinder, liquid-cooled, inline engine developing 2,000hp at take-off.

Armament: One MK 108 30mm cannon firing through the propeller boss and two MG 151 15mm cannon mounted above the engine and synchronized to fire through the propeller disc.

Performance: Maximum speed 378mph at sea level, 452mph at 19,700ft; initial rate of climb 4,800ft/min.

Normal operational take-off weight: 7,475lb.

Dimensions: Span 32ft 8½in; length 29ft 0½in; wing area 174 sq ft.

Date of first production Bf 109K-4: October 1944.

the attacking units took off and headed for their force rendezvous points. The air battles during the previous couple of weeks had taken their toll on the attack force and only 900 fighters and fighter-bombers, for the most part Messerschmitt Bf 109s and Focke Wulf FW 190s, took off for the attack. This total was somewhat less than that originally intended, but by any standard the attacking force was still a sizeable one.

Representative of the more successful attacks that morning was that mounted by *Jagdgeschwader 3* against the Royal Air Force base at Eindhoven in Holland. The airfield was home to eight squadrons of Typhoon fighter-bombers belonging to Nos 124 and 143 Wings and to three tactical reconnaissance squadrons of No 39 with Spitfires and Mustangs. Like many of the Allied forward airfields, this one was grossly overcrowded, with more than 150 aircraft dispersed around it plus visiting machines. RAF commanders would certainly have liked to have spread their units more thinly than this, but there was no choice: in the depths of the European winter only those airfields with an all-weather operating capability and hardened runways and taxiways could support sustained operations, and there were all too few of those usable in the forward areas.

The raiding force assigned to the attack on Eindhoven comprised *I, II* and *IV Gruppen* of *Jagdgeschwader 3*, the first two *Gruppen* operating Bf 109s, including some examples of the latest K-4 version, and *IV Gruppe* FW 190s. The three *Gruppen* assembled over the small town of Lippstadt and from there the eighteen four-plane sections, flying by sections in line astern, remained at low altitude, maintaining an almost straight track for Eindhoven 140 miles away. Thanks to the low-altitude approach and strict radio silence, the raiders arrived at their target with the advantage of surprise.

Jagdgeschwader 3 reached Eindhoven just as sixteen bomb-laden Typhoons of Nos 438 and 440 Squadrons were about to get airborne for an operation. The aircraft were bunched at the down-wind end of the runway and first two aircraft had begun to take off when the attackers commenced their strafing runs. The leader's Typhoon was badly shot up and the last act of its mortally wounded pilot was to cut the throttle and swing the aircraft off the runway. His wing-man continued with the take-off but was shot down and killed shortly after getting airborne. Seeing what was happening, the pilots of the remaining Typhoons unstrapped, struggled out of their cockpits and galloped clear of the planes before these too were shot up: The attacked units were both Canadian-manned, and the official Canadian history recorded that the Messerschmitts and Focke Wulfs 'attacked the field in a well-organised manner, being persistent and well-led'.

The strafing attacks on Eindhoven lasted about twenty minutes and resulted in the destruction of 30 Typhoons and reconnaissance aircraft and damage to fourteen more. Once they had overcome their initial surprise, the airfield's anti-aircraft gun defences fought back hard and, as a result of their efforts and skirmishes with Allied fighters during the withdrawal, *JG 3* lost about twenty aircraft. Similarly destructive attacks were mounted on the airfields at Brussels/Evère, Brussels/Melsbroek, St Denis-Westrem and Maldegem. At Metz-Frescaty, the most southerly airfield to be attacked, fighters of *Jagdgeschwader 53* caught the Thunderbolts of the 365th Fighter Group on the ground and destroyed about twenty of them.

Elsewhere the raiding forces were far less effective. For example, the US Army Air Force base at Asch in Belgium, home to the 352nd and 366th Fighter Groups, with Mustangs and Thunderbolts respectively, and three Royal Air Force Spitfire squadrons, came under attack from three *Gruppen* from *Jagdgeschwader 11*, two with FW 190s and one with Bf 109s. The raiders had the misfortune to arrive just after eight Thunderbolts had taken off and assembled into formation for a mission. On seeing the attackers, the American planes jettisoned their bombs and sped back to defend, their base. *Leutnant* Georg Füdreder, a Bf 109 pilot with *II Gruppe*, recalled:

Because of mist patches we took off later than planned, and I think this did a lot to impair the success of the mission. The *Gruppe* joined formation and set course for the target led by a couple of Ju 188 pathfinders . . . I did not notice whether any aircraft were hit by our own or by enemy flak on the way in, but as we neared the target I remember hearing on the radio that someone had been hit. Just short of the target we pulled up and fanned out to left and right to look over the airfield, then we went into our firing runs. I pulled up and went straight into my attack. My approach was too steep to engage the Thunderbolts on the east side of the airfield, so I aimed at four or five twin-engined planes in the north-west corner. I started a sharp 180-degree turn to go for the Thunderbolts on the east side, when tracer rounds streaked past me. At first I thought it was flak, then to my surprise I saw two Thunderbolts behind me. One was firing at me with everything but his aim was wild. I pulled sharply to port and his rounds passed astern of me. My pursuer and his No 2 gave up the chase and headed off west. I started after them, then broke away for a final run over the airfield, heading south. At this time I saw no other aircraft over or near the airfield. A pall of black smoke rose from the southern half of the airfield, coming from several burning aircraft. I made my firing run somewhat higher because of the smoke, but I still had to fly through the pall over the southern half of the airfield.

Colonel Harold Holt, Commander of the 366th, described the action from his viewpoint on the ground at Asch:

The enemy was engaged immediately by a flight of eight of our T-bolts that had just taken off and assembled. Jettisoning their bombs, they attacked the enemy planes and kept them from hitting our pitifully unprotected planes on the ground. The entire air circus took place at tree-top level directly over the strip. Roaring engines, spitting machine guns and flaming planes going down to destruction had brought the war right to our door-step! The roadways around the strip were lined with spectators who dared leave fox-holes long enough to watch the show. But a plane turning into them soon caused a mad scatter for fox-holes. Slugs from a friendly plane could do as much damage as enemy lead . . .

The attackers destroyed seven Spitfires and some Dakota trans-ports, and damaged several other aircraft; they also shot down four of the Mustangs that took off to engage them. But in achieving this *Jagdgeschwader 11* took a fearful beating from the defending fighters and anti-aircraft guns, losing nearly half of the sixty or so aircraft committed. Among the pilots lost were two skilful air defence aces, the *Geschwader* commander *Oberstleutnant* Günther Specht, credited with 32 victories, and *Hauptmann* Horst-Günther von Fassong, cred-ited with 136. In some cases the German formations failed to locate their briefed targets altogether, and as a result the attacks on Volkel, Antwerp/Deurne and Le Culot airfields were all complete failures.

Several figures have been published concerning the number of Allied aircraft destroyed as a result of the *Luftwaffe* attack. The Royal Air Force official history states that 144 aircraft were destroyed and 84 damaged 'in the British area', but there is no knowing whether the figure refers only to aircraft destroyed on the ground or includes those that fell in the course of the numerous air combats that morning. US Army Air Forces records are even more vague and they indicate that about 30 USAAF planes were destroyed and several more suffered damage, though again it is not clear whether these figures include those lost in air-to-air combat. On the best available information, it appears that the Allies lost between 174 and 250 aircraft destroyed and between 84 and 120 damaged that morning. Considering the size of the engagement, Allied pilot losses were minimal, probably fewer than twenty in total. Within a couple of weeks of the attack all the Allied combat units would be restored to full strength, following the arrival of new or repaired aircraft from storage units.

From surviving German records we knew that the attacks on the airfields cost the *Luftwaffe* 237 pilots killed, missing or captured, plus eighteen wounded. Among those lost were three *Geschwader* commanders, six *Gruppe* commanders and eleven *Staffel* commanders – experienced combat leaders who were impossible to replace. No official *Luftwaffe* figures survive for the number of aircraft that service lost in the operation. However, from the large number of pilots lost, it is reasonable to assume that these amounted to at least 300 planes or about a third of those that took part. Thus the *Luftwaffe* suffered greater losses in aircraft than those it inflicted, while its losses in pilots were more than ten times greater than those suffered by the Allied air forces. It was the greatest numerical loss, and also the highest proportional loss, ever to be suffered by a large force of attacking aircraft.

Operation 'Baseplate' was a catastrophe for the *Luftwaffe* fighter force, and several of the units involved never recovered from it. In destroying a commodity that the Allies possessed in abundance at that stage in the war, combat planes, the *Luftwaffe* expended the commodity it could least afford to lose, trained pilots. The action serves as yet another lesson about the dangers of sending airmen into action with inadequate training in their combat role. Military airfields that are well defended and at a high state of readiness are not easy targets. Even with a well-trained attack force, a low-level raid on such a target can be a risky business. Unless the operation is meticulously planned and skilfully executed, the raiding force is liable to lose more planes than it destroys. That was what happened during Operation 'Baseplate'.

Chapter 29

Target Hanoi

*On 10 May 1972 US Air Force and Navy planes resumed
their attacks on targets in North Vietnam, following a bombing
pause lasting more than 3½ years. That day Air Force F-4
Phantoms delivered set piece attacks on two targets in the
vicinity of Hanoi, one of them with the newly developed 'smart'
weapons fitted with electro-optical and laser-homing heads.
This chapter describes these actions and the force package tactics
employed by the attacking planes. An important innovation
during this war, from the point of view of historians, was the
installation of tape recorders in combat aircraft; the action conver-
sations reproduced in this chapter all come from this source.*

During the US Air Force raids on North Vietnam in the spring
of 1972 the attacking planes flew from bases in Thailand. The
F-4 Phantoms configured as bombers came from the 8th Tactical
Fighter Wing at Udorn; the Phantoms configured for reconnaissance
and air-to-air combat came from the 432nd Tactical Reconnaissance
Wing at Udorn; and the EB-66 radar jamming planes, F-105F 'Wild
Weasel' defence-suppression aircraft and EC-121 Warning Star
airborne command and control planes came from the 388th Tactical
Fighter Wing at Korat. Rescue and recovery planes to pick up crews
who had been shot down came from the 56th Special Operations
Wing at Nakhon Phanom, whilst the KC-135 tankers that supplied
fuel for the high-speed jets before they entered enemy airspace and
as they withdrew came from U Tapao and Don Muang.

On 10 May the Air Force's targets were the important Paul
Doumer Bridge over the Red River, immediately to the east of
Hanoi, and the nearby Yen Vien railway sorting yard. At 7.30 a.m.

that morning the initial wave of seven KC435 tankers (six aircraft required, plus an airborne reserve) began taking off from U Tapao each carrying 75 tons of fuel. As this was happening, an RF-4C Phantom conducted a weather reconnaissance of the Hanoi area; its coded radio report of clear skies over the targets allowed the preparations for the attacks to go ahead.

At the head of the raiding force entering enemy territory would be two four-plane units, 'Oyster' and 'Balter' Flights, with Phantoms armed for air-to-air combat. These took off from Udorn at 8.05 a.m. and headed north. Four more Phantom flights, configured in the same way, followed them into the air to escort different parts of the attack force over enemy territory. Last off from Udorn were a pair of RF-4Cs to carry out a post-strike reconnaissance of the targets.

From Korat, four EB-66 Destroyer radar jamming planes took off to provide stand-off cover for the attack. Three flights of 'Wild Weasel' F-105G Thunderchiefs followed them, to provide defence-suppression cover for the attacks; because of the importance of this mission, each 'Wild Weasel' flight took off with five planes, including an airborne reserve that would turn back just short of enemy territory if all of the others were serviceable.

From Ubon, ten four-plane flights of Phantoms took off. Two carried chaff bombs to lay out a trail of the radar-reflective strips along the route to the targets. For the attack on the important Paul Doumer Bridge over the Red River, 'Goatee' Flight's planes were loaded with two 2,000lb electro-optically guided bombs. Those of 'Napkin', 'Biloxi' and 'Jingle' Flights were loaded with two 2,000lb laser-guided bombs. It was to be the first use of the two new 'smart' weapons against a target in North Vietnam. A further four flights of Phantoms, to attack the Yen Vien railway sorting yard, carried conventional, unguided 500lb bombs.

By 8.50 a.m. the entire armada was airborne and heading north. Of the total of more than 110 aircraft, no fewer than 88 were scheduled to penetrate enemy territory. Over northern Thailand the raiders refuelled from the six KC-135 tankers waiting at the rendezvous area, then headed into Laos. Already, however, the two flights that were to spearhead the attack had been weakened. Two planes from 'Balter' Flight had suffered technical problems and had to turn back. A Phantom of 'Oyster' Flight had suffered a radar failure, but its crew opted to continue the mission though with a reduced capability.

'Oyster' and 'Balter' Flights crossed the North Vietnamese border at 9.20 a.m. and headed for their patrol lines north-west of Hanoi. The plan was to establish a barrier patrol, with 'Oyster' Flight at low altitude and 'Balter' at 22,000ft some distance behind and in full

---

McDONNELL F-4E PHANTOM

Role: Two-seat, multi-role fighter.
Powerplant: Two General Electric J79-GE-17 turbojet engines
each developing 17,900lb of thrust.
Armament: One M61A1 20mm cannon; (air-to-air) four AIM-7E
Sparrow semi-active radar missiles and four AIM-9G Sidewinder
infra-red homing missiles; (precision attack role during 10 May
1972 action) two 2,000lb electro-optically guided bombs or two
2,000lb laser-guided bombs; (normal attack role) nine 500lb bombs.
Performance: Maximum speed (clean) Mach 2.17 (1,430mph) at
36,000ft; maximum rate of climb (clean) 49,800ft/min.
Maximum operational take-off weight: 61,795lb.
Dimensions: Span 38ft 4in; length 63ft; wing area 530 sq ft.
Date of first production F-4E: June 1967.

---

view of enemy radars. Any MiGs moving against 'Balter' Flight were
therefore likely to fly over 'Oyster' Flight waiting in ambush. Three
minutes after crossing the frontier, the Phantom crews received
warning from the EC-121 Warning Star radar-picket plane over
Laos that enemy fighters were airborne. Similar warnings came from
the cruiser USS *Chicago* acting as radar-control ship in the Gulf of
Tonkin.

Initially the MiGs kept their distance from the incoming force, but
at 9.42 the North Vietnamese controller finally ordered his fighters
to go into action. A warning call from *Chicago* enabled Major Bob
Lodge, 'Oyster' Flight Leader, to turn to meet the MiGs nose-on.
That gave his flight a clear tactical advantage, for the Phantoms could
engage the MiGs at long range with their Sparrow missiles while the
enemy fighters with less advanced missiles had no effective means of
shooting back.

Down at 2,000ft the Phantoms jettisoned their external tanks and
accelerated to fighting speed. In an air combat, victory usually goes
to the side which sees its opponent first. Lodge kept his force low
to remain out of sight for as long as possible, while the four enemy
fighters ran obliquely past his nose at 15,000ft. The two forces were
not meeting exactly head-on, but even so their combined closing
speed was tremendous – more than 1,000mph, or just over a mile
every four seconds. Tape recorders in the fighters captured the words
spoken as the MiGs appeared on their radars:

'Oyster 2 has contact!'
'Oyster 1 has a contact zero-five-zero [bearing] for fifteen [miles].'

MIKOYAN-GUREVICH MiG-19 ('FARMER')

Role: Single-seat interceptor and air superiority fighter.
Powerplant: Two Tumansky RD-9B turbojets each developing
7,165lb of thrust with afterburning.
Armament: Three NR-30 30mm cannon.
Performance: Maximum speed (clean) Mach 1.4 (900mph) at
33,000ft. Operational take-off weight (clean): 16,300lb.
Dimensions: Span 29ft 6½in; length 41ft 4in; wing area 269 sq ft.
Date of first production MiG-19: 1953.

'Oyster 3 is contact, Bob!'
'Right, we got 'em!'
'Oyster 1 on the nose, twelve miles, fifteen [degrees] high . . .'

The Phantoms were fitted with 'Combat Tree', a device that worked on the same principle as the Second World War British 'Perfectos' equipment (see Chapter 10). 'Combat Tree' transmitted signals to trigger the IFF transponders in the MiGs and picked up their coded reply signals. In the context of this mission the device was vitally important, for it provided proof that the planes seen on radar were hostile. And that meant that they could be engaged from long range with radar-homing missiles, without having to close to within visual range to confirm their identity. In the three 'Oyster' fighters with serviceable radars, the back-seater locked-on to an enemy plane and made ready the Sparrow missiles.

Bob Lodge eased his fighter into a shallow climb preparatory to missile launch and the other Phantoms followed. When the leading MiG was in firing range, Lodge squeezed the trigger to launch his first Sparrow. Trailing smoke, the 450lb missile accelerated from the Phantom's 700mph to more than 2,000mph in 2.3 seconds. The motor then cut out and the weapon should have coasted on to the target, but instead it blew up in a cloud of smoke. Lodge squeezed the trigger a second time and another Sparrow streaked away from the fighter.

A few hundred yards to the right of Lodge, Lieutenant John Markle in 'Oyster 2' fired a pair of Sparrows. These gave similar results, as he later recalled:

Our first missile apparently did not get rocket motor ignition. The second missile came off the aircraft and turned slightly right as it climbed. We continued to maintain position on 'Oyster 1' in an easy right turn, slightly nose-up. As I checked

---

MIKOYAN-GUREVICH MiG-21bis ('FISHBED-J')

Role: Single-seat interceptor and air superiority fighter.
Powerplant: One Tumansky R-25 turbojet developing 16,500lb of
thrust with afterburning.
Armament: One 23mm GSh-23 cannon; up to four K-13
infra-red homing, air-to-air missiles.
Performance: Maximum speed (clean) Mach 2 (1,320mph) at
36,000ft. Maximum operational take-off weight: 22,000lb.
Dimensions: Span 23ft 6in; length 51ft 9in; wing area 247 sq ft.
Date of first production MiG-21bis: 1970.

---

the missile's progress, the trail showed a slight left turn toward
the radar target.

Captain Steve Ritchie in 'Oyster 3', 3,000yds to the left of Lodge,
also launched a Sparrow but this too was a dud: the motor failed to
ignite and it fell away from the fighter like a bomb. Thus, of the five
Sparrows fired, three had failed to function properly. The two missiles
that worked as advertised produced devastating-results, however. The
tape recorder in Markle's plane captured his reaction as he saw his
missile explode beside the enemy plane:

'Oh right! . . . Now! . . . Good! . . . *Woooohooo!*' Then came a short
pause to calm down, after which the pilot announced on the radio,
'Oyster 2's a hit!'

From the leading aircraft Lodge replied, 'I got one!'

Steve Eaves, Markle's back-seater, confirmed that he had seen the
leader's kill: 'Roger, he's burning and he's going down one o'clock!'

Captain Roger Locher, Lodge's back-seater, saw a couple of small
clouds suddenly appear as the two missiles detonated a long way in
front of him. A few seconds later he caught sight of the two stricken
North Vietnamese fighters, MiG-21s, tumbling out of the sky. One
was cartwheeling and going down in a shallow dive, the other had
part of a wing missing and was in a steep dive, rolling out of control.

The two MiG-21s that had survived the Sparrow onslaught flashed
over the top of the Phantoms, as the latter were pulling into tight turns
to the right to get behind their opponents for follow-up attacks. When
Lodge rolled out he was only 200ft behind one of the MiGs, giving
Locher in the rear seat a sight that he would never forget:

We were in his jet wash. There he was, [after]burner plume
sticking out, the shiniest airplane you've ever seen. He was
going up in a chandelle to the right, we were right behind him.

The Phantom carried no gun and it was too close for a missile attack, so Lodge eased off the turn to open the range on the enemy fighter. It seemed only a matter of time before that MiG too was smashed out of the sky. Then, without warning, a pair of MiG-19s climbed steeply from below and gate-crashed the fight. Probably flown by Lieutenants Le Thanh Dao and Vu Van Hop of the 3rd Company, the newcomers slid into firing positions behind Lodge's Phantom as Markle bellowed a warning to his leader: 'OK, there's a Bandit . . . you got a Bandit in your 10 o'clock Bob, level!' The MiG-19s passed behind Lodge then closed in from his right.

Further warning calls followed from the other Phantoms: 'Bob, reverse right, reverse right Bob. Reverse right!'

Lodge's attention was focused on the MiG-21 in front of him, which by now had opened the range sufficiently to allow a close-in missile shot. Meanwhile, behind the Phantom, the leading MiG-19 opened fire with its cannon. The hefty 30mm rounds rapidly bridged the gap between the two machines and Markle's warnings to his leader took on a more strident note: 'He's firing – he's firing at you!'

In the Phantom under attack, events now followed each other in confusingly rapid succession. Roger Locher recalled:

> One or two seconds later – *wham*! We were hit. I looked up and saw the MiG [the MiG-21 in front of him] separating away. I thought we had mid-aired because that was exactly my interpretation of how a collision would feel. We both said 'Oh shit!', and my 'Oh shit!' was because the guy in front was getting away from us.

More 30mm shells slammed into the Phantom, and at last Locher realized what was happening. The fighter decelerated rapidly and he felt it yaw violently to the right. The whole of the fighter's rear fuselage was ablaze and as the flames ate their way forwards the heat began to roast the plastic of Locher's canopy, which turned an opaque orange. Smoke seeped into the cockpit.

Around the doomed Phantom the air battle continued. The MiG-21 that Lodge had been about to engage sped clear: The fourth plane from the original enemy formation was less fortunate, however. Steve Ritchie in 'Oyster 3' rolled out of his turn about a mile behind it, in a perfect firing position, and squeezed off two Sparrows in quick succession. Once again, the first missile failed to guide, but the other homed in perfectly. It detonated immediately below the Soviet-built fighter, pieces flew off it and the MiG quickly lost speed. As the Phantom swept past its victim, Chuck DeBellevue in the rear seat saw a black shape flash past his left, less than 100ft away – the enemy pilot. DeBellevue gave a jubilant shout on the radio: 'Oyster 3's a splash [enemy plane shot down]!'

DeBellevue's triumphant call was the last thing Roger Locher heard before he ejected from his Phantom. By then the burning plane was upside down and falling fast. Locher grabbed the firing handle between his legs with both hands, and pulled hard:

> We were under negative *g* at the time. My ass was off the seat; I was pinned against the top of the canopy. I saw the canopy go, then I went out under negative *g*. There was a lot of wind blast; I started to see again. Then *thwack!* – the parachute opened. And *Zoooom!* – past me went two MiG-19s.

The other members of 'Oyster' Flight watched in horror as the Phantom fell from the sky, hoping for a glimpse of one or more parachutes to indicate that there were survivors. They saw none. The fighter was upside-down when Locher ejected and probably the plume of smoke trailing behind the aircraft screened him from their view. It seems certain that Lodge was still in his cockpit when the fighter plunged into the ground.

Shaken by the loss of their leader, the survivors of 'Oyster' Flight kept up their speed as they returned to low altitude and made a rapid withdrawal from the area. The two aircraft of 'Balter' Flight also had a tussle with MiGs, though without loss on either side. Those skirmishes were not decisive, but for the raiding force now approaching Hanoi they had an important result: they kept the MiGs to the area north-west of city, enabling the main attackers to approach their targets without interference from enemy fighters.

Now the second phase of the action could begin, with the aim of blunting the cutting edge of Hanoi's SAM and anti-aircraft gun defences. Four EB-66E stand-off jamming aircraft, four 'Wild Weasel' F-105Gs and eight F-4 chaff-bombers were assigned to this task.

The first to make their presence felt were the EB-66s. Each plane carried a battery of eighteen radar jammers and their role was similar to that of the target-support Liberators operated by No 100 Group in the Second World War (see Chapter 10). At 9.45 a.m. the aircraft arrived at their orbit positions just outside the reach of the Hanoi missile belt and, flying at 30,000ft, began jamming the enemy radars. As they did so four 'Wild Weasel' F-105Gs split into two pairs and ran into the defended area at low altitude. Their role was to strike at the radars of enemy surface-to-air missile sites as they came on the air. Each plane carried three anti-radar missiles – two short-range Shrikes and a long-range Standard ARM. One of those who flew on this type of operation, Major Don Kilgus, described the tactics used:

> Once we had found an active site we would go into afterburner and increase speed to between 450 and 520 knots [520–600mph]. Speed gave us survivability and manoeuvre potential, because when we started pulling *g* the plane would slow down. The Thud [F-105] was a super plane but it was not the tightest turner in the world and you had to plan ahead if you wanted to make a violent manoeuvre. So we would light the burner, pull up and turn at the same time to establish the firing parameters for the missile. Needles showed where the Shrike was looking and gave an indication of range plus or minus about 20 per cent. If a loft attack was necessary, for maximum range we would launch in a 30-degree climb from 15,000 feet. Or if we were close to the site we would pitch over and push the missile down his throat.

The 'Wild Weasel' aircraft were themselves likely to come under missile attack, and this was no mission for the faint-hearted.

As the F-105s played their deadly game of hide-and-seek with the SAM batteries, the next phase of the action opened. Eight Phantoms ran in towards Hanoi from the south-west at 26,000ft, each carrying nine chaff bombs. The role of these planes was similar to that of the 'Window Spoof' forces in the Second World War (again, as described in Chapter 10). At 9.47 a.m. these aircraft entered the Hanoi SAM-defended zone and each released a single chaff bomb. After a short fall the casings split open and each disgorged millions of metallized strips each thinner than a human hair. At 15-second intervals along the route to the enemy capital, each plane released a further chaff bomb.

During the run-in the Phantoms flew in the so-called 'jamming pod formation', with two lots of four aircraft flying in line abreast with 2,000ft horizontal separation and stepped up to one side with 600ft vertical separation between adjacent planes. This forma-tion offered a high degree of protection against the SA-2, the only long-range missile system then used by the North Vietnamese. Each Phantom carried a jamming pod under the fuselage, and the noise jamming from the four-plane formation produced a wedge of over-lapping strobes on the enemy gun and SAM control radars. The SAM operators could see the incoming formation, but they could not pick out the individual planes accurately to engage them.

That, at least, was the theory. It worked only if the crews held their positions in formation. As the Phantoms closed on the enemy capital the crews watched the clouds of orange or white smoke on the ground as the enemy missiles blasted away from their launchers. During its boost phase each missile left a smoke trail, but when this ended there was nothing to see until the missile itself hove into view. Captain William Byrns recalled:

A SAM came for us and someone yelled 'Look out!' I turned my head and my reaction was to pull back on the stick. That was not the normal reaction – I should have gone down. But I believe God took my hand and made me go the other way. The missile went underneath my plane, underneath the F-4 across the way and exploded on the far side of him. If I had gone down it would have hit us and we would probably not have got out.

Several of the crews experienced similar scares, and a few planes suffered a shaking as missiles detonated within a few hundred feet. Yet the protective cocoon of jamming conferred a high degree of safety: only one chaff bomber was hit by missile splinters, and these caused little damage.

Having released the last of their chaff bombs, the two flights sped away from the target area. Behind them they left more than seventy clouds of chaff that now spread out to form a corridor two miles wide, more than a mile deep and eighteen miles long. At the end of that corridor lay the Paul Doumer Bridge.

Five minutes behind the chaff bombers, the first of the main attack formations entered the Hanoi missile zone. Flying through the corridor of chaff laid to assist it, the Paul Doumer Bridge attack force headed for the target flying at 620mph at 13,000ft. 'Goatee', 'Napkin', 'Biloxi' and 'Jingle' Flights, each with four Phantoms in jamming-pod formation, followed each other at two-mile intervals.

Flying ahead of the Phantoms and far below them, a fresh team of four 'Wild Weasel' F-105Gs fanned out in pairs, looking for active SAM sites. Yet despite this harassment and the radar jamming from the Phantoms and their supporting EB-66s, the defending batteries lay on an impressive display of wrath. Holding position in a jamming-pod formation under SAM attack has been likened to the first time one snuffs out a candle with one's fingers – it was an unnatural act and it required courage to overcome one's basic instincts. Captain Lynn High commented:

We had to sit in formation and grit our teeth when the SAMs came through the formation. It took nerves of steel to watch a

SAM come straight at you, even though you knew that in all probability it would not hit you and if it detonated it would detonate too soon or too late. I watched about six SAMs do exactly that.

Meanwhile the leading attack flight, 'Goatee', commenced its bombing run on the Paul Doumer Bridge with electro-optical guided bombs (EOGBs). These weapons homed in on the image contrast of the target against its background, and the Phantoms were to attack the bridge broadside-on from the south. In each plane the back-seater operated a small hand-held controller to position the bridge under the sighting reticle on his TV screen and pressed a button to lock the target image into the first bomb. He then switched to the second bomb and repeated the process. Colonel Carl Miller, the Flight Leader, pushed his plane into a 30-degree descent and the other three planes followed. At 12,000ft the Phantoms released their bombs in a salvo.

During the recent war in the Persian Gulf the newest types of EOGBs demonstrated an impressive degree of accuracy. Earlier weapons of this type were considerably less effective, however, and on this occasion they performed miserably. The exasperated Miller watched his bombs go their separate ways:

One made a 90-degree turn and went for downtown Hanoi, I think it impacted near the train station. I don't know where the other went. The EOGB was a launch-and-leave weapon, they were supposed to stay locked-on after release. But they didn't.

After releasing their bombs, the aircraft of 'Goatee' Flight turned west and engaged their afterburners to get clear of the defended area as rapidly as possible. As this was happening, 'Biloxi' 'Jingle' and 'Napkin' Flights sped towards a point immediately to the east of the bridge, ready to attack along its length with their laser-guided bombs (LGBs). As he was about to turn in to attack, Major Bill Driggers glanced to his left to observe the result of 'Goatee' Flight's attack with EOGBs. He had expected to see them burst around the bridge and demolish parts of the structure, but the reality was quite different:

As we rolled in to attack the bridge I saw big waterspouts rising from the Red River. The first EOGBs fell short; those that made it to the bridge went through the gaps between the pylons. I saw two, maybe three, of the bombs explode in the water on the other side.

None of the EOGBs hit the target – a profoundly disappointing result during the first operational use of these expensive weapons over North Vietnam.

Two by two, the Phantoms of 'Napkin' Flight pulled into their 45-degree attack dives. The 37mm and 57mm anti-aircraft guns around the target opened up a powerful defensive fire and colourful lines of moving tracer, punctuated by stationary puffs from exploding shells, criss-crossed the sky over the eastern side of Hanoi. At 12,000ft each Phantom let go its bombs and pulled out of its dive. In the leading plane in each pair, the back-seater operated a small control stick to hold the laser-designator on the required aiming-point. A laser seeker head in the nose of each bomb steered the weapon to the point thus marked. The first salvo of four bombs exploded against the bridge or in the river beneath it, hurling smoke, spray and debris hundreds of feet into the air.

At the head of 'Biloxi' Flight, the next to attack, Captain Lynn High noticed that the enemy anti-aircraft gunners seemed to be aiming at the wrong part of the sky:

> The Vietnamese gunners obviously expected us to release from a lower altitude: they coned their fire on a point 7,500 feet to 9,000 feet above the target. It looked like an Indian tepee sitting over downtown Hanoi. But we released our bombs at a higher altitude – we kept out of it.

The Flight's eight 2,000-pounders threw up further columns of debris, smoke and spray around the bridge.

'Jingle' Flight bombed last, and Captain Mike Van Wagenen piloted the final aircraft to attack the bridge:

> There was so much going on, it was impossible to comprehend everything. The human mind cannot take that many inputs so it rules a lot of them out. The radio seemed to go quiet, the radar warning gear went quiet, everything appeared to go quiet as I tracked the Doumer Bridge underneath my sighting pipper. We just stopped thinking about the other things going on around us. My back-seater was calling off the altitudes: 15 ... 14 ... 13 [thousand feet] ... The pipper was tracking up the bridge, I had the parameters like I wanted to see them and released both bombs.

Van Wagenen hauled on the stick and watched the horizon sink rapidly past his windscreen as the *g* forces asserted themselves and pushed him hard into his seat:

As we came off the target it was like plugging in the stereo: slowly one's senses came back and one could hear the radar warning gear, the radio transmissions, everything else. The human computer was working again. I jinked hard left and right, picked up Mike [Captain Mike Messett, his element leader] and joined up on him. Then I rolled-back to the right to see where my bombs had gone. It appeared all four, Mike's and mine, had hit the first span on the east side of the river. I took one more look to see if the span was standing but I couldn't tell, there was a lot of smoke around.

As Van Wagenen left the bridge none of the spans had dropped, despite the fact that several of the laser-guided bombs had scored direct hits on the structure and caused severe damage. Two spans at the eastern end had broken apart, however, and the bridge was impassable to wheeled vehicles.

As the Phantoms sped out of the target area some of them had fleeting brushes with MiGs. Lieutenant Rick Bates recalled:

As we came off the target we passed a Thud [F-105] followed by a MiG followed by a Thud. Then I saw a MiG-21 that looked as if it was trying to turn on us. But we were going so goddarn fast he had no chance . . . Those three or four minutes was [sic] absolute and total chaos as far as I was concerned; my pulse rate was going at about eight million a minute . . .

As the Phantoms of the bridge attack force left the target, the raiding force heading for the Yen Vien rail yard began running through the chaff corridor laid earlier. The sixteen F-4 bombers followed the same route as the bridge attack force and Major Kelly Irving was surprised at the ease with which he could follow the line of chaff through the defended area:

I was impressed at how well it showed up on my air intercept radar. That was how we made sure we were positioned in it. That was a godsend – we drove up that thing like it was a highway.

The bombers ran towards their target at 15,000ft, pulled up to 20,000ft and swung into echelon right as they peeled into their 45-degree attack dives. Captain Jim Shaw, in the leading flight, recalled:

We followed the other three down the chute and Bud Pratt [his pilot] pickled [released] the bombs. When we pulled off I looked back, and saw somebody's bombs do a pretty good job across the south chokepoint. While in the target area we tried to change something – heading, altitude or speed – every ten seconds to defeat the radar-aimed fire.

This attention to detail proved necessary, for as Shaw left the target his flight suddenly came under heavy fire:

Lead got away with it, No 2 flew through some of it, No 3 could not avoid it. We broke left and came very sharply back to the right. I got an eyeful of all the standard colours of smoke puffs. The larger the calibre the darker the smoke: white puffs were 23mm, light grey puffs were 3 mm, grey were 57mm and black puffs were 85mm. Beforehand every flight leader briefs that he will fly a wide arc coming off the target, so those behind can cut off the turn and join up for mutual support. But when they were being shot at, very few leaders do it to the degree their wing-men would like. We went out scalded-ass fast and it took a while to get the flight back in order. Everybody had a distinct interest in getting away from the people they had just been nasty to!

The attacks on both targets were now complete, but there was a further chore that had to be completed. North of Hanoi a pair of RF-4C reconnaissance Phantoms moved into position to photo-graph the targets for damage assessment. The aircraft accelerated to 750mph, keeping just below the speed of sound to retain a measure of manoeuvrability, and sped towards their objectives at between 4,000 and 6,000ft, continually varying their altitude to give the enemy gunners as difficult a target as possible. Major Sid Rogers led the pair, with Captain Don Pickard flying as wing-man behind and about 1,000ft to the right of his leader. The latter recalled:

After we passed the rail yard we got everything in the world shot at us. We started jinking and as we approached Hanoi there was a trail of black puffs from bursting shells behind Sid. I said to my back-seater, Chuck Irwin, 'Good God, look at that stuff behind lead!' Chuck replied, 'It's a good thing you can't see the stuff behind us . . . !'

Moments later Pickard noticed a MiG-17 about 500yds behind and to the left, trying to get into a firing position. But the two

Phantoms soon left the slower fighter far behind. South of Hanoi a SAM battery loosed off at Pickard's aircraft. The pilot saw nothing of the missile until it detonated and the Phantom bucked under its blast:

> I didn't see the SAM but I saw a whole bunch of red things, like tracer rounds but fanning out, come past my nose [the hot splinters from the warhead]. I ducked; it looked like we were going to hit them.

Miraculously, all the warhead splinters missed the plane.

It was 10.14 a.m, and now all the bombers, the reconnaissance planes and the 'Wild Weasel' and jamming-support aircraft were heading away from the target. Four flights of Phantoms covered the withdrawal: one patrolled north-west of Hanoi, one was to the south-south-west, one was to the south-south-east and one was astride the withdrawal route near the Laotian border.

The earlier activity by MiGs had tapered off and now there was little sign of the defending fighters. Tempted by this inactivity, one flight moved west of Hanoi at 8,000ft trying to lure North Vietnamese fighters into battle. The stratagem succeeded only too well. Suddenly a MiG-19 zoomed into a firing position behind one of the Phantoms and delivered a snap attack. Exploding 30mm shells tore away chunks from the left wing and the fighter rolled into a dive and plunged into the ground. There were no survivors. The remaining Phantoms curved vengefully after their assailant and one launched missiles from extreme range, but the North Vietnamese pilot knew his business and dived away and disappeared as suddenly as he had come.

By 11.15 a.m. the whole of the raiding force was back on the ground. The 8th Tactical Fighter Wing at Ubon had sent out forty F-4s to lay the chaff corridor and deliver the attacks on the Paul Doumer Bridge and the Yen Vien railway yard; as a testimony to the effectiveness of the 'jamming-pod formation', all the planes had passed through the thickest part of the defences and all had returned, though one had suffered minor damage. The 388th Tactical Fighter Wing at Korat sent twelve F-105s, four EB-66s and an EC-121 to support the operation; all these returned safely too. The 432nd Tactical Reconnaissance Wing at Udorn had sent 28 F-4s and three RF-4Cs; its two F-4s shot down by MiG-19s were the only planes lost during the mission. Three North Vietnamese MiG-21 fighters had been shot down, all of them by 'Oyster' Flight during the initial encounter.

On the following day Phantoms delivered a second attack with laser-guided bombs on the Paul Doumer Bridge, during which they concentrated their weapons on the damaged eastern end of the structure. After further hits, the disconnected span toppled into the Red River.

Just over three weeks later there was an interesting sequel to the action. It will be remembered that Captain Roger Locher had ejected from his blazing Phantom shortly before it crashed into the ground. Although deep in enemy territory he avoided capture, living off any edible vegetation he could find. On June 1 Locher finally made radio contact with US aircraft, and the following day a large-scale rescue operation retrieved him. When he was picked up by a 'Jolly Green Giant' helicopter he had lost 30lb in weight and he was weak from starvation. For an air-crew survivor to remain at liberty, unassisted, for 23 days deep in enemy home territory and initiate a successful rescue was a record for the Vietnam War and it ranks with the most successful combat evasion episodes in history. The rescue also set a record for those who retrieved him, for it took the helicopters deeper into North Vietnam than any other such mission during the conflict.

Chapter 30

The First 'Black Buck'

*Following the Argentine capture of the Falklands Islands early
in April 1982, the British government dispatched a large naval
force to repossess the islands. At the airfield at Waddington in
Lincolnshire the three resident Avro Vulcan bomber units, Nos
44, 50 and 101 Squadrons, received orders to prepare a number of
aircraft and crews to fly extended-range missions over the South
Atlantic. The code-name for the Operation was 'Black Buck' . . .*

When Royal Air Force planners began to examine the feasibility of using the elderly Vulcan, the only available long-range bomber type, to support the operation to retake the Falklands, it became clear that this would be no easy option. The distance from Port Stanley, the capital, to the nearest available airfield on Ascension Island was 3,886 statute miles – roughly equal to the distance from London to Karachi in Pakistan. The 7,700-mile round trip was a good deal further than that flown on any previous operational bombing mission in history. Although in its time the delta-winged bomber had been modified to refuel in flight, the system had been out of use for more than a decade and scarcely any of the generation of crews then flying the bomber had received training in its use.

Even if the bomber's air-to-air refuelling system could be brought back into use, to get a Vulcan loaded with bombs to the Falklands and back again would entail an enormous supporting operation by tankers. It would require no fewer than ten Victor tanker sorties to supply the bomber and the tanker that were to accompany it to the distant south, and a further tanker would have to meet the bomber and provide fuel for the final part of the return flight. The big question was: would the damage that a single Vulcan could inflict on the enemy possibly be worth the expense and effort required to mount the operation?

While the decision whether to use the Vulcan was being pondered, work began to prepare half a dozen of the bombers for the operation, 'just in case'. The first move was to refurbish the planes' in-flight refuelling receiver systems and, as these became ready, the selected Vulcan crews began training to take fuel from Victor tankers. As the planning of the operation reached the detailed stage, a series of problems became apparent. One of the most daunting was the inadequacy of the Vulcan's navigation system for the unforeseen mission. The aircraft was equipped to operate in areas where there were plenty of land features on which its H2S bombing radar could obtain fixes, and the radar and navigational computer system were quite unsuitable for use over the featureless wastes of the South Atlantic, where fixing points were few and far between. Yet, perhaps short of fuel, the bomber would need to be able to make a rapid and accurate rendezvous with the tanker that was to replenish its tanks during the return flight. To make up for this deficiency, the Vulcans and the Victor tankers were modified to carry the Carousel inertial navigation equipment as part of the programme to prepare them for the operation.

With most complex military operations, if there is time it is usual to mount a rehearsal beforehand. In the case of the 'Black Buck' operations there was time available, but no attempt was made to make a full-scale test of the validity of the in-flight refuelling operation. As one of the pilots later explained:

> It would have been as much trouble to run a rehearsal as to fly the mission, so it was decided to fly the mission. If the problems had become too great, we would have broken off the mission and called it the rehearsal . . .

As April drew to a close it became clear that there was unlikely to be any diplomatic solution to the crisis between Great Britain and Argentina. The matter would have to be settled by force of arms. In the final week of the month two of the specially prepared Vulcans flew to Wideawake, each loaded with twenty-one 1,000lb bombs. The crews had already been briefed on their target for the initial attack, the runway at Port Stanley airfield. Soon after they arrived on Ascension Island they learned that the mission was to take place during the small hours of 1 May. One Vulcan was assigned to fly the mission; the other would take off with it, to act as a reserve in case the primary machine went unserviceable.

AVRO VULCAN B.2

Role: Five-seat medium bomber (a sixth crew member, an air-to-air refuelling expert, was carried during the 'Black Buck' missions).

Powerplant: Four Rolls-Royce (Bristol) Olympus 301 turbojet engines each developing 20,000lb of thrust.

Armament: (Conventional attack role) Normal operational bomb load 21,000lb. During some 'Black Buck' missions the aircraft carried two or four Shrike anti-radar missiles.

Performance: Cruising speed Mach 0.93 (707mph) at 45,000ft; combat radius of action without refuelling 1,725 miles; service ceiling 58,000ft.

Normal operational take-off weight: 200,000lb.

Dimensions: Span 111ft; length (inc. refuelling probe) 105ft 6in; wing area 3,964 sq ft.

Date of first production Vulcan B.2: Spring 1960.

From 10.50 p.m. Ascension time (7.50 p.m. Port Stanley time) in the evening of 30 April the two Vulcan bombers and the eleven supporting Victor tankers (including one airborne reserve) thundered into the air from Wideawake at one-minute intervals. As the aircraft headed south, their anti-collision lights blinking, the wisdom of the planners in providing airborne reserves was quickly borne out. Soon after take-off it was discovered that the primary bombing Vulcan was unable to pressurize its cabin; and that the fuel hose unit of one of the Victor tankers was unserviceable. Both planes therefore abandoned the mission and returned to Wideawake. The force, now lacking any margin in capacity if there were a further major failure, continued on its way south.

The Captain of the reserve Vulcan was Flight Lieutenant Martin Withers. When he received the news that the primary aircraft had aborted the mission, those on board the aircraft remember that there was a long and pensive silence on the intercom. Then Withers commented, 'Looks like we've got a job of work, fellers . . .' No further discussion was necessary, for the reserve crew had briefed as assiduously for the mission as had the one now forced to abandon it.

For one and three-quarter hours after take-off the gaggle of big jets headed south, then, at a point about 840 miles from Ascension, four of the Victors passed their spare fuel to four others and turned back. Another Victor passed fuel to the Vulcan.

Even at this early stage, a problem manifested itself that was to cause increasing difficulties as the operation progressed. Holding loose formation, the Vulcan and its attendant Victors flew at a compromise cruising speed that was the optimum for neither machine; moreover, their cruising altitude of 31,000ft was chosen because it was the highest at which fuel could be transferred between them, and it was somewhat lower than the height for optimum fuel consumption. The result was that both types of aircraft consumed fuel slightly faster than expected. The four Victors that had given up their fuel at the first transfer had to dip deeply into their own reserves in order to pass on the required amount to those continuing south; this would give rise to another problem a few hours later.

The second fuel transfer took place two and a half hours after take-off, about 1,150 miles south of Ascension. A Victor topped up the Vulcan's fuel tanks, then turned back. Soon afterwards two Victors passed fuel to the three Victors continuing south, then they too turned back.

Four hours after take-off there were tense scenes at Wideawake, as the four Victors that had been the first to give up their spare fuel arrived almost simultaneously at the airfield. All of the planes were low on fuel. The single east west runway runs between rocky outcrops, and it could be entered or left only at its western end. As luck would have it, the wind was from the east, which meant that each Victor's landing run took it to the end of the runway opposite from the exit. In normal circumstances each plane would have landed, then stop, turn round on the runway and taxi to the exit point and be clear of the surface before the next aircraft landed. But now the circumstances were not normal, and had the Victors followed the usual procedure the last couple of aircraft in the queue might have run out of fuel completely before they could put down.

The alternative was not ideal, but it was the only course of action that was feasible in the circumstances. The first Victor touched down, ran to the far end of the runway and stopped; the second aircraft landed and pulled up close behind the first; and the third tanker landed and pulled up close behind the second. When Squadron Leader Martin Todd made his approach, at the controls of the fourth Victor, the stage was set for the aeronautical equivalent of a motorway pile-up. Had there been any misjudgement on the part of the pilot, or a relatively minor technical failure in his aircraft, the Royal Air Force stood to lose one quarter of its available tanker force in the South Atlantic area. Furthermore, a couple of these machines were earmarked to take fuel to the aircraft that in a few hours would be returning from the distant south: if anything prevented that, the entire force heading south would have had to be recalled.

Todd placed his Victor firmly on to the runway and pulled the handle to stream the plane's huge braking parachute. He felt a reassuring push as his body was pressed against the seat straps, and the aircraft decelerated rapidly. In front of him sat the three Victors,

---

HANDLEY PAGE VICTOR K.2

Role: Five-seat in-flight refuelling tanker aircraft.
Powerplant: Four Rolls-Royce Conway 201 turbofan engines each developing 20,600lb of thrust.
Armament: Nil.
Fuel capacity: 127,000lb.
Performance: Cruising speed Mach 0.92 (700mph) at 45,000ft.
Normal operational take-off weight: 240,000lb.
Dimensions: 117ft; length 114ft 11in; wing area 2,597 sq ft.
Date of first Victor K2: March 1972 (rebuilt B.2R reconnaissance aircraft).

---

invisible in the darkness but for the insistent blinking of their anti-collision lights. Later he commented:

> There were the other three at the end of the-runway, waiting for us to stop. If our brakes had failed or anything – Christ, I hate to think of it . . .

But there was no failure. Todd pulled up well short of the other three aircraft, turned his Victor through a semi-circle and taxied to the runway exit. In relieved procession the other three tankers followed him.

As that drama was being played out, the third transfer of fuel began 1,900 miles south of Ascension. Flight Lieutenant Alan Skelton passed all his spare fuel to two of the other Victors, then turned back for Ascension. Soon afterwards, however, he discovered that his aircraft had developed a fuel leak. The quantity being lost was not large and in normal circumstances it would not have mattered, but he was a long way from Ascension and he had bitten deeply into his own fuel reserves in order to pass as much as possible to the other aircraft. One of Skelton's crew called Ascension and asked that a tanker be sent to meet them on the way back to the island.

The force heading south was now down to two Victors and the single Vulcan. Five and a half hours and 2,700 miles after take-off, there was a further transfer of fuel. And again there was an unexpected problem. Squadron Leader Bob Tuxford, captain of one of the Victors, explained:

> There is an unwritten rule in air-to-air refuelling, a variation of Sod's Law, which says, 'If you're going to find any really bumpy weather, it will be right at the point where you have to do your tanking.' Now that proved to be the case and the 'really bumpy

weather' duly appeared as a violent tropical storm at exactly the point where the final transfer of fuel between the Victors was planned to take place.

From the cockpit of the Vulcan Martin Withers observed the shadowy outline of a Victor a few hundred yards to his left trying to take fuel from another:

> It was dreadfully turbulent, we were in and out of the cloud tops, there was a lot of electrical activity with St Elmo's Fire dancing around the cockpit. The Victor was trying to refuel in that – he was having enormous problems. We could see the two aircraft bucking around, with the refuelling hose and basket going up and down about 20 feet.

Eventually, after some superb flying, Flight Lieutenant Steve Biglands succeeded in pushing his refuelling probe into the basket streamed behind Tuxford's aircraft. The fuel transfer began, but the triumph was short-lived. Suddenly Biglands gave a terse radio call to say that his refuelling probe had broken. That put the entire operation in jeopardy, for the tanker could not take on any more fuel during the flight and there could be no question of it accompanying the Vulcan to the far south. The only alternative was for the two remaining Victors to exchange roles, with Biglands giving up his spare fuel to Tuxford so that the latter could continue south with the Vulcan.

By the end of the transfer the final pair of aircraft were more than 3,000 miles south of Ascension and the Vulcan was just over an hour away from its target. In the Victor there was an earnest discussion on whether it would be possible to continue the mission. Bob Tuxford continued:

> We were considerably lower on fuel than we should have been. Now we had a decision to make: either to go on, give the Vulcan the fuel it needed to make its attack, and prejudice our own position because if we didn't pick up some more fuel on the way back we would have to ditch; or turn back at that stage while we both had sufficient fuel to get back to Ascension. I was the Captain of the aircraft and I had to make the decision, but I asked my crew what they thought. One by one they came back and said, 'We have to go on with the mission.'

Because of the need to keep radio traffic to an absolute minimum, the Vulcan crew had no inkling of the problems facing those aboard the tanker. The two aircraft linked up for the final transfer of fuel before the target, at a point about 400 miles north-east of Port Stanley. The transfer went ahead normally until, when the Vulcan's tanks were about 6,000lb short of full, Martin Withers was disconcerted to see the red indicator lights on the underside of the Victor flash on to indicate that the fuel transfer was complete. Withers broke radio silence with a brief request for more fuel, but Tuxford told him curtly that there could be no more. Later the refuelling captain commented:

> Not being familiar with the tanking game, not knowing how far I had stretched myself to put him where he was, all he knew was that he wanted a certain amount of fuel. If only he had realized how much discussion had already taken place in my aeroplane, about how far we could afford to stretch ourselves to get him there . . .

Having taken their decision, the Victor crew had now to live with its stark terms: unless they could summon another tanker to pass more fuel to them, their aircraft would inevitably crash into the sea about 400 miles south of Ascension. Moreover, because of the necessity that the Argentine forces on the Falklands should have no inkling of what was afoot, the crew could not use their high-frequency radio to inform base of their predicament until the Vulcan had completed its attack. Although Withers had less fuel than planned, the Vulcan had sufficient for the operation and he knew that a Victor tanker, plus a reserve, were scheduled to meet him during the return journey to top up his tanks.

When the bomber reached a point 290 miles from Port Stanley, Withers eased back the throttles and the Vulcan began a slow descent to keep it below the horizon of enemy early-warning radars on the Falklands. At 2,000ft he levelled off and continued towards the target. Flight Lieutenant Bob Wright, the radar operator, switched on his radar transmitter for a few seconds and observed returns from the top of Mount Usborne, the highest point on East Falkland. That brought heartening confirmation that, throughout the long over-water flight, the Carousel inertial navigation equipment had kept the bomber almost exactly on the planned track.

Shortly after 4 a.m. (local time), at a point 46 miles from the target, Withers pushed forward the throttles to bring the Vulcan's four Olympus engines to maximum thrust. As speed built up he eased the bomber into a steep climb to bring it to its briefed attack altitude of 10,000ft. Once there, the pilot levelled out and let his speed build up to 400mph before easing back on the throttles to hold that speed. Meanwhile the radar operator again turned on his transmitter and the crew settled into the bombing run. The attack was aimed at the mid-point of the runway, with the aircraft running in at an angle of 30 degrees its length. Bearing in mind the Vulcan's 1950s-vintage aiming system, that gave the greatest chance of scoring at least one hit on the runway (an attack down the length of the runway would have produced several hits if everything went perfectly, but a slight error in line would have caused all the bombs to miss).

During the bombing run Withers saw nothing of the target in the darkness below him. His job was to follow as accurately and as smoothly as possible the left/right steering signals on the display in front of him generated by the attack computer. Later he recalled:

It was a smooth night, everything was steady, the steering signals were steady and the range was coming down nicely. All of the switching had been made, and ten miles from the target we opened the bomb doors. I was expecting flak and perhaps missiles to come up but nothing happened. The AEO [Air Electronics Officer] didn't say anything about the defences and I didn't ask – I left that side of things entirely to him. I was concentrating entirely on flying the aircraft.

In fact the Argentine defenders were preparing to engage the plane bearing down on the airfield. Flight Lieutenant Hugh Prior, the Vulcan's Air Electronics Officer, picked up signals from gun-control radar trying to lock-on to the bomber; he flicked a switch to turn on his radar jammer and the signals ceased.

When the Vulcan reached the bomb-release point, the attack computer triggered the bomb-release mechanism and the twenty-one bombs were dropped at ¼-second intervals. As the last bomb left the aircraft, Withers ordered the bomb doors to be closed and he pushed open his throttles. Then he hauled the bomber into a steep turn, to get himself clear of the defended area as quickly as possible. After a fall lasting 20 seconds, the bombs exploded in a neat line across the airfield.

As the Vulcan turned away, Flying Officer Pete Taylor, the co-pilot, glanced to his right and made out the street lights in the town of Port Stanley. Then, much closer, he saw a series of flashes in quick succession below the thin layer of cloud that covered the airfield. As the last bomb exploded, the darkness returned and those in the Vulcan felt rather than heard the crump of the distant explosions.

Nobody in Port Stanley that night will ever forget the sound of those detonations. Artist Tony Chater and his wife Ann were in bed at their home in the centre of town:

I was half awake at the time and the whole house shook. It was as though there had been an earthquake, then we heard the *boom boom boom boom* of the bombs going off, very muffled. Shortly afterwards I just made out the sound of an aircraft in the distance.

To the Falklanders, the sound of that opening attack provided an enormous fillip to morale. Chater continued:

There was terrific jubilation in Stanley. From then on we really felt very confident that the British forces were going to come to our rescue.

The Vulcan was well out of range and climbing to altitude when the Argentine gun positions situated around the airfield finally came to life. Their noisy but ineffectual display of defiance continued for several minutes, then one by one the guns fell silent.

In the cabin of the bomber there were no feelings of jubilation to match those of the citizens of Port Stanley. The nervous exertions of the previous eight hours had drained the crew of much of their emotional energy, and later Withers summed up the mood:

After the attack the crew were very quiet, rather sad. We had just started a shooting war. It had all been rather cold-blooded, creeping in there at 4.30 in the morning to drop bombs on the place. But we had a job to do and we thought that job worth doing.

The bombs cut a swathe of destruction across the middle of the airfield. The first bomb landed on the runway close to its mid-point, penetrated the surface and detonated to cause a large hole with considerable 'heave' around the lip. The second bomb clipped the southern edge of the runway, causing similar damage. One of the other bombs in the stick detonated between the airfield's sole repair hangar and a Pucará attack plane parked nearby, causing damage to both. Yet another bomb blew out the windows in the control tower and gave the building a severe shaking. Three Argentine military personnel were killed and several injured. Considering the age and the known limitations of the Vulcan's attack system, the raid was as effective as might reasonably have been expected.

As the Vulcan continued its away, Hugh Prior broadcast the codeword 'Superfuse' to announce that the attack had been carried out and appeared to have been successful. That signal was the cue for Bob Tuxford's Victor to break radio silence to inform base that the aircraft had insufficient fuel to reach Ascension, urgently requesting that a tanker meet it on the way back. The crew were out on a limb – just a minor failure away from disaster. Later Tuxford commented:

> It was a long, dry journey back. We discussed a lot of things, including the practical aspects of bailing out of a Victor into the sea – you would not try to ditch it, the aircraft was the wrong shape. We had our radar on to see if there were any ships in the area, but in fact there was none in the right place.

In the event the Tuxford made a successful rendezvous with the tanker scrambled to meet him. So did Alan Skelton who, it will be remembered, had suffered a fuel leak early in the operation.

Just over four hours after the attack, the Vulcan reached its planned refuelling point off the coast of Brazil. The sun was high in the sky as Martin Withers caught sight of the white underbelly of a Victor swinging into position in front of him. The tanker levelled out with the hose trailing invitingly behind. It was, he later commented, 'the most beautiful sight in the world.'

Withers advanced slowly on the Victor and pushed his refuelling probe into the basket on the end of the hose. Initially the precious fuel flowed smoothly into the bomber's tanks, but as the pressure built up it began to spill from the connection. The translucent liquid gushed over the plane's windscreen and even with the high-speed wipers going the pilots could make out only the blurred outline of the aircraft in front. The visibility ahead was rather like that from a vehicle being driven through a car wash.

Had this been a normal training sortie Withers would have throttled back, broken contact, then moved forward again to insert the probe properly into the refuelling basket. But his bomber was low on fuel, and there was a chance that the refuelling probe or the basket had suffered damage. If he broke contact now he could not be certain that he could regain it. Although some fuel was being lost, most of it was flowing into the bomber's tanks. For each minute that Withers could maintain the precarious contact, his bomber took on a further ton of fuel.

Then help came from an unexpected quarter. Bob Wright, the Vulcan's navigator, was standing on the ladder between the pilots' seats watching the operation. As the fuel gushed over the canopy he noticed that, almost level with his eyes, at the base of the centre windscreen, the airflow was keeping a narrow strip of glass clear of fuel. Through this he could see the tanker clearly, and was able to give the pilots a running commentary on relative position of aircraft in front to assist them to hold the contact.

Withers took ten minutes to take on the fuel he needed. Then he throttled back to break contact with the tanker, and as the probe withdrew from the basket a valve shut off the supply of fuel to the hose. In an instant the airflow cleared the fuel away from the Vulcan's windscreen and suddenly there were sunshine and blue skies outside the bomber's cockpit. Withers felt as if a huge burden had been lifted from his shoulders:

> After that fuel was on board, the other four hours back to Ascension were a bit of a bore. Only then was the tension off and we knew we were going to make it. Those four hours seemed to last forever.

The Vulcan landed at Wideawake just over sixteen hours after it had taken off. Later Martin Withers received the Distinguished Flying Cross for the leadership he displayed during the attack, while Bob Tuxford received the Air Force Cross for the selfless manner in which he and his crew had supported it.

So ended the first 'Black Buck' mission by a Vulcan. The operation stretched the capabilities of the bomber, the Victor tankers and all the crews involved to the very limit. In retrospect, it is clear that the effort expended in the operation was out of all proportion to the physical damage that it inflicted on Port Stanley airfield. Yet, as is often the case in aerial warfare, the raid on Port Stanley airfield had a psychological effect on the enemy that was also out of proportion to the physical damage it caused. The attack demonstrated to the Argentine Air Force High Command that the Vulcans had the capability to strike at targets on the Argentine mainland at any time. On the following day that service's only specialized interceptor squadron, *Gruppo 8* with Mirage III fighters, was withdrawn from Rio Gallegos in the south of the country, to where it had moved to support operations over the Falklands. To meet the new threat the unit transferred to Comodoro Rivadavia much further north, and, apart from a single skirmish near the end of the conflict, *Gruppo 8* played no further part in the fighting. In effect, the Argentine Air Force had conceded defeat in the battle for air superiority over the Falklands. From then on the Royal Navy's Sea Harriers were allowed to hunt down the enemy fighter-bombers and attack planes without having to worry about themselves being preyed upon by enemy fighters. That was the 'bottom line' result of that first 'Black Buck' mission, and *that* justified the enormous effort that had been expended.

Chapter 31

Countdown to 'Desert Storm'

*At the end of November 1990 the United Nations Security
Council passed Resolution 678, which stated that unless Iraqi
forces withdrew from Kuwait by 15 January the following year
member states would be permitted to employ 'all necessary
means' to dislodge them. President Sadam Hussein believed that
his armed forces were strong enough to hold the territory he had
seized and decided to call what he considered to be the bluff of
the powers aligned against him. As the deadline approached it
became clear that no amount of diplomacy could resolve the crisis.
What the Iraqi dictator had grandiloquently termed 'The Mother
of Battles' was about to begin. The action that took place on the
first night of the conflict provided a vivid insight into the nature
of aerial warfare during the final decade of the twentieth century.*

During the latter half of 1990 the Coalition of nations arrayed
against Iraq moved large numbers of troops and a huge contingent of aircraft into Saudi Arabia and the surrounding states. By the
following January preparations were well advanced for Operation
'Desert Storm', the large-scale aerial onslaught against targets in Iraq.
As the Security Council deadline passed, the Coalition command
staffs laid final plans for the attack to begin with a massive air strike
during the small hours of 17 January.

Throughout the period of tension US and Royal Saudi Air
Force Boeing E-3 Sentry AWACS aircraft had flown round-the-
clock patrols to keep watch on the movements of Iraqi aircraft and
to provide advanced warning of a possible attack on Saudi Arabia

itself. Ready to go into action to meet such a threat were standing patrols of the most modern fighter aircraft available to the western air forces – F-14 Tomcats, F-15 Eagles, F/A-18 Hornets, Tornado F.3s and Mirage 2000s. After the deadline passed, the AWACS planes and the fighters maintained the same operating patterns as before, to keep the Iraqi defence forces in ignorance of what was in store for them.

The main attack on the Iraqi air defence system, and on military targets in that country and Kuwait, was to commence at 3.00 a.m. Baghdad time on the morning of the 17 January. This was designated 'H-Hour' for the operation. The first aircraft to get airborne specifically to attack Iraq took off from Barksdale, Louisiana, at 6.35 a.m. Central Standard Time on the morning of the 16th (H-Hour minus 11 hours 25 minutes). Seven B-52 Stratofortresses of the 2nd Bomb Wing, each loaded with five AGM-86 cruise missiles, set out for a strike on targets in northern Iraq more than 7,000 miles away. Just over seven hours later, at H minus 4 hours, a further twenty B-52s began taking off from their island base at Diego Garcia far away in the Indian Ocean.

The next to take off, at H minus 2 hours, were the slowest of the attacking aircraft scheduled to go into action that night – eight AH-64 Apache attack helicopters of Task Force 'Normandy' of the US Army's 101st Airborne Division. With them went two Air Force MH-53J 'Pave Low' heavy-lift helicopters fitted with special electronic equipment that were to serve as navigational 'mother ships' for the operation. The helicopter force left Al Jouf airfield in the northern part of Saudi Arabia at 1 a.m.

The mission of the attack helicopters was to knock out two strategically placed air-defence radars west of Baghdad, thus opening up a corridor through which high-speed jet attack planes could pass unseen on the way to their targets. The helicopters were due to hit the radars shortly before the jets entered their areas of cover. The requirement to achieve surprise and the highest possible chance of destroying the radars, and the need for an immediate assessment of damage after the attack, had led to the decision to employ attack helicopters rather than fixed-winged aircraft. In addition to a large external fuel tank, each helicopter carried eight Hellfire laser-guided missiles, a pod with nineteen 70mm unguided rockets and a built-in armament of one 30mm cannon in a turret mounted under the nose. Their crews observing the terrain around and the 'mother ships' in front of them through night-vision goggles, the blacked-out Apaches hugged the desert floor as they flew north at a stately 120mph. Soon afterwards the first of 160 tanker aircraft – KC-135s,

KC-10s, KA-6As, Victors and VC-10s – began taking off and moved into position to provide refuelling support for the initial waves of attacking aircraft.

At 1.31 a.m., H minus 1 hour 29 minutes, the first Tomahawk cruise missile roared away from the deck of the cruiser USS *San Jacinto* at the northern end of the Red Sea. Once it was clear of its launcher, the missile's wings unfolded and it descended to low altitude and made for the pin-point target programmed into its attack computer. Soon afterwards the cruiser *Bunker Hill*, then the battleships *Wisconsin* and *Missouri* in the Persian Gulf, joined in the bombardment. That night the four ships loosed off a total of 52 cruise missiles.

Shortly after the first of the sea-launched missiles had been sent on its way, the seven B-52s that had flown direct from the United States arrived at their missile-launching points over the north of Saudi Arabia. The heavy bombers launched a total of 35 cruise missiles, which were programmed to hit eight communications, air defence and airfield targets in the Mosul area. As the cruise missiles dropped to low altitude and sped across Iraq, the big bombers turned around and began the long haul back to Barksdale. Their total time airborne would be 34 hours 20 minutes, making this the longest bombing mission ever and exceeding the previous longest, those by the Vulcans to the Falkland Islands (described in the previous chapter), by a considerable margin.

At 2.15 a.m., H minus 45, the first of the bombers began to take off F-117As, F-111s, F-15Es, A-6s and Tornados, with F-14s, F-15s and F-18s 'riding shotgun' to protect them from enemy fighters. F-4G Phantoms, A-7 Corsairs, EF-111 Ravens and EA-6B Prowlers accompanied the raiders to suppress the defences in the target areas. Wing Commander John Broadbent described his take off from Muharraq airfield, Bahrain, at the head of a force of eight RAF Tornados:

> We taxied out under radio silence, and took off singly on a green light from tower. Then we climbed in trail to 10,000 feet and joined up with the Victor tankers that had taken off ahead of us. We took on fuel going along the route to the target.

As the cruise missiles flew unswervingly over their pre-programmed routes, the F-117A Stealth Fighters moved unseen into position to strike at their assigned targets and the teams of attack planes began their low-altitude penetrations into Iraqi territory, a quite different and more visible air operation unfolded high above the Iraqi SAM defences. Timed to begin shortly before the attack planes entered the missile defended zones, this involved large numbers of unmanned decoys carrying echo-enhancement equipment to give them a radar signature similar to that from a full-sized aircraft. Launched from ground sites located in the north of Saudi Arabia, 38 Northrop BQM-74 pilotless drones crossed the border into Iraq flying at medium altitudes and at speeds around 575mph. Powered by a 180lb thrust turbojet, the 5ft-span vehicle had been designed as an expendable target drone and that was now to be its task, literally. Some of the drones headed for the missile-defended zones around Basrah in the east of the country while others made for the H2 and H3 airfield complexes in the west. The drones entered the defended areas in groups of three or four, creating the illusion of combat planes flying in tactical formation.

At the same time another type of lure, the US Navy's Tactical Air Launched Decoy (TALD), was used to bring to life the missile and gun defences in the Baghdad area. Each US Navy A-6 Intruder taking part in the operation carried eight of these lightweight unpowered decoys folded up under its wings. The planes released the decoys from altitudes around 20,000ft, and once each TALD was clear of its launch aircraft its wings unfolded and it began its silent glide towards the defended area.

The incoming decoys made tantalizingly easy targets, and the Iraqi ground batteries launched salvo after salvo of expensive and irreplaceable SAMs at them. Well-trained SAM crews might not have been fooled by such a simple stratagem, but those who manned the missile sites that night were not in that category. The first independent confirmation that the war had begun came at 2.37 a.m. Baghdad time, when CNN television broadcast the now-famous pictures showing tracer rounds arcing across the night sky over the Iraqi capital punctuated by the occasional explosions from shells or missiles. That was 21 minutes before H-hour and long before the real attack on targets in the capital was scheduled to begin, and it is almost certain that the television cameras had in fact filmed the Iraqi reaction to the TALD 'attack'.

That night the ground defences enjoyed something of a 'turkey shoot', causing great slaughter among the American decoys. Unfortunately for several of the defenders, however, these particular 'turkeys' had a more sinister purpose. Once the Iraqi SAM batteries had been drawn into a full-scale defensive action, the operation entered its second phase. Flying behind the decoys, and somewhat lower, were several F-4G 'Wild Weasel' and FA-18 aircraft carrying AGM-88 HARMs (High speed Anti-Radiation Missiles). Set to

---

PANAVIA TORNADO GR.1

Role: Two-seat, swing-wing attack and reconnaissance aircraft.
Powerplant: Two Turbo-Union RB.199 turbofan engines each
rated at 15,000lb thrust with afterburners.
Armament: (Carried by all Tornado GR.1s during the first might
of the War) Two JP.233 airfield-denial weapons containers
weighing a total of 10,300lb; two Mauser 27mm cannon; two
AIM-9L Sidewinder infra-red homing missiles for self-defence.
Performance: Maximum speed (at low altitude with full weapons
load) 680mph, (at high altitude, clean) Mach 2.2 (1,450mph) plus.
Maximum gross take-off weight: 60,000lb.
Dimensions: Span (wings fully forward) 45ft 7in, (wings fully swept)
28ft 2in; length 54ft 9½in; wing area (wings fully forward) 323 sq ft.
Date of first production Tornado GR.1: June 1979.

---

home on the transmissions from the enemy fire-control radars, the
missiles were launched in large numbers. For one brief period during
the onslaught there were no fewer than two hundred HARMS in
flight and closing rapidly on the enemy emitters.

The elaborately planned 'spoof and punch' attack destroyed or
damaged the fire-control radars at several SAM sites, putting the associated missile battery out of action until the radar could be repaired
or replaced. At other sites the battery had fired off all its immediate-
use missiles, and it would take several minutes to hoist the reload
missiles on to their launchers and make them ready for action; the
sites would still be engaged in this task when the Coalition attack
forces swept past them on the way to their targets.

Meanwhile the Apache helicopters of Task Force 'Normandy'
arrived in firing positions on the two radars they were to attack (the
latter had been left alone long enough to report the approaching
decoys). The helicopter attack commenced at 2.38 a.m., H minus 22.
Using infra-red night vision systems to laser-mark the targets, the
helicopters fired their Hellcat missiles from ranges of about three
miles, then closed to a mile and a half to deliver their unguided
rockets. The various parts of targets were demolished in strict order
of priority: first the electrical generators, then the communications
facilities, then, finally, the radars themselves. In less than two minutes
the Apaches fired 27 Hellfire missiles, about a hundred 70mm rockets
and some 4,000 rounds of 30mm ammunition, which reduced both
radar stations to smoking ruins. Their task completed, the helicopters
turned round and retraced their flight paths to friendly territory.

By now the teams of attack planes were well into their low-
altitude penetrations in Iraqi territory. Initially there was no visible

reaction from the defences and several attacking crews felt an air of unreality about the proceedings. Lieutenant Dave Giachetti, Weapons System Officer in one of eight F-111Fs of the 48th Tactical Fighter Wing on their way to attack chemical weapons storage bunkers at Ad Diwaniyah near Baghdad, remembered:

> I thought it was kinda eerie, because outside everything was so calm and so quiet. We went in at low level on TFR. In the built-up areas everyone had their lights on; the street lights were on. On the way in we flew parallel to a road for some time; there were cars moving with their lights on. We were flying at 400 feet at 540 knots [620mph] towards our target and I thought, man, they don't even know we're coming!

Flight Lieutenant 'Moose' Poole, navigator in one of the RAF Tornados heading for Al Taqaddum airfield, was another of those who had difficulty coming to terms with the fact that he really was flying an operational mission that night:

> There was no moon and it was very, very dark. The ground was as flat as a witch's tit and there was little apparent movement of the aircraft. There were no visual clues outside; the only light was from my instruments. I found myself becoming detached from reality – it was just like being in the simulator flying a war sortie. I had to tell myself that this was no simulator sortie – it was for real.

Each crew caught up with the realities of the situation in its own way. Wing Commander Jerry Witts, leading four Tornados heading for an attack on Mudaysis airfield, found his moment of truth a few minutes after he crossed into Iraq when there was a chilling reminder that war could be injurious to the health:

> We had just crossed the border, lights off and sneaky beaky, when on the RHWR [radar homing and warning receiver] we got what looked like Fulcrum [MiG-29 radar] spoke at 2 o'clock. If there was anything that worried me at that stage of the war, it was the look-down/shoot-down capability of the Fulcrum. We did an evasive turn and the spoke duly trotted around the aeroplane, which is exactly what one would expect if it was moving round on to our rear. I thought, Jesus – I've only been at war for five minutes . . .

LOCKHEED F-117A

Role: Single-seat, precision-attack stealth aircraft.
Powerplant: Two General Electric F404-GE-F1D2 turbofans
without afterburners, each rated at 10,800lb thrust.
Armament: Typical operational bomb load two 2,000lb LGBs or
four 500lb LGBs. No defensive armament.
Performance: Classified, but maximum speed high subsonic.
Maximum gross take-off weight: 52,500lb.
Dimensions: Span 43ft 4in; length 65ft 11in; wing area 912.7 sq ft.
Date of first production F-117A: Spring 1982.

Soon afterwards the 'Fulcrum radar spoke' disappeared. Almost
certainly it had been a false alarm.

By now the initial salvos of cruise missiles from the ships and the
B-52s were in the final stages of their approach on their targets. Only
a relatively small proportion of these missiles carried high-explosive
warheads for the direct attack on the enemy air defence system; most
of the Tomahawks carried warloads that, while not in themselves
lethal, were designed to have a devastating effect on the Iraqi defence
system. Their payload consisted of a large number of small spools,
each measuring ½in by ¾in, wound with a long length of electrical-
conducting carbon-fibre resembling thin electrical wire. In making a
detailed analysis of the Iraqi air defence system, Coalition Intelligence
officers had discovered a major weakness that could be exploited: the
computers and the operations centres took their power from the
national electricity supply grid. If these could be deprived of mains
electrical power, the working of the entire control system would
be halted until back-up supplies could be brought on line – and
vital information on the unfolding air battle would be lost when the
computers 'crashed'. Several of the cruise missiles were programmed
to fly low over power stations and electrical power lines, spewing out
the spools as they did so. Once it was free in the airflow, each spool
unwound rapidly to lay out a serpentine length of carbon fibre that
drifted slowly to the ground. If the fibre fell across a high-voltage
electrical conductor, it produced a massive short circuit that caused
severe local damage to the electrical transmission system. In contrast
to the sophisticated electronic countermeasures systems also being
employed that night, this was a simple but extremely effective 'electrical countermeasure'.

In a further move to prepare the path for other attack forces,
at 2.51 a.m. (H minus 9) an F-117A stealth fighter dropped laser-
guided bombs on an important Iraqi air defence operations centre in

the south-west of the country. The first attack by a manned aircraft on Baghdad itself took place at 3 a.m., H-hour, when one of the stealth fighters attacked a communications centre in the city. That night F-117As attacked 34 targets associated with various aspects of the Iraqi air defence system.

As the attack forces penetrated progressively deeper into Iraq, the US fighters escorting the raiders had their first encounters with enemy planes. Captain Steve Tate of the 71st Tactical Fighter Squadron was leading a flight of four F-15C Eagles, providing cover for strike packages moving into the Baghdad area. From its patrol line over Saudi Arabia, the E-3 AWACS aircraft controlling Tate's flight reported that an unidentified aircraft was apparently closing on the No 3 aircraft in the flight. Tate later recalled:

> My Number 3 had just turned south, and I was heading north-east on a different pattern. I don't know if the bogey [unidentified aircraft] was chasing him, but I locked him up [on radar], confirmed he was hostile and fired a missile.

Launched from a range of twelve miles, Tate's AIM-7 Sparrow sped towards the rapidly closing Iraqi plane – which by then had been identified as a Mirage F.1 – and shortly afterwards the American pilot saw a fireball as the weapon impacted:

> When the airplane blew up, the whole sky lit up. It continued to burn all the way to the ground and then blew up into a thousand pieces.

McDONNELL DOUGLAS F-15C EAGLE

Role: Single-seat air superiority fighter.
Powerplant: Two Pratt & Whitney F100-PW-220 turbofans each rated at 23,450lb thrust with afterburners.
Armament: On normal operations the armament carried was four AIM-7M Sparrow semi-active radar homing missiles and four AIM-9M Sidewinder infra-red homing missiles, and an internally mounted M61A1 20mm cannon.
Performance: Maximum speed (at high altitude) Mach 2.5 (1,900mph) plus, (at low altitude) 921mph.
Normal operational take-off weight: 44,630lb.
Dimensions: Span 42ft 9¾in; length 63ft 9in; wing area 608 sq ft.
Date of first production F-15C: February 1979.

MIKOYAN-GUREVICH MiG-29 ('FULCRUM')

Role: Single-seat interceptor fighter.
Powerplant: Two Isotov ID-33 turbofan engines each rated at 19,000lb of thrust with afterburners.
Armament: Up to six air-to-air missiles on underwing pylons, usually a mixture of the R-27 medium-range, semi-active radar homing missile (AA-10 'Alamo') and the R-73 (AA-11) or R-60 (AA 8) infra-red homing dogfight missile; one 30mm cannon.
Performance: Maximum speed (at high altitude) Mach 2.3 (1,520mph).
Maximum gross take-off weight: 60,000lb.
Dimensions: Span 37ft 3¼in; length 56ft 10in; wing area 378.9 sq ft.
Date of first production Mig-29: 1982.

Following this initial success, marauding F-15s had several fleeting radar contacts with Iraqi planes. Owing to the presence of Coalition attack forces in their vicinity, however, the AWACS controller refused to give clearance for the American fighters to attack with their long-range missiles: the Sparrow could be lethal to friend or foe alike, and it was vitally important to ensure that any aircraft engaged was clear of Allied planes. Captain Larry Pitts of the 33rd Tactical Fighter Wing, one of the F-15 pilots airborne that night, recalled:

> Our radar scopes were filled with friendlies – 60 to 80 of them! Night conditions combined with bad weather made it difficult to fire missiles even if the F-15s acquired targets. There were just too many friendlies out there.

Then one of the MiG-29s moved clear of Allied planes long enough for it to be singled out for attack, and Captain Jon Kelk of the 33rd TFW destroyed it with a Sparrow. Five minutes later Captain Robert Grater of the same unit scored the first double kill of the war, with the destruction of two Mirage F1s in quick succession, also using Sparrows. Over Vietnam the performance of the semi-active radar homing missile had sometimes been disappointing, but over Iraq the improved version then in use was proving to be a highly effective weapon.

Leading the formation of Tornados making for Al Asad, Wing Commander Ian Travers Smith watched one of the Iraqi fighters go down:

> We had not seen any activity at all – no AAA. The first sign that I was really at war was when an aircraft suddenly burst into

flames in our 11 o'clock. There was scuddy cloud at medium altitude and there was this great fireball falling from the sky, with bits coming off.

A few Iraqi fighters managed to close on Coalition attack planes that night, but the latter were carrying air-to-air missiles for self-protection and they were well able to look after themselves. A twelve-plane force of F-15E Strike Eagles of the 4th Fighter Wing, running in at low level to attack a 'Scud' missile launching site near H-2 airfield, had a couple of MiG-29s approach it. It appears that, in attempting to slide into an attacking position behind an F-15E flying at high speed about 100ft above the ground, one of the Iraqi pilots misjudged his height. The MiG smashed into the ground and exploded without a shot being fired on either side.

The disruption to the Iraqi air defence control and reporting system that night prevented it from keeping track of the large number of attacking forces sweeping over the country. As a result, at several of the targets there was little or no warning of the raiders' approach until their bombs detonated. The simultaneous attack on the airfields began at H plus 1 hour, 4 a.m.

The 48th Tactical Fighter Wing, the most powerful US Air Force night precision-attack unit, sent 53 F-111Fs in forces of between four and six aircraft to hit a dozen separate targets that night. These included the major airfields at Balad and Jalibah in Iraq, and those at Ali Al Salem and Al Jaber in Kuwait, where the hardened aircraft shelters were thought to contain 'Scud' missiles. F-111Fs also attacked chemical weapons storage bunkers at H-3 airfield, Salman Pak and Ad Diwaniyah.

Six F-111Fs hit the airfield at Balad, with two aircraft launching GBU-15 electro-optical guided bombs at the maintenance complex while the other four dropped large numbers of area-denial mines at each end of the runways and among the aircraft shelters. Further west, another six F-111Fs attacked the chemical weapons storage bunkers at H-3 airfield with LGBs. As they pulled away from the target, four Royal Saudi Air Force Tornados attacked the runways. Supporting that attack was a defence-suppression force from the carrier USS *John F. Kennedy* in the Red Sea comprising three EA-6B jamming aircraft, ten A-7s carrying HARMs, and four F-14 fighters.

At the eastern end of the war zone Lieutenant-Colonel Tommy Crawford led six F-111Fs against Ali Al Salem airfield in Kuwait. His target was the hardened aircraft shelters beside the airfield, thought to house 'Scud' missiles. On the way in the bombers flew over Iraqi

Army units, which put up a disconcerting amount of tracer into the sky above them. Crawford recalled:

> We made a low-level attack because of the SAM threat – there were several SA-6 launchers in the area. Our intention was to run in at 1,000 feet until SA-6 signals on the RHWR forced us down. But there was so much AAA – I couldn't believe how much there was – we crossed the border at 2,000 feet and that was where we stayed until we delivered the bombs. It seemed like every 50 yards there was a guy with a gun who was shooting up at us it was the damnedest 4th of July show you ever saw. As we approached the border it looked like a solid wall of fire, but you have no perception of depth so it looked a lot worse than it really was. Once we had crossed the border it seemed the flak opened up in front of us as we flew along, and then it seemed as if it was worse to the sides and behind than it was in front.

The F-111Fs tossed their GBU-24 laser-guided bombs at the shelters from a range of about four miles, then curved away from the target as the WSO held the laser beam on the shelter until the bombs impacted. The crews found the flak a considerable distraction and only three shelters were hit; the unit would return to hit the other three in the days that followed.

Other F-111s crews found little difficulty from the defences. Lieutenant Dave Giachetti's target was the chemical weapons storage bunkers at Ad Diwaniyah. Four aircraft had already hit some of the bunkers with laser-guided bombs to open up the structures, then he ran in with the second section of four aircraft to deliver a follow-up attack:

> Our first mission was very straightforward. Others had penetrated the bunkers before us; four went in first to attack the bunkers. Then slightly after them our four-ship came in. Each plane tossed four canisters of CBU-89 gaiter mines [containers with large numbers of area-denial mines] at the target.

Leading the three Tornados attacking Al Asad airfield, Ian Travers Smith was another of those who enjoyed a clear run to the target:

> I had a few problems with my autopilot so I had to fly the aircraft manually. I was head-down in the cockpit as we turned on the IP [initial point] for the target run, which was almost

along the line of the valley. Then I looked up and I couldn't believe my eyes: all of the runway and taxiway lights were on – the entire airfield was lit up. We really had caught them by surprise. I could see my aiming point, no problem at all. We were absolutely spot on; all the symbology was in the right place. Until we started to drop the bombs, I don't remember being shot at. Then, when we were half way across the airfield, I looked around and saw all these flashing white lights. Not until we were about 20 miles away from the target on the way out did it dawn on me that those 'flashing lights' had been the muzzle flashes of guns firing at us.

At Al Asad the purpose of the attack was to cut the taxiways running between the hardened shelters and the runways. For this the Tornado were equipped with the specialized JP.233 runway-denial weapon. Carried in two large canisters under the fuselage, the weapon comprised 60 runway-cratering bomblets and 430 area-denial mines which were released over a period of six seconds. Once each weapon was clear of the aircraft, a small parachute opened behind it to slow its fall. Each cratering bomb weighed 57lb and was roughly the size and shape of a roadmender's pneumatic drill without the bit. When the bomb hit the surface a primary explosive charge punched a circular hole in the concrete, then a secondary warhead was fired through the hole and into the foundation supporting the surface. Detonating in the confined space between the underside of the concrete and the foundation, the secondary warhead produced an underground cavity topped with a layer of weakened concrete and large amounts of debris. If an aircraft ran over undermined area in the course of taxying, taking off or landing, the latter would collapse and probably 'amputate' one or more of the undercarriage legs. To deter teams attempting to repair the damage, the 430 mines dropped with the cratering bombs ended up among the concrete debris scattered on top of the surface. In the hours to follow they would explode at irregular intervals or if they were disturbed in any way.

At Mudaysis airfield the low-level penetration by three Tornados was similarly successful in achieving surprise, and there was no ground fire until the first of the bombs detonated. Flight Lieutenant Ian Long, bringing up the rear of the attack, watched the bombs from one of the Tornados in front detonate across the airfield:

His bombs went off in front of us with a really bright flash. That was a delight to see – it confirmed that I was heading towards my target. It looked as if everything was going according to the plan. I was not aware of any AAA being fired at me as I was running in.

A few seconds later the attack computer in Long's aircraft began dispensing the bomblets from the containers underneath the fuselage:

There were a lot of bright flashes reflected off the ground, as the weapons were fired down from the aircraft. It was incredibly light around the cockpit. As we passed over the target there were a lot of sparkling lights coming from my left and going behind us, and the odd red ball came past me. It was pretty exciting!

At the other two targets attacked by the Tornados, Tallil and Al Taqaddum, it was a different story. There other raiders had struck at the airfields before the Tornados arrived and the defenders were thoroughly alerted (the JP.233 force had to attack last, or the bombs from following aircraft might have set off the area-denial mines laid across the runways and taxiways). Flight Lieutenant Rupert Clark, piloting one of the Tornados attacking Tallil, recalled:

Ahead of us was this dense wall of AAA. Obviously the fire was not aimed, it was just waving across the sky. Some of it was huge stuff which went up like roman candles, slowly and gracefully. Other bits were whacking around. Some of it was red, some was white. As I ran in the boss's aircraft attacked on my left; I saw a carpet of explosions as the weapons came off and exploded. And then Nick Heard's. Then I saw Rickey Corbelli's burners light up in front of me as he accelerated for his attack. I could see what I was going into and I decided I was not going to turn back – I was going to go through that flak and drop my weapons. Really there was no decision to make, all of my mates had gone through and there was nothing else I could do. But actually, consciously doing it was one of the hardest things that I have ever done. It was the most frightening moment of my life. My target was in one of the thickest bits of AAA, so I moved off a bit to the right to avoid the tracer. I felt my weapons come off and saw the flashes behind me as they detonated, then I heard the thuds as the canisters came off. I applied full dry power for the escape and the jet surged forwards: we had just lost five tons of weight and one hell of a lot of drag.

As Clark and the other three Tornados cleared Tallil, a second section of four of these aircraft ran in to attack other parts in the network of taxiways. After each attacking force came away from its target there was the dreadful moment of truth as the leader sought to discover whether any of his planes had fallen victim to the enemy flak and missiles. Wing Commander John Broadbent, leading the Tallil attack, described the painful moments after he asked his crews to check in:

> I said, 'Bristol Formation, check'. Back came the replies '2, 3, 4 (pause) 6, 7, 8.' 'Bristol 5, check?' Nothing. Bristol 5 was my old mates Buckers and Paddy [Squadron Leaders Gordon Buckley and Paddy Teakle]. I thought, Jesus – they've gone down. That was really depressing and all the way back across Iraq I tried to come to terms with it. As we crossed the border we began our climb to rendezvous with the tanker. And then we heard a very faint voice on the radio: 'Bristol 5, checking in.' They had had some radio trouble, that was all.

The initial wave of air strikes on Iraq and Kuwait had been a complete success: the Coalition air forces had flown 671 sorties with manned aircraft and every plane had returned safely. So began the air war in the Gulf. The initial attacks knocked out vital parts of the Iraqi air defence command and control system, setting the stage for the Coalition to establish air superiority within a few days, and air supremacy shortly thereafter. The Iraqis were about to learn, in the cruellest possible way, about the massive destruction wrought by modern air power when there are no effective air defences to prevent it.

Chapter 32

Tornado Spyplanes go to War

Aerial reconnaissance has come a long way since the first jet reconnaissance mission in the summer of 1944 (see Chapter 8). Today it is a multi-faceted business employing aircraft and drones flying over enemy territory at ultra-low or ultra-high altitude, planes standing-off outside the reach of the defences and looking in or listening from there, and satellites orbiting high above the combat zone. During the recent war in the Persian Gulf the Royal Air Force sent its Tornado GR.1A reconnaissance aircraft into action for the first time. These state-of-the-art planes carry no conventional optical film cameras; instead, they use an electro-optical system similar in concept to the family camcorder to record the scene passing below the aircraft. Photographs are no longer the main product of aerial reconnaissance – now it is 'electro-optical imagery'.

In January 1991, a few days before the start of the aerial onslaught against Iraq, six Tornado GR.1A aircraft and nine crews drawn from Nos 2 and 13 Squadrons joined the Royal Air Force Tornado detachment at Dhahran in Saudi Arabia. The GR.1A is optimized for the low-altitude reconnaissance role flying at night or in bad weather, and it carries no optical cameras or conventional film. In the space that had been occupied by the cannon and ammunition magazines in the attack version of the Tornado, the GR.1A carries an in-built electro-optical reconnaissance system. The main sensor is the Vinten 4000 infra-red linescan equipment, which scans from side to side, perpendicular to the line of flight, from horizon to horizon, from a small blister beneath the fuselage. Supplementing this cover, looking to each side of the fuselage, are a pair of British Aerospace/Vinten sideways-looking infra-red sensors. The electronic images seen from these three sensors are fed to six separate video-recorders.

Infra-red photography using conventional film has been around for a long time. Tactically, it has the great advantage that it functions in lighting conditions ranging from bright sunlight to the darkest of nights and requires no artificial illumination (i.e. flares) that would betray the presence of the aircraft. Another well-proven technique is to link the reconnaissance system electronically to the aircraft's navigational computer, so that the latter places in the corner of each image a small block giving the aircraft's position, heading and other details at the time the image was captured; also, as he passes through the target area, the navigator can press a button to put an 'event marker' on any image of particular interest. These features are of considerable assistance to the interpreters who will later examine the imagery. In the Tornado reconnaissance system these features are incorporated and their capability is enhanced.

While the imagery produced by the infra-red electro-optical equipment lacks the crystal sharpness produced by conventional film cameras under optimum conditions, for military intelligence purposes this is a small handicap. The important advantage of the new system compared with normal photography is the reduction in the delay in getting the intelligence to those who need to use it. There is no need to develop or print the imagery before it is viewed. In the aircraft the navigator can observe the video imagery on a television screen in his cockpit in real time (and at night the screen will show things that his eyes may not see), and he can pass on, by radio, any significant discoveries that may have been made. He can even replay in flight particular parts of the imagery if he wishes to identify specific objects on the ground. After the aircraft has landed, the video cassettes can be played immediately for analysis.

During the Gulf conflict the Tornado GR.1As operated as part of a multi-faceted Coalition reconnaissance effort that included several types of drone, F-14s carrying reconnaissance pods, RF-4C Phantoms and Lockheed TR-1s and U-2s. Ground surveillance was carried out by Boeing E-8A (J-STARS) aircraft using a powerful sideways-looking radar to detect traffic movements deep in enemy territory. Electronic reconnaissance (elint) was the domain of the Boeing RC-135 'Rivet Joint', the Lockheed EP-3E 'Aries' Orion and the BAe Nimrod R.1. Overseeing the area at regular intervals were the US satellites with their own secret range of reconnaissance sensors.

Each separate system – the low- and the high-flying aircraft and drones, the radar surveillance planes, the electronic eavesdroppers and the satellites – possessed its own unique advantages for intelligence-gathering. That of the Tornado GR.1A was the ability to conduct searches of specified areas or routes at relatively short notice, and to do so at night and beneath a solid layer of low cloud (which would preclude effective optical or infra-red searches by higher-flying systems).

To avoid optically aimed anti-aircraft fire, the GR.1As operated only at night. Flying singly over enemy territory, these aircraft normally cruised at speeds around 645mph using their terrain-following radar to maintain a constant altitude of 200ft. Although the aircraft had provision to carry a couple of AIM-9L Sidewinder missiles for self-protection, the threat from Iraqi fighters was considered minimal and crews preferred to leave the missiles off and so avoid their weight and drag penalty.

The Tornado GR.1As flew their first combat mission on the third night of the war, 18/19 January. Soon after dark three of these aircraft took off from Dhahran to conduct separate searches of areas from which 'Scud' surface-to-surface missiles were being launched against Israel or Saudi Arabia. Squadron Leaders Dick Garwood and John Hill, assigned to search the area to the south of Habbaniyah, completed their mission without incident. When their imagery was examined afterwards it was found to show a 'Scud' launching vehicle in the open. F-15E attack planes were directed to the area but low cloud prevented them from finding the vehicle.

A second wave of GR.1As also took part in the 'Scud-hunting' effort that night. Flight Lieutenants Brian Robinson and Gordon Walker conducted a search in the Wadi al Khirr area. Later analysis of their imagery showed at least two camouflaged sites thought likely to contain 'Scud' support vehicles.

During the night of 19th/20th Flight Lieutenant Mike Stanway and Squadron Leader Roger Bennett had a brief tussle with the defences. Their mission was a search of the western end of the main Baghdad–Ar Rutbah highway, an area from which 'Scud' missiles were being launched against Israel. Stanway flew along the highway using the aircraft's moving map display to follow the line of the road, which, apart from the headlights of an occasional vehicle, remained unseen in the darkness. The search continued without incident until the aircraft was some 20 miles east of Ar Rutbah, then, as Bennett later explained, the mission took on a more exciting turn:

I suddenly noticed a bright glow over my left shoulder in my 8 o'clock. I thought it was an IR guided missile, either one of the shoulder-launched variety or an SA-9, and it was guiding towards us on a disconcertingly constant bearing. Mike broke hard left and climbed into it to evade. I selected flares, but the dispenser was faulty and they refused to eject. Fortunately the evasive manoeuvre by itself was enough: the missile went sailing past us and detonated some way away.

Subsequent examination of the imagery revealed a 'Scud' launching bunker with a man standing outside it. It was clear that the man or someone near to him had fired the SAM because the imagery showed that almost immediately afterwards Stanway had banked the aircraft sharply to avoid the upcoming missile.

Invariably it was the highly skilled photo-interpreters (PIs), viewing the expanded imagery on large TV screens in the Reconnaissance Intelligence Centre at Dhahran, that made all the important Scud finds rather than the aircraft navigators. As Bennett explained:

One of the PIs found the camouflaged bunker. Once he had pointed out what it was, it was almost obvious. But it required an expert to do it. Everybody tried to find the 'Scuds', but they were not left out into the open waiting to be found. After each firing, the vehicles dispersed and ran back under cover.

Mike Stanway and Roger Bennett had their most memorable sortie during the small hours of 26 February, two days after the start of the Coalition ground offensive. They took off as an airborne reserve in support of two other Tornados that had been allocated specific tasks, but on the way they received orders to fly a route reconnaissance along the main roads linking An Nasiriyah, Al Amarah, Basrah and Jalibah in eastern Iraq.

First the crew had to rendezvous with a Victor tanker over northern Saudi Arabia in order to take on fuel, and that proved no easy task. Thunderstorms in the area caused considerable turbulence, with dense cloud extending from an altitude of 26,000ft down to below 3,000ft. Bennett recalled:

Normally we would tank at around 10,000 feet. The Victor tanker had tried every level, and at 3,000 feet he was still in cloud and in turbulence. We found the tanker by using our attack radar as an AI [airborne interception radar]. Visibility was down to about 100 metres, with thunderstorms and lightning, and we tanked at 3,000 feet. There was a lot of turbulence, the tanker was moving violently up and down and there was a serious risk of mid-air collision. The weather was awful and getting worse. After a struggle Mike got the probe into the basket but it immediately fell out; he got it back in again and we started to fill up but then the probe fell out again. I looked at the fuel and said, 'Right, we've got enough.' We left the tanker with about 71 tons of fuel, climbed out the top of the weather at 26,000 feet and headed off to the north.

Just short of the Iraqi border, the Tornado let down to low altitude and headed for Tallil. Bennett continued:

Still the weather was pretty awful. We did not break cloud until we were below 1,000 feet. At 200 feet we were in the clear, with a solid overcast and no turbulence at that level – perfect conditions in which to do a reconnaissance in a GR.1A!

Near Tallil an SA-8 missile control radar locked on to the aircraft. Stanway hauled the Tornado into a tight turn and Bennett released chaff, and the lock-on ceased. Despite the two pairs of wide-open eyes quartering the sky around the aircraft, no missile was seen and it is likely that none was fired.

The initial part of the reconnaissance, of the highway from An Nasiriyah to Al Amarah, revealed little traffic. Just short of Al Amarah the aircraft turned south and followed the highway to Basrah. The crew saw a moderate amount of traffic, most of it heading north:

As we ran along that road we were fired at by AAA but fortunately it was not tracking fire – it was unaimed. It looked as if they were firing at our engine noise, and at 560 knots [645mph] at 200 feet they did not hear us until we had gone past. So all of the tracer went behind us – it looked quite pretty!

Short of Basrah the crew turned again, this time on to a westerly heading to follow the highway to An Nasiriyah:

The road to An Nasiriyah, part of the main Basrah to Baghdad highway, was chockablock with traffic. It looked like the M5 during the rush hour. I didn't need to look at the imagery: we could see the vehicles out of the canopy. They had their lights on, and as we approached they heard us and the lights went out. They probably thought they were about to be bombed. There were all types of military vehicle, including transporters with tanks, all moving west about five yards apart. They were not going very fast, about 10mph. The whole time we were looking out for SAMs, but none came up at us.

Later the crew learned that they had stumbled upon the start of the Iraqi massed withdrawal from Kuwait, later termed 'The Mother of all Retreats', ordered by President Saddam Hussein earlier that morning. Bennett reported the findings by radio to the AWACS aircraft monitoring activity in the area. The Tornado followed the highway for some 60 miles without reaching the head of the column then, its task complete, it turned south and headed for base. The crew had spent more than an hour over Iraq, all of it at low altitude. Dawn was breaking as Stanway and Bennett left enemy territory and they made the final 40 minutes of the flight in daylight. It was the only daylight operational flying time they logged during the entire war.

The build-up of Iraqi traffic was also observed by the Boeing E-8 J-STARS radar aircraft over Saudi Arabia, and several flights of B-52 bombers were diverted to attack the concentrations of vehicles.

During the Gulf conflict the Tornado GR.1A force flew 125 reconnaissance missions, the great majority of which were designated 'successful'. Like most types of intelligence-gathering operation, these carried none of the panache and spectacle associated with the more aggressive types of air operation. Nevertheless, in determining the positions of worthwhile targets, the reconnaissance planes significantly increased the effectiveness of the Coalition attack aircraft.

Finale

For this book the author has selected thirty-two noteworthy air actions intended to illustrate the truly diverse nature of aerial warfare. During the eight decades since its inception, the changes in military aviation have been far-reaching in the extreme. Indeed, military aviation has itself been a major force in driving the advances made in several areas of technology. Yet it has never been enough merely to produce clever pieces of military equipment that operate close to the limits of what is technically possible. Such equipment would be of little avail were it not for the daring, the perseverance and the ingenuity of those who fly in action. As the accounts have shown, those human qualities have never been in short supply.

Glossary

AAA	Anti-aircraft artillery.
AI	Airborne interception (radar).
ASV	Air-to-surface vessel (radar).
Chaff	Metallized strips released from aircraft to create false targets on enemy radar.
Elint	Electronic intelligence.
EOGB	Electro-Optically Guided Bomb.
Ferret	Aircraft equipped for elint missions.
Flensburg	German homing device to pick up signals from 'Monica' radar.
Fritz–X	German guided bomb designed for use against armoured warships.
GCI	Ground controlled interception (radar).
Geschwader	World War II *Luftwaffe* flying unit with an established strength of about 96 aircraft.
Gruppe	*Luftwaffe* flying unit with an established strength of about 30 aircraft.
HARM	High-speed Anti-Radiation Missile. US missile designed to home-in on the emissions from enemy fire-control radars.
HAS	Hardened aircraft shelter.
hp	Horsepower.
H2S	Generic term for microwave ground-mapping radar fitted to RAF bombers, produced in several versions between 1942 and the early 1960s.
Infra-red linescan	Reconnaissance system carried by Tornado GR.1A and other aircraft, to produce electro-optical imagery of targets on video tape for later analysis.
'Johnny Walker'	Code-name for 500lb underwater 'walking' mine, an anti-shipping weapon used by the Royal Air Force.
JP.233	Airfield-denial weapon carried by Royal Air Force Tornado GR.1 aircraft, with runway cratering munitions and anti-personnel mines to delay repair work.
LGB	Laser-guided bomb.

Mandrel	Radar jamming equipment to counter the German World War II *Freya, Mammut* and *Wassermann* early-warning equipments.
Mark 24 Mine	First-generation air-dropped anti-submarine homing torpedo.
Metox	German warning receiver fitted to U-boats, to pick up transmissions from early versions of ASV radar.
'Monica'	Tail-warning radar fitted to RAF bombers.
Naxos	German receiver and homing device to pick up signals from enemy microwave radars, carried by night fighters and naval vessels, including U-boats.
nm	Nautical miles.
PI	Photographic interpreter.
PR	Photographic reconnaissance.
RHWR	Radar homing and warning receiver.
SAM	Surface-to-air missile.
SD-2	German fragmentation bomb weighing just under 4lb, dropped in large numbers during attacks on aircraft on the ground and on other 'soft' targets. Used for the first time and in large numbers during the initial stages of the attack on the Soviet Union.
shp	Shaft horsepower.
Shrike	Early type of US anti-radiation missile used in the Vietnam War, designed to home-in on the emissions from enemy fire-control radars.
Sidewinder	US-designed air-to-air, infra-red homing guided missile.
Sparrow	US-designed air-to-air, semi-active radar homing guided missile.
Standard ARM	Standard Anti-Radiation Missile; US long-range weapon used in the Vietnam War, designed to home-in on the emissions from enemy fire-control radars.
TALD	Tactical Air Launched Decoy. An unpowered radar decoy carried by US Navy planes released from high altitude, whereupon the wings unfolded and it flew a pre-programmed track into enemy territory to lure the defences into action.
'Tallboy'	Code-name for British 12,000lb bomb.
TFR	Terrain-following radar.
'Window'	British wartime code-name for chaff.
'Window Spoof'	Feint operation in which a few aircraft dropping large amounts of chaff give an appearance on enemy radar similar to that from a large force of attacking bombers.
WSO	Weapon Systems Officer (crewman in F-111F and other US Air Force combat aircraft types).

Index